Issue

Canadian

Second Edition

Edited By

Mahfooz A. Kanwar

Don Swenson

Mount Royal College

KENDALL/HUNT PUBLISHING COMPANY

4050 Westmark Drive Dubuque, Iowa 52002

ISBN 0-7872-3647-0

Library of Congress Catalog Card Number 97-71376

Printed in the United States of America

10 9 8 7 6 5 4 3 2 1

To

Samina, Tariq and Tahir

Contents

Mahfooz Kanwar

Dr. Mahfooz Kanwar is a tenured faculty member in the Department of Behavioral Sciences, Mount Royal College (Calgary, Alberta, Canada). He holds a B.A. degree in Political Science, an M.A. degree in Sociology, another M.A. degree in Sociology/Criminology, and a Ph.D. degree in Criminology.

He has conducted research and published extensively in the sociological fields of marriage and the family, religion, crime and social problems. He has authored six books, five monographs, and a large number of academic and non-academic articles.

Dr. Kanwar has served for three consecutive terms as the chairman of the Department of Behavioral Sciences that includes the disciplines of Sociology, Psychology, Anthropology, Archaeology and Education.

He has extensive teaching experience at various universities and colleges, including the University of Waterloo, Wilfred Laurier University, the University of Calgary, South Waterloo Memorial Hospital, Drumheller Federal Penitentiary, Military Police Platoon (Canadian Forces Base in Calgary), and Mount Royal College (all in Canada); Valencia Community College in Orlando (Florida); and he has guest lectured at the University of Karachi, the Quaid-e-Azam University, the University of Punjab, and the National Police Academy, Islamabad (all four in Pakistan). He has twice received the distinguished teaching award.

Dr. Kanwar resides in Calgary and is actively involved in research in both Canada and Pakistan. He is also active in the community by participating in, and presiding over, the community and government appointed boards and committees. As well, he has responded to issues brought forth in the media, including newspapers, radio, and television.

Don Swenson

Dr. Don Swenson has been on faculty at Mount Royal College since the fall of 1992. He teaches the sociology of the family and the sociology of religion. He received his Ph.D. degree from the University of Notre Dame in Indiana, his masters degree in sociology from the University of Calgary, and his degree in Catholic theology from the University of Ottawa. His teaching experience is wide: teaching at Red Deer College, St. Thomas More College in Saskatoon and Luther College in Regina.

He has published several articles on divorce, remarriage, celibacy and marriage, and the link between religion and the family. He is currently working on a textbook in the sociology of religion and is active in the religion and family life section of the National Council of Family Relations.

About the Cover

Canada is officially recognized as a bilingual and multicultural society. In this multicultural society, there are four major segments of the population: the Aboriginal Canadians, the French Canadians, the English Canadians, and those of all other heritages. The first three groups of Canadians represent their cohesive cultural background respectively.

The fourth category of people represents a variety of cultural backgrounds. When compared with one another, they are drastically different. For instance, the East Indian-Canadians and the German-Canadians represent totally different cultural and ethnic backgrounds. They all share one thing in common: they are distinct from the three pioneer groups. Regardless of their different backgrounds, however, all four groups share the Canadian culture, and that is what the Canadian flag on the front cover symbolizes.

We have tried to make this a concise book of readings by including as much material as is deemed necessary for an introductory sociology course. We have, therefore, avoided some of the sociological jargon that normally appears in large textbooks which, in our experience, go unread by students and undiscussed by instructors.

Introduction

Sociology was born in the midst of a series of social crises in early nineteenth century Europe, and it grew as an independent discipline as a result of its response to social crises (Bottomore, 1975). Therefore, it is part of the heritage of sociology to deal with emerging social issues. The development of sociology as a profound discipline, to a great extent, depends on its ability to address important social issues. In this volume, we undertake the task of examining a series of social issues that are currently important in Canadian sociology. All the chapters included in this volume are original papers based on the most recent data.

Until the late 1960s, Canadian sociology was a "branch plant" of American sociology. Many of the early sociologists in Canada were either Americans or American-trained Canadians. Since the late 1960s, with the development of sociology departments in all major Canadian universities and the establishment of the first English language sociology journal—The Canadian Review of Anthropology and Sociology—Canadian students were exposed to sociological discussions that focus on Canadian social issues. During the last two decades, Canadian society experienced a series of social changes—the French separatist movement in Quebec, the development of the Native rights campaign, the introduction of the policies of multiculturalism and bilingualism and the women's rights movement, to mention a few—that caught the attention of sociologists. Therefore, Canadian sociologists began to develop their own research agendas in order to examine these social issues. As a result, Canadian sociology became independent from that of the United States (Forcese and Richer, 1988).

We have organized this volume on the basis of four major areas: the development of theoretical and methodological issues in Canadian sociology, social stratification, social control, family and social organizations. As social issues evolve over time, so do the theories and methods in sociology. Ideally, theoretical and methodological approaches become improved and refined in terms of the collection of data and the precision of analysis. Following World War II, the optimistic view of the future of complex industrial society in North America led to the development of the structural-functionalist perspective in sociology. However, this optimism did not last very long when it became evident that the growing industrial economic system was also responsible for growing social inequality, crimes, changes in family structure and health disorders. Therefore, by the 1960s the structural-functionalist approach was seen as inadequate to examine these emerging problems. Particularly in Canadian sociology, Marxian social theory became a widely popular approach to social issues (Forcese and Richer, 1988).

In order to demonstrate how the social inequality is based on the distribution of wealth, power and prestige, the concept of social stratification must be defined not only in terms of "social class" but also in terms of such ascribed characteristics as "ethnicity" and "gender." For example, during the last two decades, the issue of social inequality has been a dominant theme in Canadian sociology. As Canadian society developed on the basis of three major social groups—the aboriginal people, charter groups (French and English), and ethnic Canadians—the social inequality among them became increasingly evident. While the French and English Canadians continued to dominate the economic and political systems, ethnic and aboriginal Canadians still suffer from a variety of disadvantages including prejudice, discrimination and exploitation (Zeitlin and Brym, 1991). Further, with the growing campaign of the women's movement for social reforms, social inequality between men and women has been a focus of many scholarly discussions during the past two decades. Therefore, Canadian sociologists who are interested in social inequality must examine a wide range of aspects that inequality can manifest itself in a pluralistic society like Canada.

As every society has its own way of dealing with social problems, those who study these problems must be able to provide indepth sociological insights pertaining to the unique social values, customs and beliefs of that society. Canadians often emphasize their difference in values, beliefs and customs compared to their "cousins south of the border." For example, the difference in the role of law and the control of crime in the two countries has been linked to the historical emphasis on the rights and obligations of the "community" as compared to those of the "individual." The founding fathers of Canada were specifically concerned with "peace, order and good government" implying control and protection. Further, they recognized the responsibility of the state with regard to its citizens. By contrast, the United States emphasized "life, liberty, and the pursuit of happiness" suggesting the supreme rights of the individual. Hence, the emphasis on individual rights, including those accused of crime, in the United States reflects the "due process" model in which various inhibitions are imposed on the power of police and prosecutors. In Canada, however, the "crime control" model emphasizes the maintenance of law and order, and is less concerned with the rights of accused and individuals in general (Lipset, 1988).

Canadians are served by a network of social welfare programs which are often attributed to the unique character of Canadian society. Many Canadians often take these services for granted because we have grown accustomed to them. For example, state funded health care programs, unemployed insurance, and old age security programs are some of the specific services that function as safety nets in situations of ill health, unemployment and disability. Although these programs cost the taxpayers billions of dollars annually, Canadians are prepared to maintain these services. Particularly when compared to the 36 million people in the United States without any health care protection, it is important to emphasize the responsibility that the government plays on behalf of its citizens in Canada. These institutional developments reflect to some degree the fundamental social values that Canadians have cultivated with regard to fellow citizens. Therefore, Canadian sociology must address these fundamental characteristics of Canadian social life in order to provide a greater understanding of Canadian society.

As stated in the beginning of this discussion, if Canadian sociology should reflect Canadian society, it must be a problem oriented social scientific discipline (Zeitlin, 1973). However, by discussing Canadian issues, we by no means provide any alternative solutions to issues in question. We merely attempt to address these issues from a wide range of theoretical and methodological viewpoints. It is our hope that this volume will provide students with a better understanding of some of the major social concerns that affect the lives of all Canadians.

References

Bottomore, Tom (ed.)
1975 *Crisis and Contention in Sociology.* London: Sage Publication.

Forcese, Dennis and Stephen Richer (eds.)
1988 "Introduction: Social Issues and Canadian Sociology," pp. 1–9, in *Social Issues: Sociological Views of Canada,* edited by Dennis Forcese and Stephen Richer. Scarborough, Ontario: Prentice-Hall.

Lipset, Seymour Martin
1988 "Value Traditions in Canadian and U.S. Cultures," pp. 58–77, in *Readings in Sociology: An Introduction,* edited by Lorne Tepperman and James Curtis. Toronto: McGraw-Hill Ryerson Ltd.

Zeitlin, Irving M.
1973 *Rethinking Sociology.* Englewood Cliffs, N.J.: Prentice-Hall.

Zeitlin, Irving M. and Robert J. Brym
1991 *The Social Condition of Humanity.* Toronto: Oxford University Press.

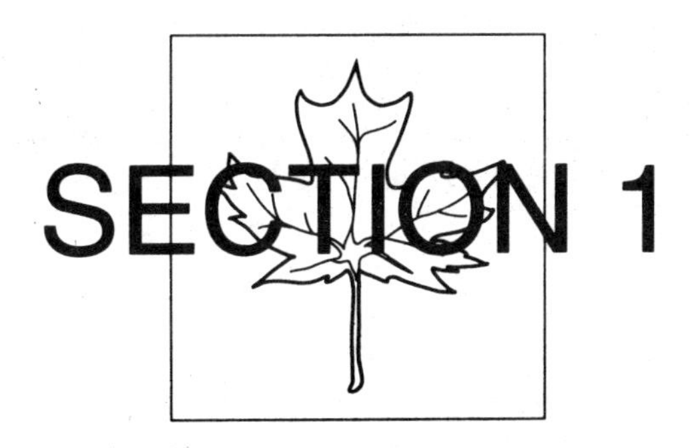

Basic Issues in Sociology

One of the fundamental characteristics of sociology is its persistent effort to maintain the classical tradition. Sociologists often remind their readers what the founding fathers of sociology set out to achieve more than a century ago. Thus, sociologists continue to ask the same questions that preoccupied Weber, Marx and Durkheim: "how a science of society can study pressing social issues." The result of this endeavour is the continuing practical relevance of sociological interpretations of various social issues. Don Swenson argues in the first chapter that in order to understand Canadian social issues, it is important to outline the basic concepts in sociology, its origins in the 19th century, and the central sociological perspectives. He continues with a discussion of what is known as the sociological imagination and the birth of the discipline in Canada.

In Chapter Two, Kanwar and Swenson outline how sociologists approach their subject as scientists. They summarize important features of research through defining basic concepts, presenting what is the research process, ethical issues, and the difficulties of sociological research.

Since the 1970s the enthusiasm among many Canadian sociologists to develop a uniquely Canadian sociological tradition was reinforced by the emerging trends in the social, political and economic spheres of the country. In Chapter Three, Bruce McGuigan argues that most Canadians consciously distinguished themselves from Americans in terms of their cultural and social values. Particularly, the Canadian policy of multiculturalism and bilingualism are examples of Canadian cultural and social diversity that, according to McGuigan, promote living in harmony with difference. Quebec separatism and regional competition in Canada indicate that nationalism has a quite different meaning for most Canadians than for Americans. During the last twenty years, these social issues have been addressed by Canadian sociologists as an important part of the Canadian sociological tradition.

In Chapter Four, Paul Divers attempts to locate these Canadian social and cultural values in the context of a broader perspective of socialization. He defines socialization as the process by which an individual acquires sense of self, knowledge, skills, attitudes, motivations and behavior patterns in order to participate in a given society or social group. He argues that although most Canadians adhere to certain common "Canadian" values and norms, the ethnic cultural characteristics in Canada, as subcultures, influence the process of socialization. This cultural diversity, however, may lead to tension among different ethnic groups. Nevertheless, cultural pluralism itself, according to Divers, is a rich heritage of Canadian society.

These authors demonstrate that social, cultural and regional issues in Canadian society are cornerstones upon which a uniquely Canadian sociological tradition has been developed. The examination of these issues by Canadian sociologists from a range of theoretical and methodological perspectives will not only contribute to the further development of Canadian sociology, but also to the better understanding of Canadian society.

1

The Theoretical Basis to Sociology: An Introduction

Don Swenson

Overview

We commence our introduction to sociology by outlining the theoretical basis to the discipline. The goal here is to introduce the neophyte of sociology to its central concepts, its social and intellectual tradition, its classical founders and the current perspectives. We shall conclude with a discussion of what is known as the sociological imagination and the birth of the discipline in Canada. The goal of this chapter is to acquaint the student with the focus as well as with the breadth of sociology.

Key Concepts

Sociologists vary considerably in how they study the social world. They agree, however, on two central concepts that capture the heart of the discipline: *social action* and *social structure*. For an understanding of these concepts, we look to a classical founder, Weber (1978) and a current theorist, Alexander (1982) for a definition of social action. For an interpretation of social structure, we look to three other classical founders, Auguste Comte (in Coser, 1977), Karl Marx (1977) and Emile Durkheim (1938) as well as another current sociologist, Anthony Giddens (1984).

Weber (1978:4) presents a definition of social action as "'action' insofar as the acting individual attaches a subjective meaning to his behaviour; be it overt or covert, omission or acquiescence. Action is 'social' insofar as its subjective meaning takes account of the behaviour of others and is thereby oriented in its course." Basic to this definition is freedom: an assumption that humans are substantially free in their personal lives and in their relationships with others and larger social arrangements (social institutions, social organizations and whole societies). Weber adds the insight that because humans are considered to be inherently rational (although they do not act so all the time!) and free when people interact with one another, they do not do so passively. There is an interpretive process occurring within the consciousness of each social actor that endeavours to interpret what the other person is thinking. It is on this basis of interpretation that people respond and act accordingly.

Alexander (1982) argues that the vital presence of the human actor is fundamental to the understanding of social phenomena. In addition, he accents the importance of the human actor attaching subjective meaning in his or her relationships with others.

From these two sources, we can construct the following definition: "Social action is human action that assumes that persons are free agents who, in their relationships with others, attach a subjective meaning to their behaviour and take into account the behaviour of others."

The second central concept of sociology is social structure. Comte (in Coser, 1977) focused his attention on the patterns of social action and used the concept to explain how social order was possible in human societies.

Marx (1977) follows with a further insight to this concept. He frames his interpretation of the concept in the development of capitalism in the western world but particularly in England. According to him, the working person for a wage (in contrast to previous workers who were more likely to share in the fruit of their labour) is an effect of the emergence of industrial capitalism commencing with significant changes in England about 1775 (we will detail this in the section on the emergence of the discipline). The behaviour of this person (joined together by many others in the same situation) was significantly restricted by the behaviours of the capitalists who controlled their actions and even exploited them. The relationships between the workers and the capitalists are structured at the expense of the workers and the benefit of the capitalists.

Durkheim (1938) expands the meaning of the concept beyond working relationships between people. His insights inform us that social structure is endemic to all social relationships. However, he does not use this term but calls it the social fact. He considers social action as being under pressure from the social environment and is defined by it:

> every way of acting, fixed or not, capable of exercising on the individual an external constraint; or again, every way of acting which is general throughout a given society, while at the same time existing it its own right independent of its individual manifestations.(1938:13)

A further insight offered by Giddens (1984) is that not only does social structure inhibit the social action of individuals but also enables it. He considers social structure to be similar to a channel, a framework of social action that both inhibits or restricts and facilitates it.

From these impressions, a definition of social structure is: "a pattern or framework of social action that is general throughout a whole society that both functions as an external constraint, sometimes from powerful social groups, and as a facilitator."

The Development of the Discipline

The roots of sociology are in the 19th century in Europe. To understand the wider picture, however, it is important to look briefly at the development of Western civilization and the concomitant history of ideas that correspond to this social development. This is done by looking at the commonly accepted division of the western history into three eras, Classical, Medieval and Modern and to add a forth era that reflects our current world or Post-Modern.

Western civilization commences (with Mesopotamian and Egyptian roots) in the emergence of Greece (c. 500 B.C.) and Rome (c. 200 B.C.). Historians agree that this period continued to the collapse of the Western Roman Empire about 400 A.D. (the Eastern one continued through the 9th century). It is from the Greeks and the Romans that reason was attached not only to social relationships but to the interpretation of what it meant to be human and what the universe stood for. Historians of intellectual history call this the Classical Paradigm.[1] The focus was rational: by using empirical observation and logical deduction, the intellectuals of this time sought to understand society, nature, the cosmos, and the human person with the light of reason.

In reference to the study of society, Nisbet (1982) informs us that Plato (427–347 B.C.), in his Republic, presented society based on ideal political ideals. Plato argued that political power, the political bond is the most distinctive and most influential types of all kinds of societies. This perspective, Nisbet notes, leads to a totalitarianism that does not allow for differences. In contrast, Aristotle (384–322 B.C.), using study, analysis, and observation of relevant facts about society, argues that the best outcomes for people is to have a pluralist-decentralist political, social community. We owe to these classical social philosophers the importance of ideals in society as well as the task to study and observe the social order to try to understand its inner workings.

A shift occurs with the emergence of Christianity as the dominant interpretive vehicle. With the collapse of the Western Roman Empire (400 A.D.), there was created a vacuum of leadership. In time, this was taken over by the Christian church which eventually became the central institution of the Medieval period and was instrumental in the emergence of Christendom. A common characterization of the relationship between religion and society was the joining of the church and secular society or a wedding of crown and altar. The central social issue was one of political power: who has social authority, the church or the secular state? When the church held political authority over the nobles and princes, we have what may be called the Medieval political paradigm. If, however, the secular prince (emperor, king, queen or prince) held the central power, we had what Weber (1978) called Caesar-papism. At several times in the Medieval period, the secular authority (particularly by Constantine [272–337 A.D.]) had greater social authority than did the church leaders.

The central intellectual struggle was between faith and reason. There appears to have been four different patterns of the relationship between faith and reason (Gilson, 1938): faith having radical precedence over reason (the Tertullian model), faith seeking understanding (the Augustian model), reason seeking faith (the Thomistic model) and reason having precedence over faith (the Averroist model). The two which held sway were the Augustian and Thomistic model which could be termed the Medieval-Intellectual paradigm.[2]

The third period in Western history is the modern one. It begins with the Protestant Reformation of the 16th century and continues through until about the middle of this century. The major social events and intellectual changes of these eras form the basis for sociology as a discipline. It is during this period that we have what may be called the modern paradigm or the positivist paradigm wherein reason combined with empirical observation of the natural and social world become central.

Five major historical events and one intellectual process account for this shift that became, upon reflection, the interpretive framework for the founders of sociology. The five historical events are: the Protestant Reformation, the Age of Discovery and colonization of non-Western societies, the English Great Rebellion of 1642–1651, the French Revolution of 1789, and the Industrial Revolution beginning in England about 1775. The shift in the history of ideas occurs with what is known as the Enlightenment from about 1650 to 1800.

The Protestant Reformation

The Reformation is critical in the development of the West. Even though it did not shift the focus from faith to reason, it did introduce a new way of looking at the person and the realignment of Europe according to religious-political regions. Weber (1958) is well known in his analysis of the Protestant ethic and the development of capitalism. He argues that with the coming of Protestantism (through Martin Luther [1483-1546] and John Calvin [1509-1564]), the Christian stands alone before his or her God without the mediation of community, symbol or sacrament. Thus, the believer becomes more self-reliant in his religion and, in turn, more self-reliant in her or his work. The Protestant ethic was one of religious individualism, frugality, hard work and serious moral effort to know if he or she was one of the chosen ones. A sign of salvation, particularly for the Calvinists, was that of worldly success: if one gained from such hard work, it was a sign that one is saved for eternal glory. The spirit of capitalism emerges from Weber's analysis of Benjamin Franklin who argued that hard work, saving, efficient use of time, and rational thinking was the way one could succeed financially. Weber used the term *elective affinity* to describe the unity of these two ways of thinking and acting to account for the growth of capitalism in the Protestant European and American societies.

The Age of Discovery and Colonization

About the same time as the Protestant Reformation, Europeans began to explore and to colonize the world. This eventually lead to the control of hundreds of societies in the Near and Far East, Africa, the Oceanic islands and North and South America. The economic effect of this was phenomenal. Wealth poured into Europe in the form of precious metals and huge profits made from agricultural products and manufactured goods produced in Europe. Marx (1977) considers this to be the reason for the emergence of a new class in Europe: the merchant class. Many of them made huge profits on the purchasing and selling of trade items. It was this class that Marx further understood to be the predecessors of the capitalists of the late 18th century and 19th century.

The Enlightenment

According to the Canadian sociologist, Zeitlin (1990), the Enlightenment takes center place in the emergence of sociology. It was part of what is know as a paradigm shift from faith and reason of the Medieval era to reason based on human experience. It includes such elements as the self-sufficiency of human experience, human freedom, social equality, the ability of humans to control their own destiny and the imperative to build a human society built on natural science, reason, democracy and the separation of the state from religion. This was a great impetus to the creation and growth of sociology as it gave it its empirical and rational basis. Zeitlin writes:

> In contrast to the Medieval era, the men of the Enlightenment regarded all aspects of human life and works as subject to critical examination—the various sciences, religious beliefs, metaphysics, aesthetics, education, and so on. Self-examination, a scrutiny of their own actions and their own society, was a essential function of thought. By gaining an understanding of the main forces and tendencies of their epoch, human beings could determine their direction and control their consequences. Through reason and science, humanity could attain ever greater degrees of freedom, and idea permeating the thinking of that era, would serve to further humanity's general progress. (1990:2)

The English Great Rebellion

Another major historical series of events was the English Great Rebellion of 1640–1650. The English social historian Stone (1972) informs us that a combination of changes in ideals, shifts in who controlled political power, and spontaneous events resulted in the transference of English political authority from a monarchial system to a parliamentary one that was to shape English society in fundamental ways. The series of events during this period resulted in what the American social historian Tilly (1981) terms *State Building* that has become a hallmark of the modern world that later sociologists would reflect on.

The French Revolution

A more radical political change occurred in France in 1789, when there was a permanent eradication of the monarchial system and the genesis of a more democratic political system. Some of the major changes included: the secularization of French society which removed social and political authority from the church to the secular leaders; the temporary expansion of divorce legislation from 1790–1803; the replacement of the regal nobility by the revolutionary leaders; the granting of the franchise to more and more French citizens; and the decline of the power of local community political institutions and the incline of the national state. Again, later sociologists reflected on these series of events as another example of State Building and the emergence of modernity.

The Industrial Revolution

Besides the French Revolution, Robert Nisbet (1966) considers the Industrial Revolution of Great Britain to be the second most critical event that permanently changed the economy of the Occidental world and, eventually, most of the globe. According to the historian Toynbee (1956), economic processes happening for many years culminated in major economic changes in the latter part of the 18th century and the first part of the 19th. As we saw above, with the Age of Discovery and Colonization, a new class of people emerged: the merchant class.

After the Great Rebellion, these persons achieved more and more political power and influence. They were able to convince the British Parliament during the 18th century to privatize common land (publicly owned) in the rural regions of England. For many years before that, most of the English in the rural areas made their living on small land holdings and cottage industries managed by women. In addition to these small private holding owned by who were known as the yeomans, these small land owners used common lands that could be publicly used for cattle grazing and cropping. With the privatization of these lands, the wealthy merchants purchased these lands and transferred them into sheep grazing holdings for wool production.

Concomitantly, technical advances (like the invention of the steam engine and the Spinning Jenny used to manufacture bolts of cloth from cotton and wool) and the mining of coal for energy made it possible for the creation of the factory system in urban areas like Preston and Lancaster. Many yeomans and their families began to migrate to these urban areas to become the English working class. Thus, according to Marx (1977), a new social-class relationship was created: the capitalists and the workers or the bourgeoisie and the proletariate.

In addition to these changes, ideological changes were occurring as well. The Scottish economist, Adam Smith (1952), published his famous book the Wealth of Nations in 1790 that became the handbook of capitalism. Thus, a combination of agricultural, technological, economic, and ideological changes occurred to result in what came to be known as the Industrial Revolution. The changes that occurred during this period were sources for further reflections by the classical sociologists on the coming of the modern world.

The Post-Industrial Revolution

As the classical foundation of sociology was laid because of these major historical and ideological processes, so also are current sociological reflections based upon what has come to be known as the post-industrial society of the West from the end of the Second World War to the present time. A combination of economic, technological, political, and ideological processes have occurred to initiate these changes.

Economically, more and more workers are being employed in service-information industries than in industrial ones. By industrial we mean the goods manufacturing sector of an economy. By service and information, we mean all those persons working in retail, sales, human services, health care, education, and finances. Currently, in Canada (1991), 70% of workers are employed in these kind of occupations. To work here, more and more education is required which accounts for the expansion of the many post-secondary educational institutions. Another major economic change is the decline of the national economic borders. Sociologists and others call this the globalization of the economy which means that raw materials, goods and services are both purchased and sold on a world market rather than a national one.[3]

Technologically, the micro-computer has revolutionalized the way we now do business, deliver human services, and educate the population. A more recent update is the Internet system which has the potential of linking millions of computer users (both at the home and in the education-work place) to information useful for a wide variety of purposes.

A combination of political and ideological changes have occurred in the former Soviet Union and Eastern Europe. Left-wing Communism is in decline except for a few strongholds in China. The "buzz-word" in many of these countries is capitalism and democracy. As yet, visible positive effects of these changes have not been witnessed.

In sociology, these changes have produced what we call paradigm shifts. Four shifts have occurred: post-positivism, feminism, post-secularism, and the inclusion of the marginalized. Post-positivist thinking in sociology refers to an alternative to using the empirical-rational method of investigation of the social world by accenting the experience of the subjects of investigation more and more. This is what the philosopher of science, Radnitzky (1973), refers to as the hermeneutic school. The argument here is that human social experience cannot be captured well using questionnaires and surveys that lend themselves to statistical analysis. Using a case study approach and personal interviews, the life experience of the people studied can be much more rooted in their own stories.

Feminism, or "Honouring the Feminine," is a major paradigm shift. The Canadian sociologist, Dorothy Smith (1990), argues for a "standpoint theory." She means that sociology needs to recognize that women have a unique experience in contrast to men and that their voice should be heard from their own standpoint. In essence, this approach in sociology is to both make relevant the unique experience of women in society as well as to critique male power which dominates much of the familial, economic, educational, and political life of people.

A third paradigm shift that has not received much reflection by current sociological thinking is the re-emergence of the experience of the sacred. An assumption of the modern world is that as science and technology grew, the belief systems of people would decline. This has not occurred even though there are signs of increased secularization in educational and political systems in the Western world.

A fourth paradigm shift for sociologists comes from a sister discipline, anthropology. These researchers have long been doing research on marginalized peoples both in Western and non-Western societies. One might call this approach the "Post Caucasian" one which includes the experience of vast numbers of people who are not Caucasian. One may use the term "Pedagogy of the Oppressed" that reflects how we need to honour the social experience of those who have been oppressed by political, economic and religious institutions.

We thus conclude our discussion on the background to sociology or the social world that led to its emergence. We now will give a brief introduction to the classical founders of the discipline, Auguste Comte, Karl Marx, Emile Durkheim and Max Weber.[4] The sources for this investigation are Lewis Coser (1977) and Anthony Giddens (1971).

The Classical Foundation

August Comte

The French philosopher turned sociologist, August Comte (1798–1857), was the first of the classical founders to reflect on 18th and 19th century historical and social events in Western World. The impetus to his work was what he percieved to be the major social problems that occurred in the wake of the industrial and French revolutions. He thought that if one applied the method of the natural sciences (observation, experimentation, comparison and historical research) to the social world, one would be able to discover not only the causes to the social problems but also the solutions.

To him we owe the term sociology which means the study (the Greek *logos*) of the social (the Latin *socio*). In addition, he gave to us as an inheritance in the discipline that the true unit of investigation is not the individual but the social or, at least, the dyad. He believed that the individual person was too much subject to individualism and egoism and the these propensities needed to be curbed by social processes in social groups. For social order to be possible, there needs to be some mechanisms that bind people together: language, religion (for him, this was a secular religion), and occupational groups.

Finally, we also owe to Comte a vision of society that is like a living organism: the division of several parts that form a system of interrelated parts that function for the whole. This came to be known later as structural functionalism.

Karl Marx

Although Karl Marx (1818–1883) is known as a philosopher, an historian and a revolutionary, he is best known as a sociologist who, like Comte, and as we shall see with Durkheim, believed that the basic unit of study is not the individual but the social group. For Comte, the primary social group was the family but for Marx, it was the working social group. It is from work that humans find not only subsistence but also the potential to create ideas and to find meaning to life. The relations of production (relations that people establish with each other when they utilize existing raw materials) constitute the real foundation upon which the whole society, including culture, is erected. Marx, together with Engels (1947:47) writes: "It is not the consciousness of men that determines their being, but, on the contrary, their social being that determines their consciousness."

His focus of investigation was on the modern world of capitalism, particularly in England, where he lived out his last days studying in the London Museum. He argues that the relationships between people are shaped by their relative positions in regard to the means of production and their differential access to the scarce resources and scarce power. Human life is struggle—struggle to access these resources and power. In pre-capitalist times, this access was shared more by all members of a society. In capitalism, these resources and power have become concentrated into the hands of a few who were known as the bourgeoisie and exploited those, the proletarians, who had less access. The latter experienced alienation and suffered from this alienation.

It was difficult for these proletarians. This class was something they were born into and they had little control over their lives. What was needed was a change. Marx's view of humanity was not a passive view. He believed that humans are essentially creative beings whose 'natural' propensities are denied by the restrictive character of capitalism. Even though he knew that capitalism was an economic structure of control, it is still the human agent who is the focus of change and he believed that humans make their own history. It is here were we meet Marx the revolutionary. He called, with Engels (1932), to have the proletarians unite in one major revolution against the bourgeoisie and take control of the means of production from them. Thereafter, all citizens and workers would, together, own the means of production and there would be equality and justice for all.

Marx's views are central to sociology. Particularily in Canada, we owe to Marx the seeds of what is known as the political economic approach to the study of the modern world that focuses on the economic system, the work environment and the political mechanisms of social control.

Emile Durkheim

Although we do not have any indication that Emile Durkheim (1858–1917) read Marx, we do know that he read Comte. With Comte and Marx, he considers that the basic unit of society is not the individual person but the social group. In fact, Durkheim spent much of his time arguing for this position against a reductionism that took the position that what really matters in social life is individual consciousness. Durkheim is also remembered in the disciipline to have become the first professional sociologist at Sorbonne University in Paris.

He believed that the key social problem that the modern age faced was to reconcile individual freedom which sprung from the dissolution of traditional society with the maintenance of moral control upon which the very existence of society depended. He applauds this new freedom and does not look with nostalgia to the past. However, this new freedom can easily lead to what he calls *egoistical individualism*. There needs to be some sort of external control that curbs this kind of egoism. This control is what he refers to as the social fact which has coercive power that impose itself on the individual independent of personal will. In this way, the individual person becomes integrated into society and regulated by society. If this does not happen, an individual may experience what he calls *anomie* which is a social state of normlessness wherein the individual is cast on a sea of humanity with no moorings or direction.

Durkheim is a functionalist. The goal of the modern society is social order that is achieved by a delicate balance of individual freedom and control through mechanisms of cohesion, solidarity, integration, the proper use of authority (that was just) and ritual. By ritual he means, primarily, religion for it is in religion that is found the par excellence source against egotistical individualism.

These functions are fulfilled not through nebulous forces in society but through social institutions which are sets of beliefs and practices that have become normative and that were focused on a recurrent and continuing social concern. The central institutions to achieve this are work occupations and the state. He is the first to give us a generic definition of sociology and to paraphrase, sociology is the science of institutions, of their genesis and of their functioning (Durkheim, 1938).

A final major contribution Durkheim made to the discipline was to take Comte's desire to make sociology a science. In his work *The Rules of Sociological Methods*, he said that one needs to consider social facts in the same way as one would consider natural facts and to observe them, describe them, to classify them and, finally, to explain them. He was the first to do an empirical study in the field when he analysed census data to test a theory of suicide. His key theory and finding was that suicide is rooted not so much in individual sources but in social factors (Durkheim, 1938).

Max Weber

The last classical founder of the discipline that we investigate here is the German Max Weber (1864–1920). While Comte, Durkheim and Marx considered that the unit of study of sociology was the social group, Weber argued that the unit of study was the social actor.[5] In fact, for him, sociology is a comprehensive science of social action. In addition, unlike these co-founders who all accented social structure, his work focused on social action (see the section, above, on basic concepts).

Another important feature distinguishes Weber from his predecessors. Comte, Marx, and Durkheim all agreed that social phenomena were similar to natural phenomena and that they could be observed, analysed and explained just as were natural events. Weber disagrees. He believed that the human agent was unique and that because of his or her consciousness, one needs to *enter into* the mind of the social actor to try to understand (*versthen*) what the actor is thinking. He, like Durkheim, offers us a definition of sociology: "that science which concerns itself with the interpretive understanding (read *versthen*) of social action and thereby with a causal explanation of its course and consequences" (Weber, 1978:4).

Even though his focus was on the individual social actor, he did not spend time in investigating the micro nature of society but was much more concerned with the larger picture. Coser (1977:218), quoting Mannheim (1951:52), notes: "Max Weber's whole work is in the last analysis directed toward the question: 'Which social factors have brought about the rationalization of the Western civilization?'" His work was voluminous and comprehensive. He studied such topics and subjects as the city, the Roman Empire, law, art, the state and major religions like Catholicism, Protestantism, Judaism, and Islam in the West and Hinduism, Buddhism and Taoism in the East. The overall attempt of this investigation was to try to understand why capitalism and the modern state occurred in Western Europe and not in other parts of the world.

His work was more comprehensive than Marx in that he looked for factors besides economic to account for the growth of Western modernity: religion, politics, technology, and ideologies. Even though his focus was on the social actor, he did acknowledge the importance of social structures especially when he investigated social class, statuses, bureaucracy and religion. In fact, he considered that the single most important problem of modernity was not social disorder (Comte), alienation (Marx), or anomie (Durkheim) but the imprisonment of the individual in social structures so powerful (as reflected in political and economic bureaucracies) that they would lead the social actor to depression and disillusionment. In this way, Weber is more like a post-modern sociologist than a modernist thinker. His predecessors were all optimistic about the ability of science to solve the social problems of modernity but Weber put little hope in the sciences. He, in fact, looks to the future with little hope. He writes in the *Protestant Ethic and the Spirit of Capitalism*:

> No one knows who will live in this cage (bureaucracy) in the future, or whether at the end of this tremendous development entirely new prophets will arise, or there will be a great rebirth of old ideas and ideals, or, if neither, mechanized, petrification, embellished with a sort of convulsive self-importance. For of the last stage of this cultural development, it might well be truly said: "Specialists without spirit, sensualists without heart; this nullity imagines that it has attained a level of civilization never before achieved." (1958:182)

Summary

From our outline of the central concepts of sociology and a look at the classical founders, we are now in a position to compose a definition of sociology. In a word, "sociology is the science of the social group that ranges from a dyad of two persons to whole societies and accents understanding social action and social structure."

The Current Main Perspectives

With some variation, most sociologists consider four main perspectives to be the central ones in interpreting the modern world: structural functionalism, symbolic interactionism, conflict theory or the political economic perspective, and feminism.[6] As Figures 1:1 and 1:2 illustrate, all are linked to the classical founders: structural functionalism to Comte, Durkheim and Weber, conflict theory and feminism to Marx, and symbolic interactionism to Weber. We begin with outlining structural functionalism.

Structural Functionalism

Relying on the Enlightenment philosopher, Thomas Hobbes (1952), Comte and Durkheim laid the foundation of this perspective. Using a biological analogy, the modern society is

Figure 1:1. Classical Founders

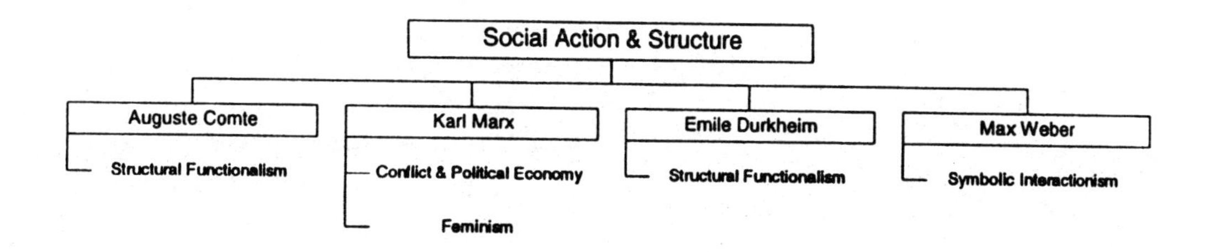

Figure 1:2. Key Concepts and Perspectives

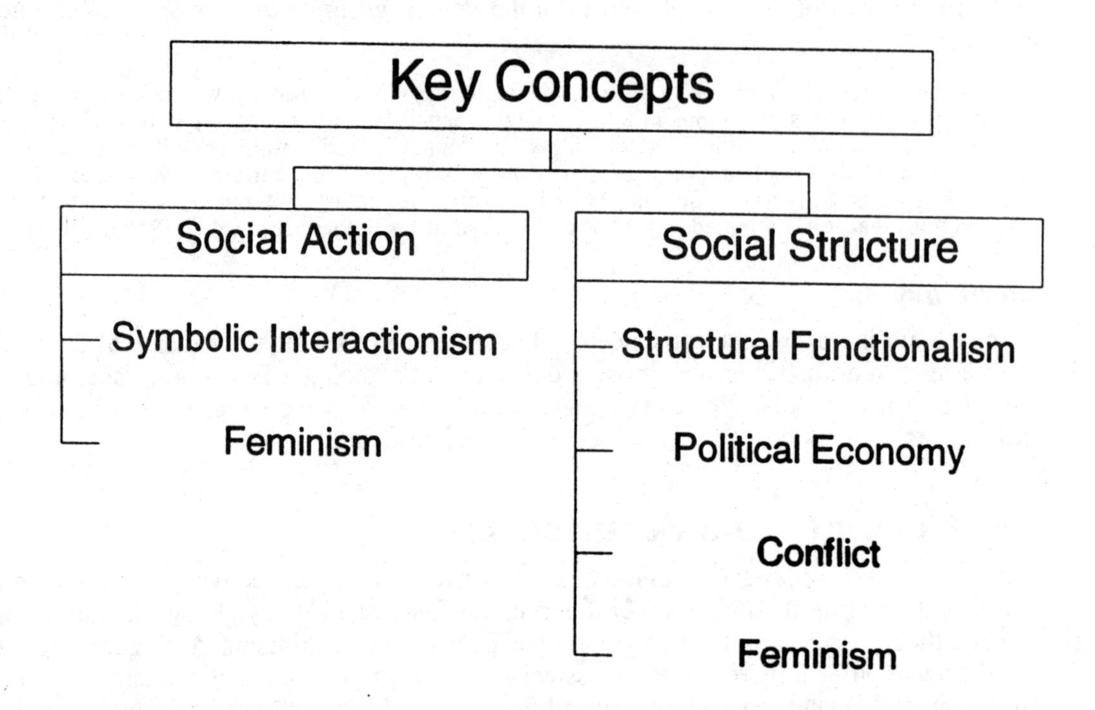

like a living organism that is a system of structures (like the respiratory, digestive, reproduction structures) which all have function to fulfill. Each of these structures have a specific function and together and working in unison, function for the good of the whole. Biologists and structural functionalists would all say that the "whole is greater than the sum of its parts."

In sociology, the various structures of a society have a unique function to perform and together, as a system, function to supply social order to all members of that particular society. For example, the political structure is present to provide a just social system for all members, or the family is to provide for the socialization needs of societal members. In a vital, interconnecting linkage with all other structures, order is achieved and individuals, in connections to others, can live relatively peaceful lives.

The perspective was augmented by several American sociologists who researched and worked in the first to middle part of the 20th century: Talcott Parsons (1937), Robert Merton (1949), Kingsley Davis (1949). To outline this perspective and the subsquent ones, I am again, relying on Coser (1977).

Structural functionalism rests on an understanding of functional analysis which refers to the interpretation of the interrelationships between social phenomena and the effects of given items for the larger structures in which they are embedded. Functions are seen as effects that make for the adaptation of given structures and dysfunctions that lessen or eliminate adaptation. Parsons' (1937) contribution is his understanding that human actors have a potential to make choices of courses of action (thus the view is voluntaristic) but these choices are constrained by biological and social environmental conditions. It was his hope to provide a comprehensive and complete picture of the modern society that would compare to the attempts made by Newton in physics.

Merton was not nearly as optimistic. He termed his theoretical outlook as Middle Range, meaning that theory needs to be abstract enough to cover several social types but concrete enough that it could be testable with specific hypotheses.

Like Parsons, Merton considers the human actor to be free but restrained by social structures and institutions. In this light, he studied crime, the current sources of anomie, the sociology of science, political institutions, and reference groups. He, unlike Parsons, looked how some social structures did not function well for people. In addition, human actors face many dilemmas and contradictions. Coser (1977:567), relying on Merton's (1976) insights, comments: "social actors are always faced by sociological ambivalence, ambiguities, conflicting expectations, and dilemmas of choice; and societies, far from being rigidly unified wholes, contain in their structures discrepancies and incongruities that preclude the possibility of treating them as unambiguously unified wholes."

The continuation of a structural functionalist perspective occurs in the work of Davis (1949). In his work, the *Human Society*, he outlines a thorough and systematic view of social structure and social functions in the light both of Parsons and Merton.

Symbolic Interactionism

Emerging from the theoretical positions of George H. Mead and Charles Cooley (who we shall meet in the chapter on socialization) and more currently from Herbert Blumer (1969), who gave this perspective its name, symbolic interactionism focuses on social action and not on social structure. Johnathan Turner writes:

> individuals ... are considered to be players in a 'game.' When conceptualized as a game, interaction is more likely to be seen as unstructured and as influenced by the wide range of tactics available to participants ... symbolic interactions tend to conceptualize human interaction and society in terms of the strategic adjustments and readjustments of players in a game. (1974:177)

Some of the assumptions of the theory are that social actors are relatively independent and that they act in response to stimuli rom others and do so by interpreting these stimuli according to their own meanings. In addition, the social world is constructed from interpretive processes arising out of interactions between individuals and the role of social science is less the search for patterns of these interactions but more so for an awareness of the uniqueness of each interaction.

This perspective was later nuanced by the American social psychologists, Sheldon Stryker and Anne Statham (1985). They add role theory to the perspective to include structural elements that account for the organization and continuity found in social life, for a consensus among social action, and for an integration of the various structural elements of a society.

Conflict Theory or the Political Economic Perspective

Historically, the beginnings of sociology in the United States was dominated by the kind of sociology that emerged from the University of Chicago that latter became known as symbolic interactionism. With the work of Parsons and later by Merton, the Chicago school lost its hegemony as the dominant sociological perspective. However, by the 1960s, structural functionalism itself began to lose its hegemony to be challenged, especially, by the conflict perspective. Conflict theory includes several authors ranging from classical Marxism to include such sociologists as Ralf Dahrendorf (1959) and Lewis Coser (1967). Those closest to the Marxist model are termed political economists whereas the term conflict theorists includes those influenced by Dahrendorf and Coser.

Collins (1988) presents us with a summary of the political economic perspective and conflict theory. The political economic perspective is a hybrid of classical Marxist sociology and some current theorists. The classical model is a combination of the relationships between capitalists, workers, technology and the state. It is argued that capitalists use workers for profit from their labour. However, in the never ending quest for profits, technology takes over much of the labour. This is a problem, for if workers do not work there is no one left to purchase the products produced by the capitalists. Thus, we have a crisis of overproduction and frequent downturns of the economy. In addition, the state is supported by the capitalists and it is much more likely to be influenced by them than the workers even though the latter control the votes.[7]

The perspective is augmented with ideas from world system theory which notes that the capitalist system is now a world system and that the bourgeoisie search the world for cheap raw materials and inexpensive labour to increase profit. Additional theorists accent how the capitalist class does not only control the means of production but also the ideological or cultural systems as well. Lastly, the state is seen to be more of an independent actor which is a major employer and economic actor in its own right.

Conflict theory emphasizes that conflict is endemic to social relationships and that even though conflict can never be completely eliminated, it can be controlled. In addition, according to Dharendorf and Coser, there is conflict between a wide number of social groups beyond just the classes as pronounced by the political economists. Coser argues that there is a positive function of conflict that if not pushed to the extreme results in consensus within a social system.

Feminism

The final major perspective to look at here is feminism. Although there have been feminist thinkers for centuries,[8] it was not until about the 1970s that it made significant strides in academic circles, particularly psychology, sociology, philosophy, history and religion.

This perspective has two primary roots: in political economy and cultural analysis. The political economic root is understood to be that women's economic power (their income and possession of property) affects their personal lives. Collins (1988) notes that the more economic power women have, the more freedom do they experience in their personal life.

Those who search to explain gender inequality in the cultural system focus upon patriarchy (men ruling women). Simply put, the majority of known human societies place women in inferior positions of authority both in the private sphere and the public sphere. Patriarchy has been the pattern. Feminists not only try to understand why this is the case but also endeavour to liberate women from this inequality. This will be outlined in much more detail in the chapter on gender.

Summary

It is important to understand that no one theory can account for the wide variety of human social experience. It depends upon what one is trying to understand. If one is searching for causes and effects of micro social phenomena, symbolic interaction can be a useful tool. On the other hand, if you are interested in macro social phenomena, structural functionalism and political economy-conflict perspectives are useful. If, however, your concern is how social systems achieve consensus and equilibrium, then structural functionalism may be the route. And, if your interest is in power, justice, social inequality, the political economy-conflict perspectives are useful. Lastly, if your interest is on female-male relationships (gender), both on a micro level and a macro level, then feminism would be the likely choice.

The Sociological Imagination

Coser (1977) considers C. Wright Mills to be not only a conflict theorist but one of the most important sociologists of this century. His work on stratification presented a powerful challenge to the structural functionalist perspective. He is remembered, mostly, however, for his offering a particular vision of society that he terms the *sociological imagination.* Four elements constitute the imagination: social structure, culture, history and biography.

Social structure has been explained in the first part of this chapter. Culture is to be understood as a system of values, ideas and codes of behaviour of a particular society. History refers to the impact that the past has had on the present world will inhabit. Biography means one's own personal social experience.

Mills (1959) argues that if one can understand one's own story in the light of social structures, culture and history, then one is in a better position to have some level of control over one's destiny. The sociological imagination may accomplish the following goals (1959:5–7): (1), it enables its possessor to understand the wider historical scene in terms of its meaning for the inner life of the individual and the external life of a number of individuals; (2) it helps us to grasp history and biography and the relations between the two within a particular society; and, (3) it is the ability to move in one's understanding from the most impersonal and remote transformations to the most intimate of our personal lives.

He adds to this two other important terms: personal troubles of milieu and public issues of social structure. Personal troubles tend to occur within the character of the individual and in range of immediate contact with other persons. Public issues concern

Figure 1:3. The Sociological Imagination

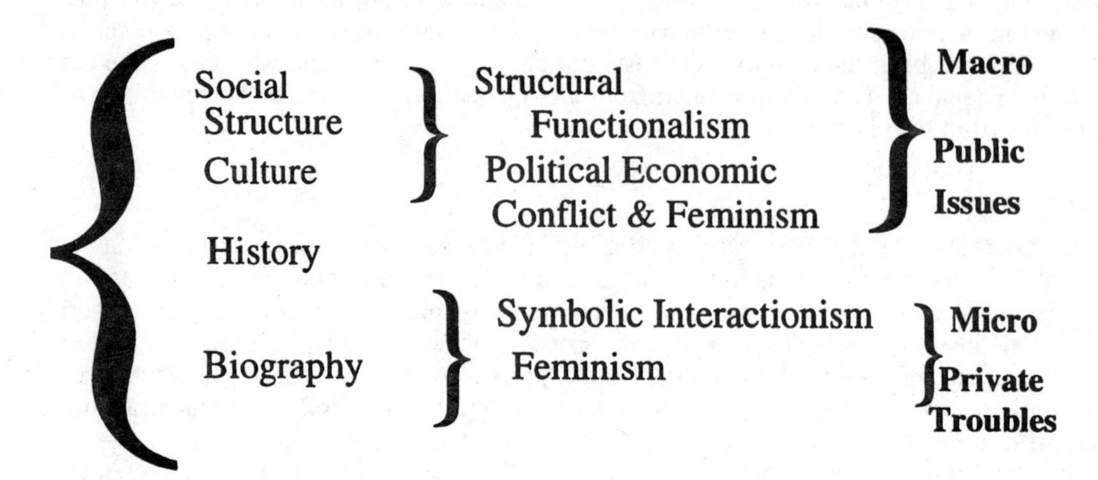

those matters which transcend these local social environments and are beyond the range of one's personal life. An example in Canada would be the high unemployment rate in Newfoundland that has come as a result of the closure of the fishing industry on the East coast. A personal problem would be an unemployed person in an economic environment of high employment because he or she had a drinking problem.

In an attempt to connect Mills' sociological imagination to the various classical founders and current perspectives, Figure 1:3 was constructed. Note that micro refers to one's proximate social environment whereas macro indicates the social structures which are distant from personal contact and control.

The Emergence of Sociology in Canada

Sociology originated in Canada both in Quebec and in English Canada. Forcese and Richer (1982) note that sociology in Quebec began with a merger of Roman Catholic social teaching and practice, European sociology and American social thinking. Leo Gerin, using the work of the 19th century European sociologist, Frederic LePlay (1982), did research on the changing family in rural and urban Quebec.

Beyond that, the major influence to formal sociology within the universities came from the Catholic social action movement. This movement was a religious response to social problems and to challenge the more radical left-wing movement from Marxism. The focus was to try to understand the social problems which emerged as a result of a transformation of Quebec society from rural to urban.

Sociology in English Canada also had religious roots. However, the impetus did not come from Roman Catholicism but, rather, from the social gospel movement of Protestantism. This movement used sociology and its reformist attitude as an extension of the

Christian missionary and social services interests. The most well known was Christopher Dawson from the University of Chicago who originally was a Baptist minister and later become sociologist. He founded the first Canadian sociology department at McGill University in 1922 (Forcese and Richer, 1982).

Gradually, the religious influence in sociology began to wane as years passed. Macionis, Nancarrow Clark, and Gerber (1994) add that the new emphasis was on social, political and economic history. The most influential sociologist during this period was Harold Innis who developed a theory of the growth of the Canadian economy. Then, in the 1960s, the political economist perspective begins to be dominant with the monumental work of John Porter (1965), the Vertical Mosaic—a study of power, ethnicity, class and economy. More currently, especially through the work of Dorothy Smith (1990), mentioned above, feminism has become increasingly center-fold in Canadian sociology.

Summary

What this chapter has attempted to do is to present to the student what were the key concepts of the discipline: social action and social structure. Thereafter, several historical events, processes and ideologies were presented that provided background for the classical founders to construct the rudiments of sociology. These included the Protestant reformation, the age of discovery and colonization, the Enlightenment, the English Great Rebellion, The French Revolution, the industrial revolution, and the post-industrial revolution. The central classical founders included Comte, Marx, Durkheim, and Weber. Thereafter, four current perspectives were presented: structural functionalism, symbolic interactionism, conflict theory or the political economic perspective, and feminism. Mills' sociological imagination provided a summary statement to the goal of sociology and the chapter concluded with a brief introduction to the genesis and development of the discipline in Canada.

Notes

1. Paradigm refers to a pattern, example or a model (Webster, 1968).

2. Tertullian was a 3rd century theologian who taught a radical form of Christianity and believed that reason was a "work of the devil." Augustine was a famous father of Christianity of the 3rd and 4th centuries who considered reason to be useful only if it was enlightened by faith. Thomas Aquinas of the 13th century is the most famous of all Roman Catholic theologians. He felt that reason was flawed but basically good and able to perceive the divine presence in creation. Averroes lived in the 12th century and was an Islamic philosopher. He argued that faith is important but needs to be subservient to reason.

3. *The Canadian Review of Sociology* has devoted its August 1995 issue to the topic.

4. Other sociologists may add others like Herbert Spencer (1820–1903), Georg Simmel (1858–1918), Thorstein Veblen (1857–1929), Charles Cooley (1864–1924), George H.

Mead (1863–1931), and Vilfredo Pareto (1848–1923). We are restricting our study to those who have been known as the major classical founders of the discipline.

5. In this light, Weber is more akin to social psychology than to sociology.

6. Other common ones are exchange theories (or rational choice), ethnomethodology, and phenomenology.

7. A recent example of this is the Canadian federal government's decision to radically reduce the deficit at the call of the world dominant capitalists centered in the United States and other more powerful nations.

8. Stone (1979), a social historian of the family, discovered several feminist movements during the English Great Rebellion. Thompson (1980), a social historian of social class, noted a prominent feminist thinker by the name of Mary Wollstonecraft who published a book in the late 18th century entitled *Rights of Women*. She spoke for the need of a female voice in the economy and the state. Feminism, called "social feminism," was part of prohibition of the latter part of the 19th century and the first part of the 20th in the United States and Canada.

References

Alexander, J.
1982 *Theoretical Logic in Sociology: Positivism, Presuppositions, and Current Controversies*. Volume I. Berkeley, CA: University of California Press.

Blumer, H.
1969 *Symbolic Interactionism: Perspectives and Method*. Englewood Cliffs, NJ: Prentice-Hall.

Collins, R.
1988 *Theoretical Sociology*. New York: Harcourt Brace Jovanovich College Publishers.

Comte, A.
1896 *The Positivist Philosophy of Auguste Comte*. London: Bell.

Coser, L.
1967 *Continuities in the Study of Social Conflict*. New York: Free Press.

Coser, L.
1977 *Masters of Sociological Thought: Ideas in Historical and Social Context*. Second Edition. New York: Harcourt Brace Jovanovich College Publishers.

Dahrendorf, R.
1959 *Class and Class Conflict in Industrial Society*. Stanford, CA: Stanford University Press.

Davis, K.
1949 *Human Society*. New York: Macmillan.

Durkheim, E.
1938 *The Rules of Sociological Method*. New York: The Free Press.

Forcese, D. and S. Richer
1982 "Introduction: Social Issues and Canadian Sociology." Pp. 2–14. D. Forcese and S. Richer eds. *Social Issues: Sociological Views of Canada*. Scarborough: Prentice-Hall.

Giddens, A.
1971 *Capitalism and Modern Social Theory*. London: Cambridge University Press.

Giddens, A.
1984 *The Constitution of Society*. Cambridge: Polity Press.

Gilson, E.
1938 *Reason and Revelation in the Middle Ages*. New York: C. Scribner's and Sons.

Hobbes, T.
1952 *Leviathan, or Matter, Form, and Power of a Commonwealth, Ecclesiastical and Civil*. Chicago: Great Books of the Western World, Britannica Inc.

LePlay, F.
1982 *On Family, Work, and Social Change*. Chicago: The University of Chicago Press.

Macionis, J., J. Nancarrow Clark, and L. Gerber
1994 *Sociology: Canadian Edition*. Scarborough: Prentice-Hall.

Mannheim, K.
1951 *Man and Society in an Age of Reconstruction*. New York: Harcourt Brace Jovanovich College Publishers.

Marx, K. and F. Engels
1932 *The Communist Manifesto and Other Writings*. New York: International Publishers.

Marx, K. and F. Engels
1947 *The German Ideology*. New York: International Publishers.

Marx, K.
1977 *Karl Marx Selected Writings*. Edited by D. McLellan. New York: Oxford University Press.

Merton, R.
1949 *Social Theory and Social Structure*. New York: Free Press.

Merton, R.
1976 *Sociological Ambivalence and Other Essays*. New York: Free Press.

Mills, C.W.
1959 *The Sociological Imagination*. New York: The Oxford University Press.

Nisbet, R.
1966 *The Sociological Tradition*. New York: Basic Books.

Nisbet, R.
1982 *The Social Philosophers*. New York: Pocket Books.

Parsons, T.
1937 *The Structure of Social Action*. New York: Free Press.

Porter, J.
1965 *The Vertical Mosaic: An Analysis of Social Class and Power in Canada* Toronto: The University of Toronto Press.

Radnitzky, G.
1973 *Contemporary Schools of Metascience*. Chicago: Henry Regnery, Co.

Smith, A.
1952 *An Inquiry into the Nature and Causes of the Wealth of Nations*. Chicago: The Great Books, Britannica Inc.

Smith, D.
1990 *Texts, Facts, and the Feminine: Exploring the Relations of Ruling*. New York: Routledge.

Stone, L.
1972 *The Causes of the English Revolution, 1524–1642*. New York: Harper and Row.

Stone, L.
1979 *The Family, Sex and Marriage in England 1500–1800*. New York: Harper and Row.

Stryker, S. and A. Statham
1985 "Symbolic Interaction and Role Theory." Pp. 311–378. In G. Lindzey and E. Aronson (eds.). *The Handbook of Social Psychology*. New York: Random House.

Thompson, E.P.
1980 *The Making of the English Working Class*. London: Penguin Books.

Tilly, C.
1981 *When Sociology Meets History*. New York: Academic Press.

Toynbee, A.
1956 *The Industrial Revolution*. Boston: Beacon Press.

Turner, J.
1974 *The Structure of Sociological Theory*. Homewood Ill.: The Dorsey Press.

Weber, M.
1958 *The Protestant Ethic and the Spirit of Capitalism*. New York: C. Scribner's and Sons.

Webster, N.
1968 *Webster's New Twentieth Century Dictionary of the English Language*. Unabridged. New York: The World Publishing Company.

Zeitlin, I.
1990 *Ideology and the Development of Sociological Theory*. Englewood Cliffs, NJ: Prentice-Hall.

2

An Introduction to Sociological Methodology

Mahfooz Kanwar and Don Swenson

Orientation

Like many other social sciences, sociology is based on scientific inquiry that deals with theory and research. No study is considered sociological if it does not result from empirical data gathered through scientific methods. Scientific methodology is, therefore, an integral part of sociology and its domain. All studies in the discipline of sociology are based on what we see or observe and discover; there is no room for assumptions in sociology. Our hypotheses may result from common knowledge or even general assumptions, but they must be verified by our data collected through scientific methods.

Scientific data lead us into building sociological theories. Scientific research is thus used to verify or disprove, confirm or reject an hypothesis as well as theory. Sociological research methods also help us build new theories or modify the existing theories; it is the cumulative aspect of sociology. Assumptions based on general knowledge, guesses based on common sense, and personal opinions based on intuition provide a lead into a sociological research; but in sociology, they are meaningless without empirical evidence collected through scientific methods.

Sociological methodology is based on certain rules and procedures that lead us into sociological investigations. The scientific methodology is used by many disciplines, social and natural sciences, but sociology in particular emphasizes on the question why? Sociological methodology provides an explanation as to what happens and why it happens. The sociologist is supposed to be interested in finding out what happens and what causes it to happen. Therefore, the relationship between cause and effect becomes the main focus of a sociologist.

Sociological methodology is a complex and extensive area in the discipline. However, for students in introductory sociology, it may suffice to introduce some pertinent aspects and terminology. We shall introduce key concepts, then look how sociologists gather data that is both qualitative and quantitative in nature, outline the research process, discuss ethics and research, and, then, conclude by presenting some of the difficulties of doing sociological research.

Terminology

Construct. The most basic term is called a construct. It is defined as "a term that is a theoretical creation based on observations but which cannot be observed directly or indirectly" (Babbie, 1989:109). An example is religion that was used by Max Weber (1958) in his classic book, the *Protestant Ethic and the Spirit of Capitalism*. He divides this construct into two minor constructs or categories, Protestant and traditional (meaning Roman Catholicism, Judaism, and the various Eastern religions). Another example of a construct is the economy that he further subdivides into capitalism and traditional.

Proposition. When one proposes a link between two constructs, a proposition is the result. In the case of the Weberian tradition, religion is connected to the economy in that religion is a factor that proceeds the economy and that the economy is somehow a result of religion.

Variable. A measurement of a construct is called a variable. Dane (1990:339) refers to it as "the extent to which a measurable construct exhibits more than one value." A construct is too abstract and can only be used in a theoretical sense. From Weber, examples of variables include, under Protestant, the Protestant ethic (an internal way of thinking religiously) and under the construct capitalism, the spirit of capitalism.

Hypothesis. As a proposition is a link between two constructs on a theoretical level, so also are hypotheses measurable constructs or variables proposed connections between two or more variables. Within hypotheses, two kinds of variables are common. An independent variable is the characteristic that becomes a cause or is a creation of an effect. The variable that is caused by an independent variable is called a dependent variable.

An example from Weber's work is that the Protestant ethic was a cause of the spirit of capitalism. Other examples include the following real life situations. If one goes to the bar and drinks more than his limit, drives his car and causes an accident, then the extent of his drunkenness is an independent variable and the resulting accident is a dependent variable. Both can be measured (thus they are variables) and one can establish an empirical link between the two. Medical scientists can relate poor diet, lack of exercise, the use of drugs including smoking and the use of alcohol and genetics to some diseases like heart attacks and cancer.

Correlation. If one tests a hypothesis with data and there is a verification of the hypothesis, one has what is called a correlation. A correlation is an ongoing relationship between two variables. If one can establish a consistent relationship between drunk driving and accidents, a sociologist can argue that there is a correlation between the two. Here, the correlation is more than a variation between two variables for one can predict that drunk driving causes (as an independent variable) car accidents. Here, one can generalize that the more one drinks, the more likely one is likely to cause an accident.

Control variables. An additional question can be asked, however. In doing research and analyzing data, one may consider other factors to be the cause of the accident.

Possibly, the accident is caused by poor road conditions, the weather, or someone else in the vehicle. Sociologists use the term control variable to describe those other factors that may be other independent variables which may explain the changes in the dependent variable. In the example of drunk driving, we are interested in knowing that even if one takes into account other reasons for car accidents (lack of training, listening to a cellular phone while driving, having mechanical problems with the car etc.), driving while intoxicated is still the primary cause of accidents.

Sociological theory. Sociologists are not only interested in predicting and testing to see if two variables are linked. They are also interested in developing a theory that includes many other potential reasons or causes of a social phenomena. In the example here of car accidents, to get a fuller picture of what causes car accidents, one may extend the number of propositions and hypotheses to include more than one cause or reason. Or in the case of Weber's theory of the development of capitalism in the early modern period, there would likely be many more reasons for its emergence.

Merton presents us with a definition of theory:

> It is only when such concepts are interrelated in the form of a scheme that a theory begins to emerge. Concepts, then, constitute the definitions (or prescriptions) of what is to be observed; they are the variables between which empirical relationships are to be sought. When propositions are logically interrelated, a theory has been instituted. (1968:89)

In the chapter on theory, three main theories were presented, structural functionalism, conflict and symbolic interactionism. In the chapter in deviance (Schiessel), the author outlines how these theories endeavour to explain deviance. Many articles have used the propositions derived from these three theories, then have been translated into testable hypotheses and, subsequently, tested with data. A notable example is the work of Merton (1968) who, from structural functionalism, developed the strain theory (see the chapter on Deviance by Bernard Schissel) of deviance. His theory has received empirical support by finding that anomie[1] is higher among lower social classes and that members of these classes do have less access to institutionalized means to success (Bell, 1957 and Tumin and Collins, 1959 and cited in Henslin and Nelson, 1996).

How Data Are Gathered

After one creates adequate constructs, propositions, variables, and hypotheses and before one can test them, data necessarily needs to be collected. In the tradition of research in sociology, data are gathered using three main means: historical, qualitative or quantitative. Historical research, as the name implies, reviews historical materials to test hypotheses. Weber's work on the Protestant ethic and the spirit of capitalism is a case in point.

Qualitative research consists in data that are not easily quantifiable or translated into numbers. Findings from this research is more of a generic nature. Quantitative methods are the more common ones used in the discipline. Concepts are operationalized so that they can be measured. These numbers are later analyzed using statistical methodologies.

Westhues (1982) provides us with those methods which are most commonly used by sociologists: the analysis of historical records, the analysis of contemporary records, fieldwork, demographic techniques, and survey research.

Historical Methods

We shall first of all explain what these methods mean and then present, from Westhues, research examples that have tested the Weberian theory of the rise of capitalism in general and its applicability more recently.

Historical records provide an abundance of data from people who lived in the past and have now passed on. The disciplinary domain of this kind of research is social history or the study of common people from the past.[2] Several historical studies give credibility to Weber's contention that Protestantism preceded the emergence of capitalism. Jonassen (1947) found that in the development of modern Norway, late 19th century capitalism succeeded Protestant revivalist movements in earlier decades. In the creation of capitalism in the United States, Tiryakian (1975) traced its development to its Puritan origins which was one of the Protestant groups that Weber originally targeted as being special carriers of the Protestant ethic.

Qualitative Methods

Analysis of Contemporary Records[3]

The range of the kinds of contemporary records is extensive. It includes such documents as: newspapers; news magazines; legislative acts; directories of prominent people; governmental reports on such data as crime, migration, housing, industry, public health, social welfare; and various kinds of media including TV, movies, Internet sources, and radio. Weshues (1982) notes that each source provides diverse, rich, and varied forms of measures of sociological variables that a sociologist could discover patterns of human, social behavior.

Two well known studies, one by the Canadian sociologist Porter (1965) and the American Anderson (1970), were based on these kinds of data. To present evidence for the continual presence of the linkage between Protestantism and capitalism, in the Canadian study, Porter documented that among the 985 economic elites in Canada, only 10% of them were Roman Catholic. In the American counterpart, Anderson discovered that there was systematic evidence pointing to the white Protestant over representation in the political, economic, and scientific elites in the United States.

Fieldwork

Fieldwork is only possible when the sociologist gets his or her "hands dirty." In this method, the researcher becomes acquainted with the people she or he hopes to study. The field worker may interview people, search for non-verbal indicators of group life, and may even take on a role that is acceptable to the community. In this way, the researcher becomes a participant observer.

One of the obligations of the participant observer is not to influence what happens and record objectively what is observed. Although they overlap, psychologists are likely to conduct observational study in a relatively more controlled atmosphere in a laboratory but sociologists and anthropologists are more likely to do so in the field.

The analysis of qualitative data is quite different from quantitative. Typically, the researcher has vast amounts of written documents. To search for patterns and consistencies in these documents prove to be very difficult. However, recent computer programs have been developed to facilitate the process. One such program is called NUDIST (published by Sage Publications) that has been shown to be very useful in this search.

Another term to describe fieldwork is the case study. It is important that the researcher conducts a detached observation so that what is recorded is as close as possible a mirror of the real social life of the people who are subjects.

Unstructured questionnaires are used in this kind of research. They consist of wide open ended questions wherein respondents are encouraged to answer in any way they want.

This research is very costly both in time and money. Yet, it has the potential of revealing many rich details of a people's social life that could not be discovered in any other way.

Two ethnographers,[4] Redfield and Rojas (1953) went to live among descendants of the Mayan people in Mexico's Yucatan peninsula. In their research, they found one village that thrived on industry, hard work, frugality, and productive effort. The researchers discovered that the elite people of the village had earlier become Protestant because of some missionaries' efforts.

Quantitative Research

This kind of research is the closest approximation to the kind of research used by the natural scientists. This was the dream of Comte who hoped to be able to study human societies as well a physicists, for example, studied inorganic matter. Durkheim extended Comte's vision and actually did a study of suicide in Western Europe using census data (Durkheim, 1951).

In the social sciences, the basic kind of research method that is of a quantitative nature is the experiment. The researcher is interested in discovering or testing for causes of social phenomena using very controlled environments. It is typically done in a laboratory or in a natural setting. There are typically two groups of subjects: the experimental group and control group. The experimental group consists of those subjects who are exposed to the independent variable while the control group are subjects not exposed to the independent variable. After subjects have been randomly assigned to the two groups, measurements on the dependent variable is made on both groups. Then, the independent variable is introduced to the experimental group but not to the control group. As second set of measures is applied to the dependent variable. If there are changes in the dependent variable, then one can safely assume that this difference is a result of the independent variable.

In sociology, this method is rarely used because sociologists are more interested in broad issues in society that cannot be discovered or tested in a laboratory. The experiment is outlined here to illustrate that survey methods are an attempt to approximate the experiment in searching for causes of social phenomena.

Demographic Techniques

Demographers are those social scientists who have specialized in the study of whole populations through national census. They frequently investigate fertility rates, marriage rates, migration rates and mortality rates. Their advantage is that the whole of a population is included in the collection of data. In Canada, one is held every ten years.

Porter (1965), in the same study referred to above, found that there was a strong correlation between Protestant affiliates and higher levels of income. This gives further credibility to the linkage between Protestantism and capitalism.

Survey Research

This technique is one that is most commonly used by sociologists. It is similar to demographic research in that a large number of cases can be included in the data as well as a large number of variables. However, if differs on two accounts. First, the sociologist is the designer of the survey (not state officials) and can include many questions that are relevant to her or his research. Secondly, and more importantly, surveys do not ask questions of whole populations but only of a select few of that population. This is done through a technique called random sampling which means that all individuals within a population have an equal chance of being selected. A special feature of this kind of sampling is that one can generalize to the whole population.

The kinds of questions asked can be either a structured interview or an unstructured one. The former involves written questions that require a predefined set of answers to be responded to. Four common ways for this to happen is to mail out questionnaires to the sample, personally interview them, telephone them or tape record their answers for further recording and analysis. This is the kind of questionnaire that is used in either demographic or survey research.

Surveys are like opinion poles that news magazines use frequently. In social sciences, surveys are used to obtain various characteristics of a population (age, sex, income, religious affiliation, attitudes, beliefs, behaviors). In this way, one can obtain numerical measures of variables that can be used later to see if two variable correlate with one another, or one or more can be found to predict (as independent variables) a dependent variable.

A well known survey that tested the Weberian thesis was done by Gerhard Lenski (1963) in the late 1950s. He was well acquainted with Weber's work in that he searched for questions that would measure the spirit of capitalism or capitalistic attitudes and values. The way he measured this was to ask respondents if they are more happy working or taking life easy. The scale he used was one that measured positive, neutral or negative responses. His measure of Protestantism was simply affiliation. His analysis indicated that there were small but relatively consistent differences between white Protestants and Catholics in their economic attitudes.

The Research Process

For students in an introductory course, if will suffice to learn a general guideline of a research model. The researcher begins with a topic that may help us to understand some aspect of our complex society. After this initial stage, one needs to refer to the existing literature to see what has been found out about this topic before. It also provides background information and a clue to a theoretical perspective.

A second stage is to specify the meaning of the constructs and variables that one is to include within the process. From these constructs and variables, propositions and hypotheses are further developed. A third stage is to choose which research method would best be used to measure these variables and hypotheses. From the last section, these include: the analysis of historical records, the analysis of contemporary records, fieldwork, demographic techniques, and survey research.

If the study is a quantitative one using survey methods, a population needs to be specified. Babbie (1989:97) describes it as that group of people about whom we want to be able to draw conclusions. If for example, one is interested in studying divorce in Alberta, the target population would be all adults who are currently married or have been married and are now divorced. One would not include children or anyone who is not married or has never been married.

From that population, a random sample is to be drawn. This means that a method is selected that does not have any bias (like the use of the 20th number in a phone book, having access to SIN's and having a computer program randomly select the sample). The important feature of this is that every kind of person within the population has an equal chance of being included in the sample (on characteristics of gender, age, social class, religion, ethnicity, race, and the like).

This is followed by the construction of a questionnaire (structured as in the case of a survey and unstructured for field work) that focuses on creating questions that reflect the constructs that were originally established. The methodological term used is called "operationalization." Once the data are collected, the researcher begins to analyze them. This analysis of data leads to the interpretations and evaluation which must be as objective as possible. The final stage is the conclusion or application that consists in the reporting of the results and assessing their application.

Ethics in Sociological Research

Ethics in this case refer to professional standards that a sociologist (indeed any scientist) is required to adhere to. Some of these moral codes consist of openness (offer to share findings with colleagues), honesty, truth, refusing to falsify findings and committing plagiarism. Another code includes confidentiality. To encourage subjects in a study to be honest, researchers promise confidentiality. The American Sociological Association Code of Ethics stipulates: "Confidential information provided by research participants must be treated as such by sociologists, even when this information enjoys no legal protection or privilege and legal force is applied" (quoted in Henslin and Nelson, 1996:137).

Further codes include activities that protect the rights of subjects. For example, informing subjects that they are part of a study, making sure that no harm comes to the subjects, and giving them freedom to respond or not. Participants must be free to be part of a study or not to maintain their integrity.

A good example of the integrity of a researcher who refused to divulge information that he had gathered in a research project to state authorities is provided by Henslin and Nelson (1996). This researcher, Rik Scarce, was studying a radical environmental movement. While he was engaged in his research, a group calling itself the Animal Liberation Front broke into the laboratory of a university, did damage to the facility, and freed some of the animals. Police investigators questioned Scare thinking that he might have some information that would lead them to the guilty parties. He cooperated to the extent of providing information of a generic nature but would not violate his agreements of confidentiality to his subjects. He later was subpoenaed but still refused. For his refusal to cooperate with these authorities, he spent 159 days in prison.

Difficulties in Sociological Research

Like in many other disciplines, there are some difficulties in sociological research. Some subjects may provide the wrong information. They may intentionally create their own answer or they may shy away from the real information. Also, they may be intimidated by a researcher or may provide information that they think the investigator wants to hear rather than being honest with what is truthful. This is what is called "social desirability."

In a study by Kanwar (1980) on satisfaction in marriage and the family, one of the questions asked was if the couple were to marry again, would they marry the same person if they had a personal choice in the matter? When together, they all responded in the affirmative. When questioned separately, however, 57% of husbands and 87% of wives said they would not marry the same person. Likely, in each other's presence, they are not being honest for fear of offending their spouse.

One way to reduce socially desirable answers to questions is to include items in a questionnaire that tests for it. If it is found to be present in the answers given from a subject, that subject's answers are eliminated from the project. An example is the research done by Larson and his colleagues (1994). In this study, many questions were asked of evangelical clergy and their spouses across Canada. A social desirability question was included that went something like this: On a scale of 1 to 7 (1 meaning poor and 7, fantastic), how would you rate your marriage? If a subject answered 7, we would realize that no one really has a fantastic marriage. The respondent was answering this question to please the researcher or give to him or her what the subject thought they would like to hear. The subject was eliminated from the other data because if this question was false, then there is a likelihood that other questions could also be wrong.

Another method to protect information from social desirability responses is to have different ways of receiving the information. In a well known study on human sexuality in the United States by Laumann and his colleagues (1994), a question was asked twice as to the number of sexual partners the subject had in past year. The interviewer wrote on the code book the subject's response. Much later in the interview (these interviews lasted about 2 hours), the same question was asked again. This time, however, the subject was asked to write the answer on a piece of paper. This answer was then put into a sealed envelope and handed to the interviewer. Later, in the laboratory, the responses were compared. If there was discrepancy, the case was not included in the study.

In addition, the presence of the researcher, an outsider, may affect how people respond to certain questions or may change certain behaviors just because of the presence of the reseacher. This has become known as the Hawthorne effect. Babbie (1989) explains.

> During the 1920s and 1930s, two researchers, F. J. Roethlisberger and W. J. Dickson studied working conditions in the telephone "bank wiring room" in the Western Electric Works in Chicago. Their intent was to see if an improved work environment would result in higher levels of productivity. Initially, they found that to be the case. In this room, they improved the lighting conditions and productivity increased. However, when they made the lighting conditions even worse than they were before any of the changes, they found that productivity increased again. Their hypotheses were not substantiated by their research. What really increased productivity was not improved working conditions but, rather, the fact that they were being observed by the researchers. The independent variable, then, was not a change in the work conditions but the presence of the researchers! The lesson from this research is that one needs to be careful in not allowing information to be distorted by the visible presence of the researcher.[5]

Summary

This has been a simple introduction to sociological methodology. Its use may not be translated directly into personal research that the student may do. Much more needs to be learnt. However, one important fruit of this chapter could be that the student is in a better position to judge research that she or he reads in articles or books. Also, many agencies use statistics to tell their stories. Knowing good methodology from poor will enable the student to be more critical and more aware of erroneous information in the public domain.

Notes

1. Durkheim's term and used by Merton to describe a condition of society in which individuals become disconnected from others and detached from the norms that ordinarily guide their social action.

2. The social historian Tilly (1981) assists us in understanding what social history is. According to him, the central question asked by social historians is how did the development of the modern world (like democracy, capitalism or socialism) affect the ways that ordinary people act together in their common interests?

3. Another term used to describe this is content analysis.

4. A person who does ethnographic research. Ethnography is a field of anthropological research based on direct observation of and reporting on a people's way of life. As such, ethnography is the core method of cultural anthropology. Ethnographic subjects are usually cultural groups, such as communities, tribes, or dialect groups. However, classes or institutions within complex urban societies are also subjects of study. Ethnography consists of two phases: the process of observing and recording data, usually called fieldwork, followed by the preparation of a written description and analysis of the subject under study (Grolier Multimedia Encyclopedia).

5. In a laboratory setting, in studying the behaviors of subjects, researchers sometimes stand behind one-way windows wherein the observers can see the subjects but not vice versa. This eliminates the probability of the Hawthorne effect.

References

Anderson, C.
1970 *White Protestant Americans*. Englewood Cliffs, NJ: Prentice-Hall.

Babbie, E.
1989 *The Practice of Social Research*. Belmont, CA: Wadsworth Publishing Company.

Bell, W.
1957 "Anomie, Social Isolation, and the Class Structure." *Sociometry* 20:105–116.

Dane, F.
1990 *Research Methods*. Pacific Grove, CA: Brooks/Cole Publishing Company.

Durkheim, E.
1951 *Suicide: A Study in Sociology*. New York: The Free Press.

Grolier
1996 Grolier Mulitmedia Encyclopedia. Grolier Incorporated and Microsoft Corporation.

Henslin, J. and A. Nelson
1996 *Sociology: A Down to Earth Approach. Canadian Edition*. Toronto: Allyn and Bacon.

Kanwar, M.
1980 "Marriage, Family, and the Social System in Pakistan." Research funded by Mount Royal College and conducted in Pakistan in June-December, 1979.

Laumann, E., R. Michael, J. Gagnon and S. Michaels
1994 *The Social Organization of Sexuality: Sexual Practices in the United States*. Chicago: The University of Chicago Press.

Jonassen, C. T.
1947 "The Protestant Ethic and the Spirit of Captialism in Norway." *American Sociological Review* 12:676-686.

Larson, L., J. Goltz, I. Barker, M. Driedger, T. LeBlanc, B. Rennick, and D. Swenson
1994 *Clergy Families in Canada: An Initial Report.* New Market, ON: Evangelical Fellowship of Canada.

Lenski, G.
1963 *The Religious Factor*. New York: Doubleday.

Merton, R.
1968 *Social Theory and Social Structure*. Glencoe, Il.: The Free Press.

Porter, J.
1965 *The Vertical Mosaic*. Toronto: The University of Toronto Press.

Redfield, R. and V. Rojas
1953 A Village That Chose Progress. Chicago: The University of Chicago Press.

Tilly, C.
1981 *When Sociology Meets History*. New York: Academic Press.

Tiryakian, E.
1975 "Neither Marx or Durkheim ... Perhaps Weber." *American Sociological Review* 81:1–33.

Tummin, M. and R. Collins
1959 "Status Mobility and Anomie: A Study in Readiness for Desegration." *British Journal of Sociology* 10:253–267.

Weber, M.
1958 *The Protestant Ethic and the Spirit of Capitalism*. New York: Scribners and Sons.

Westhues, K.
1982 *First Sociology*. New York: McGraw-Hill.

3

Issues in Canadian Culture

Bruce McGuigan

As we saw in Chapter One, the concept "culture" is at the very heart of sociology along with social action, social structure and social history. Culture provides people with a kind of mental "roadmap" of social life, a sense of meaning and identity.

To understand culture within sociological discourse, it is useful to view sociology as seen through the eyes of Max Weber, who chooses to call sociology an "interpretative sociology." By this he meant that the sociologist accomplishes her or his task by endeavouring to interpret or understand (in the German, *versthen*) the inner thoughts, ideas, values and perspectives of the people he or she is studying. Once this is done, one is in a better position to make sense of the social action and the social structures that emerge from those social actions. This is why sociologists consider culture to have several dimensions, which we outline in this chapter: cognitive (the way people think and communicate), normative (the way people behave or evaluate the behaviour of others), and material (artifacts produced by human, social activity).

In the first section of this chapter we will look at how sociologists discuss and analyze culture. Following this, we will trace the main current issues in Canadian culture. The goal of this chapter is to both acquaint students with the sociological analysis of culture as well as with the current major issues in Canadian society which can be attributed to culture. By the end of this chapter, you should understand the basic concepts and issues in the sociological discussion of culture as well as the current central issues in Canadian society and their cultural importance.

Studying Culture

Introduction

The term culture brings to mind a variety of images. We may imagine a way of life, an art form, a language, a civilization or all four at once. For many, the word culture engenders images of Mozart, Brahms, Da Vinci, Picasso and other prominent figures in what is commonly referred to as "high culture." Some of us may relate the term culture to "popular culture" or "mass culture." Distinctions between these terms are hard to make. High culture has the common shared meaning discussed above. John Fisk, one of the most prominent scholars of popular and mass culture, makes the following distinction between the two:

> what industries produce is mass culture, what the people produce out of mass culture is popular culture. All industrial products can be taken into popular culture, but most are not. (Galbo, 1991:4)

Fisk suggests that mass culture is composed of the products of industries such as the music industry, fashion industry, television and film industry, even the automotive industry. What people do with these products is what constitutes popular culture. These usages of the term culture focus on what is produced by a culture and transitory usages of these products and ignore the fact that culture is a constant component of daily human existence for all of us.

The popular conceptions of the word "culture" leaves us unaware of the extent to which individual human lives are shaped by culture. We tend to take for granted the extent to which everything we do in our daily lives is culturally determined. Some of these things may be specific to our culture, others may be shared by almost all human cultures.

In the first few minutes after waking up, we all perform a number of actions which are culturally determined. The time we wake up frequently conforms to what is an accepted and common time to wake up in our culture. The device we may use, an alarm clock or clock radio, is a cultural product and is not common to all cultures, so too are our bed and bed clothes. If we shower or brush our teeth after waking up it is because this is an appropriate daily morning activity in our culture. What clothing we put on, what we eat and drink for breakfast, and everything we do for the rest of the day including work, recreation and family activities, are elements of our culture.

Usually, one does not become aware of the all encompassing nature of culture until we are placed in an unfamiliar cultural context. Even very minor cultural differences can suddenly produce in us the awareness that we are in a foreign culture. Certainly, in many regards, Canada is similar to the United States. But Canadians who travel to the United States almost invariably have something to say about how Americans differ from us. The generalizations we make after this kind of contact are indications of how unfamiliar the cultural setting is to us. We may say that Americans are friendlier, more direct, more aggressive, more nationalistic or just speak funny. These are indications that American culture varies in discernible ways from ours in values and practices.

Exposure to extreme cultural differences can produce in us the perception that we are not at all capable of coping in a social environment. This is often referred to as *Culture Shock.* Language is frequently the first thing we notice because an unfamiliar language environment makes it impossible for us to communicate clearly and accurately. However, culture shock can also leave us feeling that we have no idea of how to behave or act. Norms of appropriate conduct vary substantially between human cultures. For example, standards of dress for men and women, appropriate public conduct, table manners and a host of other components of culture are substantially different in the Arab world than they are in the West.

Social scientists generally use culture to refer to all of those learned aspects of being human. This would include language, beliefs, values and ideas as well as all activities and practices including things like science and technology. To put it differently, it would include all of those things that are both the product and subject of human beings interacting with one another. Cultures develop as a consequence of a social group's shared experiences and the meanings they commonly attach to the world around them. Cultures also consist in part of a social group's shared experiences and shared meanings. Culture shapes much of what we are able to perceive because by giving us language, values and ideas it gives us the tools with which we both perceive and communicate perception. We are not born with all of the characteristics of a fully developed human. Everything, from language to attitudes, to how to go about performing simple common human actions, must be learned. Human survival is a cultural activity. We create tools and technology, methods and patterns of social interaction, and all of the things we need to survive as a cultural activity. Without culture, there would be very little about us that we could call "human." Genetics give humans the potential to develop, culture *is* that development, both in terms of process and content.

One of the most important issues in discussing culture is that any statement we make by way of definition is also comparative. Logically, we can not define without comparing. What we say about one culture by way of definition are frequently those things which we perceive to be distinguishing characteristics of that culture. Naturally, we are implying that other cultures either do not have these characteristics, have them to a lesser extent, or do not have them in similar combinations with other characteristics. There are very few elements of human cultures that are found in the identical form in all cultures. There is tremendous variation. However, similarities can be noticed in certain well defined general areas.

Anthropologist George Murdock examined and compared over two hundred cultures and found a number of "universal" components of human culture. These universals refer to equivalencies between cultures, not identical components. Among other things, Murdock identified humor, dancing, folklore, mourning, religion, athletic sports and hospitality as common to all of the cultures he examined. However, it is critically important to remember that the precise content of these components of culture varied substantially.

For the purpose of study or analysis, culture can be divided into several categories. These categories are somewhat arbitrary in that any element from one may be closely related to others. However, it is useful to talk about culture as the way people think and communicate (cognitive), the way people behave or evaluate the behavior of others (normative) and the things people produce (material). Sociologists generally focus on the cognitive and normative elements of culture. It is useful to think of both of these elements as being similar to a code.

Culture as a Code

Culture is like a code in two ways. First, it is like a radio or secret code. All cultures contain ways of creating, transmitting and interpreting meaning that are unique to that culture. This is usually referred to as the *cognitive* element of culture. Second, cultures are like a legal code. All cultures contain *values*. This may include general ideas about what is good or bad, normal or abnormal, acceptable or unacceptable, desirable or undesirable, or more generally, what is valued. This is referred to as the *normative* element of culture. To be able to function in a culture, we have to know the *code*.

Cognitive

The creation, transmission and interpretation of meaning is accomplished through the use of symbols. A *symbol* is something that refers to something else. Written and spoken words, signs, gestures, facial expressions are some examples of symbols. They represent things like actions, objects, ideas or attitudes. They are not these things themselves, but something else which we all understand to *mean* that thing.

For example, when we want someone to sit in a chair we do not necessarily have to push them into a sitting position on a chair. If we say "Sit in the chair" we use sounds which are accepted by both that person and ourselves to be symbols for the object (chair) and the action (sitting). Of course, what happens if the person does not speak our language? What if they cannot speak or hear at all?

For this communication to work, we must both understand and agree upon the symbols and be able to understand them. Symbols are not universal or permanent. Languages are systems of symbols which members of different cultures use to create and communicate meaning. If we use the word "chair" in conversation with someone from a culture without chairs and who has never had the concept "chair" explained to him, it will have no meaning to him. Even more awkward for communication, cultures may use the same sound or a similar sound to communicate something quite different. If I was to say that I was "embarrassed" English speakers may understand that I felt distressingly self conscious. A native Spanish speaker might confuse the word "embarrass" with "*embarazado*" from his or her language and believe that I was pregnant.

However, languages are not just methods of communication including the use of sound or gesture. To varying extents, languages contain ways of seeing or ordering physical and social reality which are unique to a culture. For example, we identify *things* by the symbols we use in language. Most of us are aware that the Inuit have several words for snow, while we have only the one. This is not an over complicated perception of frozen water on the part of the Inuit. It enables the Inuit to *perceive* several things where we only perceive one. These culture specific systems of symbols are not just important for communication between any individual and others, but also for internal intellectual and psychological activity—communication within individuals. The eminent social psychologist George Herbert Mead asserted that ". . . [I]n order that thought may exist there must be symbols, vocal gestures generally.... (Mead, 1962 [1934]:73).

Part of this idea that language communicates a perception of the physical and social reality around us is contained within the idiomatic phrase "To speak someone's language." If I say "I speak Fred's language," what is usually meant and understood is seldom, if ever, that I share the ability to speak a certain language with Fred. What I mean, and what people in our culture would generally comprehend, is that I understand how Fred views the world, what his values are, and how he is likely to respond to different objects and ideas.

Most English speaking Canadians have at one time or another struggled to learn French. Something which you may have immediately recognized is that part of what French speakers communicate in conversation with one another is the relative status of those communicating. As you are probably aware, in French one uses the pronoun *vous* when addressing a person of superior status and *tu* to speak to a person of equal or inferior status. Similarly, in Spanish the verb form *Usted* is used with those of superior status. There is no equivalent to these structures in English. English speakers may find it difficult to understand why it is that in French one speaks to an individual such as a policeman or a professor as if there was more than one of them and why it is in Spanish that one speaks to these people in a manner which to us suggests that they are not even in the room and that we are communicating through an intermediary.

Language is not the only symbol system for a culture. There are cultures which differ in many regards yet share the same language. Every culture has symbols with shared meanings other than words and gestures. Actions have "symbolic" meaning. As Mead noted, offering someone a chair may also be interpreted as a symbolic gesture of hospitality or good manners (Mead, 1962 [1934]:15).

Most cultures have objects to which symbolic meaning is attached. We can easily imagine that to many Americans, the maple leaf is the foliage of a tree of the family *Aceraceae.* To Canadians, it is a symbol for their nation. We have other symbols as Canadians which we understand to have special meaning to us: The Mountie; The Beaver; The Blue Nose; O Canada; etc. To Canadians, the Mountie is not just a policeman, the Beaver is not just a large rodent with a weird tale; and O Canada is not just a song. These objects become symbols when we as members of a culture attach meaning to them above and beyond what they are as objects or things. Their symbolic meaning is not intrinsic, it is not a basic physical property. Similarly, it is possible to give an interpretation of what symbols in a culture mean in terms of the values of the members of that culture. Many sociologists interpret symbols such as the Mountie and the Beaver to mean that the normative structure of Canadian society places a high value on lawfulness and diligence.

Normative

The normative element of culture are those aspects of a culture that are relevant to how members of that culture behave. They go from very general statements about what actions, ideas or attitudes are appropriate, to specific statements about what is good or bad.

In the most general terms, a society's values are those things which members of that society consider to be important—what they value. *Values* are general ideas about what is appropriate or inappropriate, good or bad, desirable or undesirable. If we say that a Canadian value is honesty, what we are saying is that there is some level of agreement between Canadians that not lying or cheating is important and that anything gained by cheating or lying is of less or no worth. We may also be saying that relative to another unspecified culture we either place more emphasis on honesty, or perceive ourselves to do so. Values are "ideal" kinds of behavior and general attitudes. They are as frequently goals or aspirations of how we should or should not think, act or behave and less frequently descriptions of how we actually behave.

Norms are more specific than values. *Norms* are those ideas about what members of a culture should or should not do in a given situation. Norms include all of what may be considered to be right and wrong. We conform to the norms of our culture constantly without really thinking about it. We do not have to actively recall and apply norms as we go through varying social experiences. We usually regard them as simply how things are done—frequently without question or consideration that there may be alternatives. For example, you may have noticed that on elevators passengers face the door and do not interact with strangers in any way. Why? What happens if someone doesn't do this? Will he or she be treated severely?

We encourage compliance with norms and discourage noncompliance through the use of *sanctions.* Simply put, sanctions are rewards for conformity and penalties for nonconformity. A negative sanction may include staring at someone or even refusing to look them in the eye, it may also include cutting off their head.

Of course, there are actions or attitudes which may be regarded as right or wrong and are of varying importance. Defrauding a bank is a serious violation of a norm against stealing, which can be argued to be a specific application of a society's general values regarding honesty. Keeping a hundred dollars that we may find on the street may be dishonest, but it is not regarded by most members of our society to be as serious as robbing a bank.

The early social scientist William Graham Sumner differentiated between three kinds of norms. These distinctions have become conventional in social science and are largely based on how they are defined and what kinds of sanctions are applied when they are violated (Sumner, 1906). If violating a norm is considered to be a serious act for which there should be serious consequences social scientists label those norms as *Mores* (pronounced *moraze*). Mores are standards which members of a society consider to be an obligation. Those norms which when violated generate a less serious response are referred to as *Folkways.* Folkways are not obligatory; responses on the part of members of a society when a folkway is violated are likely to be mild or nonexistent.

Folkways are informal customs to which most people in a culture generally conform. Violating a folkway is not a serious act and in some cases there may be no response at all on the part of other members of a society. Folkways include such things as styles of dress, manners, conventional behavior, where and how to stand in an elevator, how to eat, what to eat and when, etc. When we violate a folkway, we may be considered to be rude, strange or inept and someone may do something to communicate their displeasure to us, but we will not usually be considered a threat and response is not likely to be severe or violent.

Facing the door in an elevator and not speaking to or looking at fellow passengers is a norm, a rule of social conduct for that situation. It is classified as a folkway because facing the wrong way in an elevator and talking to strangers would not result in other members of society applying any serious sanctions or even any sanctions at all.

Folkways are not universal or permanent. They change, appear and disappear within a culture. Even when they are present, they are not in effect in every social situation or location. Facing the door and not making eye contact or speaking in an elevator is appropriate behavior for that situation and location, it would not be appropriate at a dinner party.

Mores can usually be recognized as a more powerful or important norm by the sanctions (or consequences) enacted by members of a culture when these norms are breached (violated). Mores are almost never situational. There are seldom places or situations in which they are suspended. Members of a culture share very strong feelings about mores, this is why they are unlikely to tolerate any breaches. Examples of mores are things like murder, rape, theft or incest. It is easy to believe that mores are universal or do not change, but this is not true. In some cultures, pre-marital sex is severely punishable and in the past in our own culture serious sanctions have been applied to violators of this norm. Currently, however, it would be difficult to view norms against pre-marital sex as a more strongly held by all those who share our culture. There are few if any serious social sanctions applied in our culture to this kind of activity. The most serious response to those who engage in this kind of behavior, mild reproach, ostracism, etc., suggest that this norm may be on the way to becoming a folkway or even that pre-marital sex is now a norm itself, rather than a deviant act.

Laws are norms which have been formally defined and enacted. This formalization process can involve the actions of religious institutes, governments, or both. Legal formalization involves the clear definition of the act, and a definition of the sanctions applied to an individual who breaches the norm. Cultures with formal religious or political institutes create laws, most often out of mores, and in cultures with well established political or religious institutions most mores are covered by laws. In these cultures, specialists of the law—lawyers—are found. However, preliterate cultures have mores without necessarily having what we would recognize as laws or lawyers.

Taboos are the most strongly prohibited social acts. The term has generally been used in the past to not only imply severity but also imply universality. That is, that they are often considered to exist in all cultures. The most often discussed taboo is the norm prohibiting sexual contact with family members—incest. However, it is important to note that although all known human cultures have prohibitions against sexual activity with certain kin, the content of these taboos vary enormously. What is incest in some cultures is *required* in other cultures. For example, in our culture sexual activity with a first cousin is generally regarded as incest. In the Yaruro culture of South America, male members *must* marry their mother's brother's daughter or their father's sister's daughter—their first cousin (Freeman, 1974).

Frequently, human cultures have systems of ideas which allow them to disregard norms under certain specified circumstances. Ideologies are ideas or systems of ideas which justify actions against certain individuals in violation of norms. Put more simply, ideologies frequently justify the breaching of mores. A good example of this would be national ideologies which legitimate breaches of mores such as murder under certain circumstances, such as war. Racism can be an ideology which justifies breaching general norms of conduct against specific individuals on the basis of their membership in certain racial or ethnic groups. Of course, ideologies do not have to be that complex. For example, what ideology would you use to justify keeping money you found in the street?

Cultural Change and Transmission

When considering culture, we must recognize that culture is not only how ideas are transmitted, culture itself is also transmitted. One of the consequences of the transmission of culture is that it is changed. There are two processes of change. Individuals may reinterpret cultural elements which have been transmitted to them and transmit this reinterpretation to others. The other process is that cultures may come into contact with foreign cultures and adopt elements of that culture. Both occur constantly.

Change

Cultures change very slowly. We can see in written history statements of ideas, values and perceptions of the world that are not tremendously different from our own. For example, what may be most striking to many the first time they read Shakespeare is the clearly visible difference in language. This is an obvious change in culture over time. However, once difficulties with the language are overcome, we may notice that Shakespeare's ideas and sentiments do not differ substantially from those expressed in our own time. However, it is not difficult to recognize cultural change. For several hundred years, and perhaps for all of human history, values as well as language have been undergoing perceptible change within the lifetime of individuals. Simply studying a ten or twenty year old movie will yield a bewildering variety of variations in cognitive and normative culture, in the way people talk and behave.

Excellent examples of changing norms in Canadian society can be found in Canadian behavior in the area of marriage. Norms govern all kinds of marriage related behavior. The age at which we marry, divorce and cohabitation without marriage are all activities covered by norms. Norms in some of these activities, such as divorce, have been formalized as laws.

There are two clear indications that norms in Canada regarding divorce have changed. The first is that laws in Canada regarding divorce have undergone substantial revision twice in the last 25 years, in 1968 and in 1985. In both cases, a substantial amount of pressure was successfully exerted by groups within Canadian society to bring about legal revisions consisting of making it easier to get a divorce. The other indication that norms regarding divorce have changed is that the divorce rate (divorces per 100,000 married women), has been steadily increasing since about 1960. It is currently estimated that one third of marriages in Canada will end in divorce, up from an estimate of one in five in 1971 (Adams, 1990:147).

In general, values in Canadian society regarding marriage have been undergoing change. Fewer people than ever before are choosing to marry, more are divorcing, and increasingly high numbers of couples choose to live together without marrying.

Cultural Transmission

Culture is transmitted. It is taught to each member of a society, and shared between different cultural groups. This process is called *Acculturation.* We are all acculturalized from birth to be members of our culture. We learn language, beliefs, values and norms in the process of acculturalization. The term is also applied to situations when cultures adopt elements of other cultures, and when individuals learn to cope in a new and previously unfamiliar culture.

Acculturalization is accomplished through a wide variety of processes. The process in which we are taught to be members of a culture from birth (also called socialization) occurs primarily through direct contact with other members of the culture, parents, siblings, friends and teachers. However, cultural transmission also occurs through other processes. The media, including the written word and the electronic media, also transmits culture. All of these communication processes may occur simultaneously for someone who has been emersed in a new and unfamiliar culture, those who travel, or those who emigrate to new cultures.

Written language was a tremendous cultural innovation. It allowed a very accurate transmission of culture over time and distance. For example, our culture maintains values and symbolic meanings from the written records of religions established thousands of years ago. Because these records exist, accurate transmission of cultural values has been accomplished across thousands of years. Books, letters and newspapers also allow the transmission of ideas—and therefore culture—accurately across vast distances (Innis, 1971). For example, the ideas that became the foundation of the American revolution were in part transmitted in the form of books from France and England and by immigration from England, they were applied and became an important component of culture in the United States (Lipset, 1989:10).

As a consequence of electronic media, instant global communication has become possible. It was the Canadian social scientist Marshal McLuhan who coined the phrase "Global Village" (McLuhan, 1964) to explain the social consequences of the technological innovations. Communication with individuals on the other side of the planet has become almost as easy as with someone in our own town, we just pick up the phone.

It is important to recognize that this transmission of culture is by no means equal. If one society produces more cultural objects, films, television shows, music, books, etc., than another, it will likely "give" more than it "receives" in terms of cultural influence. The United States is the most prolific society in the world in producing cultural objects. As a consequence, American culture and values have become profoundly influential. Objects produced by American culture, such as posters, music, and television can be found in the most remote parts of the world. American television programs, for example, constitute as much as 30% of programming in industrialized nations and 90% in non-industrialized nations (Hindley et al, 1977 in Hiller, 1991:60). Add to this the influence of newspapers, magazines, books, movies and it should be apparent that American cultural influence is not solely a problem in Canada (Hiller, 1991:60).

Subcultures and Countercultures

Most modern industrial societies are not culturally homogenous. Most contain a considerable amount of cultural variation. Groups within a society may have different values, attitudes, norms, and lifestyles from the dominant culture. These groups are called *subcultures.* Their culture usually contains a number of variations from the dominant culture. For example, the diet, values, beliefs and lifestyles of Italian Canadian may vary in identifiable ways from the dominant Anglo-Canadian culture. These variations identify this group as a subculture. Many countries such as Canada and the United States have a tremendous number of subcultures. They do not exist solely on the basis of ethnic identity. Subcultures can also form around other symbol systems. In Canada, the "barriers" between dominant culture and subculture form on the basis of a wide variety of factors including religion, class, ethnicity and regional variations which may themselves also include ethnicity, class and religion with differences in economic activity. To some extent, we can even also talk about subcultures as forming around musical taste. Those of us who live in large urban centers may be able to identify a variety of subcultures centred on music. We may be able to identify bars, restaurants and businesses that cater to country and western or punk subcultures. We may even be able to make certain reasonable generalizations about the patrons of these establishments, in terms of beliefs and values. In some cases, it is possible to identify parts of town where members of these cultures congregate and live and where their more visible cultural practices take place.

In a complex society such as ours, it is possible to be capable of functioning in several cultures. Some individuals may be able to understand and adhere to the cognitive and normative elements of Italian-Canadian culture, Punk culture and the dominant culture equally well. It is not difficult to imagine someone who appears to be a member of the dominant Anglo-Canadian culture during the week at work, Italian-Canadian culture at home with his or her family, and Punk culture when out with friends.

Countercultures vary from subcultures in that their members hold values that are in direct opposition to those of the dominant culture. The "Hippy" subculture that was so visible during the 1960s and early 1970s was openly opposed to what they perceived to be a violent, materialistic, and repressive dominant culture. They peacefully protested the Vietnam war, lived with few material possessions, and experimented with drugs and sexuality in a manner not condoned by the dominant culture. Certainly, contact between this counter-culture and the dominant culture resulted in acculturation in both directions. Most hippies eventually gave up their lifestyle and some of their values regarding peace and love and anti-materialism influenced the dominant culture.

Nature versus Nurture

So far the position clearly taken in this chapter is that human culture is quite independent of human biology. That is, that human-ness is culturally determined, not biologically. At least one opposing perspective exists. There exists a limited debate over how much of human behavior is shaped by culture, and how much is determined by the biological fact of human-ness. This debate is usually referred to as *Nature versus Nurture.*

Sociobiology is the study of the biological basis of human behavior. The perspective's leading proponent was Edward O. Wilson, a Harvard entomologist who specialized in the study of ants (Wilson, 1975). Wilson applied Darwin's theory of evolution to human cultural traits, not just physical ones. He suggested that some human behaviors have been passed on genetically and that some physical characteristics may exist because of past and continuing cultural values. The core assertion of sociobiology is that social behavior among humans, like ants, has evolved as a mechanism to ensure the survival of the species. Sociobiologists assert that humans are genetically predisposed to a variety of social behaviors and even attitudes to ensure the perpetuation of mankind. These would include norms regarding incest, homosexuality, sex-role differences, to name just a few. More often than not, critics of sociobiology simplify it's assertions to facilitate easy criticism. The fact is, Wilson's own position was that the vast majority of the range of possible variations in human social behavior is culturally determined. His concern was that social science has an overwhelming tendency to underestimate the role of biology in human social behavior.

Ethnocentrism and Cultural Relativism

Contained within cultures, and also varying substantially within our own culture, are attitudes toward other cultures. There are two opposite ends to the possible spectrum on attitudes to other cultures: ethnocentrism and *cultural relativism.*

To be ethnocentric is to view one's culture's values and norms as superior, and the values and norms of other cultures as inferior. Ethnocentrism also involves evaluating the actions and attitudes of members of another culture by the norms and values of one's own culture. In such cases, someone who is ethnocentric is acting without regard for the fact that members of that culture may be behaving in a way that, from the perspective of their own culture, is completely appropriate. Since our view of the world around us, especially the social world, is shaped almost entirely by our culture, ethnocentrism is an understandable and perhaps even inevitable response to contact with conspicuously different cultures.

Cultural relativism is the opposite of ethnocentrism. To be culturally relativistic is to believe that the values, norms or customs of all cultures are equally valid, and that none are inherently good or bad. While it is easy to imagine someone who is ethnocentric, it is difficult to imagine that anyone could be completely culturally relativistic. This is because the "original equipment" that we have to view the world around us is provided by our own culture. Some common cultural practices in some other cultures are likely to be startlingly disharmonious with our own. To be fully culturally relativistic would mean that we literally have no opinion or consider acceptable the practices of other cultures which would be serious violations of mores within our own. For example, until very recently female infanticide was a common practice in parts of northern India, so too was the social norm that widows commit suicide by throwing themselves on their husbands funeral pyres. It would be hard to imagine any Canadian woman who would not view these as unacceptable practices in our society and suggest that they be allowed because they are the part of the values of a different culture.

Canadian Culture

Canadian culture is often discussed as difficult to define. Most discussions of Canadian culture emphasise diversity. There is tremendous variety in culture in Canada by ethnicity and region. Canadian culture, especially in the English speaking parts of the country, is also similar in many regards to other English speaking societies such as the United States, Australia, and Great Britain. As stated earlier in this chapter, the definition of a culture for social scientists necessarily means comparison. Comparison can be explicit, in that elements of other cultures are directly compared, or implicit, in which inherently comparative terms are used for definition (big, small, peaceful, aggressive, etc.). It has been frequently argued that, more than Americans, Canadians construct their sense of nationhood, their shared identity as a country, in reaction to their neighbour. One prominent American sociologist, Seymour Martin Lipset, has conducted a great deal of comparative analyses of Canada and the United States over the last forty years and concludes that Canadians "frequently seek to describe what Canada is about by stressing what it is not: the United States" (Lipset, 1990:XV). This is understandable. Lipset, himself conducted his comparisons of American and Canadian culture for the purpose of developing a better understanding of the United States.

The United States not only borders Canada, but as has been stated earlier, is the most productive culture in the world in terms of cultural products such as music, films, and literature. From these products, Canadians have shown a tendency to define their society by reference to how they differ from the United States rather than by reference to explicit and shared symbols of Canadian society developed by Canadians. For a very long time the traditional interpretation of our shared origin as a people, which is an important element of culture, is that we are the country that formed out of the rejection of the American Revolution. This point has been emphasised in the past by Canadian historians, arts and literature critics, and social scientists (Lipset, 1990). It can therefore be argued that the Canadian preoccupation with defining ourselves by comparison to the United States is itself an aspect of our culture.

This comparative preoccupation shows up clearly in opinion polls in Canada. What is more, we not only compare ourselves to the United States, we have almost unanimously decided that we come out on top of the comparison. More than 75% of us are certain that we are culturally distinct from the United States and over the last ten years never less than 75% consider Canada to be a superior place to live, largely based upon these cultural differences (Gregg and Posner, 1990:17-20). Interestingly however, when they are not being explicitly comparative, the way respondents on questionnaires describe our culture is not clearly different from the way Americans describe theirs.

Culture comparison is difficult. One of the problems is choosing and precisely defining what aspects of a culture are going to be compared. The difference between French and German culture are obvious and easy to identify. Language, history and other aspects of culture such as food, architecture and customs make it easy to make clear and generally agreed upon distinctions between these two countries and cultures on what are apparent and obvious structural differences alone. Comparison and definition are much more difficult when the cultures being compared share a language, are in close physical proximity and have both been formed by similar processes of immigration. The paradox is that Canada is so structurally similar to the United States, so similar in the "externals," but so clearly different in the internals of who we are as to be as different from the United States as France is from Germany (Gwyn, 1985 quoted in Gregg and Posner, 1990:18).

When social scientists compare cultures they cannot rely solely upon common perceptions. Granted, these common perceptions are themselves part of the cultural content of a society whether or not they are measurable or accurate. Since the late 1950s, a number of sociologists have compared Canadian and American culture by attempting to measure and compare values. To do this, they have used a wide variety of data from opinion polls as well as the analysis of institutional structures, government policy and literature. Unquestionably, the American sociologist Seymour Martin Lipset has been the most prolific scholar in this area of comparison. Throughout most of the 1960s and 1970s his conclusions have represented what can be called the conventional perspective on Canadian-American differences within Canadian sociology (Brym, 1989:2, 24). Although his conclusions are no longer widely supported by Canadian social scientists, Lipset's most recent book, *Continental Divide: The Values and Institutions of the United States and Canada*, was a best seller in Canada for more than a month after it's February 1990 release.

We can beneficially look at Lipset's conclusions in greater detail for two reasons. The first is that it does represent a detailed and exhaustive study from an American perspective on how Canada and the United States differ. Lipset's comparisons are explicitly cultural since they rely almost entirely on a comparison of values and how these values shaped the institutional structures of the two societies. Secondly, it can be used to stimulate thought and discussion on how Canadian culture differs from that of the United States. Criticisms of Lipset's work will also be briefly reviewed to show that alternative perspectives do exist and that the definition of Canadian culture is an ongoing process of discussion and debate.

Although he compared other aspects of Canadian and American society (Lipset, 1950), Lipset began his comparisons of Canadian and American values in 1963. In his first publication, Lipset compared values in Canada and the United States as well as Australia and Great Britain using information from opinion poles, nationwide statistics such as crime rates, literary commentaries and political discussions. To do this, he constructed a series of four opposite or contrasting possible value continuums and ranked the four cultures on their relative emphasis on these values. This comparative model was derived and adapted from the work of Talcott Parsons and is called the "Pattern Variables" (Lipset, 1963; Parsons, 1951).

Lipset's pattern variables were: Elitism—Egalitarianism; Ascription—Achievement; Particularism—Universalism; and Specificity—Diffuseness (Lipset, 1963). Elitism means that a society may stress the superiority of some individuals based upon their position of power or prestige while egalitarianism emphasises that all individuals be accorded similar respect. Ascription means that individuals are judged on the basis of their ascribed or inherited qualities while achievement orientation means that individuals are judged on the basis of what they have done. Particularism means that there are different standards on the treatment of individuals which depend upon their social positions or class while universalism means that the society emphasises treating all individuals in the same way. Specificity means that individuals are dealt with according to the position that they occupy while diffuseness means that individuals may be regarded with reference to their membership in collectivities such as ethnic groups, linguistic or racial groups (Lipset, 1962:209-211).

Lipset interpreted differences between Canada and the United States such as higher American crime rates to mean that Americans were more achievement oriented and egalitarian. He interpreted the Canadian emphasis on the ethnic mosaic as contrasting with the American emphasis on the melting pot to mean that Canadians were more particularistic and diffuse (Lipset, 1963).

What may be immediately apparent is that all of the values which Lipset chose to look at as defining a society can be seen to be different dimensions of the same issue: equality. Societies which are egalitarian, achievement oriented, universalistic and specificity oriented are ones in which a high emphasis is placed on individual equality. On all but one of these dimensions, Lipset ranked the United States as closer to the equality side than the other three English speaking societies. On egalitarianism, Lipset ranked the United States behind Australia. On all four of these equality variables, Lipset ranked the United States ahead of Canada (Lipset, 1963:249). Lipset published nine more comparisons focusing only on Canada and the United States over the following twenty-seven years without changing the relative rankings of Canada and the United States (Lipset, 1964; 1968; 1970; 1976; 1979; 1985; 1986; 1988; 1990). This body of research represents the most exhaustive comparison of Canadian and American culture conducted by a single scholar.

Lipset's conclusion after over twenty-five years of researching on the subject is that despite substantial change in the United States and Canada, these two societies have kept their relative cultural distinctiveness. He suggests that they are like "trains on parallel tracks," they have both gone a long way but are no more closer to one another than when they started out (Lipset, 1990:212). To Lipset, the cultural values which constitute the distinction between Canada and the United States originate in the founding process of the two societies and have become part of the social institutional structure. Therefore change is slow and occurs within the parameters laid down by the historical definition of that culture. The founding process for the United States is argued by Lipset to be the American Revolution and its democratic individualistic ideals. In Canada, the counterrevolution and the rejection of the break with the British Empire are argued to form the basis of our culture. (Lipset, 1963:86). In addition, the founding documents of the United States institutionalized the cultural values of individual liberty and equality. By contrast, the BNA Act articulates values which emphasize the rights of linguistic groups, religions and provinces, not individuals (Lipset, 1990:225).

Generally, critical responses to Lipset's comparisons by Canadian scholars emphasize two factors. The first is that Lipset's conclusions about Canadian values may have been accurate up to World War II, but since then are inaccurate (eg., Clark, 1975; Porter, 1979). Secondly, Lipset's comparisons offer very little real understanding because they are influenced by an American perspective so profound as to be viewed as an attempt to develop an ideologically motivated defence of American society (eg., Davis, 1970: Romalis, 1973). This second category of criticisms tend to emphasize the researchers' mistrust of Lipset's consistent findings that there exists greater equality in the United States. They reference racial inequality and the civil rights movement of the period as evidence for their argument.

The sociological discussion of Canadian culture can extend far beyond cultural values on equality. However, current issues in Canadian society and culture, the subject of this text, are dominated by subjects such as multiculturalism, Quebec separatism and the problem of regionalism. From a macro social cultural viewpoint (a perspective that emphasizes nationwide issues and subjects), the cultural importance of equality and inequality become a linking theme in the major problems currently facing the nation. Therefore, this element of Canadian culture, the strength of our value of equality, is emphasised in the following sections. Two things become apparent from this discussion. The first is that Canadians do place profound emphasis on equality. The motivating value for both government action and public dissatisfaction with the government is the profound strength of the Canadian value of equality. Second, that diversity in regions, linguistic groups, and minority cultures make it difficult if not impossible to make generalizations about Canadian culture that have equivalent meanings in all regions of Canada and for all Canadians. What can be argued is that this diversity itself is an essential defining characteristic of Canadian culture.

Regionalism

The term "region" usually engenders differences in the geography of areas. In Canada, we frequently divide the country into five regions, largely on the basis of geographical differences. Common perceptions of the regions of Canada are: British Columbia; The Prairies (Alberta, Saskatchewan and Manitoba); Ontario; Quebec; and the Maritimes (New Brunswick, Nova Scotia, Prince Edward Island, and Newfoundland) (Ornstein, 1986:57). We could also argue that the North is another geographically large, although demographically small, region. It is natural to identify these regions by the geographical features which distinguish them from one another. British Columbia is associated with mountains and the Pacific Ocean, the Prairies are associated with huge expanses of flat grasslands, Ontario with the Great Lakes, Quebec with the Saint Lawrence River and the Maritimes with the Atlantic Ocean.

There are several problems with these conceptions of Canadian regions. The first is that each of these divisions contain within them substantial variation. Frequently as much variation in cultures exists within a Canadian region as between regions (Ornstein, 1986:56). Each of these regional divisions is larger than the largest European country. Ontario and Quebec are more than twice as big as France. The North West Territories is more than twice as big as Spain, France, and Germany combined. Due to their sheer size, tremendous variations exist within each region, geographically and socially, which are minimalized by grouping them together as regions. Some of these regions contain within them an artificial grouping of provinces or diverse populations.

Although geography is unquestionably a contributing factor, sociologists are concerned with the social aspects of regional variation within Canada. The diversity of human populations between these regions is at the core of the study of regional variation to sociologists. Canada does have regional diversity. As stated earlier in this chapter, "Cultures develop as a consequence of a social group's shared experiences and the meanings they commonly attach to the world around them. Cultures also consist in part of a social group's shared experiences and shared meanings." Using this definition, it is not at all difficult to understand that the culture of Newfoundlanders and that of residents of Saskatchewan might vary in perceptible ways. Over 90% of Newfoundlanders are the descendants of immigrants from the British Isles who began establishing permanent settlement on the island in the 18th century (White, 1990:6). Historically and until today, fishing has been a primary economic activity. They live on a rocky and mountainous island that is the most economically deprived area of the country and which did not join Confederation until 1949. By contrast, only about one third of the population of Saskatchewan are solely the descendants of British settlers and nearly twenty percent are of Ukrainian and German descent (White, 1990:6). Large scale settlement of the Prairies didn't begin until the turn of the century and from that point until today wheat farming has been the backbone of the Saskatchewan economy. From these simple and general characteristics alone, it is easy to imagine that people in these areas would have perceivable differences in lifestyles and beliefs, and many argue that indeed they do.

Regionalism is defined by two researchers on the topic, Ralph Mathews and J. Campbell Davis, as a consequence of the fact that:

> people do come to identify with their region of residence and with those who live there with them. Furthermore, this identification may in turn lead them to "think differently" about certain things (i.e., have different attitudes and values with regard to them) than residents of other regions. In time, this regionally distinctive set of attitudes and values may lead them to behave differently as well. (Mathews and Davis, 1986:92)

The foundation of identification with region and it's people may include any of the factors in the Saskatchewan and Newfoundland example discussed above: shared ethnic origin, history, geography or economy. Although, as the example above shows, it is easy to imagine differences in regional culture, the extent of cultural variation between regions is difficult to measure. Those who have attempted, by measuring differences in values between regions, have found weak support for the idea that cultures vary substantially between regions (Mathews and Davis, 1986:93; Ornstein, 1986:51). However, it has been shown that part of the culture of the regions of Canada is the shared *perception* of residents of the regions of Canada that they differ from one another. They may not differ greatly in values, but they perceive themselves to be different from one another and this perception is based on identifiable shared institutions and symbols (Hiller, 1991:139). This shared perception of distinction is itself an important part of regional culture.

The term *regionalism*, within the context of the Canadian discussion of the issue, implies strong attachments to locals, a sense of rivalry between regions and is usually discussed within the context of a problem of Canadian unity. In fact, the term "regionalism" is frequently used in the Canadian context to describe the problem of differences in levels of economic development and underdevelopment (Guindon, 1988:96). Regional differences in cultures, although interesting, of themselves would not necessarily lead to this kind of regionalism. Differences of themselves do not necessarily lead to preferential attachment, inter-regional rivalry, disunity and inequality.

Davis and Mathews (1986) conducted research on level of commitment to, and level of satisfaction with, province of residence as well as whether respondents considered themselves "Canadian first," "provincial resident first," or both equally. Based on data from 1977, they found that Canadians, including Quebecers, were generally most likely to consider themselves "Canadians first" (Mathews and Davis, 1986:103). Newfoundland residents were the only ones to have a majority of respondents not in the "Canadian first" category (57.4% "both equally"). However, and perhaps more important in terms of developing an understanding of regionalism, substantial proportions of the population of most provinces expressed affinity for "both equally" or "province first." Only in Ontario was the total of the two latter categories less than 10% (5.2% and 4.3%, respectively). In total, 26.5% of Canadians identified with Canada and their province equally or with their province first.

Sociological explanations for this kind of regionalism are tremendously varied. Sociologist Harry Hiller divides the existing explanations into four general categories:

Uneven development; elite control; north south linkages; and political structures (Hiller, 1991:130-137).

Uneven development, elite control, and political structures all refer to the fact that central Canada is the centre of political and economic power in the country. The political power of the centre of the country exists in large part because seats in the Canadian Parliament are allocated on the basis of population, and most Canadians live in Central Canada. Uneven development is partly the consequence of the fact that not all of the regions of Canada are endowed with similar opportunities for development. It is also argued to be partly the consequence of 100 years of Federal Government policy favouring industrial development in central Canada at the expense of the Maritimes and Western Canada (Hiller, 1991:132). Most of the Canadian political and economic elites are also residents of central Canada. Economic elites in Central Canada are in a position to influence the political decision making process to ensure that their interests are met regardless of the interests of the far flung provinces or the consequences of these decisions to the residents of those provinces. Finally, North American geography is frequently described as more befitting nations with boarders running North-South than East-West. The natural boundaries of Canada, the Rocky Mountains, the expanse of Prairie and The Canadian Shield make East-West communication and contact much more difficult than North-South. Shared environments and economies make for powerful cross-border "North-South linkages."

Regional discord and a sense of regional attachment above national attachment has been exacerbated by attempts to resist and counter the power of central Canadian elites. Not just the elites, but also the growing middle classes in provinces such as Quebec and Alberta have encouraged their provincial governments to expand and to "fight Ottawa" for more legislative autonomy as a way of supporting regional economic interests against Central Canadian interests (Brym, 1986:31). This support for regional economic interests creates divisiveness in that regional interests may be quite incompatible with the interests of central Canadian economic elites, labour, and politicians.

Equality is a core issue in Regionalism in Canada. Part of the "world view" or shared perceptions of the residents of many of Canada's regions has clearly become this belief in an adversarial relationship with central Canada. There is probably very little variation between regions in Canada in terms of cultural emphasis on equality, however, the regional cultural shared perception of inequality is reenforced by the fact that residents of the various regions in Canada are not equal. Furthermore, especially in the West, Canadians frequently perceive this inequality to be unjust (Gregg and Posner, 1990:37). In very tangible ways, the residents of central Canada, especially the Toronto and Montreal areas, are much better off in terms of income and political influence than other Canadians. As shown in chapter 12 of this text (Divers, 1992) there are tremendous variations in unemployment rates in Canada by region (Table 12:5). In the last nine years, Newfoundland residents have had an average of nearly 20 percent unemployment and residents of British Columbia have averaged 13 percent. During the same period, residents of Ontario have had an average unemployment rate of only 8 percent (average calculated from Table 12:5).

Quebec

Quebec represents a special case in the discussion of regional variation within Canada. The fact that more than 80% of residents of Quebec have French as a first language (Albert, 1990:14) should make it clear to English Canadians that Quebec does vary in at least one obvious way from the rest of Canada. However, the distinctiveness of Quebec culture does not rest solely on language. Culture consists not only of language but also shared history, symbols, ideas and perceptions of reality. In all of these areas, Quebec is clearly a distinct culture.

Quebecers view their history as a people in North America and the development of Canadian confederation from a perspective that is quite different than of English Canadians. Even before the rise of powerful Separatist sentiments in the 1970s, Quebecers had established for themselves a sense of shared history that emphasized experiences and perspectives quite distinct from the rest of Canada. What's more, this sense of distinctiveness had by that time been established and cultivated for over two hundred years. This sense of shared identity as distinct from the rest of Canada is well formed and evident in the way young Quebecers are acculturalized. For example, the treatment of the Conquest, French Canadian heroes and significant historical events have all been substantially different in the Quebec French school curriculum since long before the success of the Parti Quebecois (Bell and Tepperman, 1979:109). Historical education in Quebec has emphasized the pre-Conquest period, viewed the conquest as a tragedy rather than a victory, and has made explicit reference to the Anglo domination of Canadian and especially Quebec society.

For a brief period after the Conquest of New France in 1763, the goal of the British conquerors was to assimilate the French population by denying them any of their cultural or religious institutions and by encouraging British settlement. This was eventually deemed impractical. The Quebec Act of 1774 can be characterized as a compromise that facilitated British rule by gaining the cooperation of the Church and the land owning Seigneurs (Breton, 1988:562). The Quebec Act allowed the Church religious freedom and the right to maintain control over much of French Canadian social life. It also recognized the property rights of the Seigneurs and allowed them to continue collecting rents, thereby gaining their support for British rule.

The cultural distinctiveness of Quebec has always been asserted and maintained not as an "ends" in itself, but as a means to an ends. At first, the maintenance of French language and culture was viewed by the Catholic Church hierarchy as a means of keeping Quebec Catholic in what they perceived to be an English speaking and Protestant British North America. The conquest of New France by the British provided the Catholic hierarchy with a means of isolating Quebec from the social and cultural change in France brought about by the Enlightenment and the French Revolution. Keeping Quebecers French provided them with a means of isolating them from similar ideas and cultural changes which were part of the liberal rhetoric of the American Revolution and increasingly an aspect of British political culture (Bell and Tepperman, 1979:110–111). This sentiment is embodied in the often cited slogan "*la langue gardienne de la foi,*" the language guardian of the faith (Guindon, 1988:105).

The period of the early 1960s is identified as the turning point for Quebec culture. The "Quiet Revolution" was a period of rapid cultural change in Quebec. The traditional view of Quebec which emphasised a rural, conservative and Catholic society were abandoned in favour an ethic of *Rattrapage,* catching up, with social, political and economic development in the rest of Canada and the western world (McRoberts and Posgate, 1984:95). It is in this period that the French language and the shared cultural heritage of Quebecois were celebrated as valuable in their own right, rather than as a means to isolate Catholic Quebec from the liberalizing and Protestant influences of Anglo North America.

The Quiet Revolution was first a change in culture, and consequently brought about changes in the institutional structure of Quebec which facilitated the extension of this new interpretation of Quebec itself. In the late 1940s and the 1950s, Quebec intellectuals, including a minority within the church, were already highly critical of the traditionalist, ultra-conservative Catholic and rural ethos of Quebec culture (McRoberts, 1988:84). From their positions in the Quebec French language media and universities they shared a new vision of Quebec culture with a growing number of young Quebecers. The growth of the Quebec government in the areas of social services and education beginning in 1960 provided opportunities for this new well educated Quebec middle class. Lacking opportunity in the English controlled economy, they became government bureaucrats in a rapidly growing government bureaucracy. For this reason, the Quiet Revolution has been called a "bureaucratic revolution" (Guindon, 1988:31). From their positions in the bureaucracy, this new Quebec middle class used the Quebec state to counter the economic power of English Canadians in an effort to become *maîtres chez nous,* masters in [their] own house (McRoberts and Posgate, 1986:106).

This desire for French speakers equality in a province where they were the majority is the foundation of modern Quebec nationalism (McRoberts, 1988:14). Legislation to protect the French language in Quebec cannot now be understood as only intended to ensure the survival of the language itself. It is also to protect against the necessity of French speaking Quebecers having to assimilate to English culture, and thereby threaten the survival of their own culture, to have full equality in a province where they are a majority. Although it may appear to English Canadians that the defence of Quebec culture is an end in itself, to Quebecers it is also and perhaps most importantly an issue of equality.

Already some analysts are describing what is currently happening in Quebec as a "Second Quiet Revolution." Quebecers are well on their way to controlling their own economy as well as government bureaucracy. The highest level for support of the Canada-United States free trade agreement was in Quebec, reflecting a higher degree of confidence in the increasingly Francophone controlled economy than English speaking Canadians had in their own economic ability (Gregg and Posner, 1990:36). This does indicate a change in Quebec culture. Clearly Quebec culture now also includes a belief in their capacity in business and industry, which some analysts argued was missing well into the 1960s.

Multiculturalism

Multiculturalism refers to the conception of a social group as composed by a variety of contributing cultures. The most literal interpretation of the meaning of the term is explicit cultural relativism. It would imply that all of these contributing groups fully maintain all of the elements of their culture, and that all of these elements of culture are regarded as having equal status within a group. Following this definition, it would mean that if Canada were a fully multicultural society it would mean that the cognitive and normative, or language and laws, components of all immigrant groups and Native Canadians would all have official status and recognition. Of course, this is not the case. Only the cultures of English and French speaking groups have this kind of full official recognition, and, as is clear from the discussion above, even French does not enjoy anything near full equality within Canada.

Though it was not until relatively recently that the idea of Canadian multiculturalism was supported by government policy or legislation, the conception of Canada as a "mosaic" of cultures has a long history. The term "mosaic" has been used in the North American context since at least the early part of this century and been part of the definition of Canada since before the Second World War (Kallen, 1982:162). Mosaic is in most regards interchangeable with "multicultural" and is usually contrasted in meaning with "melting-pot" (Lipset, 1990). Part of the identification of the differences in these terms as meaningful is a comparison of the American emphasis on ethnic assimilation contained in the term "melting-pot," and the Canadian emphasis on "mosaic," the maintenance of ethnic identity.

Implicit in the term melting pot is the idea that all of the cultures of a society contribute to the development of a new and unitary culture. Also suggested by the term is the idea that all of the cultures contribute to the new synthesised culture in a measure proportionate to their population representation (Kallen, 1982:161). In reality, melting pot, at least in the United States, can more appropriately be defined as the expectation that new immigrants should assimilate to the pre-existing dominant culture (Li, 1988:6). Part of the supporting ideology of the melting pot ethic is the emphasis placed on individual rights rather than a recognition of the shared conditions and rights of identifiable groups, such as Black Americans or Chicanos.

The mosaic ethic can be interpreted as a reflection of the perception that individual concerns and circumstances may be shared by identifiable groups and that therefore to address these concerns, the rights of groups must be recognized. The mosaic ethic is pluralistic. It is the recognition and legitimation of the existence of divisions within a society. In Canada, the legitimacy of group concerns as opposed to the individual rights emphasis of the melting pot can be traced to the formation of the nation. The BNA Act allocated rights to citizens on the bases of their membership in two substantially overlapping kinds of social groupings, French and English and Catholic and Protestant. Cultural pluralism is argued to be an extension of this structural reality of dualism reflected in the constitutional provisions made for French and English Canadians in the founding document of the nation (Kallen, 1982:163).

The mosaic nature of Canadian society and the melting pot of American society are both commonly overstated. In reality, very little difference exists between these two nations in cultural maintenance or cultural assimilation. The melting pot emphasis on assimilation and individual achievement in the United States is not reflected in social and economic reality. The very existence of differences in equality on the bases of race or ethnicity in the United States demonstrates that individual achievement by assimilation, the promise of the melting pot, is not occurring (Li, 1988:6). The same can be said about Canada. The pluralistic ideal of multiculturalism assigns equality to groups. Again, there is no shortage of data indicating that differences in equality between groups exist (Kallen, 1982; Li, 1988). However, the fact that these two contrasting ideas have themselves become part of the respective cultures of the United States and Canada permits different bases of legitimation for similar actions to address this inequality. As we shall see later in this section, arguably, the recognition of diversity in Canada may permit more effective action.

It is important to note that multiculturalism is part of the regional diversity of Canada. Canadian regions differ substantially in ethnic composition. As has already been discussed, over 90% of Newfoundlanders are of British extraction while less than a third of residents of Saskatchewan are, and over three quarters of the population of Quebec are of French descent. Multiculturalism means different things to the residents of different regions of Canada in terms of both minority and majority ethnic composition. Ethnic groups which seem proportionally small in the Canadian population may be a large minority in some regions. For example, Canadians of German extraction constituted 3.6% of the total population in 1986. However, in Saskatchewan they made up 12.9% of the population while in Newfoundland only 0.2% (White, 1990:6).

It is also important to note that the ethnic composition of Canada has been changing since the beginning of this century. At different times and in different regions, this change has been dramatic. For example, at the end of World War II, the overwhelming majority of residents of Toronto (88%) were descended from immigrants from the British Isles. By 1989, the majority of Torontonians, 51%, were foreign born (Lipset, 1990:187).

Perhaps the most significant difference between Canada and the United States on this issue of mosaic and melting pot is that although these ideas form part of the cultural definitions of these societies, only in Canada is the ethnic ideal made official and supported by government policy and legislation. In Canada, an official policy of Multiculturalism was proclaimed in 1971 and set forth four objectives:

1. The Government of Canada will support all of Canada's cultures and will seek to assist, resources permitting, the development of those cultural groups which have demonstrated a desire and effort to continue to develop a capacity to grow and contribute to Canada, as well as a clear need for assistance.
2. The Government will assist members of all cultural groups to overcome cultural barriers to full participation in Canadian society.
3. The Government will promote creative encounters and interchange among all Canadian cultural groups in the interest of national unity.
4. The Government will continue to assist immigrants to acquire at least one of Canada's official languages in order to become full participants in Canadian

society. (House of Commons Debates, August 10, 1971; quoted in Kallen, 1982:166)

Canada's multicultural policy was never intended to grant full equality to all cultures. Officially, it is defined as multiculturalism within a bilingual framework (Kallen, 1982:165). This is evident in the above listed goals of the policy which, although containing provisions for the maintenance of minority cultural identity, are explicitly oriented towards partly assimilating immigrants to one of the dominant linguistic groups for the purpose of "full participation." However, the policy was intended to promote equality by reducing discrimination and emphasising "fair play" (Li, 1988:9).

Perhaps the clearest contrast between the ethics of the mosaic and the melting pot is found in the constitutions of Canada and the United States. Multiculturalism is entrenched in the 1982 Charter of Rights and Freedoms. Section 27 of the constitution states that: "This charter shall be interpreted in a manner consistent with the presentation and enhancement of the multicultural heritage of Canadians." More specifically, although guaranteeing individual equality and protection in subsection 15.1, under subsection 15.2 the Charter specifically allows government actions and programs oriented toward "the amelioration of conditions of disadvantaged individuals or groups including those who are disadvantaged because of race, national or ethnic origin, colour, religion, sex, age, or mental or physical disability."

The content of Canadian legislation in the area of minority rights contrasts vividly with the American assimilationist melting pot ideology. American legislation recognizes only the rights of individuals, not of groups, nor of individuals as members of groups. Although both countries have had affirmative action programs, and the United States had them before Canada, American programs and government actions have been weakened and reversed during the 1980s and 1990s due to the American constitutional and cultural emphasis on individual rights and freedoms superseding group rights (Lipset, 1990:180-182).

Precisely what the multicultural emphasis within Canadian culture ultimately means is the subject of debate. Certainly, the dominant culture outside Quebec is English and within Quebec is French. Most minority ethnic groups are expected to at least partly assimilate by learning the language of one of these two dominant cultures. There is also very little opportunity for minorities to ignore the normative structures of the dominant cultural groups. Minorities in Canada do not have the opportunity to maintain their cultures as a full "way of life." This is the source of criticisms that the ultimate result of the Canadian multicultural policy is little more than an "ethnic zoo" where members of minority cultures are encouraged only to occasionally put on presentations of their traditional dance, styles of dress, and food (Kallen, 1982:167).

These kinds of criticisms may miss important aspects of culture. The opportunity for the maintenance of some aspects of minority culture may provide many individuals with a means of maintaining a sense of who they are by conserving their cultural history and thereby enabling them to cope in an increasingly complicated world (Kallen, 1982:166). Also important, is the fact that it is a reflection of the dominant culture's value of equality, which as stated above, was an important motivation for the establishment of the policy.

A Canadian Crisis

A popular self perception of Canadians which forms part of our culture is that we are a tolerant people (Gregg and Posner, 1990:18). It can therefore be said that this is a "value" of Canadian culture. Currently, Canadian society is perceived to be undergoing a crisis which threatens both national unity and challenges our self perception as a tolerant people. Canadians are expressing what many regard as surprisingly hostile attitudes to multiculturalism, regionalism is increasingly viewed as a problem, and the demands of Quebec for cultural autonomy are encountering rising resistance in English Canada. As a consequence, some social scientists describe current trends in Canadian society as an "identity crisis" (Gregg and Posner, 1990:26). The idea of a Canadian "identity crisis" bears directly upon culture as it has been defined in this chapter. To what extent do Canadians share a culture if we cannot agree upon what we share in common as a nation? Our commonly expressed shared values and self image as "more tolerant, more charitable and more humane than Americans," which has been argued in this chapter to be part of Canadian culture, is described by some analysts as no longer consonant with reality (Gregg and Posner, 1990:26). This gap between the espoused Canadian values which most Canadians use to define our cultural distinctiveness and the reality of our behaviour can be considered to be both the source and the content of the current Canadian Identity Crisis.

Despite the cultural emphasis we perceive ourselves to place on tolerance, and the institutionalization of this value in government policies such as multiculturalism, in recent surveys Canadians give *less* support to the maintenance of minority ethnic identity than Americans. Survey evidence as recent as 1989 indicates that more Americans than Canadians view the retention of minority ethnic identity as positive and more Canadians than Americans expect immigrants to assimilate to the dominant culture (Gregg, 1989; quoted in Lipset, 1990:187).

English Canadian opinions on issues of Quebec culture are varied, but negative attitudes are held by half of English speaking Canadians. In 1989, nearly half (49%) of Canadians agreed with the statement "I am tired of giving special treatment to French-speaking residents of Quebec" (Gregg and Posner, 1990:25). The same year, more than three quarters of all Canadians were opposed to Bill 178, the Quebec French language sign law. Most felt that it would hurt Francophone minorities outside Quebec and inflame anti-French sentiment (Gregg and Posner, 1990:20). Clearly, a substantial proportion of the Canadian population outside Quebec no longer have any tolerance for efforts by the residents of Quebec to protect the viability of their culture. This increasing lack of tolerance was represented in public sentiments over the Meech Lake Constitutional Accord. However, special considerations granted Quebec in the Accord are not the only reasons for its failure.

Regional discontent is also argued by many to be the force behind the collapse of the Meech Lake Constitutional Accord in the summer of 1990. This constituted the failure to obtain a Canadian Constitution with the consent of all ten provinces. The Accord failed to be ratified by both Newfoundland and Manitoba and encountered strong resistance throughout the West. Public opinion poles from the period indicated that opposition to the Accord in Newfoundland was 75%, and in Manitoba was 69% (Gregg and Posner, 1990:48). It is possible that hostility to the Accord in peripheral Canadian regions reflects a dissatisfaction with a perceived Central Canadian emphasis on Quebec's interests and issues, at the expense of an understanding of what is going on in the West or Maritimes.

Negative responses to what in the past have been called the essential characteristics defining Canada are not limited solely to the results of opinion poles. In his 1990 book, *Mosaic Madness: The Poverty and Potential of Life in Canada*, prominent Canadian sociologist Reginald Bibby decries the consequences of Canadian ethnic, linguistic, and regional pluralism. Bibby states that:

> Since the 1960s, Canada has been encouraging the freedom of groups and individuals without simultaneously laying down cultural expectations. . . . Our expectation has been that fragments of the mosaic will somehow add up to a healthy and cohesive society. It is not at all clear why we should expect such an outcome. (Bibby, 1990:10)

Bibby views what he regards as the excessive emphasis on pluralism in Canada as ultimately crippling to the development of a national culture by emphasizing the interests of small group association without regard for the national interests and identity.

Ultimately, to Bibby, this problem is not solely limited to a lack of national cultural symbols or individual recognition of national interests. It goes beyond symbolic or cognitive elements of Canadian culture to influence normative culture as well.

> Relativism has slain moral consensus. It has stripped us of all of our ethical and moral guidelines, leaving us with no authoritative instruments to measure social life. . . . Relativism, taken to an extreme, erases agreement on the norms that are essential to social life. (Bibby, 1990:14)

Bibby's analysis is a highly impressionistic interpretation of available data. However it does appear to be in concordance with much of Canadian public opinion.

The Final Report of the *Citizens Forum on Canada's Future* (following Canadian tradition, also called "The Spicer Commission" for its chairman) was presented on Canada Day, 1991. Both Canadian self perceptions and social scientists findings discussed in this chapter are substantiated by the Report. It is apparent that Canadians are facing a crisis of identity, the lack of a clearly shared culture. Furthermore, this identity crisis seems to extend at least in part from those characteristics which we have in the past selected as our shared identity and national culture.

The Forum on Canadian Unity

The Forum's consultation with Canadian citizens involved over 400,000 participants from all over the country. Comments from these participants on such subjects as Canadian values and identity, as well as Canadian problems echo research findings and sociological interpretations cited above. Contributing discussions on Canadian values emphasised tolerance, real equality and fair play (Spicer, 1991:35–44). Also consistent with the sociological research cited above, the Forum's commissioners noted that Canadians had a tendency to define their national values with direct comparison to the United States.

Participants in the Forums meetings raised issues not commonly noted by sociologists in current research. They placed tremendous value upon Canadian cultural institutions such as the Canadian Broadcasting Corporation. They were also dissatisfied with the government cutbacks in national institutions which they perceived worked to maintain a sense of Canadian unity such as the national rail passenger service (VIA) and Canada Post. The commissioner referred to the institutions as "Unifying Institutions" (Spicer, 1991:45). What was apparent from the Report was that many Canadians perceived Federal government institutions as essential for the maintenance of a shared sense of cultural identity.

Not surprisingly, considering the body of sociological information on the subject, many participants were dissatisfied by the impact of Canada's multicultural policy. They thought it had two kinds of negative consequences. The first was that it harmed unity by emphasising diversity rather than shared identity. Secondly, they thought that the application of laws derived out of this policy threatened Canadian identity by destroying shared cultural symbols such as the R.C.M.P. uniform (Spicer, 1991:85–87).

These are not trivial concerns. Arguably, what has happened in recent Canadian history is that the application of agreed upon Canadian values in government policy has threatened a sense of unity. It seems that this occurred because the unintended consequences of government action for many, has been the accentuation of divisions in Canadian society out of a genuine interest to ameliorate equality differences; between French and English, minority cultures and regions. At the same time, diminished emphasis has been placed on shared identity and culture. In the end, those very values which motivated government themselves became threatened by consequent change.

As the Commissioners report put it:

> We must...somehow reconcile two very different elements of nation building: the power of shared mythology or symbols, with the effectiveness of genuine, pragmatic programs. These are inevitably intertwined as our transportation and communications systems have so effectively displayed. We have to understand that the pragmatic concerns of managing programs—closing a rural post office—can have symbolic consequences far more powerful than the bottom line. But we must also recognize that innovative, sensible programs that engage Canadians in accordance with their values may be a key to effective nation building....Whatever our future directions, we must ensure that fundamental Canadian values are not jeopardized. (Spicer, 1991:118)

What is perhaps most interesting about the Spicer Commission's report is that it is taken for granted that Canadian shared cultural identity needs government action to be maintained. The problems of assimilating large foreign born segments of the population, and the problem of living next to an enormous and globally influential culture, necessitate active interpretation and promulgation of shared Canadian meanings.

Most Canadian cultural issues are not unique. In fact, in a global comparative context, Canadian problems of ethnic diversity, regionalism and bi or multi-lingualism are common if not pervasive (Hiller, 1991:213–246). Even "old world" countries, which appear to external observers to be culturally unitary, deal with issues of minority ethnic nationalist movements, economic regionalism and the assimilation of high numbers of recent immigration. Spain, France, England and most European countries have had more problems with separatist movements and regional economic underdevelopment than Canada. In fact, if the violence that is frequently associated with regional or ethnic tensions is any indication of the severity of the problem, Canada is doing rather well by comparison to most countries. What may be unique, is that what has apparently become a part of Canadian culture is the perception that these issues currently constitute a serious problem that requires ongoing direct government action. Perhaps our shared perception that characteristics such as regional disparities, bilingualism and multiculturalism are problems that threaten a shared sense of cultural identity, or even the viability of the Canadian nation, stem from the fact that we live next to one of the very few nations that apparently does not have serious issues to address in these areas. We constantly compare ourselves to that nation, the United States, rather than develop a sense of our own shared identity out of our common experience.

Conclusion

This chapter has focused on what are arguably the current critical issues in Canadian culture of shared cultural identity and nationhood. These issues are all "macro-social," in that they are observed at the level of large groups, rather than face to face interaction. Unfortunately, this leaves out much but conforms to the limits of length imposed in publications of this sort. Readers are encouraged to extend their understanding of Canadian culture and the sociological study of Canadian culture by use of the list of suggested readings found below.

Canada clearly has a unique culture. A great part of this cultural distinctiveness consists in the almost overwhelming variations present in Canadian society and the pervasive emphasis in Canadian culture placed upon living in harmony despite these variations. The vast majority of Canadians, as has been shown from a number of sources, are certain that we are culturally distinct from the United States, that this distinctiveness is "good," and that they would have it no other way. This too, is part of Canadian culture. The current crisis in Canadian society is a cultural one. Perhaps it can be characterized as indicative of a process of "working out" and maintaining the Canadian cultural identity in an increasingly complex and "global" social world.

Suggested Readings

Atwood, Margaret
1972 *Survival: A Thematic Guide to Canadian Literature.* Boston: Beacon Press. Atwood traces major themes in French and English Canadian literature and, following the Canadian preoccupation, compares them to those found in American literature. This book shows that a shared distinctly Canadian cultural identity is evident in both French and English language literature.

Brym, Robert (with Bonnie Fox)
1989 *From Culture to Power: The Sociology of English Canada.* Toronto: Oxford University Press.
Brym traces the shift in Canadian sociology from the emphasis on the study of culture prevalent in the 1960s to the current emphasis on the study social/economic bases of power in Canadian society. This is an excellent book which describes why the study of culture, especially in comparison to the United States, became important in the 1960s and why it was supplanted by the political economy perspective beginning in the 1970s. It should be required reading for Canadian students of sociology.

Guindon, Hubert
1988 *Quebec Society: Tradition, Modernity, and Nationhood.* Toronto: University of Toronto Press.
Guindon's book is an historical sociological analysis which traces structural and cultural changes in Quebec society. For students who lack an understanding of these processes, it can contribute a foundational sociological understanding of Quebec society.

Hiller, Harry H.
1991 *Canadian Society: A Macro Analysis* (2nd Ed.). Scarborough, Ontario: Prentice-Hall.
Hiller's book provides an excellent overview of structural and cultural elements of Canadian society. Particularly useful is Hiller's comparisons of Canadian society to other societies, and the fact that in this process he makes only limited use of the United States.

Kallen, Evelyn
1982 *Ethnicity and Human Rights in Canada.* Toronto: Gage Publishing Ltd.
Although now nearly ten years old, this book does supply the best description and analysis of the association of the issues of equality and ethnicity in Canadian society. Kallen pays particular attention to the evolution of these issues in Canadian cultural mythology and in Canadian legislation.

Lipset, Seymour Martin
1990 *Continental Divide: The Values and Institutions of the United States and Canada.* New York: Routledge.
This book is Lipset's ultimate work in Canadian-American social comparisons. Although many Canadian readers will not agree with his conclusions or

evidence, it provides interesting conclusions on Canadian-American differences from a decidedly American perspective. Lipset's contrasts of American and Canadian beliefs and mythologies is particularly interesting.

References

Adams, Owen
1990 "Divorce Rates in Canada," in *Canadian Social Trends.* Craig McKie and Keith Thompson, eds. Toronto: Thompson Educational Publishing Inc.

Albert, Luc
1990 "Language in Canada," in *Canadian Social Trends.* Craig McKie and Keith Thompson, eds. Toronto: Thompson Educational Publishing Inc.

Atwood, Margeret
1972 *Survival: A Thematic Guide to Canadian Literature.* Boston: Beacon Press.

Bell, David and Lorne Tepperman
1979 *The Roots of Disunity.* Toronto: McClelland and Stewart.

Bibby, Reginald W.
1990 *Mosaic Maddness: The Poverty and Potential of Life in Canada.* Toronto: Stoddart Publishing Co. Ltd.

Breton, Raymond
1988 "French-English Relations" in *Understanding Canadian Society.* James Curtis and Lorne Tepperman, eds. Toronto: McGraw-Hill Ryerson.

Brym, Robert J.
1986 "An Introduction to the Regional Question in Canada," in *Regionalism in Canada.* Robert Brym, ed. Toronto: Irwin Publishing.

Brym, Robert J. (with Bonnie J. Fox)
1989 *From Culture to Power: The Sociology of English Canada.* Toronto: Oxford University Press.

Clark, S.D.
1975 "The Post Second World War Canadian Society," in *Canadian Review of Sociology and Anthropology* Vol. 12, No. 1.

Davis, Arthur
1970 "Canadian Society and History as Hinterland versus Metropole," in *Canadian Society, Pluralism, Change and Conflict.* Richard J. Ossenberg, ed.

Freeman, Linton C.
1974 "Marriage Without Love: Mate Selection in Non-Western Societies," in *Selected Studies in Marriage and the Family* (4th Ed.) Robert F. Winch and Grahan B. Spanier, eds. New York: Holt, Rinehart and Winston.

Galbo, John
1991 "An Interview with John Fisk," in *Border/Lines* 20/21, Winter 1990/91.

Gregg, Allen R. and Micheal Posner
1990 *The Big Picture: What Canadians Think about Almost Everything.* Toronto: MacFarlane, Walter and Ross.

Guindon, Hubert
1988 *Quebec Society: Tradition, Modernity and Nationhood.* Toronto: University of Toronto Press.

Hiller, Harry H.
1991 *Canadian Society: A Macro Analysis.* Scarborough, Ontario: Prentice-Hall.

Innis, Harold
1971 *The Bias of Communication.* Toronto: University of Toronto Press.

Kallen, Evelyn
1982 *Ethnicity and Human Rights in Canada.* Toronto: Gage Publishing Ltd.

Li, Peter S.
1988 *Ethnic Inequality in a Class Society.* Toronto: Wall and Thompson.

Lipset, Seymour Martin
1950 *Agrarian Socialism: The Cooperative Commonwealth in Saskatchewan.* Berkeley: The University of California Press.

1963 *The First New Nation.* New York: Basic Books.

1964 "Canada and the United States: A Comparative View," in *Canadian Review of Sociology and Anthropology,* 1.

1968 *Revolution and Counterrevolution.* New York: Basic Books.

1970 "Revolution and Counterrevolution: The United States and Canada," in, *The Canadian Political Process.* Orest Krulak, Richard Schultz and Sidney Pobihushchy, eds. Toronto: Holt, Rinehart and Winston of Canada.

1976 "Radicalism in North America: A Comparative View of the Party Systems of Canada and the United States" in *Transactions of the Royal Society of Canada,* IV, 14, 1976.

1979 "Revolution and Counterrevolution: Some Comments at a Conference Analyzing the Bicentennial of a Celebrated North American Divorce," in *Perspectives on Revolution and Evolution* Richard A. Preston, ed. North Carolina: Duke University Press.

1985 "Canada and the United States: The Cultural Dimension" in *Canada and the United States: Enduring Friendship, Persistent Stress.* Charles F. Doran and John H. Sigler, eds. New Jersey: Prentice-Hall.

1986 "Historical Traditions and National Characteristics: A Comparative Analysis of Canada and the United States," in *The Canadian Journal of Sociology,* Vol 1, No. 2, 1986.

1988 *Distinctive Neighbors (sic): Values and Culture in the United States and Canada.* (Mimeo)

1989 *American Exceptionalism Reaffirmed.* (Mimeo)

1990 *Continental Divide: The Values and Institutions of the United States and Canada*. New York: Routledge.

McLuhan, Marshal
1964 *Understanding Media.* New York: McGraw-Hill.

McRoberts, Kenneth and Dale Posgate
1984 *Quebec: Social Change and Political Crisis* (Revised Edition). Toronto: McClelland and Stewart.

McRoberts, Kenneth
1988 *Quebec: Social Change and Political Crisis* (3rd Edition). Toronto: McClelland and Stewart.

Mathews, Ralph and J. Campbell Davis
1986 "The Comparative Influence of Region, Status, Class and Ethnicity on Canadian Attitudes and Values," in *Regionalism in Canada*. Robert Brym, ed. Toronto: Irwin Publishing.

Mead, George Herbert
1934 *Mind, Self and Society.* Chicago: University of Chicago Press.

Murdock, George
1967 *Ethnographic Atlas.* Pittsburgh: University of Pittsburgh Press.

Parsons, Talcott
1951 *The Social System.* Glencoe: The Free Press.

Porter, John
1979 *The Measure of Canadian Society: Education, Equality and Opportunity.* Toronto: Gage Publishing Company.

Ornstein, Micheal D.
1986 "Regional Politics and Ideologies," in *Regionalism in Canada*. Robert Brym, ed. Toronto: Irwin Publishing.

Romalis, Coleman
1973 "A Man of His Time and Place: A Selective Appraisal of S.M. Lipset's Comparative Sociology," in *Perspectives in Political Sociology.* Andrew Effrat, ed. New York: Bobbs-Merril Company Inc.

Spicer, Keith
1991 (Chair) *Citizens' Forum on Canada's Future: Report to the People and the Government of Canada*. Ottawa: Government of Canada.

Sumner, W.G.
1906 *Folkways.* New York: Ginn.

Wison, Edward O.
1975 *Sociobiology: The New Synthesis.* Cambridge MA: Harvard University Press.

White, Pamela M.
1990 "Ethnic Origins of the Canadian Population," in *Canadian Social Trends.* Craig McKie and Keith Thompson, eds. Toronto: Thompson Educational Publishing Inc.

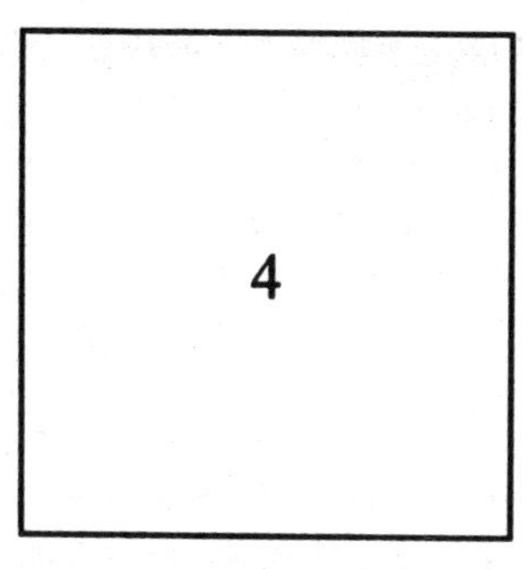

Socialization

Paul P. Divers

In this chapter, the student is to be introduced to the topic of socialization. It is here that sociology meets psychology in what is commonly known as social psychology. Social psychology is "the study of individual behaviour and psychological structures and processes as outcomes of and influences upon interpersonal relationships, the functioning of groups and other collective forms, and culturally defined macrosocial structures and processes" (Borgatta and Borgatta, 1992:1921). It is in socialization that members learn a culture (as described in Chapter Two), become adept in interaction with others, and adapt to social structures such as ethnicity, gender, and social class.

Introduction

> Every year our nation is invaded by several million "things" (one searches for the right word) that are immense, incalculable threats to the social order. They threaten total chaos. They are barbaric. They do not love democracy and suspect communism. They hold no brief for the Judao-Christian tradition. They have no modesty. They do not speak our language, nor our history, nor value our customs. They lack any motive or knowledge that leads them to share, to give and take, to compromise, to accommodate, to cooperate. They are impulsive and demanding. They do not respect authority, show respect to their elders, or express deference.... These invaders are human infants. (Campbell, 1975:1)

In Canada 386,114 infants were born in 1990 (Statistics Canada). We depend on them as much as they depend on us since without them our society would be unable to survive for very long. One central fact about infants is that they are not prepared for the life that lies before them. At birth, infants are unable to cooperate; they have only the potentiality for doing so (Handel, 1988). The process of getting them to cooperate on our terms is called *socialization*. Socialization can be defined as the process by which someone develops a

The author would like to express his appreciation to Paul Zipursky and Elaine Grandin for their suggestions and editorial comments on earlier drafts of this chapter.

sense of self and acquires the knowledge, skills, attitudes, motivations, and behaviour required to participate in a given society or social group so they can function within it. Although the socialization process largely takes place through face-to-face interaction in small groups, its purpose is to enlist children into their particular society. Socialization is, then, a process that helps to explain two different types of phenomena: (i) the way that an individual is capable of participating in society; and (ii) how society is possible at all (Elkin and Handel, 1984).

Socialization is not confined to childhood. It is a lifelong cumulative process whereby individuals learn how to adapt existing knowledge, skills, attitudes, motivations, and behaviour to new and changing circumstances. In other words, as individuals move through life they are faced with situations and circumstances that they have not previously experienced. At the beginning of their working lives, the young steel worker, teacher, and secretary soon learn to adapt to the particular circumstances of the occupational role and environment. Should they change jobs in later life, they will join a different occupational group and may have to learn new skills and adopt different mannerisms and styles of dress. The ability to adapt to these changes is based on earlier socialization processes and new ones soon to be acquired. The content of the various forms of socialization are not mutually exclusive, nor are the agents of socialization necessarily working in harmony, so the process actually experienced by individuals is exceedingly complex.

In this chapter we will explore the topic of socialization with emphasis on: (i) the major theories of child development; (ii) the types of socialization experienced over the life course; (iii) the relationship between socialization and society, including the various agencies of socialization that enable us to become part of society; and (iv) subcultural variation in socialization practices. Initially, our attention will focus on childhood socialization since this is the most crucial time period during which individuals learn how to participate in society. Thereafter, we will open our discussion to the complexities of socialization and the social roles adopted by individuals over the life course.

We will begin with a discussion of the theories of child development and socialization to society. In this chapter only five such theories are discussed. You should be aware, however, that there are a myriad of theories dealing with this process in the literature. Nevertheless, the theories presented here should provide you with a general understanding of some of the work that has been done in this area.

Theories of Child Development and Socialization

Cognitive Development Approach

Jean Piaget: Cognitive Development

The cognitive development approach to child development has as its chief spokesperson, Swiss psychologist Jean Piaget (1896–1990), whose general theory is a stage theory focused on the cognitive or intellectual development of children. Piaget's main stages of intellectual development are presented in Table 4:1. You should keep in mind that the age range highlighted in each stage are approximate age ranges. Some children develop intellectually faster and reach each stage sooner than other children of the same age.

Piaget assumes that thinking follows its own developmental style in children, with the development of language usually coming after the attainment of a certain level of thinking. Piaget has provided substantial experimental evidence of some of the intricate ways that thinking and language are interrelated. It seems from Piaget's studies that even though attempts are made to train young children in special ways of language to talk about problem-solving, such training is of very little use to children whose capacity for thinking has not developed to the state, point, or level at which they can meaningfully consider concepts represented in the special language. However, Piaget's work also demonstrates that the capacities for thought and language do begin to interpenetrate one another in very young children, from about eighteen months to two years of age. Subsequently, this process becomes so interwoven that by the age of five to six years it is exceedingly difficult to sort out the primary causal influences of either thought or language.

Table 4:1
Piaget's Stages of Intellectual Development

Stage	Approximate Ages[1]	Characterization
1. Sensorimotor	Birth–2 years	Infants differentiate themselves from objects; gradually become aware of the relationship between their actions and their effects on the environment so that they can act intentionally and make interesting events last longer; learn that objects continue to exist though no longer visible.
2. Preoperational	2–7 years	Uses language and can represent objects by images and words; are still *egocentric,* the world revolves around them and they have difficulty taking the viewpoint of others; classifies objects by single salient: if A is like B in one respect, it must be like B in other respects.
3. Concrete Operational	7–12 years	Become capable of logical thought; achieve conservation concepts in the following order: number (age 6), mass (age 7), weight (age 9); can classify objects, order them in series along a dimension (such as size), and understand relational terms (A is longer than B).
4. Formal Operational	12 and older	Can think in abstract terms, follow logical propositions and reason by hypothesis; isolates the elements of a problem and systematically explores all possible solutions; becomes concerned with the hypothetical, the future, and ideological problems.

1. The ages corresponding to each stage are approximations. Some children develop at different rates, often associated with socioeconomic background and ethnicity. All children pass through each stage in the same sequence according to Piaget.

Source: Adapted from Piaget, Jean (1928). *Judgement and Reasoning in the Child.* New York: Harcourt.

Sensorimotor Stage. Piaget emphasizes the close relationship between motor activity and perception in infants during the first two years. During this period infants are busy discovering the relationship between sensations and motor behaviour. Examples of what infants learn include: how far they have to reach to grasp an object, what happens when they push their food to the edge of a table, and that their hands are a part of themselves while the crib rail is not. Naturally as infants grow older they acquire many new abilities. One important discovery during this stage is the concept of **object permanence**: an awareness that an object continues to exist even when it is not present to the senses. For example, if you were to place a cloth over a toy for which a six-month-old is reaching, they will lose interest and act as if the toy were not there. In contrast, a ten-month-old infant will actively search for the object because they know the object does exist.

Preoperational Stage. The preoperational stage gradually takes place between the ages of two and seven. The key change in the intellectual development of children during this stage is the concept of **conservation**, the ability to understand that objects and quantities remain constant despite changes in their appearance. By the end of this stage children learn that the amount (mass) of a substance is not altered when its shape is changed. For example, if you were to have two identical balls of silly putty, children age four will tell you that they are the same. Now, if you were to roll one ball out into a log, children aged four will tell you that they are different; in fact, the log consists of more silly putty! However, by age six or seven children no longer simply rely on visual impression but have developed greater cognitive ability to know that two items that were identical remain the same in mass, regardless of their different shapes.

Operational Stages. Between the ages of seven and twelve, the *concrete operational stage,* children master various conservation concepts and begin to perform additional logical manipulations. For instance, children in this stage are capable of drawing maps to their friend's house and can provide verbal directions. In contrast, a five year old could not give verbal directions since their ability to do so is based on visual places of reference. Children younger than seven or eight are seldom capable of creating the mental images necessary to draw a map or provide verbal directions to a specific place; although they can physically take you there. Not until the final stage of cognitive development, the *formal operational stage,* which begins around seven or twelve, are children able to reason in purely symbolic terms. During this stage children are able to deal with several alternatives that are not immediately present in a conversation. They are able to reason about the consequences to their behaviour and offer compromises that are reasonably well thought out. In addition, children around age twelve have the capacity to give directions, using abstract terminology such as north, south, east, and west.

Jean Piaget: Moral Reasoning and Judgement

Piaget's work also extended to include the examination of moral reasoning (the sense of what is right and wrong) in child development. According to Piaget (1932) the moral reasoning of children is best exemplified in their response to paired stories illustrating different degrees of responsibility for damage done. For example, in one story a girl named Marie decided that she wanted to surprise her mother by sewing a present for her. Since she did not know how to use the scissors properly she cut a big hole in her dress. In its companion story, a girl named Margaret decided to play with some scissors while her mother was out of the house. She also did not know how to use the scissors properly and made a small hole in her dress. Piaget asked children of various ages which girl was more at fault. In comparing the responses to these paired stories, Piaget found that children under the age of nine tended to measure the gravity of the deed in terms of the amount of damage done. In most cases, children under nine years of age insist that Marie was more wrong because she made a bigger bole in her dress. These children also felt that Marie should be more severely punished than Margaret even though Marie's intent was to surprise her mother, whereas the little hole in Margaret's dress was made because she was playing with the scissors. According to Piaget, young children base their morality on objective standards. Thus, the greater the damage, the greater the guilt. This view Piaget considers a direct outgrowth of what he calls **moral realism,** a view that the severity of punishment should depend on the amount of damage done, regardless of intent. In other words, moral realism demands that "the letter rather than the spirit of the law shall be observed." (Piaget, 1962:207).

At about age nine, however, children gradually lose this sense of objective responsibility and begin to place more emphasis on subjective intentions. These children in response to the same paired stories felt that Margaret was more at fault for the hole in her dress since her accident was due to careless play; whereas, Marie's accident was due to an unintentional act while trying to surprise her mother. Piaget calls this **moral autonomy**, a view that the severity of the punishment should depend on the intent of the act.

According to Piaget, very young children learn from their parents objective responses to situations during the early stage of moral realism. During this time period they learn that parents make the rules and offer few explanations for their decisions (i.e., "Don't touch that Bethany or you'll get a spanking" or "Ryan, you will be grounded if I find you playing with the Stafford boys"). Piaget believes that children tend to learn that broken rules are acts of consequence. It is not until they begin to play more actively with peers that they learn that rules are social constructions and are flexible under certain circumstances. Piaget believes that the development of children's cognitive capacities enables them to reach a level of moral thought that is consistent with society's.

The Psychoanalytic Explanation

Sigmund Freud: Father of Psychoanalysis

Freud (1856–1939) is clearly the founder of psychoanalysis. His theories developed over a forty year period of clinical work culminating in 24 volumes of text. Freud frequently used the analogy that the mind was like an iceberg. The small part above the surface of the sea represents *conscious experience,* while the larger mass—below sea level—represents the *unconscious:* a store of impulses, passions, and primitive instincts that affect our thoughts and behaviour. According to Freud, the roots of human behaviour lie in the unconscious (*instinctive*) aspect of the human mind. Consequently, for the individual to function effectively in society, personality development requires that the unconscious (*instinctive*) aspects of the human mind be tempered and controlled. In Freud's view, the

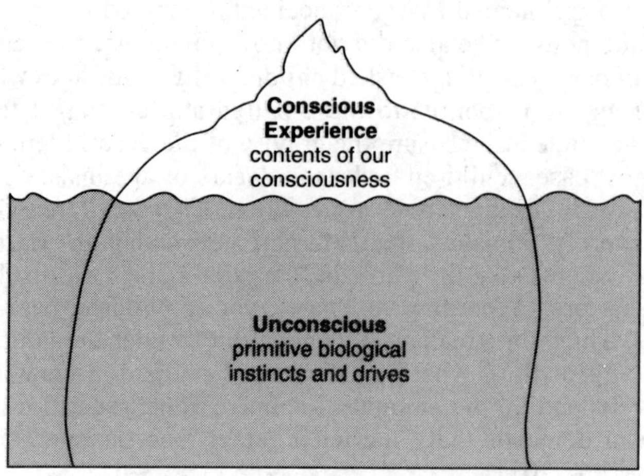

Freud compared the human mind to an iceberg.

individual is mainly governed by irrational instincts where conscious and rational dimensions constitute only a fragment of the total personality.

In this psychoanalytic view, the personality is composed of three major energy systems with each trying to exert itself over the others: the **Id**, the **Ego**, and the **Superego**. The **Id** is the original source of personality, present in the newborn infant, from which the ego and superego later develop. It consists of everything that is inherited, including the reservoir of primitive biological instincts that are continually striving for expression. Thus, the id seeks immediate gratification of primitive, pleasure-seeking impulses. The id, like the newborn infant, operates on the *pleasure principle:* it strives to obtain pleasure and to avoid pain regardless of any external considerations. For example, newborns showing little regard for their sleeping parents, will awaken during the night crying because they are hungry and wet. According to Freud, the id operates in each of us even as adults.

The **Ego** (or *self),* on the other hand, is that aspect of the human personality which is readily available to the individual in their conscious or waking state. It includes the normal functions of memory, perception, and thinking. The ego develops out of the id because of the necessity for dealing with the real world. For example, a hungry college student may not be able to immediately satisfy her hunger pangs until the lecture is over. Thus, the ego obeys the *reality principle,* which requires it to test reality and delay gratification until the appropriate conditions are available. The ego, therefore, takes the real world into consideration; including, what actions are appropriate, which id instincts will be satisfied, and in what way. As such the ego mediates between the demands of the id, the realities of the world, and the demands of the superego. The ego, according to Freud, attempts to reconcile the demands of the id and the superego by means of defense mechanisms (i.e., rationalization, repression, and projection).

The third energy system of the personality, the **Superego** (or *conscience*), represents the internalized values of society which oppose the expression of unacceptable impulses, such as sexual and aggressive drives. The superego judges what is right and wrong according to the standards of society. For example, although you may be very tempted to physically assault your sociology instructor after they give you a lower grade than you had expected, you do not because striking another individual—especially your sociology instructor—is in violation of our societal standards of acceptable conduct.

Often, the distinction made between the three energy systems of the personality can best be thought of as the difference between the child (id), the adult (ego), and the parent (superego). In other words, the child is spontaneous, the adult is responsible, and the parent imparts appropriate morals, values and constraints.

Erik Erickson: Psychosocial Development

Erickson, a trained psychoanalyst from the Viennese Psychoanalytic Institute under Anna Freud (daughter of Sigmund Freud), is well-known for his conception of socialization over the entire life cycle, from birth to death. Erickson felt that the social problems encountered in the course of development were more important than biological ones. He described a progression of *psychosocial stages* in which the individual faces a wider range of human relationships as they mature and have specific socialization issues to solve at each of these stages (refer to Table 4:2). Successful transition and development at each stage requires that the individual resolve the particular issues that are faced. Inadequate resolution of issues at each stage leads to incomplete development and possible problems in the future.

For Erickson, it is not a question of the individual adapting to society nor of society moulding the individual. The individual and the society form a unity which cannot be artificially separated. According to Erickson, the separation of individual development from society is impossible since both are necessary for socialization.

The Symbolic Interaction Explanation

At the turn of the century American sociologists attempted to establish the discipline of sociology by theorizing about the social self from a perspective that came to be known as symbolic interaction. This theorizing differed from that done in psychology since it focused on the social individual interacting with society rather than on the individual and the internal development of psyche. These symbolic interactionists argued that individuals possess only a general capacity for thought. This capacity, therefore, must be shaped and reshaped in the process of social interaction. Such a view leads the symbolic interactionists to focus on a special form of social interaction—socialization (Ritzer, 1988). To the symbolic interactionists, socialization is a dynamic process that enables individuals to think, learn, and act. Furthermore, socialization is not simply a unidirectional process whereby individuals receive information, but is a dynamic process in which the individual shapes and adapts the information to their own needs (Manis and Meltzer, 1978:6).

The intellectual roots of this perspective are most often associated with Charles Horton Cooley (1864-1929) and George Herbert Mead (1863–1931). Cooley is best known for his conception of the **looking-glass self,** while Mead is best known for his work on **role-taking.** In general, both argue that the self could not exist without society since society is in the mind. In this section, we will specifically focus our attention on

Table 4:2
Erickson's Psychosocial Stages of Development

Stage/Age	Psychosocial Issue	Characterization
1. Birth–first year	Trust vs. mistrust	Emotional attachment to the mother is vital for a favorable outcome. Infants need to recognize that even though the mother is not in sight, they have not been abandoned.
2. Second year	Autonomy vs. shame and doubt	Children during this stage begin to physically grow and gain control over bowel functions. This provides the child with a sense of autonomy and control. If the child is unable to control bowel movement and is subjected to too much parental control, they are vulnerable to shame or doubt for not having self-control and willpower.
3. Third year–fifth year	Initiative vs. guilt	Children during this stage seek direction and purpose. The capacity for language and understanding is sufficient enough to relate to parents and significant others, though they frequently misunderstand. Children explore continuously, both verbally and in their actions. Children who are made to feel that exploration is desirable will move through this stage successfully. Children who are made to feel that exploration is undesirable may experience guilt for their desire to do so.
4. Sixth year–onset of puberty	Industry vs. inferiority	During this stage, children are ready to learn, cooperate and form attachments to parents, relatives, teachers, and other children. Children are able to relate to roles that they can identify, i.e., policeman, firefighters, astronauts, and so on. Successful development during this stage enables the child to feel that they can work at tasks. Children who do not experience success during this stage may develop a sense of inferiority.
5. Adolescence	Identity and repudiation vs. identity diffusion	For Erickson, the adolescent period is a crucial stage in the socialization process. During this stage adolescents are maturing physically, mentally, and sexually. Success at this point requires that individuals establish roles for themselves, develop a coherent sense of self, and find their place in society.
6. Early adulthood	Intimacy and solidarity vs. isolation	As individuals begin to emerge from their identity struggles, they are faced with developing the ability to establish relationships such as intimate love and friendship.
7. Young and middle adulthood	Generativity vs. stagnation	This stage involves the establishment of satisfying social roles. Generativity, according to Erickson, is the interest in directing and guiding the next generation. Naturally, this is not a satisfying interest for all adults. Stagnation occurs if the individual is not involved with some role that fosters development, whether that be raising children, involvement in research and development, planting a garden, etc.
8. Later adulthood	Integrity vs. despair	This stage involves individuals reflecting back on their lives. Feelings of integrity, a sense of wholeness/completeness, or a sense of despair, lost opportunities and incompleteness.

Source: Modified from original; Erickson, Erik. 1963. *Childhood and Society,* second edition. New York: Norton.

these two theorists and their views on how children experience the socialization process in our society.

Charles Horton Cooley: The Looking-Glass Self

Cooley began his work by observing children playing with what appeared to be imaginary friends. To Cooley, children may appear to be physically by themselves, but in their imaginations they are in the presence of others. Cooley suggests that this is how the mind initially develops because thinking consists of imaginary conversation that is carried on silently in the mind, even among adults. The mind, then, interacts with external stimuli from the social world through silent talk and interpretation of what is received.

Cooley called his social model *the looking-glass self* because the mind is like a mirror in that individuals receive from others what they believe others to think and see. The general premise is that we see ourselves as others see us and we depend on some reasonable consensus of friends and associates to maintain a consistent sense of self *(self image).* According to Cooley, there are three components to the looking-glass self:

1. we imagine how we appear to others;
2. we imagine what their judgement of that appearance must be;
3. we develop some self-feeling, such as pride or mortification, as a result of our imagining other's judgement (Cooley, 1902).

Therefore, the development of self is not individual in nature as it is within the psychoanalytic models since the "mirror in the mind" is based on social interaction with the external world. For instance, when young children tell adults a story, their satisfaction with the storytelling experience is not with the story itself but with the response they receive from those that are present. If the adults were not to say anything to the child after the story was told, the child receives the message—through the looking-glass self—that (s)he did not please the adults or what (s)he had to say was not valued.

The power of the looking-glass self has both short and long term effects. Children who are told they are attractive, intelligent, funny, and creative throughout their childhood may internalize that they are. Similarly, children who are told that they are fat, stupid, dull, and have no creativity may also internalize that image of themselves in their personality structure. This is also true of adults who experience relationships where they are continually made to feel inadequate and worthless as human beings. If this view is received from those that they encounter repeatedly, there is a much reduced opportunity that they will sustain or develop a positive self.

The empirical evidence available tends to support Cooley's conception of the looking-glass self. Rosenberg (1981) has shown that individuals do see themselves as others see them. Similarly, there is evidence that individuals believe others think more highly of them than they actually do. Individuals, then, tend to side in the egocentric direction in their views of how others see them, unless they are repeatedly made to feel differently. Finally, many individuals from minority groups that have suffered discrimination such as Blacks in the U.S. and Jews around the world, tend not to have negative views of themselves. The reason for this is that they tend to identify with other group members, resulting in a realistic appraisal of self (Rosenberg, 1981).

George Herbert Mead: Taking the Role of the Other (Role-Taking)

Mead, a philosopher by training, was one of the most influential figures to carve out the groundwork for the symbolic interaction perspective. As one of the most notable figures in this tradition, it is interesting to note that he never went to graduate school. Nevertheless, Mead was best known during his career as having a powerful impact on his students. It was not until after his death that his most famous work was published, *Mind, Self, and Society: From the Standpoint of a Social Behaviourist (1934/1962).* This publication, however, was not written by Mead himself but was compiled from lecture notes taken by his former graduate students. One of his former students, T.V. Smith, once stated, "Conversation was his best medium, writing was a poor second" (Ritzer, 1988:176).

Mead's general theory of the stages of socialization begins with Cooley's description of children's imaginary friends. According to Mead, children's play moves through two distinguishable stages. The earliest form of play, known as the play stage, is characterized by children playing make-believe. Undoubtedly you have seen young children pretend to be a mother or a father by imitating behaviour and conversation. In the play stage children take on the roles of people who are significant to them. They will play as doctors, police officers, astronauts, and the like because they identify with them. At times, children will take on two complementary roles at once. Thus, children may say things to themselves that their mothers have said to them, then reply in their own words (Elkin and Handel, 1984).

The second stage of play is known as the game stage because children as they develop learn the organization of roles. Children learn how to distinguish one role from another. They learn how they should act at school with teachers, how to act around their friends, and how to act with their parents. Very young children are not capable of making this distinction. Let me try and clarify this point. If you ever have been to a young child's t-ball game you probably remember laughing after a child finally hit the ball because all the children on the playing field would chase the ball simultaneously or one would catch the ball and chase the base runner around the bases instead of throwing the ball to another player ahead of the runner. To Mead, very young children have not yet learned that for organized games to be properly played requires that people play various positions (roles). Mead also emphasizes that during this stage children learn the norms and values of society from their parents and significant others.

During the game stage children also become cognizant of the **generalized other.** By this, Mead is referring to the child's ability to take the role of the other. In our baseball example, older children know that if the ball is hit to the left field, the left fielder alone will chase the ball while the other players bold their positions and await the throw from the fielder after the ball has been caught. The generalized other represents our capacity to take a viewpoint by putting ourselves mentally in the role of the other. That is, we know what the left fielder will do by understanding the role of the left fielder on certain plays. The self to Mead is at first unsocialized since it is poorly developed and external to children. It is established once children learn to take the role of the other and internalize society's norms and values. In other words, the socialized self emerges once society is internalized which occurs in the game stage of socialization.

Mead also goes beyond Cooley by partitioning the self into two components: the "**I**" and the "**Me**"; however, he later identifies a third component, the **generalized other** which completes the process of developing a socialized self. For Mead, one of the essential qualities of the self is its reflexive ability: the ability to be self conscious (White, 1977). This quality enables individuals to stand apart from themselves (that is, as they see themselves) in order to see how others view them. The reflexive nature of the self enables individuals to react to the imagined "other person's judgement." According to Mead, individuals acquire a sense of self through the processes of communication and interaction with others.

The "**I**" in Mead's self represents the individual's ability to project oneself outside of the body. In other words, the "**I**" is that part of the self that we usually do not think about. For example, when you are chasing a baseball you do not think of what your body is doing during the action. To do so would make you clumsy, therefore, you concentrate on chasing the ball. The "**I**" as a component of self is the part of which we are unaware until the act is completed. You probably remember as a child—as I do—rolling your eyes after your parents stated something that you did not like or could not agree with. This act often occurred unknowingly to you, but was usually brought to your awareness by your parents. Restated, this part of the self is spontaneous, provides us with our individuality, and expresses itself without our conscious awareness until after the act.

The "**Me**" in Mead's conception of the self consists of those conscious thoughts and actions that are in our awareness. More accurately, it is the organized set of attitudes of others which individuals assume themselves. The "**Me**" is our ability to be appropriate and meet societal expectations. For example, when you are invited out on a dinner date to a lavish restaurant, you usually know how to behave—even if you have never been to a lavish restaurant—and what silverware is used for what purpose. On the other hand, when you go out with your friends for pizza, how you behave and whether or not you eat your pizza in hand or with a knife and fork is usually not of any real consequence. The "**Me**," then, attempts to adopt the proper response to the situation encountered. The "**I**," the spontaneous side of self, and the "**Me**," the social self, represent separated but complementary components of the same self. In our previous example of rolling your eyes at a comment made by your parents, the "**I**" is expressing itself since you were not aware of it, even though your social self, the "**Me**," recognizes that this is not acceptable behaviour toward your parents. The self-reflexive nature of the self is evident when the act is made conscious to you since you recognize that this is not considered appropriate behaviour when you put yourself in the role of the other.

Theories of Development: A Recapitulation

In this section we discussed a variety of theoretical views on child development. Although each of these views are different in detail, each emphasize that the self emerges through social interaction with others. Each view attempts to demonstrate how the individual comes to understand societal standards. Piaget specifically dealt with the cognitive development and morality in children. Freud was particularly interested in the unconscious and its effect on the human personality. Erickson's work takes us beyond Freud since it explores stages in personality development over the life cycle. Finally, Cooley and Mead suggest how society is internalized in us through social interaction with others.

Each of these theoretical views should not be perceived as competing views of socialization but complementary since each theorist addresses different components of development and socialization. The theories of Freud, Erickson, Cooley, and Mead, however, tend to be more applicable to adulthood socialization than Piaget's. Overall, the importance of these theoretical views on childhood socialization become especially relevant once we explore the types of socialization experienced by individuals in our society. More importantly, these views lay the foundation for understanding the processes of socialization experienced by members of any society.

Types of Socialization

As suggested earlier, socialization is not a uniform concept but one that has enormous range over the life cycle. Socialization processes vary over the life cycle resulting in a cumulative effect that enables us to function in pro-social ways rather than in anti-social ways. To fully understand the processes of socialization, we need to further delineate the types of socialization experienced by all individuals during their lifetimes.

Primary Socialization

Primary socialization takes place during infancy and early childhood usually within the family. Initially, children's view of the social world is very general and primarily seen through the eyes of their parents. It is through primary socialization that individuals learn language, symbols, mores, norms, and values and develop a diverse set of cognitive skills, enabling them to act productively in society.

As children move through the primary socialization process, their referent shifts from the specific to the general. This abstraction is necessary for them to come to understand what others in general expect. Children slowly begin to learn that the views they hear first about the social world may not necessarily be consistent with others they are now in contact with. According to Berger and Luckmann (1967), primary socialization is the most important since it is during the early years that an individual's social construction of the world takes place. Primary socialization alone, however, cannot entirely prepare children for roles and experiences in the adult world.

Secondary Socialization

Secondary socialization refers to the social training received by children, often in institutional or formal school settings and which continues throughout their lives. In contrast to primary socialization, secondary socialization typically involves socialization by other adults, i.e., teachers. Secondary socialization later in life (also known as *adult socialization*) takes place when individual's become involved with new dimensions of life: raising a family, entering a professional school, starting a job, and retiring. You will recall that we suggested that socialization in adulthood requires individuals to adapt to changing circumstances. This is especially apparent in such cases as marital breakdown (see Family chapter) and occupational obsolescence (see The Organization of Work chapter). In general, the skills initially developed through primary socialization provides adults with the basis to acquire the adaptation skills necessary during their life time experience with secondary socialization. We will return to the notion of adult socialization later in this chapter in section five.

Anticipatory Socialization

Anticipatory socialization is considered by sociologists a rehearsal or preparatory process enabling individuals to anticipate what it will be like to play particular roles in life. For example, if you were to enter nursing school or teaching, you probably have anticipated what it would be like to be a nurse or a teacher. Often, imagery operates to enable individuals to consider how they will play out social roles prior to engaging in them; including, what will be worn and used (symbols of the position), anticipation of how various situations that may arise would be handled, and the language (technical jargon) that is necessarily attributed to the occupation. Anticipatory socialization can be an intermediary stage between primary socialization and secondary socialization. Most often, however, anticipatory socialization occurs during the period most often associated with secondary socialization.

Wheeler (1967) argues:

> A practical question facing most agencies of socialization [i.e., the school system] is how to manage the advance preparation so as to increase the probability of successful outcome....Since much activity may go on between the decision to enter a program and actual participation, it seems likely that a considerable amount of socialization affect is achieved before the person enters. (p.84)

Simply put, the agencies of socialization, such as the school system (teachers and guidance counsellors) and the mass media, are actually providing individuals with preparation for anticipated future social roles as a way to ensure that individuals are socialized to carry them out as expected.

Resocialization

Resocialization is based upon unlearning and replacing old attitudes, beliefs, and behaviours with new ones. This type of socialization is especially relevant to adults since throughout the adulthood life cycle, people are constantly required to adapt to changing circumstances and situations. Resocialization is usually more difficult than the original socialization experience since it entails the unlearning of old and familiar ways of behaving. This is obvious when we think of how adults adapt to changing job roles that have been instituted by organizations, i.e., the transition to computer technology. Similarly, individuals who lose their jobs, retire, or go back to school after a prolonged absence, experience the process of resocialization. In each case, the identity of the individual may change, or at minimum, their social role may become altered leading to the necessity to adapt to changed circumstances.

The resocialization process is also evident among individuals who enter **total institutions** (Goffman, 1967) or **carceral organizations** such as correctional or psychiatric institutions for any length of time. In most respects, individuality and freedom to act as one desires is removed. Individuals living under such circumstances lose the freedom to eat, sleep and exercise when they so choose, express themselves freely, and leave when they would like. Prior to and immediately following discharges after prolonged incarceration from such institutions obviously requires that the individual undergoes the process of resocialization in order to adapt to community life once again.

Individuals in extreme situational isolation and stress, usually known as **critical situations** are also subject to the process of resocialization. Bettelheim (1943) and Cohen (1953) studied concentration camp behaviour of individuals imprisoned in Nazi concentration camps during the second world war. Bettelheim, imprisoned himself, witnessed in many of his fellow prisoners a continuous resocialization process taking place. In the camps the first response of many prisoners was to pay the minutest attention to every sign of harm, to each guard, to the prisoner foreman, to each noise in the distance, and to each abrupt or large-scale movement. Finally, after long-term stress caused by such concerns, prisoners either "converted" themselves from their Judaic religion to a synthetic faith and action or moved on to a form of psychological adaptation which involved paying less attention to lethal danger and more to self-preservation actions such as trying to find "safe" or less difficult job assignments, making friends to share a confidence with, and finding a better place to sleep. Coben's research confirms Bettelheim's findings and suggests that extreme situational isolation leads to a deculturation process. According to Cohen, prisoners strive to adjust new and peculiar circumstances to be congruent with values ordinarily learned in the process of socialization.

Atypical Cases: Blocked Socialization

To this point we have described socialization patterns common to most children and adults. These patterns typically involve situations that are established to enable individuals to become productive members of society. Many individuals, in particular children, are not so fortunate. Some children are raised in crowded institutions, others are raised by unresponsive adults or parents who are absent for long periods of time. Studies of these less than ideal situations provide contrasting evidence for understanding the importance of primary socialization.

Blocked socialization, represents one type of socialization which results when the child is withheld social interaction and social support for prolonged periods of time. One study, among many aimed at determining the effects of parental deprivation, compared the development of infants with and without maternal stimulation. In this study, Spitz (1964) compared infants who were abandoned and receiving hospital care with infants who resided in a nursery for infants who had mothers incarcerated in prison. Spitz found that the infants who were abandoned received minimal stimulation in the hospital setting since nurses were responsible for numerous children at once. In fact, of the 45 infants under the age of eighteen months, 6 died in a measles epidemic. In another ward containing 43 infants eighteen to thirty months of age, 17 died of measles and only two of the 26 surviving infants could speak.

In contrast, the children who were in the prison nursery and were placed with their mothers for a portion of each day, were reported to be healthy, vigorous, and developmentally on track. Spinx's study showed that physical stimulation alone is insufficient to ensure adequate development and socialization. Those infants that were in contact with an adult who cared and provided consistent emotional support were able to acquire the primary socialization necessary to develop emotional and social attachments.

Studies have also traced the long-term effects of children deprived of adult attention. Children raised in isolation or near isolation are termed *feral* (or unsocialized) children. Such cases as the "Wild Boy of Aveyron" and the "Wolf Girls of Agra" have been reported in the literature. These were purported cases of children raised by wolves and who were later found by humans. Bettelheim (1959) has studied the documentation of these cases and has concluded that the reports actually suggest cases of abandoned children suffering from autism or feeble-mindedness. Bettelheim concludes that there is no scientific evidence available to demonstrate that any animal, including adult primates, could care adequately for a human infant, especially in terms of meeting the demands of species-characteristic behaviour, reflexes, and drives, to enable them simply to survive the time of their utter dependency.

More recent reports of feral children point to instances of children who were raised in the attics of houses with little to no human social contact. The best known case of a feral child raised in social isolation was reported in the United States by Kingsley Davis (1940). The girl in this case became known as "Anna of the Attic" since she was raised since birth in a dark attic by her grandfather because she was an illegitimate child. Anna reportedly received minimal physical care and virtually no social or emotional care. At age six Anna was discovered by social workers who reported that she could not walk, talk or feed herself. Prior to her death, approximately five years later, Anna was able to walk and could communicate in a limited way. This case, however bizarre it may seem, points to the importance of human social contact for child development and socialization.

Blocked socialization most frequently occurs in less extreme situations. It may occur to individuals living in situations where sexual and verbal abuse is a constant feature of everyday life. Cooley's looking-glass self may help us understand how individuals develop inadequate senses of self and emotional attachments to others in these situations. You will recall that Cooley suggested that we develop a sense of self through our experiences with the social world as well as in silent talk and interpretation of what others say to us. Individuals living in the situations alluded to may develop a distorted view of human relationships in the social world.

For an example of blocked socialization, see Inset 4:1.

Inset 4:1
Child Needs a Family

The following newspaper clipping is based on a neglected child in need of an adoptive family. The description demonstrates the negative effects of a child neglected early in life. Even short-term blocked socialization can impede a child's development and ability to socialize with others.

Melissa is a three-year old who needs an adoptive family. She has come a long way in the past year but functions at the level of a one-year-old.

This little girl enjoys good physical health. She can drink from a cup and can feed herself with a spoon. Despite significant delays, Melissa has responded well to a daily infant stimulation program and to a caring and structured home.

While Melissa does not yet interact with other people, as she gains confidence, her eye contact with those around her improves. She is learning to talk with the help of a speech therapist.

Melissa will need continued stimulation programs and medical supervision. She also needs a family who will provide her with love, understanding and patience.

***The Calgary Sun*, Sunday, June 9, 1991, p. 4.**

Socialization and Society

Socialization and Social Control

Society requires that the individual should respond in appropriate ways to certain stimuli. From this single premise it is reasonable to conclude that the socialization process is closely related to a system of social control. According to White (1977), "...it might be possible to conceive of socialization as a pervasive yet covert mechanism designed to ensure cultural continuity, and social control as its more overt counterpart" (p.16). By way of the mechanisms of socialization social control can operate. In childhood, patterns of attitudes and action are established which suit the need for people to interact meaningfully and harmoniously. Later in life after some view of "self" has become well established, mechanisms of socialization still operate to dispose individuals to behave in appropriate ways, and to help them either to select the right attitudes and actions from their mental bank, or to learn new appropriate responses. The notion of oneself becomes enhanced throughout socialization, and both childhood and adulthood can become part of an overt social control system. For example, parents and teachers will often appeal to what they believe is an adolescent's self image by invoking standards of adult behaviour (i.e., "As an adult, what do you think are the consequences?"), or readiness to accept responsibility (i.e., "Since you're an adult now, I'll leave you in charge"), when trying to coerce the young person into what may be considered a desired behaviour. The social control form in this respect attempts to appeal to the individual in terms of what she perceives as being worthy of herself.

The internalized controls which are established throughout socialization ensure that individuals know in broad terms how to behave in any social situation, or at least have the necessary knowledge potential for proper behaviour. Ultimately, social control is achieved when self-control (or, the *internalized social conscience*) is mastered, and individuals are able to exercise discipline over their own actions and behaviour. This does not mean that the social conscience is necessarily obeyed each time, nor even does this conscience provide the individual with the precise response demanded by the particular social circumstances, only that what is plausible is available. For instance, individuals in our society understand that driving under the influence of alcohol violates both social and legal codes of conduct, nevertheless, many still do drink and drive; even though the appropriate response is evident and available to them. Nevertheless the socialization process plays a vital social control function and helps to ensure the reasonably smooth continuity of society.

If socialization responds to the needs of society the question of who does the socializing is of considerable importance. It is likely that socialization will greatly be influenced by the individuals and institutions conducting it. Let us now turn to these agencies of socialization in our society.

Agencies of Socialization

The process of socialization obviously does not occur in a vacuum. Throughout the lives of children, as well as adults, various individuals and institutions participate in influencing future attitudes and actions. An important aspect of socialization is the acquisition of social meaning and behaviour from experiences with families, schools, peer groups, work settings, and the mass media (Peterson and Peters, 1983). The separate influences of these and other *socializing agents* have been the focus of most of the existing scholarship on socialization (Gecas, 1981; Inkeles, 1968). Initially, the family is the primary socialization agent during the early years. As children come into contact with the larger society, the school system, peer groups, and the mass media affect how they learn about society and future social expectations. These agencies, however, do not have a sequential influence on children, with the exception of the first two or three years of a child's life. Most of the agencies influence children in a concurrent and complementary fashion.

The Family

The first agent of socialization for infants is their immediate family. Children are not only provided with physical care but also care that initiates emotional bonds with their parents. Almost immediately, most infants learn that they can rely on their parents for care, security and comfort. As infants grow older parents begin to take on the role of educating them to human and social ways. This process is extensive and requires that children attain requisite levels of cognitive development before they can acquire language, become toilet trained, learn how to delay gratification, and so on. Initially, children are socialized to familial ways, rather than what is socially acceptable to society at large. Parents, in particular, teach their children about society based on their own experiences, biases, and modes of conduct. Later children learn that their parents ways may not necessarily be the universal way to achieve functional membership in society. Nevertheless, children are still strongly influenced by their parents as agents of socialization.

The family into which children are born act as their first reference group (commonly called the *family of orientation).* The family, as a social institution, stresses particular values, norms, and attitudes specific to itself and are used as referents for children in enunciating and evaluating their own values, norms, and attitudes. Parsons and Bales (1955) have suggested that children identify with the family as a group; therefore, their practices become part of children's conception of self. Specifically, Parsons and Bales suggest that not only do children identify with individual members of the group as role models, but they use interaction within and between group members as models for future ways of acting and building strong identities of themselves. The pattern of interaction that takes place within the family setting has future implications for how the individual will act in the future. Interestingly, during the late adolescence and into the early twenties young people can readily identify those qualities of their parents or interactions within the family unit that they will exclude from their own family life in the future. Nevertheless, many will fall into similar patterns of behavior simply because they have learned from their parents only certain ways of resolving a problem or accomplishing a task. For example, if a parent turns to alcohol every time there is a crisis, it is not unusual for children of that parent to turn to similar vices to deal with conflicts in their lives. Often, the interaction patterns developed within a family are not practiced by the offspring, but frequently they will marry someone who does cope in similar ways without immediately recognizing it.

At birth children inherit the status (or statuses) of their parents, in the community and in society. Most importantly, the family's position in the social class structure becomes the child's position. This affects not only bow the child will be responded to during the childhood years but their status as an adult as well (Elkin and Handel, 1984). One of the first major studies looking at the factors affecting occupational attainment in the United States was that by Blau and Duncan (1967). These researchers found that "the family into which a man is born exerts a profound influence on his career, because his occupational life is conditioned by his education, and his education depends to a considerable extent on his family" (p. 330). Evidence in Canada would suggest that this is even more true compared to the United States (Wanner, 1986). Wanner's study comparing the educational attainment of individuals in Canada and the U.S. found that "in Canada parental SES [socioeconomic status] is a more potent determinant of the likelihood of extending schooling beyond high school, particularly to university" (p. 62). The evidence shows that the family does influence the values, attitudes, and future actions of children. Children born into more affluent and educated families tend to adopt similar values that emphasize the necessity of future education throughout children's lives. Children born into families of less affluence and education tend to adopt value structures geared towards obtaining "good paying and secure" employment.

More recently, sociologists have come to recognize that much of their work on families as socialization agents has been centered on the nuclear family, married adults and their offspring. Today, however, our nation has experienced what has been termed as *pluralistic* family structures. Some of these family structures include: single parent headed families, blended families, homosexual headed families, and so on (for a more comprehensive discussion on changing family structures see chapter 10). Conventional wisdom suggests that children from these families will be maladjusted to "normal" functioning in society. Presently, there is no compelling evidence that these family structures result in more or less well-adjusted children than the typical nuclear family. In fact, the evidence would suggest that the adjustment of children to these alternative family structures typically depends on the ability of adults to adjust to them and how they deal with these relationships with children (Eiduson et al, 1988).

Our knowledge of child socialization within the family usually led us to believe that socialization was a one-way process: parent-to-child. During the last fifteen years or so we have come to realize that children are not passive recipients to the influence of their parents, but do in fact act as socialization agents to their parents (Bell and Harper, 1977; Mackie, 1984). As much as parents impart knowledge and the ways of society to their children, the process is reciprocated by children. Many parents of adolescent children learn the ways of the changing world through the eyes and experiences of their children. Times change and parents tend not to experience the changing realities confronted by their offspring. This phenomenon is commonly called the "generation gap" implying that parents seldom understand the pressures experienced by youth today. Pressures such as early sexual and drug exploration, conflicting values, development of self-concept, or changing gender roles, were not experienced to the same degree by many of their parents; consequently, they are not understood.

Although families are still perceived as having a major influence on the socialization of their children, parental involvement with children in the last decade has declined. More recently, parents argue back and forth that it is not the amount of time spent with children that is important, but the quality of time. We will not debate this point here, but will emphasize that alternative agents of socialization have replaced the parent to a greater or lesser extent in socializing children. Some of these include day care centres (see Inset 4:2), mass media (i.e., television), school, and organized activity and sports clubs.

The Peer Group

Up until about the age of two, children who are seemingly playing together, are essentially only playing in close proximity with each other; which consists of them doing their own particular things. By the time this independence ends, children have learned how to respond to the orders, requests or needs of other children (White, 1977). Peer groups tend to be the first contact children have with others outside of their family. It is in these groups that children socialize through playing with each other and begin to exert their independence from family. During the early years of childhood, children usually play together under the supervision of an adult or an older child, to whom reference is frequently made for direction, assistance, approval, and mediation as disagreements emerge between playmates. Play between very young children tends to be *egocentric,* all vying to exert their own interests and desires. Adults and older children while supervising young children act as agents of socialization, establishing how children should play together. As children mature, adult supervision is required to a lesser extent as children learn the social rules of play, cooperation, and negotiation.

The peer group, according to Elkin and Handel (1984), has certain distinctive characteristics:

1. by definition, it consists of similar ages;
2. participants in the group have varied power and prestige;
3. the peer group establishes its own interests and concerns, quite apart from adults concerns with appropriate social values, norms, and expectations; and,
4. their intent for long-term socialization is unintentional, yet their interactions serve an important function for preparing them for the adult world.

Children usually participate in more than one peer group. Sometimes they include siblings and cousins, others consist of neighbourbood children, still others involve schoolmates. Participation in a variety of peer groups prepare children for future relations with a variety of adults. Each peer group usually has its own rules, norms, and purpose. Children learn to adapt to varying circumstances and roles that they assume within each group, much in the same way that adults adjust to groups that they are in contact with.

Inset 4:2

Child Day Care Provision: Socializing Agent?

Since World War II one of the most striking demographic changes in North America has been the number of women entering the work force. During the first half of this century, few women worked outside of the home after starting a family. Today, this is no longer true. A major consequence of this development is that infants and pre-school children (ranging from three weeks to five years of age) are being placed in various types of day care; receiving primary care from adults other than parents, at least for a portion of each day.

The number of licensed day care spaces in Canada in 1990 was 320,624, an increase of 22,541 spaces from the year before (Health and Welfare Canada, 1991). These day care spaces, however, do not include the number of children receiving primary care from non-licensed private or casual day care arrangements established between parents and care providers (i.e., babysitters).

Professionals and parents alike have debated the consequences and benefits of children receiving care from adults other than the parents of procreation. Here, our concern is not with entering into this debate but to suggest that this new form of child care for our nation's children has resulted in the creation of a new socialization agent. Care providers today receive children during their informative years. Many are responsible for providing care to many children at once.

Presently, we have little empircal data to confirm or disconfirm the effects that these arrangements have on child development and socialization to familiy and societal values. Part of the problem, of course, is that children cared for in private and casual day care arrangements are difficult to assess and access. Further, longitudinal studies would be required to determine if children in day care facilities develop differently than children receiving care from their parents on a full-time basis.

What do you think? Does it make a difference if children are cared for by adults other than their parents?

Peer groups for older children serve some very important functions. First, it is in these groups that children establish their own rules for dealing with membership inclusion/exclusion, conflicts, trust, and other forms of normative behavior. For older children, the peer group is separate from the watchful eyes of adults. In these groups, children take on adult roles such as decision-makers and leaders. In addition, children learn their own special place within the group. Children learn to be followers, leaders, comedians, negotiators, scapegoats, and so on. For this reason, children in multiple peer group situations tend to have greater opportunity to experience a variety of roles. That is, the roles they occupy may vary by peer group.

Peer groups among adolescents take on special significance since adolescence is the time period in young people's lives when they struggle between parental/family dependence and establishing their own independence and sense of self. In a national study conducted in Canada, Bibby and Posterski (1985) found that adolescents commonly perceived adults to be insensitive to their problems. Many claimed that they were not taken seriously. Whether these views are real or perceived is irrelevant to the fact that they are felt. Peer group socialization then, is most prominent during adolescence because it is in the peer group that teenagers sense self-importance and acceptance.

Socialization during this stage of the life cycle involves dealing with both positive and negative peer influences. Adolescents tend to deal with issues around "fitting in," dating, sexuality, drugs and alcohol use, personal independence, future educational and occupational prospects, and so on. Peer influence plays a major role in how these issues are resolved. Parents of adolescents tend to want to help their children make decisions, but often their values are initially rejected as adolescents exercise their own individual identity and independence.

As a socialization agent adolescent peer groups not only develop their own understandings of the world but complement the views of their families in many respects, particularly in late adolescence. Adolescents, although often rejecting many of their familial values also accept many others. These values are usually shared in discussions with their peers resulting in a socialization process that broadens adolescents' views of society beyond that of their parents. Overall, the peer group is an influential socialization agent, but it is still not the primary socialization agency in our society. According to Mackie (1983), the peer group is the second most potent socialization agency behind that of the family. Bibby and Posterski found support for Mackie's insight. Table 4:3 shows that even during adolescence, teenagers still perceive their family as having a major influence on their lives. Teachers and the media have a less perceived influence on the lives of adolescents. Although parents have the greatest influence on their adolescent children, many adolescents reportedly receive more satisfaction from their peer group than their families (see Table 4:4). Most of this satisfaction stems from adolescents feeling that their parents do not understand them nor treat them as adults, whereas their peer group is "in touch" with them, according to Bibby and Posterski. Nonetheless, the family is still the predominant socialization agent.

Table 4:3
Perceived Sources of Influence among Adolescents, Canada, 1984[1]
"To what extent do you think your life is influenced by:"

	A Great Deal	Quite a Bit	Some	Little or None	Totals
Family	55%	30%	11%	4%	100%
Your Friends	30	43	23	4	100
Teachers	9	32	43	16	100
Media	8	26	45	21	100

[1]Number of respondents = 3500
Source: Modified from original. Bibby, Reginald W. and Posterski, Donald C. (1985). *The Emerging Generation: An Inside Look at Canada's Teenagers*. Toronto: Irwin Publishing, p.101.

Table 4:4
Perceived Sources of Enjoyment among Adolescents, Canada, 1984[1]
"How much enjoyment do you receive from the following:"

	Canada	B.C.	Prairies	Ontario	Quebec	Atlantic
Peer Group	59.7%	59.7%	58.7%	62.3%	56.0	61.7
Family	33.0	33.4	28.6	34.4	35.8	31.0
Television	29.0	30.0	27.0	31.0	26.0	36.0
School	15.0	17.0	11.0	17.0	15.0	16.0

[1]Number of respondents = 3500
Source: Modified from original. Bibby, Reginald W. and Posterski, Donald C. (1985). *The Emerging Generation: An Inside Look at Canada's Teenagers*. Toronto: Irwin Publishing, p.32.

The School

With the increase in the social complexity of our society, socializing experiences within the family setting and the peer group alone are insufficient to prepare children for later experiences in the adult world. Consequently, it is in school that children systematically are taught the ways of the whole culture. "From entry in the first grade until entry in the labour force or marriage the school class may be regarded as the focal socializing agency" (Parsons, 1964:130). Ishwarin (1979) estimates that from kindergarten through grade six children spend approximately 7,000 hours in school (p. 23). Evidently, the school system has the potential to influence children.

According to Parsons (1964) the school system simultaneously serves four functions:

1. It emancipates the child from primary emotional attachment to the family;
2. it drives home societal values and norms beyond those that can be given in the family;
3. it imposes a differential valuation and reward of achievement; and,

4. from society's point of view it provides a selection and allocation of its human resources relative to the adult role system (p. 143).

The school system, then, as a formal socialization agency imparts more to children than just knowledge about reading, writing, and arithmetic. It is also a time and place for developing those social skills that are necessary if they are to use the formally learned knowledge in satisfying ways for themselves and in acceptable way for others. It is also the place where children experience a whole set of new constraints. Children must adapt to new and unfamiliar surroundings, new people, time-tabled work and play, and possibly a new range of behavioral expectations.

As children move through school, they slowly adapt their processes of thought and logic to a more objective recognition of others in their social environment. Children learn to recognize the difference and the independence of their own views and feelings from those of others. More importantly, children begin to experience in the school system their relative abilities compared to the students around them. Prior to the school years, children may have been raised with praise and feelings of their importance as members of a family. During the school years however, they come into contact with other children vying for similar praise and attention. Teachers tend to reinforce the differences between children through grading and providing rewards to the "better" students, while offering few incentives for "weaker" students, whether intentionally or not, to compete in the educational marketplace. Typically, class size is very large limiting the amount of time that a teacher can spend with a child experiencing difficulty mastering the fundamentals of a subject matter. Often, these processes lead to feelings of low self-worth, competitiveness, and, finally, to future roles in life becoming clearer to children well before they actually assume them.

Children initially experience extrafamilial social control and authority in the school system. Early in the school career children learn that the teacher has authority and control over them. Most often, teachers must maintain uniform standards in terms of evaluation, behaviour, and social expectations to which all students must adhere to. The effect of this process is that students learn to be constrained in their attitudes so they are accepted by both the authority figure and their peers. Children also learn about authority figures and social control outside of both the classroom and their families while they are in the school system. For instance, older children in the school system come into contact with even more teachers than they experienced during their earlier school years. These teachers, along with teachers involved with extracurricular activities such as sports teams and activity clubs, act as socializing agents in moulding students to societal expectations. Children learn how to compete with others in socially appropriate ways. They learn the pleasure of winning and the pain of losing. This process prepares them to adapt to adult life with flexibility and recognition that winning and losing will be constants in the years to come.

The socializing influence of the school system is not only experienced by children but also by young adults pursuing post-secondary school training. Numerous studies have shown that young adults are socialized in nursing schools (Davis, 1968; Ross, 1961; Simpson, 1967), graduate training (Bates, 1967; Becker and Carper, 1956), and to professional training such as medical schools (Bucher and Stelling, 1977; Friedson, 1970; Haas and Shaffir, 1981), chiropractic schools (Kelner et al, 1980; Mills and Larson, 1981), and law schools (Lortie, 1968), to assume the occupational roles that they are being trained for. All of these studies point to the way that self-identity is transformed, feelings of competency are developed, collegiality and competitiveness are reinforced, and how uncertainty is managed, during the schooling years.

The school system as a formal socialization agent begins early in children's lives and lasts upwards of twenty or more years for some. It not only teaches the knowledge necessary for individuals to function adequately in adult life, but also operates as a primary disseminator of appropriate values, norms, and social expectations to members of society. Functionally, this is important to society but not necessarily to all of its members. The school system as a socialization agent also acts as a credential granting agency; that is one that grants certification to individuals for succeeding on their terms. Employers in the work world have passed through this system and accept its legitimacy. Unfortunately, many students are not able to remain in the school system until they reach the minimal level of education—high school diploma—for a variety of reasons. Individuals who fall into this category tend to receive fewer employment prospects compared to their graduating counterparts. For example, individuals with grade twelve diplomas tend to have greater employment opportunities compared to individuals who have grade ten or eleven completed. Presently, there is no compelling evidence to suggest that an extra year in school actually leads to higher calibre labourers or salespersons. Nonetheless, individuals who do not achieve the minimum standards accepted today, often find themselves at a disadvantage when seeking employment.

The Mass Media

The influence of the mass media (i.e., television, music videos, magazines, newspapers, and advertisements) has unquestionably been a powerful socializing force of both the young and old in our society. The mass media invades our senses while we are at home and when we are out in public areas. In today's society, it has become increasingly difficult not to have been exposed to the mass media in one form or another on a daily basis. According to Rosengren and Windahl (1989), the mass media play very important roles:

1. as carriers of society's overall culture and also of specific subcultures;
2. as political arenas of conflict and consensus;
3. as evermore ubiquitous and powerful agents of socialization;
4. as a means to express group identity and group affiliation; and,
5. as individual instruments of knowledge and pleasure, power and subjugation (p. xix).

Our concern here is with how the mass media *acts* as a potential socialization agent in society. We will pay particular attention to the medium of television since it is the most potent catalyst in disseminating and reinforcing cultural values, norms, and attitudes in modern day life.

When a medium such as television has the power to transmit and reflect the values of society and when, as Leifer *et al.* (1974) suggest, it serves a normative reference point, it assumes some of the characteristics of an agent of socialization. If the premise that television has some of these characteristics is accepted, it becomes crucial to examine television's impact on the minds of those who are subjected to its influence. The statistics on the television viewing patterns of children have stimulated much interest. Comstock (1975), synthesizing the findings of a number of studies, points out that:

1. Children typically begin viewing television regularly 3 or 4 years before entering the first grade.
2. Most children watch some television every day, and most watch 2 hours or more per day.

Spurlock (1982:73) further suggests that the evidence on television viewing shows that by the time children are 16, they have watched from 12,000 to 15,000 hours of television. This is equivalent to viewing approximately 15-20 months of television, 24 hours a day! The influence of television for socializing children cannot be repudiated. Rosengren and Windahl (1989) went as far to say that television as a source of general information may have a greater impact on children's social development than school. This is alarming considering that the television programs viewed by children seldom serve an educational function. According to Spurlock (1982), the heaviest period of television viewing by children is during prime time. Frequent television viewers can testify to the fact that there are far more half-hour sitcoms, game shows, sporting events, and "cops and robbers" shows during prime time than programs that would serve educational value to children.

The invention of the television has also met with mixed blessings in our society since it not only provides us with needed up-to-date information on what is happening around the world, across the country, and in our city, but it also reinforces cultural stereotypes, codifies social roles, and constructs gender identity (see Estep, 1982; Lindsey, 1990; Mackie, 1991; Rosengren and Windahl, 1989). Television shows typically portray men in positions of power, domination, and control; whereas women are typically portrayed as weak, submissive, emotional, and as sex-objects (Lindsey, 1990). Moreover, both adult and children's shows revolve around men, with male characters outnumbering females 3 to 1 (Signorielli, 1982 quoted in Lindsey, 1990). When females do outnumber males it is usually in the context of multiple females hanging off the arms of a male, with the accent on women as object. Studies (Fruch and McGhee, 1975; Gross and Jeffries-Fox, 1978) have shown that the degree of television viewing is associated with conceptions of gender stereotypes. These studies show that both pre-schoolers and older children who are heavy consumers of television viewing hold more traditional gender stereotypes than pre-schoolers and children who view television less frequently. Coupled with the gender stereotypes are children's perceptions of social roles available to them in the future. Heavy consumers of television programming often felt that men performed instrumental roles (i.e., providers and decision-makers) while women performed expressive roles (i.e., nurturers and childrearing functions), which limited their conceptions of occupations available to men and women and contributed toward a view that males were superior to females. The major consequence of these findings is that the vulnerability of children leads them to believe that what is on television is an accurate depiction of reality.

Television also acts as an agent that reinforces the values and norms of a society. Most programming emphasizes the importance of the family, the consequences of deviant behaviour, and the extent of cultural diversity in our society. More recently, television networks have taken steps to address these issues, however, most of these efforts are ineffective since the majority of the programming still exhibit sexism and violent acts. Until television network executives realize the impact of their programming on viewers, little progress will be made toward the advancement of the equality of the sexes and sensitizing us toward the consequences of the victimization of others.

Patterns of Subcultural Variation in Canada

Throughout this chapter we have alluded to socialization as a complex process. You should be aware, however, that the patterns of socialization, or the ways that individuals become socialized to society can, and often do, vary by such factors as ethnic background, social class, and region of the country. In this section we will briefly convey how these factors contribute to different socialization practices and their effects on society and the individual.

Ethnicity

Canada as a nation was founded on immigrants. Today, Canada is considered to be a multicultural society with distinct ethnic subcultures remaining intact. Since 1980 19% of Canada's immigrant population have predominantly come from Asian and other non-European countries (McKie and Thompson, 1990). This fact accompanied with our aboriginal population, French Canadian and English Canadian distinction, and earlier immigrant populations, has resulted in a cultural mix unseen in many industrialized nations. Naturally, then, this process leads to varied cultural and socialization patterns among the various ethnic groupings in the country. Here our concern is with bringing to your attention that the socialization patterns discussed throughout this chapter differs by ethnic grouping. It is true that most members in our population do support the general values and norms in our society, however, many do vary in terms of socializing their children, the importance of the family, the value of education, and strength of their cultural identity.

One of the consequences of a rich cultural mix is tension between various ethnic and race groups. As pointed out in McGuigan's chapter on Culture, ethnic and race relations has been a source of tension and common misconceptions between groups. Prejudicial and discriminatory attitudes and actions tend to be reinforced during childhood socialization. For example, think of yourself as a young child overhearing your parents discussing the violent behaviour of some Asian gangs or the French separatist movement. If your parents believe that the violent actions of some Asian gang members represents the violent nature of Asians in general or that we should let Quebec separate because they are nothing but a society of complainers, then you too as an impressionable young child may adopt similar beliefs about these groups without having a clear understanding of the issues and problems faced by these groups. Socialization, then, not only is a necessary and beneficial societal requirement, it also has detrimental effects when the socializee is influenced by socializers who maintain egocentric postures or base their views of others on generalizations.

Social Class

The concept social class is a complex concept that has been variously defined in sociology and related disciplines. The concept of social class, however, invariably suggests that different groups possess unequal amounts of wealth, influence, prestige, and "life chances" (Elkin and Handel, 1983). For our purpose we will define social class as the social standing an individual has in their community based on their education, occupational prestige, and income level. Undoubtedly, you have heard of such classes as lower class, working class, middle class, and upper class groups in society. Social class becomes an important factor in understanding how individuals are socialized to society since it contributes toward self-identity, extent of political influence, social contacts, as well as economic and educational aspirations and opportunities.

Research in social class differences in Canada and elsewhere frequently point to the varied socialization practices across the classes. For example, in a study conducted in Hamilton, Ontario, Pineo and Looker (1983) found evidence to suggest that the socioeconomic status of parents had bearing on whether or not the value of self-direction in children was supported by parents. The researchers found that middle-class parents were more likely to encourage self-direction in their adolescent children than working-class parents. Lambert (1981) in his study of the social influences among English-Canadian and French-Canadian parents on child development found that there were more similarities between French-Canadian and English-Canadian parents of the same social class in child-rearing values than either group are with same-ethnic parents of a different social class.

Earlier we discussed the work of Blau and Duncan (1967) and Wanner (1983) showing that the education level of parents influenced the educational aspirations of their children. These studies demonstrated indirectly that the social experiences of children from families to different social classes are socialized differently, resulting in divergent values toward education.

Oversocialization

Our discussion on socialization may lead you to conclude that the individual is a more or less passive object of socialization by society as represented by its various socialization agents. It is true that individuals are often constrained in their actions because of these socialization forces, but they still have free will to act on their own. If individuals did not have the free will to act, then we would have a society with very little variation in personality and action. In one of the most quoted articles dealing with this concern "The Oversocialized Conception of Man in Modern Sociology," Dennis Wrong (1961) argues in a complex way that the individual is not totally driven by internalized norms and values. In other words, Wrong suggests (not to the extent that Freud did in earlier writings) that the individual is a social, but never a fully socialized creature. If the norms and values of the environment that they experienced growing up, then all actions would not be the responsibility of the individual. In other words, if an individual were raised in a poor neighbourhood and had negative role models, does this mean that they should not be held responsible for their actions in society?

In our society, most individuals are socialized by the various agencies discussed. However, we also know that all agencies do not socialize all individuals in the same way. For example, the school system socializes children in different ways depending on the attentiveness of the student and their individual academic ability. Similarly, not all families are the same; therefore, we should expect variation in the content of socialization to society. Wrong is quite right in his argument: we do place too much emphasis on the internalization of values and norms, and less on the variety of ways that individuals experience these influences. It seems reasonable to conclude that the internalization of societal norms and values are experienced by most individuals in our society but that the process by which it is experienced, as well as, the personalities of the individuals subjected to these processes will affect the extent of social constraint internalized.

Socialization and Social Roles

Socialization to society from early infancy onward is important in preparing individuals for future social roles. In primary socialization, children learn the general aspects of participating in society. As children mature, secondary socialization enables children to learn the specific elements of the activities and social roles that people play in society. In this section, we will briefly discuss the concept of social roles and how socialization enables individuals to carry them out. We will also discuss the effects of gender role socialization as well as socialization to occupational roles.

Performing Social Roles

> All the world's a stage,
> And all the men and women merely players:
> They all have their exits and their entrances;
> And one man in his life time plays many parts.
> (*As You Like It,* Act II, Scene VII)

This excerpt from William Shakespeare's 1599 play, *As You Like It,* summarizes what we engage in on a daily basis. All the world is a stage in the sense that we play many roles that demand certain requirements of us. As a mother you act differently to your children than you do toward your husband, employer, closest friend, parents, and those you meet at school. Each time we enter a social encounter with others, we wear different hats depending on who it is we are interacting with at the time. The act of wearing different hats is called performing **social roles.** *Social roles* can be defined as "a pattern of behaviour, structured around specific rights and duties and associated with a particular status position within a group or social situation" (Theodorson and Theodorson, 1969). Notice that social roles are not people but are the parts played by people in social situations. Social roles enable us to predict the behaviour of others and for individuals to pattern their actions accordingly. Social roles, then, are sets of norms that allow and limit our behaviour.

Erving Goffman, an Albertan-born sociologist, is probably the best known theorist who has worked in the area of social role performances. Goffman in an important work *Presentation of Self in Everyday Life* (1959) frequently used the analogy that everyday interactions with others was similar to performing on a stage. According to Goffman, there were **front stages** and **backstages.** The *front-stage* was that part of yourself that you acted out for social audiences. If you were talking to your employer, for example, you would probably act confident, knowledgeable, and skilled. Away from your employer, the *backstage,* is where you drop the "act" or take off the mask, perhaps even tell a loved one how worried you are about being able to do the tasks ahead of you. Goffman believed that performing social roles represented the "crucial discrepancy between our all-too-human selves and our socialized selves" (1959:56). According to Goffman, we spend a good part of every day playing multiple social roles and have to take off and put on the different masks warranted to play the role required. For Goffman, this was all a part of **impression management,** the art of guarding against a series of unexpected actions, such as unintended gestures, verbal slips, and inappropriate behaviour required by the situation. *Impression management* requires that we maintain the social role intact until we leave the setting or situation. In addition, impression management requires that we do not allow others into our backstage since it then becomes frontstage knowledge about ourselves. For instance, even if you invite your employer over to your house for dinner, you still do not act as you normally would when your employer was not present. In general, we attempt to keep a controlled front of who we are to others. Only certain individuals have the opportunity to see other sides of our same self, but no one ever really has the opportunity to see all our backstage behaviour. Overall Goffman does recognize that some backstage parts of ourselves are revealed on occasion. Instructors will sometimes communicate differently to students when they see them in the cafeteria, in contrast to the way they act in the lecture hall. Similarly, if you frequent the same night spot, the waiter or waitress may act differently to you, in contrast to a patron they have not served before.

Social role performance is possible since individuals are socialized to the society they live in. We learn all about social roles through secondary socialization processes and the agents of socialization. In addition, particular norms, values, and attitudes are adopted and reinforced by the different groups to which we belong. As you learned in the chapter on culture, norm violations are recognized by members of social groups. We learn through our own errors, and those of others, how to play social roles and control what it is we want others to see of ourselves.

Gender Role Socialization

Gender role socialization, unlike social roles, begins at the moment of birth. Whether you liked it or not, your parents in all probability treated you different than your opposite sex sibling. Since parents are socialized into the same society, albeit at a different period of time, they react differently towards you depending on whether you were a boy or a girl. Fox (1977:809) found that studies of gender learning show that "even as infants, girls are expected to be, thought to be, and rewarded for being quieter, more passive, more controlled—in short, 'nicer' babies—than are boys" (quoted in Mackie, 1991). This process, no matter how harmless it may appear at first, is the beginning stages of gender role socialization. Gender *role socialization is* the process whereby individuals are socialized to take on the roles that are deemed "sex-appropriate" for the society they live in. These roles are often defined in terms of their degree of masculinity and femininity. This process limits the range of possible behaviour seen to be acceptable of a man or a woman. Boys learn not to cry, girls learn that crying is acceptable. Boys learn that aggressive play is natural and fun, girls learn that aggressive play is not lady-like and unacceptable. Boys learn that playing house with dolls is sissy-like and girls learn that playing house with dolls is rewarded with praise—"you're a good little mother." Each of these situations socializes boys and girls to particular gender roles. Boys learn to hold back their emotions, to be aggressive and competitive, and to believe that they cannot nurture like a female. Similarly, females learn to express their emotions, be passive and pacify, and to believe that it is their mothering "instinct" to be good nurturers.

At school boys and girls learn that their abilities are differentially assessed by teachers. Boys are good at mathematics and sciences, girls are better at english and spelling. Until recently, textbooks assigned to school classes reinforced sex role stereotypes; often portraying women as intellectual inferiors to men (Weitzman, 1979). In addition, vocational tracking often resulted in males and females entering classes that reflected stereotypical biases of their predecessors—boys learned machine shop, woodwork, and automobile mechanics; girls learned home economics, secretarial skills, and hairdressing—under the guise that it would be useful to them later in life. What children actually learned was a narrow range of skills that made them dependent on the other sex. In addition, boys were able to learn the skills that paid better later in life compared to those of girls.

As boys and girls become young adults, boys are perceived as a "good catch" if they are single and educated; females, on the other hand, are considered to be "old maids" and must be undesirable if they are still single at a certain age. Even though times are changing, these descriptions of men and women are still common perceptions of many individuals in our society. Young men and women, even if they do not accept these stereotypical notions, are often the envy of others or the recipient of sympathy of others because of their status—which is usually sex-based.

More recently in the sociological literature there has been discussion on the connection between the early socialization of males and violence. Given that the vast majority of violent crimes are committed by males, researchers have looked for possible sources of violent behaviour in the particular expectations of parents and significant others have for young boys; that is, expectations that will lead them to become a particular type of "man."

A recent example of such research is Myriam Miedzian's work, *Boys Will Be Boys: Breaking the Link between Masculinity and Violence* (1991). Miedzian continues the tradition established by Chodorow (1978) and Dinnerstein (1977) which argues that it is exclusive female mothering which is a major factor in the creation and maintenance of a violent masculinity. Miedzian maintains that young boys must deny the warmer, softer, and more intimate world of the mother if they are to take on a masculine identity. Because males have been absent from the world of nurturing, masculinity is understood by young boys as that which is not feminine, and given that the feminine is so strongly tied to mothering, that which is not warm, soft, intimate, and nurturing. According to Miedzian, young boys must separate themselves from the world of women and mothers, denying all that is feminine inside of them, in order to take on the fruits of masculinity which are concerned with toughness, domination, and the suppression of emotions. Miedzian documents how these tendencies, established in the family context, are translated into violence and reinforced by contemporary sports, television, music videos, and toys.

Miedzian calls for a wholesale change in how adults parent. In particular, that it is crucial that fathers become more actively involved in nurturing children so that young boys identify with nurturing and caring as normal human action and emotion. Miedzian also points to concrete programs in schools and elsewhere that could be instituted to encourage young boys to take on care-giving roles and to develop nurturing skills. In this way the masculine mystique will lose its violent edge.

For some, gender role socialization is not perceived to be problematic, for others it is deleterious to both males and females and has made our society less rich than it could otherwise be. Our intent here is not to take issue with this practice but simply to point out that gender role socialization from birth onward affects how men and women view the world, their perception of the opportunities available to them, and so on (later chapters in this book specifically address the issues pertinent to this process). Gender role socialization, particularly during adult life, takes the form of social roles. Men and women play different social roles primarily because they were socialized into them (see chapters of The Family and The Organization of Work).

Socialization to Occupational Roles

Socialization to occupational roles consists of both psychological and social adjustments of people to their work and work setting. This process often originates well before people actively enact the role that they will play at work and will be an ongoing feature throughout their careers. Naturally, socialization to occupational roles does not imply that all people are content and satisfied with their careers, but it does suggest how people learn to adapt to the formal and informal norms, values, and codes of conduct of the role they will or presently do occupy. Socialization to work roles consists of three phases according to Chen and Regan (1985). These phases consist of

1. the neophyte learning the knowledge and skills of the work that is necessary to perform the activities of the occupational role;
2. the neophyte learning the subculture of the work setting, including the code of conduct that is shared by the work group; and,
3. the neophyte's transformation of identity, whether recognized or not, through the internalization of the occupational role (pp. 63–73).

These phases are equally applicable to janitors, ministers, steel workers, salespersons, librarians, and physicians since each must learn the skills, adapt to the ways of the work setting, and identify with the work group and occupational role. In *Men and Their Work* (1958) Everett C. Hughes identified that all of these occupational roles are occupied by actors facing similar kinds of problems associated with adapting to a different status, unfamiliar expectations, and new work environments when moving into new occupational roles. Let us clarify this point by looking at two different examples.

In their study of medical students, Haas and Shaffir (1980) found that the socialization of medical students to the profession involved two sets of problems. The first problem was based on acquiring the vast body of knowledge and skill necessary to become a competent physician. The second, and more immediate, was to convince their evaluators that they were competent in their knowledge and skills. According to Haas and Shaffir, these medical students attempted on a daily basis to direct their evaluators away from the areas in which they felt least competent during hospital rounds and volunteered to answer or raise insights or express knowledge when they knew the area under discussion. Haas and Shaffir suggested that these students were becoming socialized to demonstrate their competence through impression management either by being competent (*instrumental abilities*) or by appearing to be competent (*expressive abilities*). Eventually, as the medical students acquired greater areas of competence they spent less time managing their expressive demonstration of competence and more time demonstrating their instrumental abilities. Finally, as the medical students gained greater levels of competency, their self-identity was transformed through detaching themselves from emotional involvement with their patients, enabling them to align themselves with their occupational role and away from that of a lay person.

The work of Jack Haas in 1977 studying high steel ironworkers, those individuals who construct the structural beams for high-story buildings, demonstrates the socialization experiences of newcomers and experienced ironworkers in managing their personal fears and work conditions in a highly dangerous occupation. These workers, like the medical students, managed their role competency by never discussing their fears and inadequacies. Haas suggested that these workers depended on each other for safety, resulting in a culture that required workers to manage their feelings of fear while on the job. According to Haas, apprentices are ridiculed and are expected to perform some of the most demeaning and dangerous jobs. For the ironworker, apprentices are treated in this fashion to test their ability to "take it" and to determine if they were "made of the right stuff." Apprentices, on the other hand, take many calculated risks in demonstrating their acts of bravado. Most of these risks, however, demonstrated to the experienced ironworkers that the apprentice was fearless, dependable, and could be trusted while "running the iron"—the colloquial term for assembling beams.

The two examples provided illustrate that although the demands of the occupational roles are different, both require managing the presentation of self in demonstrating ability to others. It is through the process of socialization that individuals learn to acquire the knowledge, skills, abilities, motivations, and attitudes to successfully transform their identity to be consistent with the occupational role performed.

Socialization to occupational roles is an ongoing process during the work career. Many organizations indoctrinate incoming employees with orientation sessions directed at the operation, policies, and procedures of the setting. Similarly, most organizations today have ongoing training seminars for employees to retrain or reorient employees to changes in the work setting. All of these formal practices are developed to socialize employees to the ways of the organization.

One area of socialization to be discussed later in this book is that of the informal socialization to deviant occupations. During the last twenty years, sociologists working in the area of deviant subcultures have analyzed how individuals are recruited and trained for deviant occupational roles such as illicit drug trafficking, prostitution, exotic dancing, street gang membership, and so on. In this book, Brannigan *et al* discuss, among other things, the occupational careers of prostitutes; in particular, how they are socialized into the business and manage their identities which are in direct conflict with the wider mainstream society.

Summary

1. Socialization may be defined as the process by which individuals develop a sense of self and acquire the knowledge, skills, attitudes, motivations, and behaviour required to participate in a given society or social group so that they can function within it. It is a process that helps to explain two different types of phenomena: (i) the way that an individual is capable of participating in society; and, (ii) how society is possible at all (Elkin and Handel, 1984). The socialization process is not confined to childhood. It is a lifelong cumulative process requiring individuals to adapt to changing circumstances.
2. Piaget's cognitive development approach to child development emphasizes that children move through four stages of development. Each stage usually requires the former since cognitive development requires that children achieve certain mental abilities to move to the next level. Piaget also contributed to our understanding of child development by studying moral reasoning in children. Piaget found that children under the age of nine exercise moral realism in judging the acts of others: that is, the severity of punishment should depend on the amount of damage done. Children around nine years of age believe that the severity of the punishment should depend on the intent of the act. For Piaget, this is a direct outgrowth of what he calls *moral autonomy*. Piaget believes that the development of children's cognitive capacities enables them to reach a level of moral thought that is consistent with society's.
3. The psychoanalytic explanation is best exemplified by the works of Sigmund Freud. According to Freud, the roots of human behaviour lie in the unconscious (instinctive) aspect of the human mind. Consequently, for the individual to function effectively in society, personality development requires that the unconscious aspects of the mind be tempered and controlled. According to Freud, the human personality has three major energy systems: the *id, ego,* and *superego.* The distinction between the three energy systems of the personality can best be thought of as the difference between the child (id), the adult (ego), and the parent (superego); wherein the child

is spontaneous, the adult is responsible, and the parent imparts appropriate morals, values and constraints.

4. Erik Erickson's psychoanalytic theory of personality development extends Freud's work. He describes a series of psychosocial stages in which the individual faces a wide range of human relationships as they mature and have specific socialization issues to solve at each of these stages. Successful transition at each state requires that the individual resolve the particular issues that are faced. Inadequate resolution of issues at any stage leads to incomplete development and possible problems in the future.
5. The symbolic interaction explanation of socialization is best exemplified by the works of Charles Horton Cooley and George Herbert Mead. Cooley's model is based on the *looking-glass self.* According to Cooley, the mind is like a mirror in that individuals receive from others what they believe others to think and see. The general premise is that we see ourselves as others see us and we depend on some reasonable consensus of friends and associates to maintain a consistent sense of self. Mead's work starts with Cooley's description of children's imaginary friends. According to Mead, children's play moves through two distinguishable stages: the *play stage* and the *game stage.* The play stage is characterized by children playing make-believe, while the game stage is characterized by children learning the organization of roles. During the game stage children become cognizant of the *generalized other.* Mead also goes beyond Cooley by partitioning the self into two components: the "I" and the "Me." The "I" represents the spontaneous side of self, and the "Me," the social self.
6. Socialization is not a unitary concept. In our discussion, we identified four types of socialization experienced by individuals: *primary, secondary, anticipatory, and resocialization.* In addition, we suggested that some individuals experience what is known as *blocked* socialization. Primary socialization is probably the most important of the types identified but it is not enough to complete the socialization process.
7. Four agencies of socialization were identified: the *family*, the *peer group,* the *school,* and the *mass media.* Each of these agencies influences the development of the child's personality and socialization to society. In addition, each agency may be a more potent socialization agent than the others during certain periods of the life cycle. Overall, however, the family is still the most important socialization agent in our society today.
8. Variation in socialization practices is evident across social class and ethnic groups. Overall, the studies suggest that social class in Canada seems to be more influential when we look at child development between French-Canadian and English-Canadian families.
9. Dennis Wrong argues that sociologists have what he calls an "oversocialized conception of man," whereby the influence of the socialization process is exaggerated in effect. Wrong suggests that individuals do have free will to act and that all individuals do not experience society in the same way. For Wrong, individuals do internalize societal values and norms, but do so to varying degrees.

10. Social roles can be defined as a pattern of behaviour, structured around specific rights and duties and associated with a particular status position within a group or social situation (Theodorson and Theodorson, 1969). Social roles are the parts played by actors on a daily basis governed by sets of norms that allow and limit behaviour. Goffman's analysis of social roles led him to conclude that the self orchestrates frontstage and backstage behaviour. Frontstage behaviour is that which others see when we are acting out our social roles. Backstage behaviour is that which particular others do not see. The difference between the two, according to Goffman, is that we guide our behaviour around our socialized self, whereas, few people see our all-too-human self. For Goffman, frontstage behaviour required impression management whereby we maintain the social role intact until we leave the setting or situation.
11. Gender role socialization is the process whereby individuals are socialized to take on the roles that are deemed "sex-appropriate" for the society they live in. These roles are often defined in terms of the degree of masculinity and femininity. Generally, this process begins at birth at which time the newborn is sex-typed a boy or a girl.
12. Socialization to occupational roles consists of psychological and social adjustments of people to their work and work setting. Socialization to work roles consists of the novice learning the knowledge and skills of the work, learning the subculture of the work setting, and a transformation of self-identity. All individuals who work are subject to these adjustments. In addition, many individuals will experience a variety of occupational roles throughout their work careers.

References

Bates, Alan P.
1967 *The Sociological Enterprise.* Boston: Houghton Mifflin.

Becker, Howard S. and James W. Carper
1956 "The Development of Identification with a Profession." *American Journal of Sociology,* 61:289–298.

Bell, Richard O. and Laurence V. Harper
1977 *Child Effects on Adults.* New York: John Wiley.

Berger, Peter and Thomas Luckmann
1967 *The Social Construction of Reality.* New York: Doubleday.

Berry, Gordon L. and Claudia Mitchell-Kernan eds.
1982 *Television and the Socialization of the Minority Child.* New York: Academic Press.

Bettelheim, Bruno
1943 "Individual and Mass Behavior in Extreme Situations." *Journal of Abnormal and Social Psychology,* 38:417–452.

1959 "Feral Children and Autistic Children." *American Journal of Sociology,* 64:455–467.

Bibby, Reginald W. and Donald C. Posterski
1985 *The Emerging Generation: An Inside Look at Canada's Teenagers.* Toronto: Irwin Publishing.

Blau, Peter and Otis D. Duncan
1967 *The American Occupational Structure.* New York: Wiley.

Borgatta, E. and M. Borgatta eds.
1992 *Enclycodpedia of Sociology*. New York: MacMillan Publishing Company.

Bucher, Rue and Joan Stelling
1977 *Becoming Professional*. Beverly Hills: Sage Publications.

Campbell, Ernest Q.
1975 *Socialization: Culture and Personality.* Iowa: Wm. C. Brown Company Publishers.

Chen, Mervin Y. T. and Thomas G. Regan
1985 *Work in the Changing Canadian Context.* Toronto: Butterworths.

Chodorow, Nancy
1978 *The Reproduction of Mothering: Psychoanalysis and the Sociology of Gender.* Berkeley: The University of California Press.

Comstock, George A.
1975 *Television and Human Behavior: The Key Studies.* Santa Monica, Calif.: Rand Corporation.

Cooley, Charles H.
1902/ *Human Nature and the Social Order.* New York: Scribner's.
1964

Davis, Fred
1968 "Professional Socialization as Subjective Experience: The Process of Doctrinal Conversion among Nursing Students," in Howard S. Becker, Blanche Geer, Davis Reisman, and Robert S. Weiss eds. *Institutions and the Person: Papers Presented to Everett C. Hughes.* Chicago: Aldine.

Dinnerstein, Dorothy
1977 *The Mermaid and the Minoteur: Sexual Arrangements and the Human Malaise.* New York: Harper and Row.

Eiduson, Bernice T., M. Kornfein, I. L. Zimmerman, and T. Weisner
1988 "Comparative Socialization Practices in Traditional and Alternative Families," in Gerald Handel ed. *Childhood Socialization.* New York: Aldine De Gruyter.

Elkin, Frederick and Gerald Handel
1984 *The Child and Society: The Process of Socialization,* Fourth edition. New York: Random House.

Erickson, Erik
1963 *Childhood and Society,* Second edition. New York: Norton

1968 *Identity: Youth and Crisis.* New York: Norton.

Estep, Rhoda
1982 "Women's Roles in Crimes as Depicted by Television and Newspapers." *Journal of Popular Culture,* 16(Winter):151–56.

Fox, Greer Litton
1977 "Nice Girl: Social Control of Women through a Value Construct." Signs, 2:805–817.

Freidson, Eliot
1970 *Profession of Medicine: A Study of the Sociology of Applied Knowledge.* New York: Harper and Row Publishers.

Fruch, T. and P. McGhee
1975 "TraditionAl Sex Role Development and the Amount of Time Watching Television." *Developmental Psychology,* 11:109.

Gamble, Thomas J. and Edward Zigler
1986 "Effects of Infant Day Care: Another Look at the Evidence," *American Journal of Orthopsychiatry,* 56(1):26–42.

Gecas, Victor
1981 "Contexts of Socialization," in Rosenberg, M. and Turner, R. eds. *Sociological Perspectives in Social Psychology.* New York: Basic Books.

Goffman, Erving
1967 *Interaction Ritual: Essays on Face-to-Face Behaviour.* Garden City, New York: Doubleday Anchor Books.

1959 *The Presentation of Self in Everyday Life.* Garden City, New York: Doubleday Anchor Books.

Gross, L. and S. Jeffries-Fox
1978 "What Do You Want to Be When You Grow Up, Little Girl?" in Tuchman, G., Daniels A., and Benet, J. eds. *Hearth and Home.* New York: Oxford University Press.

Haas, Jack and William Shaffir
1978 *Shaping Identity in Canadian Society.* Scarborough: Prentice-Hall.

1981 "The Professionalization of Medical Students: Developing Competence and a Cloak of Competence," in David Coburn, Carl D'Arcy, Peter New and George Torrance eds. *Health and Canadian Society: Sociological Perspectives.* Don Mills, Ont.: Fitzhenry and Whiteside.

Haas, Jack
1977 "Learning Real Feelings: A Study of High Steel Ironworkers' Reactions to Fear and Danger." *Sociology of Work and Occupations,* 4(2):147–170.

Handel, Gerald
1988 *Childhood Socialization.* New York: Aldine De Gruyter.

Health and Welfare Canada
1991 *Status of Day Care in Canada 1990: A Review of the Major Findings of the National Day Care Study.* Ottawa: National Child Care Information Centre, Child Care Programs Division.

Inkeles, Alex
1968 "Society, Social Structure and Child Socialization," in Claussen, J. A. ed. *Socialization and Society.* Boston: Little, Brown.

Ishwarin, K
1979 "Childhood and Adolescence in Canada: An Overview of Theory and Research," in Ishwarin K ed. *Childhood and Adolescence in Canada.* Toronto: McGraw-Hill Ryerson.

Kelner, Merrijoy, Oswald Hall and Ian Coulter
1980 *Chiropractors: A Study of Their Education and Practice.* Toronto: Fitzhenry and Whiteside.

Lambert, Wallace
1981 "Social Influences on the Child's Development," in Gardner, Robert C. and Kalin, Rudolf eds. *A Canadian Social Psychology of Ethnic Relations.* Toronto: Metheun.

Leifer, A. D., N. J. Gordon and S.B. Graves
1974 "Children's Television: More Than Mere Entertainment." *Harvard Educational Review,* 44(2):213–245.

Lindsey, Linda L.
1990 *Gender Roles: A Sociological Perspective.* Englewood Cliffs, New Jersey: Prentice Hall.

Lortie, Dan C.
1968 "Shared Ordeal and Induction to Work," in Howard S. Becker, Blanche Geer, Davis Reisman, and Robert S. Weiss eds. *Institutions and the Person: Papers Presented to Everett C. Hughes.* Chicago: Aldine.

Mackie, Marlene
1983 "Socialization." Chapter 3 in Robert Hagedorn ed. *Sociology.* Toronto. Holt, Rinehart, and Winston.

1984 "Socialization: Changing Views of Child Rearing and Adolescence," in Maureen Baker ed. *The Family: Changing Trends in Canada.* Toronto: McGraw-Hill Ryerson Limited, pp. 35–62.

1991 *Gender Relations in Canada: Further Explorations,* Second edition. Toronto: Butterworths.

Mandell, Nancy
1988 "Socialization, Subcultures, and Identity," in Curtis, James and Tepperman, Lorne eds. *Understanding Canadian Society.* Toronto: McGraw-Hill Ryerson Limited, pp. 395–422.

Manis, Jerome and Bernard Meltzer
1978 *Symbolic Interaction: A Reader in Social Psychology,* third edition. Boston: Allyn and Bacon.

McKie, Craig and Keith Thompson
1990 *Canadian Social Trends.* Toronto: Thompson Educational Publishing Inc.

Mead, George Herbert
1934 *Mind, Self, and Society: From the Standpoint of a Social Behaviorist.* Chicago: The University of Chicago Press.

Miedziam, Myriam
1991 *Boys Will Be Boys: Breaking the Link between Masculinity and Violence.* New York: Doubleday.

Mills, Donald L. and Donald E. Larson
1981 "The Professionalization of Canadian Chiropractic," in David Coburn, Carl D'Arcy, Peter New and George Torrance eds. *Health and Canadian Society: Sociological Perspectives.* Don Mills, Ont.: Fitzhenry and Whiteside.

Parsons, Talcott
1964 *Social Structure and Personality.* Glencoe, Illinois: The Free Press.

Parsons, Talcott and Robert F. Bales
1955 *Family, Socialization and Interaction Process.* Glencoe, Illinois: The Free Press.

Peterson, Gary W. and David F. Peters
1983 "Adolescents' Construction of Social Reality: The Impact of Television and Peers." *Youth and Society,* 15(l):67–85.

Piaget, Jean
1928 *Judgement and Reasoning in the Child.* New York: Harcourt.

1960 *The Moral Judgement of the Child* [1932], 3rd Impression. New York: Harcourt.

1962 *Play, Dreams and Imitation in Children.* New York: W. W. Norton and Company.

Pineo, Peter C. and E. Dianne Looker
1983 "Class and Conformity in the Canadian Setting." *Canadian Journal of Sociology,* 8:293–317.

Ramu, G. N.
1979 *Courtship, Marriage and the Family in Canada.* Toronto: The Macmillan Company of Canada.

Ritzer, George
1988 *Contemporary Social Theory,* second edition. New York: Alfred A. Knopf

Rosengren, Karl Erik and Sven Windahl
1989 *Media Matter: TV Use in Childhood and Adolescence.* Norwood, New Jersey: Ablex Publishing Corporation.

Ross, Aileen D.
1961 *Becoming a Nurse: Professional Nurses in Canadian Hospitals.* Toronto Macmillan Company of Canada.

Simpson, Ida Harper
1967 "Patterns of Socialization into Professions: The Case of Student Nurses," *Sociological Inquiry,* 37:47–54.

Spurlock, Jeanne
1982 "Television, Ethnic Minorities and Mental Health: An Overview," in Berry, Gordon L. and Mitchell-Kernan, Claudia eds. *Television and the Socialization of the Minority Child.* New York: Academic Press.

Wanner, Richard A.
1986 "Educational inequality: Trends in twentieth century Canada and the United States." *Comparative Social Research,* 9:47–66.

Weitzman, Lenore J.
1979 *Sex Role Socialization.* Palo Alto, Calif.: Mayfield Publishing Company.

White, Graham
1977 *Socialisation.* London: Longman Group Limited.

Williams, Thomas Rhys
1972 *Introduction to Socialization: Human Culture Transmitted.* Saint Louis: The C. V. Mosby Company.

Social Stratification

Social stratification is a broad conceptualization of social inequalities among various groups. Within this broader term, sociologists identify a number of manifest social inequalities such as social class, ethnicity, gender, age and region, to mention a few. The distribution of wealth, power and prestige among various groups can be influenced by these identifiable characteristics which ultimately determine the life chances of an individual. In this section, we focus on three major types of social inequalities in Canadian society to highlight the social, political and economic domination of certain groups over others. In chapter four, Bruce Arai and Neil Guppy examine some of the major characteristics of class formation and class relations in Canada. They maintain, that in comparison with the United States and Britain, most Canadians consider themselves as belonging to the middle class. In general, Canadians are protected by a number of social safety nets in the event of ill health, loss of employment and minimum wage regulations which enable Canadians to maintain a minimum standard of living. For example, they point out that those who earn the least amount of income in Canada, still acquire a slightly greater proportion of national income than the lowest quintile of American earners. On the other hand, the highest quintile in the United States receives a larger share of the national income than its counterpart in Canada. By using national data provided by Statistics Canada, Arai and Guppy demonstrate a wide range of issues related to the distribution of wealth, social class structure, and social mobility in Canadian society during the past few decades. Further, they show the concentration of political power among the working class, the middle class and the corporate elites within the political party establishments in Canada.

In modern societies like Canada, social class is not the only manifestation of social inequality. Ethnic background is a particularly important dimension of an individual's life chances. Canada is a pluralistic society where different ethnic groups have established their home over the years. In chapter five, Elizabeth Moravec Hewa examines how the ethnic background can influence the distribution of wealth, power and prestige in Canada. She discusses the historical establishment of the British and the French as two dominant groups which form the majority of political and economic elites in Canada. However, as Moravec Hewa shows, the relationship between these two groups has always been a struggle for power. Further, she examines the long struggle of the Aboriginal people for political and economic survival within the Anglo-French domination in Canada. Particularly in recent years, Aboriginal people have posed an unprecedented challenge to the established power structure. Recent social and political campaigns of native groups for the protection of their cultural heritage and the settlement of their land claims have attracted a wider audience within the Canadian society. Moravec Hewa presents these recent developments in the context of current constitutional reforms in Canada

Last but not least, gender is the other important aspect of this manifestation of social inequality in modern societies. For centuries, the social and economic contribution of women has been undervalued and their ability to play a greater role in social and political spheres have been hampered by male domination in social institutions. As Gisele Thibault points out in chapter six, the women's movement, particularly since the 1960s in Canada and the United States, has contributed to the development of political consciousness among women for a greater campaign to win their equality with men. She examines the development of women studies in post-secondary education and its influence on the understanding of women's issues. These programs have been able to demonstrate a number of social, political and economic concerns of women. By examining the inherent limitations of the classical and contemporary sociological theories to interpret women's issues, Thibault demonstrates the emerging theoretical orientations in feminist scholarship. However, she recognizes the need for further theoretical expansion in feminist studies in order to provide an in depth understanding of women's issues.

These three chapters discuss micro and macro levels of social inequalities in Canada. However, these are not the only aspects of possible manifestations of inequality among Canadians; age and place of residency (e.g. region and province etc.) considerably influence an individual's life chances. In this volume, the limited space makes it impossible for us to address all these issues.

5

Social Class and Economic Inequality

A. Bruce Arai and Neil Guppy

This chapter introduces our first major investigation into a social structure that frames every member of modern societies: social class. Social class refers to the type of stratification system that allocates rewards to those members who succeed well on a number of social indicators; namely, income, education and prestige. Thus, those persons who have the highest incomes, the most education, and occupations that carry with them maximum prestige are members of elite or upper classes. In this chapter, they are assumed under the section entitled "Rich Canadians." On the other end of the spectrum, those who have the least on these number of indicators are the "Poor Canadians." Mid-way are "Middle Class" Canadians who have various levels of education, income and prestige.

When the topic of the consequences of social inequality is covered here, we will see what real effect that the social structure of class has upon the life chances of Canadian women, men and children.

Introduction

In this chapter we will introduce you to some of the basic issues involved in the study of social class and economic inequality. The chapter consists of four broad sections. First, we tackle class divisions in Canada—do classes exist? We describe a "classless" vision of Canada, and outline some "common-sense" reasons often used to dispute the existence of different social classes in Canada. Second, after showing that, at the very least, there are significant economic inequalities between Canadians, we examine some of the major formulations of class analysis, as proposed by people such as Karl Marx, Max Weber, and Erik Olin Wright.

In our third section we deal with mobility, the movement of people within and between classes. Finally we explore how class analysis can be used to understand various aspects of Canadian society, such as the pension system, and other social services. As well we briefly show how other factors, notably gender, are related to inequality.

The Classless Vision of Canada

When many people think about Canada, they see a country without large class differences, even when compared to similar countries such as Britain or the United States. For example, there is no Canadian nobility of very rich lords as there is in Britain (e.g. the Duke of Wellington). Nor do there seem to be very many wealthy Canadians comparable to the Rockefellers, Carnegies, or Donald Trump of the United States.

Similarly, Canada supposedly does not have many poor people. Inhabitants of inner-city neighbourboods in Canada are significantly better off than those who inhabit the ghettoes of the larger British and American cities. Homelessness in Canada is a minor concern compared to the rapidly rising number of Americans forced onto the street. The overall impression of Canadians is that the vast majority of us are "middle-class." We can afford a car, and often a house. Almost everyone lives a comfortable life.

Most of us are able to give reasons as to why we do not see the extremes of rich and poor in Canada. For example, we share with Britain and the U.S., a system of government based on democracy and equality. This allows us as individuals to pursue our goals to the best of our abilities and it gives us a say in how our society is organized.

In addition, Canada, the U.S. and Britain all have free market economies. In the market, all people can compete on an equal basis to earn a living. On those occasions when the market has failed, politicians in all three countries have drafted laws to preclude some people from gaining an unfair advantage over others. Therefore, Canadians, Americans and the British have laws preventing people from fixing the prices of their goods or services at artificially high levels, or forming monopolies to control the market. We also have minimum wage laws to ensure that people are paid a fair wage, and a taxation system whereby rich people redistribute a portion of their income to the less fortunate.

Furthermore, in comparison to Britain and the U.S., we often perceive that inequality in Canada is lower because of our extensive social service "safety net" to protect people against the possibility of poverty. Our social services generally compare very favourably to those in the U.S. or U.K, which mitigates against the class divisions we see in these other two countries.

When people lose their job in Canada they are entitled to unemployment insurance, and, as a last resort when they cannot get a job, we have a generous welfare system. When Canadians fall ill, their medical costs are paid by the government to ensure that people are not ruined financially by an illness. In addition, educational institutions in Canada are predominately funded by the state to allow everyone an equal opportunity to attain their desired level of training.

This situation is markedly different from the U.S. and Britain. In some cases in the U.S., paying for hospital bills has reduced families to absolute poverty. Similarly, many British and American schools, colleges and universities depend in large part upon one's ability to pay high tuition fees. Therefore, inequalities are entrenched as the rich can afford to send their children to "the better schools," which gives them an advantage over poorer kids who attend regular schools.

In sum, in the classless vision of Canada, the free market, when combined with the Canadian social services system and the ideals of equality and democracy, ensure that class divisions in Canada are minor in comparison to other countries. Further, any economic divisions which do exist are seen to be the simple result of the normal operation of the economy and therefore justifiable. Those who are rich have earned their money on the basis of their hard work and they are thus entitled to a fair reward. Those who are poor have simply not applied themselves with sufficient vigour, and raising their standard of living is simply a matter of effort and determination.

Reasons for Studying Social Class

Although many of us may subscribe to the notion of Canada as a classless and relatively equal society, that belief rests largely on our common-sense impressions. In most cases, we have no data to back up these claims. By studying social class, as opposed to relying on conjecture, we are able to get a better picture of the extent of economic inequality and refute or confirm the classless vision of Canada. Second, the study of social class allows us to compare Canada with other countries in actual, not speculative terms. Is it true that there is more economic inequality in Britain or the U.S. than in Canada? This question is difficult to answer without looking at social class.

Finally, studying social class gives us insight into other sources of inequality which are often expressed in class or economic terms. For example, women, members of ethnic minorities and the elderly often receive less income than white men, not because they are less competent, but because they are victims of systematic discrimination.

Canada in Comparison with Other Countries

One way to examine differences in the degree of economic inequality between different countries is to look at the proportion of the total income earned by all earners in each country that falls to various "percentile groups." Percentile groups, as shown in Table 5:1 are constructed by ranking all income earners from highest to lowest, and then dividing these people into five equal groups. Thus, for example, the 20% of earners who earn the least amount of income comprise the "lowest quintile." Table 5:1 shows the percentage of total national income which falls to the various percentile groups in six selected countries.

Our impression of Canada as more egalitarian than the U.S. in terms of income distribution is marginally confirmed in Table 5:1. Those Canadians who earn the least, acquire a slightly greater proportion (5.7%) of national income than the lowest quintile of American earners (4.7%). Moreover, the highest quintile in the U.S. receives 1.7% (41.9–40.2) more national income than its Canadian counterpart.

However, when compared to the United Kingdom, the distribution of earnings in Canada is more concentrated, less egalitarian. The top 20% of earners in Canada receive 40.2% of the national income compared to 39.5% in the U.K. Additionally, the poorest

Table 5:1
Percentage Distribution of Income in Lowest Quintile, Highest Quintile and Highest Decile for Selected Countries

Country	Year	Lowest 20%	Top 20%	Top 10%
Brazil	1983	2.4	62.6	46.2
Canada	1987	5.7	40.2	24.1
Japan	1979	8.7	37.5	22.4
Sweden	1981	8.0	36.9	20.8
United Kingdom	1979	5.8	39.5	23.3
United States	1985	4.7	41.9	25.0

Source: Adapted from *World Development Report 1990: Poverty*. Pp. 236–237.

people in the U.K are marginally better off than the poorest Canadians, garnering 0.1% (5.8–5.7) more of the national income than the lowest quintile of Canadian earners. Therefore, we can conclude that economic inequality in Canada, despite our impressions, is not very different from the situation in the U.S. or the U.K, and it may even be more unequal (see Banting, 1987).

Furthermore, contrary to the classless vision of Canadian society, there is very little redistribution of income in this country. The Canadian state does *not* act like Robin Hood and take from the rich to give to the poor. The Canadian tax system is such that the rich stay rich and the poor stay poor (see Banting, 1987; Hunter, 1993).

What Is the Extent of Economic Inequality in Canada?

If we focus attention specifically on Canada and examine income distribution over the past decade, we find quite striking differences between the rich and the poor. Table 5:2 shows the percentages of total personal income which accrues to each quintile for selected years between 1979 and 1989. What this table shows is that, over the entire decade, those Canadians in the lowest quintile earn less than 5% of the total income earned by all individuals and families. In contrast, those people in the highest quintile consistently earned over 40% of the total personal income. Put another way, on average, each individual or family in the highest income quintile earns approximately eight times the amount of money of each individual or family in the lowest bracket. Not only has this income distribution persisted over the last decade, it has remained fixed ever since World War II (see Hunter, 1993).

Table 5:3, which shows the upper dividing lines between each quintile, also reveals a large gap between the lower and higher income brackets. For example, in 1979 the highest earners in the lowest quintile had a gross income of $7,818, which is roughly one-quarter what the highest earners in the fourth quintile accumulated. This gap too stays constant throughout the decade.

Table 5:2
Percentage Distribution of Income of Families and Unattached Individuals by Quintile, 1979–1989

Year	Lowest Quintile	Second Quintile	Middle Quintile	Fourth Quintile	Highest Quintile
1979	4.3	10.8	17.7	25.2	41.9
1981	4.6	10.9	17.6	25.1	41.7
1983	4.3	10.3	17.1	25.0	43.2
1985	4.6	10.4	17.0	24.9	43.0
1987	4.7	10.4	16.9	24.8	43.2
1989	4.8	10.5	16.9	24.6	43.2

Source: Adapted from Statistics Canada, Cat. No. 13–207, 1989, p.47.

Table 5:3
Upper Income Dividing Lines between Quintiles, in Current Dollars

Year	Lowest Quintile	Second Quintile	Middle Quintile	Fourth Quintile	Highest Quintile
1979	7,818	14,777	21,994	31,000	NO
1981	10,064	18,570	27,581	38,610	
1983	10,648	19,909	30,107	43,810	LI
1985	12,117	21,929	33,507	48,450	MI
1987	13,476	24,349	36,740	53,532	T
1989	15,497	27,997	41,888	61,100	

Source: Adapted from Statistics Canada, Cat. No. 13–207, 1989, p. 147.

Rich Canadians

The tables above clearly show that there is a high degree of economic inequality in Canada. This idea is further supported when we examine the average compensation of top Canadian executives. For example, in 1986, the average total compensation for various types of chief executive officers (CEO's) ranged from $88,941 for Canadian Operations Managers to $160,174 for CEO's in finance/banking and insurance (Sobeco-Chapman, 1986:4). Further, the average total compensation for second executive officers (just below CEO'S) was $107,460 (Sobeco-Chapman, 1988:64). To put these salaries in perspective someone who worked 40 hours/week, for 52 weeks, at $4.50/hour (a good minimum wage in the 1980s) would earn $9,360 annually.

The CEO salaries may seem minuscule in relation to the vast wealth held by people such as Queen Elizabeth II or even Donald Trump. However, when we examine a list of the ten richest people in the world, we find that three of them are Canadians! Albert Reichmann, Kenneth Colin Irving and Kenneth R. Thompson all possess over six billion dollars worth of assets, while people like Donald Trump do not even make the list (see Grabb, 1990; Davies, 1993).

Poor Canadians

In contrast to the very rich, there are also a large number of poor people in Canada, many of whom are forced to rely on food banks and/or transient houses for sustenance and shelter. In the 1986/87 fiscal year, 26 transient houses provided beds for 110,061 people (Health Reports, 1989).

The rise in the number of food banks since 1981 also points to the existence of a substantial number of poor people in Canada. For example, in 1989 an average of 175,000 families per month depended on food bank grocery bundles to supplement their inadequate food supplies (Bolaria and Wotherspoon, 1991:473). The majority of these people (72%) were also forced to rely on welfare assistance to cover their other costs of living.

A final measure of the condition of the poor in Canada is provided in Table 5:4 which documents the incidence of families and individuals who are forced to live on "low income." Low income families and individuals are defined as those people who spend 58.5% or more of their total income on food, clothing and shelter. This official definition is often taken by researchers as an estimate of the amount of poverty in Canada (Ross and Shillington, 1989:6). The percentages of all families and individuals categorized as poor in 1989 were 11.1% for families (more than 1 in 10 Canadian families) and 34.4% for individuals (i.e., individuals not in families).

If we break these figures down by age and sex, we can see evidence of the operation of other sources of inequality expressed in class or economic terms. We see that women and the elderly fare significantly worse than men and younger people in virtually every

Table 5:4
Low Income Families and Individuals as a Percentage of Total Families and Individuals by Sex and Age, 1989

Characteristic	Families*	Individuals
Males (average)	8.1	26.9
- Under 65	7.8	26.2
- Over 65	10.4	30.7
Females (average)	35.5	40.6
- Under 65	39.1	34.5
- Over 65	15.0	50.0
Percent of Total	11.1	34.4

*The "male" and "female" categories refer to the sex of the head of the household.
Source: Adapted from Statistics Canada, Cat. No. 13-207, 1989, p. 181.

category. For example, only 8.1% of families headed by males are low income, whereas 35.5% of families headed by females live below the poverty line. Additionally, individuals over the age of 65 are more likely to fall into the low income bracket than individuals under retirement age. In other words, being a woman and/or being old generally increases one's chances of living in poverty.

As indicators of poverty in Canada, the number of transients in transient houses, the percentage of low income families and individuals, and the extent of food bank use, clearly show that many Canadians fall well below the "middle class." Also, the salaries of CEO's and top managers, the wealth of people like the Reichmann's, Irvings, and Kenneth Thompson, and the proportion of the country's total income garnered by the top quintile reveals the existence of a distinct upper stratum in Canadian society. How, then, are we to explain these differences between Canadians? One of the most useful approaches is that of class analysis.

Class Analysis

The concept of class is rooted in the writings of Karl Marx. Marx was born in 1818 and lived through the turmoil of the "Industrial Revolution" in his native Germany, France and England. He was expelled from both Germany and France for his writings and participation in protest movements. In 1848 he moved to England where he saw firsthand the world's then most advanced industrial economy.

The British economy presented Marx with an extraordinary contradiction. On the one hand Marx saw the tremendous wealth that was generated through the application of machinery to the process of goods production. On the other hand be also saw that most of this wealth accrued to a small group of people while others lived in abject poverty. The wealthy often lived extremely well while the poor worked up to eighteen hours a day in the dangerous working conditions of mines and factories. In many cases, women and children were forced to find jobs, usually in "sweatshops" or mines, just to provide the family with the bare minimum of food, clothing and shelter.

What could possibly account for these incredible differences in wealth, prestige and lifestyle? For Marx, the answer lay in the power that a person derived from their **relationship to the economy**. Marx saw that the people who owned the land, factories and machines were generally wealthy while those who did not were poor. Thus, he reasoned that the private ownership of productive property was the basis for the creation of two great classes in capitalist society; the class of rich owners known as the **bourgeoisie**, and the class of poor workers called the **proletariat**.[1]

Marx argued that on the basis of its ownership of productive property, the bourgeoisie was able to exploit the proletariat through the mechanism of profit. Marx felt that the labour power of workers was the source of the extra value of a commodity after it had been transformed from raw materials into a finished product. Therefore, he thought that these workers should be compensated for their efforts. However, in capitalist production this extra value is appropriated by the bourgeoisie in the form of profits.

According to Marx, private ownership gave the bourgeoisie tremendous power over the proletariat because the working people could only make a living through the sale of their labour power (i.e. they had to become employees). They did not own the land or equipment to produce commodities, and therefore were forced to work for others to survive. Conversely, the bourgeoisie did not need the aid of others because they could work their own property to make a living.

The implication of this situation was that owners could deny workers an ability to survive, simply by not allowing others to use their productive property. In order to live, then, workers were forced to compete with each other for the right to work. The surest way to "win" a job in this situation was to offer the most amount of work for the least amount of money. Under these conditions, owners were quite happy to lend out their productive property because they could make more money by hiring workers at low wages.

Marx also claimed that there was another reason that owners paid the lowest possible wages to their workers. This was because intense competition also existed within the bourgeoisie. Owners were forced to generate as much profit as possible to protect themselves from their competitors. For example, if an owner paid her/his workers "excess wages" s/he might not have enough capital to buy cost-cutting machinery, which would put that owner at a disadvantage in relation to her/his competition." Marx felt that capitalism inevitably tended towards monopoly as the less successful businesses went bankrupt in the face of recession, or were bought out by more successful companies. This tendency swelled the ranks of the working class as more and more people were forced to sell off their holdings and work for others.

As working people became more aware of the increasing gap between the rich and the poor, members of this class would begin to understand the real nature of capitalism. This understanding, known as *class consciousness,* involved an identification of the real problem of capitalism (i.e. ownership of private property) and a recognition of the means by which the problem could be solved. According to Marx, this usually involved a violent revolution in which the power of the owning class was wrested away by force.

This revolution, for Marx, involved crucially the abolition of private property, because this was the way in which owners exploited workers. Once private property was eliminated, exploitation would cease to exist and a more egalitarian, communist society could be created.

As is clear from this brief review of Marx's thought, his major focus is on the power that people derive from their position in the economic sphere. For him, one's power was determined by one's class, and all social inequality can ultimately be reduced to one's relationship to the economy, as either an owner or worker. Many people have criticized him as an *economic determinist*, arguing that he paid too little attention to other sources of power and social change.

Max Weber (pronounced "Vay-ber") was one of the first people to argue that while Marx's ideas were generally right, his understanding of the sources of social change was too narrow. Weber felt that people derived power from two other sources besides their economic position. First, people gained power from the prestige they held among members of their community. The more prestige a person had, the more ability that person had to influence the decisions of others. Weber classified this as power based upon one's *status.* The second alternate source of power which Weber identified was the arena of politics. A person's connection with politics and political figures at all levels also influenced their ability to affect change. This power, Weber called *party.* For him, the triumvirate of class, status and party provided a much better explanation of inequality in social life than a reliance on one single factor (Giddens, [19791 provides a good discussion of class analysis, and he offers a more detailed examination of the views of Marx and Weber).

More recently, others have criticised many of Marx's ideas as being outdated. Dahrendorf (1959) for example, has argued that Marx's theories may have been applicable to nineteenth century Britain, but they are inadequate for the study of modern societies. Marx's notions of class cannot explain the development of the joint-stock company and the "middle classes" of managers, supervisors and professionals. How, Dahrendorf asks, can we fit supervisors into Marx's notions of class? They are not part of the ownership class because they are not owners, yet neither are they members of the working class because they control other workers. Additionally, how do we classify people who own stocks in a company while working for that company at the same time?

Marx has also been criticised on other grounds. On the one hand, the rise of feminist sociology has questioned the usefulness of the concept of class in explaining inequalities between men and women in two ways. First, is it true, as Marx claimed, that all inequality can be reduced to a class basis? Many feminists argue convincingly that gender is an important source of power and difference in its own right. One of the best examples of this is that many women, whether they are owners or workers, remain subject to abuse and oppression at the bands of men (e.g., rape).

The second criticism raised in the feminist literature concerns the class position of someone who does not participate in the paid labour force (e.g., housewives). Do these women just assume the class position of their husbands, in the same way in which they have traditionally taken on their husbands' surnames? If so, then the concept of class is inherently sexist because it does not recognize the value of women's work to either the family, or industrial capitalism.

In a similar vein, many researchers have questioned the applicability of class analysis to numerous other groups who have only indirect ties to paid employment and the market. Do retirees maintain the class position they occupied during their working lives, or do they fall into a different class, reflecting their changed circumstances? Similarly, what is the class position of students who are, in many cases, simply training themselves for labour force participation? Can we assume, for example, that business students will become business people and therefore should be in a higher class than say, forestry or nursing students?

Finally, the tremendous growth in state bureaucracies calls into question Marx's basic two-class system. Are public-sector workers exploited in the same way as private-sector labourers, even though the majority of them do not work in organizations run for profit? That is, if profit is the mechanism by which the surplus value of workers is extracted, do public-sector employees retain the value of their work? The question then becomes whether or not public-sector workers are members of the same class as private-sector workers.

The numerous criticisms of the Marxian definition of class would seem to render the concept ineffectual. However, ideas of class have undergone a resurgence due to the work of people like Erik Olin Wright (1985). Wright modified Marx's two class system to accommodate some of the changes brought on by the rise of monopoly or finance capitalism.

Wright accepts Marx's basic distinction between owners and workers, but further subdivides these two "great classes" to account for what he calls "contradictory class locations" (Wright, 1985). The bourgeoisie can be split into three groups based roughly on the amount of assets they own and control. The proletariat can be separated into numerous groups or class locations based on control over two specific types of assets: "assets in skill" and "assets in organization."

People may possess assets in skill which differentiate them from other workers. For example, secretaries and factory workers possess more skill assets than garbage collectors, and thus occupy different class locations. Additionally, people may possess assets in organization in that they are located higher in an organizational hierarchy. For instance, managers and supervisors possess more organizational assets than secretaries, factory workers or manual labourers. The acquisition of both types of assets usually involves formal schooling or apprenticeship followed by job experience.

Sociologists have employed numerous definitions of social class. Marx, Weber, Dahrendorf and Wright are four men whose ideas have been particularly influential. However, there is no one "right" definition of the concept which can be employed in all situations. Moreover, there is extensive debate about the amount of explanatory weight which should be given to social class versus other social categories such as race and gender. In the following sections we will illustrate the ways in which various definitions of social class have been used, in connection with race and especially gender, to explain different issues of inequality in Canada.

The Canadian Class Structure

The pie chart (Figure 5:1) gives estimates of the percentages of workers and owners in the Canadian economy loosely following Wright's class schema. Very few Canadians are principally owners, only about 4%. The size of the working class is about ten times larger (43%), although still a minority. Indeed, the other three groups combined, what might loosely be called the middle class, comprise the majority of participants in the economy (53%).

Managers and supervisors (25%) make up the bulk of this middle group. These are people who control the work of others but who are not owners. Another large middle class contingent is semi-autonomous workers, people like college teachers, most social workers, and some engineers, who do not supervise the employment of others, but who are themselves employees. The last segment of the middle class is the self-employed, people who work for themselves and employ no helpers (e.g., many farmers, artists).

This chart captures at a glance both what Marx foresaw and what he missed. The concentrated form of ownership which Marx predicted has emerged. Very few Canadians are the outright owners of large business enterprises, employing the labour of others to

Figure 5:1 The Canadian Class Structure

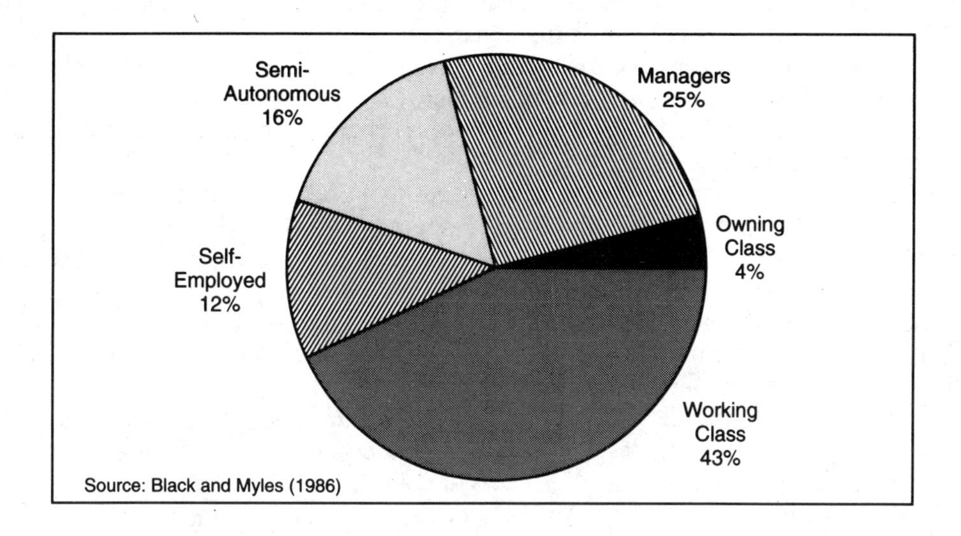

generate profit. But the growing working class that Marx also predicted is not in evidence. While a significant number of Canadians are workers, there are important divisions within this group, especially around issues of authority, supervision, and education.

In spite of these divisions, Canadian workers have all experienced relatively high standards of living. Most Canadian families own their own home and enjoy vacation travel. Almost every Canadian family owns a car, a television set, and a score of other household appliances. While the quality of housing and leisure varies enormously, patterns of consumption, not patterns of class, seem to matter most to Canadians. In the age of advertising and mass marketing, allegiance to consumption over class is hardly surprising.

Opportunities and Mobility

Issues of class may be less important to Canadians because, as we noted above, the ideal of equality is a strong part of our heritage. Canadians pride themselves on being fair-minded, on stressing issues of equality. Canada is seen as a good place to live because of the opportunities available.

Equality of opportunity captures this stress. But just how equal are the opportunities of Canadians? Does the child of a wealthy, urban family have opportunities equal to those of a child from a poor, farming family?

In a qualified manner, the answer to this question must be yes. All Canadians attend schools. The public funds to support education are also relatively equal across all school boards, whether the neighbourhood is rich or poor, rural or urban. In this manner, equality of educational opportunity exists. We are also fortunate in this country to have a health care system which provides access to quality care independent of the size of your bank account.

These examples demonstrate that opportunities to participate are equal, everyone has access. This does not, however, mean that everyone has an equal opportunity at success. Here is an analogy to illustrate the difference between participation and the likelihood of success. Any horse can enter a horse race (there is equality of opportunity). But all bettor's know that the likelihood of victory (success) is not equal, and consequently some horses have better odds than others.

A parallel situation exists in the school system. All children may participate, but the likelihood of success differs. The children of poorer parents face many hurdles, all of which diminish their chances of success. Relative to children from more wealthy homes they have poorer nutrition, they have fewer (if any) educated role models, they are exposed to fewer educational resources (e.g., reading material, travel experiences), and their families have less money to spend on tutors, private lessons, and other educational experiences (e.g., summer camps, pre-schools).

Certainly these hurdles do not prevent children from less privileged backgrounds from succeeding at school. Just as the long-shot at the horse race occasionally wins, so too do some children from poor families excel at college and university. The point is that the odds of succeeding are stacked against children from poorer backgrounds.

Sociologists talk about these hurdles in terms of equality of condition. The skills and abilities that children bring to the school environment differ, their initial conditions are unequal, and so their chances of success in the school system vary. Figure 5:2 illustrates these differences by examining the effect of a mother's education on the schooling of her sons and daughters.

Figure 5:2. Post-Secondary Attainment by Mother's Level of Education, 1986 (25–44 Year-old Age Group)

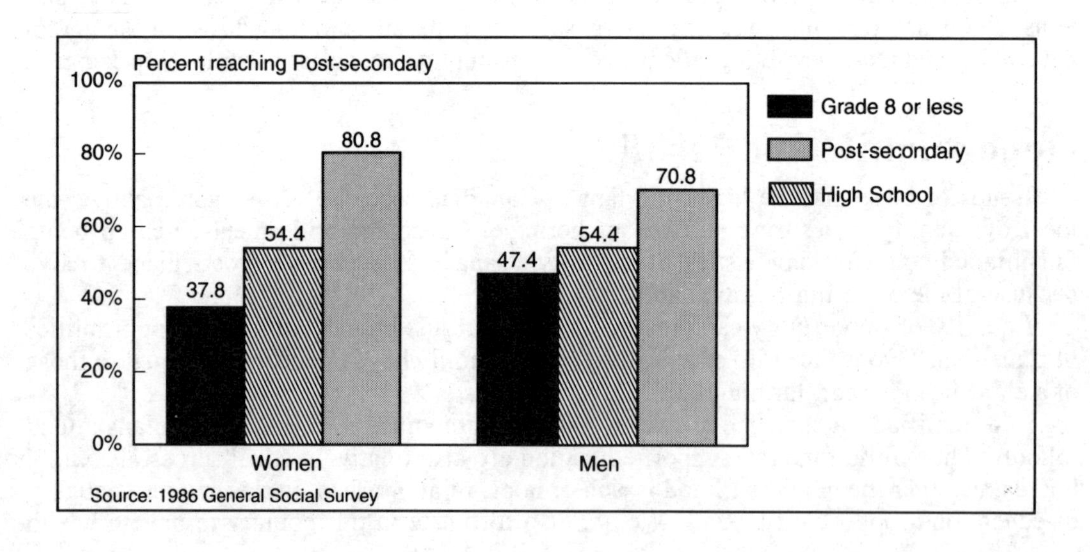

The levels of education of mothers are divided into three groups: those mothers with grade 8 or less, mothers who have completed high school, and mothers with post-secondary education. The likelihood of a daughter attaining post-secondary schooling rises from 37.8% to 54.4% and then to 80.8% across the three categories of mother's schooling, a difference of 43% between the two extremes.

The figure also shows that a son's schooling is influenced by his mother's education, although the effect is not quite as strong (a 23.4% difference between the extremes). This is clear evidence that mother's schooling has a strong bearing on the educational attainment of her daughters and sons. While Figure 5:2 does not tell us which of the hurdles listed above are operative, it provides compelling evidence that barriers to educational attainment exist (see also Guppy and Arai, 1993; Turritin, Anisef, and MacKinnon, 1983).

The importance of these barriers to educational attainment is not limited just to a person's level of formal training. Past research has shown that one's level of educational achievement is strongly *changed* over time, but clearly a significant difference remains by 1989 with women still earning only 65.8% of men's average pay. The amount of pay inequity remains large because despite some change.

Some of the earnings difference between the sexes is attributable to differences in the occupations women hold, the greater frequency of career interruptions among women (for children mainly), and the greater likelihood of women being in the service sector labour market. But even when relative earnings are adjusted for these factors, women still earn 20-30% less than men (Robb, 1987).

These comparisons of average wages between women and men add a further dimension to the patterns of poverty we documented in Table 5:4. That is, not only do women have a much greater chance than men of living in poverty, even when they live above the poverty line the average woman can expect to earn only a portion of the income of the average man.

Sociologists have typically interpreted gender inequalities of this sort by distinguishing between *ascription* and *achievement*. Ascription refers to characteristics of groups based on birthright and/or personal attributes determined at conception. To the extent that others interact with us, or make judgments about us, based on our sex or race (for example), then ascriptive processes are at work.

In contrast, when people judge us on the basis of what we do, as opposed to who we are, they are evaluating us according to principles of achievement. A frequent measure of social progress, of enlightenment, is the degree to which performance and ability related to both their occupation and amount of income (Boyd *et al.*, 1985). Consequently, the existence of obstacles to educational attainment not only prevents people from less educated backgrounds from acquiring superior schooling, it also perpetuates economic and occupational inequality between Canadians.

An alternative perspective on issues of opportunity in Canadian society focuses upon occupational mobility. By comparing the occupations of parents and their children, we can identify how much social mobility occurs (see Creese, Guppy, and Meissner, 1991). The mobility process is more open, more democratic if someone's occupational position does not depend upon the social class into which they were born.

Table 5:5
Occupational Mobility in Canada: Father to Son Mobility in Selected Occupational Groups

Father's Occupational Group	Son's Occupational Group			
	Prof/Managerial	White Collar	Blue Collar	Row%
Professional/Managerial	50%	25%	25%	100%
Blue collar	20%	25%	55%	100%

Source: Summarized from Creese, Guppy, and Meissner, 1991.

Table 5:5 provides some evidence on the degree of occupational mobility among Canadian men. The table is constructed in order to examine the occupational destinies of the sons of fathers who held either professional/managerial jobs or blue collar jobs (for simplicity we ignore the range of other jobs held by fathers, e.g., white collar, farm). An obvious feature of the table is that not all sons follow in the occupational footsteps of their fathers. However, there is a substantial amount of occupational "inheritance" since 55% of the sons of blue collar fathers are themselves blue collar workers and 50% of the sons of fathers in professional and managerial positions hold similar jobs.

The general lessons from mobility research can be summarized as follows. First, many more people are mobile than immobile. Second, there is generally more upward than downward mobility in Canada, because historically jobs in the professional, managerial, and white collar sector have expanded while work in farming and blue collar jobs has shrunk. Third, most of the mobility that does occur is short range, with very few people going from "rags to riches" (or vice versa).

In addition, patterns of mobility in Canada are relatively similar to those in the U.K or the U.S. Finally, the evidence also points to a modest increase in the openness of the occupational structure, suggesting that over time an individual's life chances have become less tied to their social origins. Although inequality of opportunity continues, this evidence suggests it is declining, possibly because of the expanded opportunities available from the growing numbers of people attaining post-secondary education (see Wanner, 1993).

Ascription and Achievement

It is important that two issues be kept separate: the *amount of inequality* versus patterns of *change in inequality.* It is very important not to think of decreases in inequality as equivalent to the eradication of inequality. The gap in pay between women and men is a useful way of illustrating this point.

Table 5:6
Historical Change in the Earnings of Women Relative to Men (for Full-time, full-year Workers)

Year	Relative Earnings
1967	58.4
1971	59.6
1975	60.1
1979	63.3
1983	64.6
1987	65.9
1989	65.8

Source: Earnings of Men & Women, Statistics Canada (13–217) Annual.

Table 5:6 shows, for the period 1967 to 1989, the average wages paid to women and men who worked full-time, full-year. In 1967 the average wage paid to women was 58.4% of the average wage of men. Put another way, the *amount* of pay inequality between women and men in 1967 was 4¢ ($1.00-$0.58). This gap in average wages has indicators (achievement) take preference over ascribed stereotypes in judging or evaluating people.

The very, very slow erosion of pay differences between women and men suggests that many women are judged on the basis of their sex not their abilities. Here is an important contrast to put these pay differences in perspective. Recently 10,000 more women than men have earned university degrees each year. Yet a sizable wage gap remains. In fact, even among women and men who have recently graduated from university, there was still a wage gap of $7,000 in 1987 (Wannell, 1990). Since these women and men were of similar age, all university graduates, possessing equivalent years of experience, the earnings gap is hard to explain using achievement principles.

Class, Social Movements, and the State

The distribution of income is a key measure of the extent of inequality in a country. As shown in Table 5:1, income distributions vary considerably in different countries. This variability suggests that different national policies influence the income distribution. For example, by altering tax policies (e.g., income taxes, wealth taxes, sales taxes) and public expenditures (e.g., welfare, family allowance, state pensions), governments can influence the national income distribution.

Governments, however, do not have an entirely free hand in taxation and expenditure decisions. Taxpayers are also voters. As well, business owners resist attempts by governments to intervene in the economic marketplace, arguing that the free market is the best means of insuring fair income distribution. Organized labour also applies pressure to governments, lobbying for social legislation such as unemployment and universal health insurance to provide a social safety net when the blind forces of the market deal harsh blows to particular individuals or families.

Government strategy is thus the product of bargaining and negotiation between contending parties. On the one hand business groups such as the Business Council on National Issues, the Canadian Manufacturers Association, and the Canadian Chamber of Commerce press the government to pursue policies sensitive to the needs of business. This is effectively the voice of capital, the lobbying arm of an ownership class. In contrast, the Canadian Labour Congress (CLC) puts forward a labour agenda, speaking on behalf of the approximately 3.5 million union members in Canada. On issues of income distribution and economic inequality the CLC is often joined by the Canadian Council on Social Development and the National Anti-Poverty Organization. This is effectively the voice of working people, the pressure groups urging a redistribution of income and wealth in Canada.

A concrete example of the struggle between business and labour occurs over pension entitlements. Labour views pensions as a form of deferred wage, a pot of money set aside to provide working people with a source of economic support upon retirement. Business leaders share that view but worry that pension income drains funds out of business investment and increases government deficits.

What makes the pension question particularly contentious now is the growing size of Canada's elderly population. One view is that a demographic time bomb is ticking and that as the baby boomers of the 1950s and 1960s reach retirement age (in 2010 to 2030), the amount of money required to fund their pensions will bankrupt the Canadian state. Business leaders fear that unless the state drastically reduces public pension provisions (e.g., the Canada Pension Plan, the Guaranteed Income Supplement, and Old Age Security), current financial obligations for these pensions will greatly inflate government debt.

Labour groups counter by arguing that adequate pension packages were freely negotiated and that any rearrangements would violate the democratic process by which these provisions were made. Government and business leaders helped devise and implement current pension provisions. Labour argues that to alter those agreements now, just prior to many workers retiring, would be to effectively, and unfairly, change the rules of the game at the last minute. For labour the problem is one of democracy, not one of demography.

Assessing the quality of pension provisions in fifteen capitalist democracies, John Myles (1989) has shown that the power of the working class to mobilize and assert its influence dramatically improves pension quality. The single most important factor effecting the quality of a nation's pension system is working class mobilization (e.g., the size and organization of the labour movement), not corporate concentration, the size of the elderly population, or the level of economic development. Myles found that the quality of Canadian pensions is relatively low in comparative perspective and he argues that if the government were to emphasize a business agenda even more than it now does, then poverty among the elderly (see Table 5:4) would significantly worsen.

If these government policies are to be understood as the result of struggles between owners and workers, between capital and labour, then it is important to consider the relationship between these three groups—owners, workers, and political leaders. First, the two federal parties which have formed recent governments are financed primarily by business. The large election budgets of both the Conservative and Liberal parties come primarily from cooperations or individual business people. It would be wrong to see this money as direct bribes for political favours, but the funding clearly is given in the expectation that the ruling party will favour business interests. This does not deny the intimate links between the NDP and labour. Our point is that business, rather than labour, has, at least in terms of financial support, greater influence on federal parties (see Stanbury, 1986).

Second, politicians are not recruited equally from the different social classes. In the 1980s federally elected politicians were overwhelmingly (almost 90%) from upper class origins (Guppy *et al.*, 1987). At the level of Cabinet Ministers, the concentration of upper class representation was even higher. In addition, Fox and Ornstein (1986) demonstrate the existence of direct linkages between politicians and private corporations. They show that, for the period 1946 to 1976, strong ties were present between both federal and provincial cabinets and private organizations (a trend that has not weakened, in our judgment, in the last two decades). These linkages add further evidence to the argument that business holds a stronger position than labour in influencing political decisions.

Now, of course, politicians are influenced by groups other than capital and labour. Over the past few decades many other groups have formed to press for specific political concessions. These groups include the National Action Committee on the Status of Women, the Assembly of First Nations, the National Advisory Council on Aging, and the Canadian Civil Liberties Association. One tangible result of this growth of *new social movements* (i.e., pressure groups not aligned with capital or labour) can be seen in section 15.1 of the *Canadian Charter of Rights and Freedoms:*

> Every individual is equal before and under the law and has the right to the equal protection and equal benefit of the law without discrimination and, in particular, without discrimination based on race, national or ethnic origin, colour, religion, sex, age or mental or physical disability.

The policies of various federal and provincial governments introducing laws on employment and pay equity, on family matters, and on sexual harassment have been inspired in large part by the women's movement. Feminists looking at trends such as those in Table 5:6, have argued that equality for women will not come if market forces are allowed to dictate the relative wage rates of women and men (Armstrong and Armstrong, 1990). Due to the obstacles women face in the workplace (e.g., promotion), in education (e.g., male bias as in engineering), or in the home (e.g., wife abuse), women cannot be expected to attain wages that truly reflect their levels of productivity (see Abella, 1984).

Consequences of Inequality: Real Life Chances

We are all aware of social inequality. We all share some idea of what it means to be rich or to be poor. Here, though, is a graphic way of depicting just what consequences follow from inequality. Above we showed how your *life chances* are influenced by your social background. In contrast, Figure 5:3 shows how your *chances of life* are influenced by your social background. The likelihood of surviving at birth varies dramatically by social class origins. Twice as many children born in poor neighbourhoods die in infancy compared to children born in the richest of Canadian neighbourhoods.

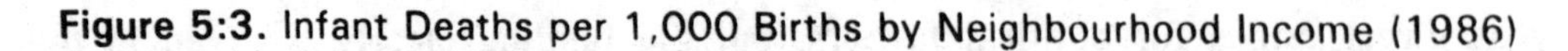

Figure 5:3. Infant Deaths per 1,000 Births by Neighbourhood Income (1986)

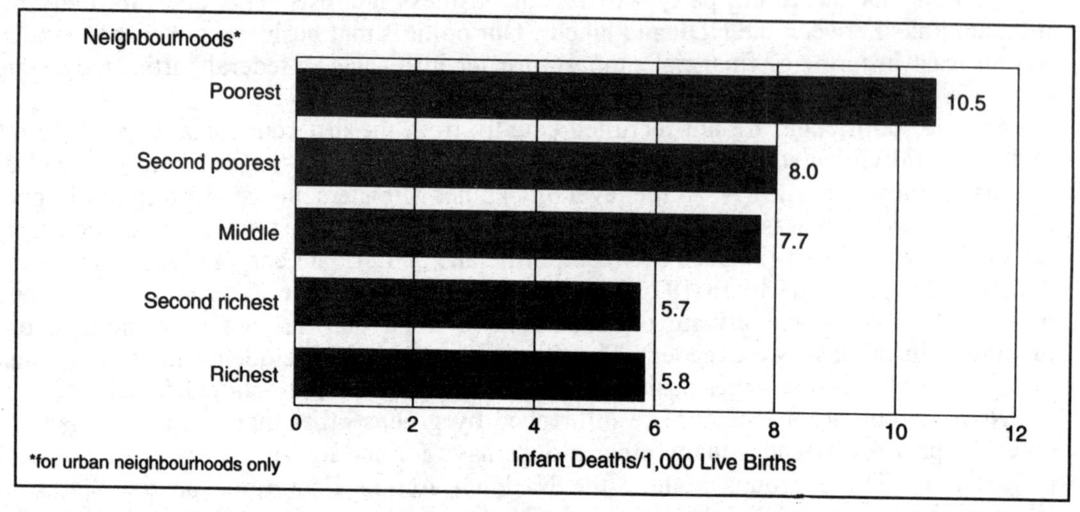

Comparing these infant mortality rates for various racial and ethnic groups produces still larger differences. Among Native Indians in Canada the infant mortality rate for children up to 12 months of age was 17.2 death per thousand live births in 1986 (Bobet, 1989). If we compare this to the rates for urban Canadians in Figure 5:3, we find that significantly higher mortality rates among Native Indians than even among the poorest city dwellers (10.5/1,000). As an alternative measure, the life expectancy of Native Indian women is 73 years as compared to an average for all Canadian women of 81.4 years. For men the respective averages are 65.7 versus 74.1 years.

Furthermore the link between *life* expectancy and income also occurs for *health* expectancy and income. People from low-income families experience many more health ailments than do individuals born to more affluent families. The health problems of poor children begin before birth and often continue throughout life. There is a poverty of health as well as a poverty of income (see the National Council of Welfare, 1990).

"There but for the grace of God go I:" of all life's unknowns, the lottery of birth is the most telling. We do not choose our parents, but fortune is on our side if we are so lucky as to be born in a privileged family. This is a real life chance that we have all experienced, although too few of us reflect on the consequences.

The lottery of birth is a personal problem or personal fortune, depending upon your luck in the lottery. It is also something over which an individual has no control. Children born in poor families have no choice in the matter, they cannot be faulted for their personal misfortune any more than can children born to wealthy families be lauded for their foresight. Sociologists view these different real life chances not as *personal troubles,* but as *public issues.*

We cannot adequately explain the fact that over a million children in Canada currently live in poverty by blaming them. Poor children are the victims of poverty, and they deserve no blame for their misfortune. Issues of effort, or motivation, or personality are totally inadequate to account for their predicament. Rather, the explanation must lie with the way in which we collectively have allowed the distribution of income and power to occur. It is thus a public issue, an issue of social organization in which we all share.

High rates of poverty result not from some deficit or some inadequacy among the victims of poverty. To argue so is to blame the victim (Ryan, 1976). The growing feminization of poverty (depicted in Table 5:4) is not the fault of poor women, it the result of practices (e.g., domestic responsibilities, lower pay for work of equal value) and policies (e.g., alimony defaulting) that we all permit to continue.

Conclusion

In this chapter we have attempted to provide an idea of the way sociologists examine inequalities in Canada. We began by showing that a "classless" or middle-class vision of Canada is naive and unrealistic. We then outlined the notion of social class, and showed how it has evolved and been used in different ways to help make sense of differences in power and wealth. However, throughout the chapter we have tried to show that while some forms of inequality are expressed in class terms (e.g. differences in wealth), other social divisions such as sex and race also remain fundamental to the creation and maintenance of these inequalities. Finally, we have tried to make it clear that the victims of inequality (women, the elderly, Native Indians, the poor, etc.) deserve no blame for their plight. Rather, the causes of these disadvantages lie in the social organization of Canadian society, which we all help create, and for which we all share responsibility.

Notes

1. Marx made mention of two other classes which are unimportant for the present discussion: the petite bourgeoisie which was a class of people who owned their own productive property but did not employ anyone (e.g. small shopkeepers and farmers); and the lumpenproletariat, made up of people whom Marx said did not contribute anything to society such as criminals, drifters, con-artists and the mentally ill.

References

Abella, Rosalie
1984 *Equality in Employment:* A *Royal Commission Report.* Ottawa: Supply and Services.

Armstrong, Pat and Hugh Armstrong
1990 *Theorizing Women's Work* Toronto: Garamond.

Banting, Keith
1987 "The Welfare State and Inequality in the 1980s." *Canadian Review of Sociology and Anthropology,* Vol. 24(3), 309–38.

Black, Don and John Myles
1986 "Dependent Industrialization and the Canadian Class Structure: A Comparative Analysis of Canada, the United States and Sweden." *Canadian Review of Sociology and Anthropology*, Vol. 23(2), 157–81.

Bobet, Ellen
1989 "Indian Mortality." *Canadian Social Trends*, Winter, 12–13.

Bolaria, Singh and Terry Wotherspoon
1991 "Income Inequality, Poverty, and Hunger," in S. Bolaria ed. *Social Issues and Contradictions in Canadian Society*. Toronto: Harcourt Brace Jovanovich.

Boyd, Monica and 5 others
1985 *Ascription and Achievement: Studies in Mobility and Status Attainment in Canada.* Ottawa: Carleton University Press.

Clement, Wallace and John Myles
1992 *Relations of Ruling: Class, Gender and Postindustrialism in Comparative Perspective.* (forthcoming).

Creese, Gillian, Neil Guppy, and Martin Meissner
1991 *Ups and Downs on the Ladder of Success: Social Mobility in Canada.* Ottawa: Statistics Canada.

Dahrendorf, Ralph
1959 *Classes and Class Conflict in Industrial Society.* Stanford: Stanford University Press.

Davies, James
1993 "The Distribution of Wealth and Economic Inequality in Canada," in J. Curtis *et al.* eds. *Social Inequality in Canada: Patterns, Problems, Policies,* 2nd edition, Toronto: Prentice-Hall.

Fox, John and Michael Ornstein
1986 "The Canadian State and the Corporate Elites in the Post-War Period." *Canadian Review of Sociology and Anthropology*, Vol. 23(4), 481–506.

Giddens, Anthony
1979 *The Class Structure of Advanced Societies,* 2nd edition. New York: Harper and Row.

Grabb, Ed
1990 "Who Owns Canada? Concentration of Ownership and the Distribution of Economic Assets, 1975–1985." *Journal of Canadian Studies,* Vol. 25(2), 72–93.

Guppy, Neil and Bruce Arai
1993 "Who Benefits from Higher Education? Differences by Sex, Social Class, and Ethnic Background," in J. Curtis *et al.* eds. *Social Inequality in Canada: Patterns, Problems, Policies,* 2nd edition, Toronto: Prentice-Hall.

Guppy, Neil, Sabrina Freeman, and Shari Buchan
1987 "Representing Canadians: Changes in the Economic Backgrounds of Federal Politicians." *Canadian Review of Sociology and Anthropology,* Vol. 24(3), 417-30.

Health Reports
1989 *Health Reports.* Vol. l(l), Ottawa: Statistics Canada, Cat. # 82-003 S19.

Hunter, Alfred
1993 "The Changing Distribution of Income," in J. Curtis *et al.* eds. *Social Inequality in Canada: Patterns, Problems, Policies,* 2nd edition, Toronto: Prentice-Hall.

Myles,John
1989 *Old Age in the Welfare State: The Political Economy of Public Pensions.* Lawrence, Kansas: University of Kansas Press.

National Council of Welfare
1990 *Health, Health Care and Medicare.* Ottawa: National Council of Welfare.

Robb, Roberta
1987 "Equal Pay for Work of Equal Value: Issues and Policies." *Canadian Public Policy-Analyse de Politiques,* XIII(4), 445–61.

Ross, David and Richard Shillington
1989 *The Canadian Fact Book on Poverty.* Toronto: Canadian Council for Social Development.

Ryan, William
1976 *Blaming the Victim.* New York: Vintage Press.

Sobeco-Chapman
Annual "Sobeco Management Compensation in Canada." Toronto: Sobeco-Chapman Inc.

Stanbury, William
1986 *Business-Government Relations in Canada* .Toronto: Methuen.

Turritin, Anton, Paul Anisef, and Neil MacKinnon
1983 "Gender Differences in Educational Attainment: A Study of Social Inequality." Canadian *Journal of Sociology,* Vol. 8(4), 395–319.

Wanner, Richard
1993 "Patterns and Trends in Occupational Mobility," in J. Curtis *et al.* eds. *Social Inequality in Canada: Patterns, Problems, Policies*, 2nd edition, Toronto: Prentice-Hall.

Wannell, Ted
1990 "Male-Female Earnings Gap among Recent University Graduates." *Perspectives on Labour and Income,* Vol. 2(2), 19–31.

Wright, Erik-Olin
1985 *Classes.* London: Verso.

6

Race and Ethnicity in Canada

Elizabeth Moravec Hewa

In the topic of race and ethnicity we find another place where sociology meets psychology resulting in social psychology. We shall see that ethnicity and race are major social structures which frame our lives in many ways. They are also sources of personal identity illustrated when a child knows that the colour of his or her skin is different from others or when a grade school child is ostracized from age mates because they "speak funny" because their parents come from an ethnic group who have recently immigrated to Canada.

In the study of stereotypes, prejudice, and racism, we are introduced to a social psychology of ethnicity and race. The literature on ideologies links us to culture that frequently provides rationale for much of the negative impact that prejudice and discrimination has upon so many Canadians.

Introduction

Canada is recognized as a democratic country that has established policies to protect and promote the full participation of all citizens in Canadian society. The multi-cultural policy appears to offer equal opportunities to all regardless of race, colour or creed. Race and ethnicity are key terms used in these policies. These terms will be explored as ideological constructs which are based on relations of power between dominant and subordinate groups. In this regard, it is argued, the stereotype plays an important role in maintaining the status quo.

The social and political relationships of the major groups which make up Canadian society highlight some of these assertions. The relationship between the French and the English as the dominant groups in Canada will be discussed. The history of domination of the aboriginal people in Canadian society will be presented. It will be argued that the current problems facing the aboriginal people are a result of this long historical relationship.

Finally, a brief discussion of the immigration and settlement patterns of the ethnic groups in Canada will be provided to show the existence of prejudice and discrimination in Canadian society.

Ethnicity, Race and the Role of the Stereotype

Interpretations and Concepts of Ethnicity

Max Weber (1864-1920), who is considered to be one of the founding fathers of modern sociology, provides a broad definition of ethnicity. He explains how individuals come to see themselves as part of an ethnic group:

> The belief in group affinity, regardless of whether it has any objective foundation, can have important consequences especially for the formation of a political community. We shall call "ethnic groups" those human groups that entertain a subjective belief in their common descent because of similarities of physical type or of customs or both, or because of memories of colonization and migration; this belief must be important for the propagation of group formation; conversely, it does not matter whether or not an objective blood relationship exists.... In our sense, ethnic membership does not constitute a group; it only facilitates group formation of any kind, particularly in the political sphere. (Weber, 1978:389).

The characteristics of ethnicity that Weber emphasizes are those of subjectivity and the role of the political institution. The belief that one belongs to a certain ethnic group arises from such things as common customs, language, physical characteristics and interpersonal relationships. Once the individual has internalized his/her ethnic identity it is difficult to change. The process is involuntary because the person is born into an ethnic group and becomes related to it through emotional and symbolic ties.

The political aspect of ethnicity, however, is much more complex. Under different historical circumstances various ethnic groups can emerge as one nation with a strong collective identity. For example, the aboriginal people in Canada were not members of one tribe, cultural or linguistic community when they were colonized. However, over a long period of oppression, and the institution of the term "Indian" by the government as a legal term, they have developed a collective identity as being Indian in addition to their own cultural roots (Lambert, 1978).

Although the definitions of ethnicity are not well defined, the most common characteristic of ethnicity is the belief in common ancestry. Common ancestry can refer to common ancestors, heritage or geographic location. The practice of common customs, language and religion are also considered to be important elements in forming an ethnic identity. Specifically, it is the belief of a shared heritage that contributes most to the formation of an ethnic group. The persistence of these beliefs over generations and the involuntary nature of being born into an ethnic group facilitates ethnic consciousness (Isajiw, 1985; Manyoni, 1978; Marger, 1985).

The definitions of ethnicity, therefore, can be divided into two different approaches. The *ascriptive* approach defines members of the same ethnic group as a group of people having or believing that they have common descendants, a common culture, language and physical characteristics. Secondly, these attitudes and behaviour are acquired by being born into a group rather than acquiring the ethnic status through a special act.

The opposing view, known as the *situational* approach, argues that what really matters is people's definition of themselves as culturally or physically distinct from others. In this view, ethnicity is flexible and capable of taking on different meanings. This approach shifts the study of ethnicity from a single ethnic group to the *relationship* between groups (Smooha in Kuper and Kuper, 1985). Therefore, it is this approach which is most useful to discover the distribution of power and resources among the various groups in Canada.

The Concept of Race: Biological or Sociological?

The definition of "race" is more specific than "ethnicity." The characteristics of race are usually concerned with the visible physical traits such as skin colour, hair texture, body and facial shape. In addition, common internal physiological traits such as metabolic rate, genetic diseases, hormonal activity and blood composition can be examined (Marger, 1985). It is the combination of these physical characteristics that have been used to classify people into a specific race. Physical differences between people exist, and these differences can be statistically studied. However, these statistical categories should not be interpreted as clearly differentiated human groups. The genetic "boundaries" between races have invariably changed over many generations. It has been shown that racial categories form a gradual range of differentially shared human characteristics. Thus the popular division of the human race into three major racial groups—Caucasian, Mongoloid and Negroid—essentially are arbitrary. The majority of people are a mixture of these categories (Marger, 1985). East Indians, Indonesians and Europeans are each a mixture of races. Their subjective ethnicity sets them apart from each other through language, culture and ideology. In reality, racial groups are highly variable entities; there are no pure races.

Although the biological basis of race cannot be denied, the more important sociological issue is how the characteristics of each race are constructed within a particular social setting. As Robert Redfield (1958:67) clearly states: "It is on the level of habit, custom, sentiment and attitude that race as a matter of practical significance is to be understood. Race is, so to speak, a human invention." Correspondingly, the classification of race can be used in many ways. For example, van den Berghe (1985) has explained that there is an inherent desire among human beings to distinguish "us" from "them" as a basic part of kin selection. A human group will give priority to their nearest kin and close kin over distant kin. Altruism to other people or groups is greater if there are more similarities and the outcome is related to a cost/benefit ratio. The criteria most often used to determine affinity are the easily identifiable physical characteristics such as skin colour, hair texture, body shape and facial features. Consequently, the concept of race is used by those who share the same physical attributes. We learn to classify ourselves as belonging to a particular race and learn how to distinguish those who are not part of our race.

In conclusion, although the idea of ethnicity can be seen as "subjective" and the notion of race is "imposed," both are learned in the social setting to which we are born. The general understanding of race and ethnicity in society influences the way people develop social relations and interactions. Often such understandings arise from popular beliefs and are reinforced through selective perception. That means people take note of only those cases that confirm their stereotypical attitudes and ignore those that refute them.

Stereotypes and Ideology

It was with the publication of *Public Opinion* by journalist and political analyst Walter Lippmann in 1922 that the term "stereotype" was brought to the attention of social scientists. Lippmann defined "stereotype" as cognitive structures that help individuals to process information about the environment. He argued that the stereotype is a form of perception which imposed certain preconceived ideas "before the data reaches the intelligence." Because we learn stereotypes in a cultural setting we also internalize the value laden aspects of the stereotype. The individual learns stereotypes through mass media, peer groups and others who influence the process of socialization. Although the individual has some control of the stereotypes that they learn, they essentially conform to society's dominant ideology which helps to maintain the status quo (Ashmore and Del Boca, 1981). The dominant ideology is the values and beliefs of the dominant group which controls fundamental social, political and economic institutions in society. Ideology creates and legitimizes the stereotype. Therefore, stereotype can be seen as a socially shared system of beliefs which regulates social interactions among individuals (Dyer, 1977). For example, in North America, it is generally believed, the ideal typical social values are those of white male Anglo-Saxon Protestant, and all other value systems are measured against this archetype. It is believed that by emulating these bourgeois values one can achieve a greater acceptance by the dominant group (Seiter, 1986). The dominant group perpetuates the status quo through stereotypes. That is, they justify their power, wealth and status through positive stereotypes, while negative stereotypes are attributed to subordinate groups to justify their lower social and economic positions. As the subordinate groups are powerless to counteract these negative stereotypes, they begin to behave as predicted by the dominant group.

Race and Ethnicity in Canada

The Relationship between the French and the English

Canada was created over two hundred years ago amidst the conflict of British and French colonial powers. Although the victory of the British General Wolfe over the French General Montcalm at the Plains of Abraham in 1759 marked the end of French colonialism it did not eliminate the French people, their culture and language. The language and religious differences between the French and English communities soon created tension, and greater autonomy was demanded by the French to preserve their language and culture within the English-dominant Canada.

A number of legislations were passed by the British to calm tensions in New France, which is now Quebec. The most important was the introduction of the Quebec Act in 1774, which restored the civil laws of New France and the freedom of worship. This gave the French a feeling of security in their own laws and religion. Following the American Revolution, the British sympathizers (the Loyalists) who settled in Quebec established a substantial English-speaking population. This rapid increase of English-speaking people in Quebec quickly developed into economic and political conflicts. Britain and France tried to resolve the conflict with the introduction of the Constitutional Act in 1791. The Act established two territories, each with an elected assembly: Upper Canada where most of the English resided and Lower Canada where most of the French lived. The most important outcome of this action was that the French and the English were given clearly demarcated geographical territories. This inspired an even stronger sense of community among the French population in Quebec with a distinct linguistic and cultural identity.

Although the French in Quebec gained considerable linguistic and cultural autonomy, economically they remained dependent on agriculture. The financial and commercial sectors of the Quebec economy were largely controlled by the English. The economic disparity between the two communities resulted in a growing nationalism among French Quebecers which eventually lead to the 1837 Rebellion in order to gain independence. Once the Rebellion was subdued, the British in 1840, moved to consolidate Upper and Lower Canada into a single union. The underlying objective of the Act of the Union was to eventually assimilate the French into the dominant English population.

The clergy in Quebec reacted by assuring its people that the French language and culture could be sustained only through the church. Hence, the church assumed a dominant role in promoting the French language and the Roman Catholic faith within the territory of Quebec as a means of survival of the French community (Rioux and Martin, 1978). This staunch agricultural, Catholic way of life was the driving force of Quebecers until the mid-twentieth century (Juteau Lee, 1979). The English in Quebec, on the other hand, because of their religious and educational backgrounds, as well as their political and economic connections with the rest of the country, became the dominant force in Lower Canada. Although the French were the numerical majority in Quebec they remained an economic minority in their own province.

After Confederation in 1867, the creation of a large English territory further threatened the minority status of the French. Although the French language was officially recognized in the British North America Act, in practice, the English could continue to work in the English language, while the French who wanted to improve their economic standing were compelled to learn English language and customs. In spite of the industrial growth in Quebec in the early 20th century, the educational system was largely dominated by the Catholic Church. The Church insisted that the survival of the French language and culture could only be assured through loyalty to the Church. The emphasis on humanities, classics, and religion, in the formal education ill-prepared those who wanted to participate in the financial industrial economic activities of the province. As industry took on a central role in the economy of Quebec, the Francophones occupied the lower-skilled jobs. By the 1960's the French Canadians were the most poorly paid workers in Quebec. Their incomes were even lower than the newly arrived English speaking immigrants (Royal Commission on Bilingualism and Biculturalism, 1969).

The Quiet Revolution of the 1960's was the culmination of the strong nationalist ideology which had permeated Quebec since its creation. The emerging middle class in

Quebec comprising of French professionals, many who had studied in English universities, aspired to political, economic and ideological change. They wanted to be in charge of their own house (*maîtres chez nous)* by separating from the rest of Canada. The Parti Québécois led by the former Liberal, Rene Levesque became the driving force of this ideological change. In 1976, eight years after its formation, it became the provincial government of Quebec. The ideology of sovereignty and self-determination, that is, to be independent from English domination, continues to be the issue.

The cultural and language differences should not be seen as the basis of the conflict between the English and the French in Canada. The distribution of political and economic opportunities did not satisfy the aspirations of French Quebecers who were educated and trained according to the values and beliefs of the Catholic Church. In order to meet the changing needs and aspirations of the new generation in Quebec, political and economic relationships between Quebec and Canada must be changed. Although this may require a new formula of redistributing power between provinces, this solution would be preferable to the eventual breakup of Canada on the basis of linguistic and cultural differences. As Canada is already a multi-ethnic, multi-lingual and multi-cultural nation, any solution to the Quebec problem would be an important precedent for other nations with similar problems.

The Aboriginal People of Canada

The history of relationship between colonizers and Native populations is usually a history of resistance, violence and oppression. Canada has not been an exception. Although the early history of contact between the British and French settlers and the Native people was marked by mutual cooperation it was always to the benefit of the colonizers. Enterprises like the Hudson's Bay Company were able to make huge profits and expand their operations throughout the country because of the expertise of the Native hunters (Marger, 1985; Bolaria and Li, 1988). The British, concerned to keep the Native population cooperative, issued the Proclamation of King George III in 1763 recognizing the rights of the aboriginal people. This historical document defined land areas which belonged to the Indians and clearly obligated the Crown to obtain negotiated agreements in changes to land use, status and rights by way of treaties (Frideres, 1988; Venne, 1989).

The Proclamation was soon forgotten in the face of western expansion after Confederation in 1867. The British North America Act not only created a country called Canada but also dramatically changed the relationship between the government and the Native people. Cooperation turned into domination as the government quickly realized the value of the land and resources occupied by the various native groups. Treaties were drawn up by the federal government with the various native groups in order to relegate them to areas of land called reserves. These reserves were usually isolated from the mainstream society, were of poor quality land and were otherwise seen as useless to the government. The government assumed a patronizing role, increasingly regulating and controlling life on the reserves. The introduction of the Indian Act in 1876 formally entrenched the future relationships with the indigenous population. The Act was set up to administer the colonized people. According to the Act, the authorities determined who could be called "Indian" and how the land reserved for Indians would be used. Indians were officially designated as being "status" or "non-status." Status Indians fell under the provisions of the Indian Act and were allowed to live on reserve lands. However, they did not have title to the land but they had access to federal funding. Status Indians were further subdivided into Treaty and non-Treaty Indians (McMillan, 1988; Frideres, 1988).

There are also about half a million others who consider themselves to be aboriginal people who are termed non-status Indians and are not officially recognized by the government. The majority of these people call themselves the Metis, who are the offspring of mostly French fur traders and Native women, particularly Cree (McMillan, 1988). The growing Metis population soon developed a strong ethnic identity, particularly in western Canada because of geographic and social isolation. The Metis, under the leadership of Louis Riel, even declared themselves a nation which culminated in the crushed Rebellion of 1885. However the Metis never stopped considering themselves as an ethnic group and are now re-emerging as a political force. Their concerns are related to the discrimination they receive because of their Native background and the lack of any support from the Canadian government because they are not officially recognized as "status Indians" (Sealey and Lussier, 1975; McMillan, 1988).

The Indian Act is the key document to understanding the historical relationship between the government and the aboriginal people in Canada. For example, the Act contained the concept of "enfranchisement." Enfranchisement literally means to set free, to liberate from slavery, to admit to citizenship. Individuals or a whole band could surrender their Indian status and become Canadian citizens thereby gaining the right to vote, own property and purchase liquor. To obtain this right, an Indian had to be baptized a Christian, he had to be married according to European customs and he had to have a reasonable knowledge of English. Essentially, European customs were built into the requirements for freedom (Robertson, 1970).

Indian women who married non-aboriginal men along with their children, lost their Indian status while Indian men who married non-Indian women not only retained their status but could pass on their status to their wives and children. This act of sexual discrimination was overruled in 1985 after many complaints by Indian women to the Human Rights Commission.

The Indian Act has changed very little from its inception. The major changes made in 1951 included repealing:

1. the ban on potlatches and sundances which were and still are essential ways in which religious and social ties are strengthened among the various tribes and bands,
2. the 1927 amendment which prohibited the raising of money for political purposes (in particular for land claims) and
3. allowing Indians to consume alcohol in public places (McMillan. 1988; Morrison and Wilson, 1988).

In 1960, the government changed the Indian Act to extend federal voting rights to all Indians making it possible to be both an Indian and a Canadian citizen; but it was only 1985 that the offensive "enfranchisement" clause was removed (McMillan, 1988). In

1969, the infamous White Paper on Indian Policy proposed a radical restructuring of its relationship with the aboriginal people in Canada. It proposed to abolish the Indian Act. The major recommendations of the White Paper were: all native reserves would be eliminated, treaties terminated, federal recognition of any special status for Indians would be withdrawn and any constitutional references made to "Indian and Indian lands" would be abolished (Venne, 1989).

From the outset, the Indian Act aimed to assimilate a colonized people. The Act and the consequent changes were imposed on the Indian population without negotiation or consent. The "bestowing of citizenship" in 1960 was done without approval of the Indians themselves. Decisions were made without respect to the Indians' needs or wishes. The federal government, has had full control of the lives of the Native people. Therefore the proposal in 1969 to abolish the Indian Act was seen by the Indian leaders as not only a denial of the government of any responsibility for the circumstances in which most Indians found themselves but also as the ultimate solution to fully assimilate the aboriginal groups into the mainstream society. Harold Cardinal, a Cree Indian leader from Alberta (and appointed Regional Director General for the Alberta Division of Indian Affairs in 1977) argued that the proposal was "a thinly disguised programme of extermination through assimilation." The government was eventually forced to withdraw the proposal (Venne, 1989; Morrison and Wilson, 1988; McMillan, 1988; Frideres, 1988).

This event can be seen as the start of true negotiations between the aboriginal people and government to be treated as equals in Canadian society. However, there are still serious problems facing the many native communities in Canada.

The Legacy of the Reservations

The aboriginal people were living in this country for thousands of years developing and maintaining their own culture and a way of life with little interference. The invasion of the Europeans has severely strained their cultural identity because of the deliberate attempts to dissipate, assimilate and annihilate them for possession of their land and resources. The assumption that somehow the aboriginal people have not been able to adapt to the new culture or that their own culture is not useful for the modern world is quite common among many Canadians. In a national survey conducted in 1976, respondents were asked to attribute qualities to members of various ethnic groups. In the ranking of the 12 ethnic groups classified, the aboriginal people were ranked 10th in having the least desirable traits. A majority of non-Indians in Kenora, Ontario, for example, evaluated the Ojibwa Indian band from the nearby reservation of Grassy Narrows that "Indians are poor because they are shiftless, lazy, unreliable, irresponsible, profligate with money and material goods. At the same time, they insist that Indians are this way because they have given up their old customs and values and have not yet adopted the new ones prized by the dominant society" (Shkilnyk, 1985:129).

Anastasia Shkilnyk's study of the Ojibwa people living in Grassy Narrows reservation in Ontario is a clear example how government policies can disrupt the way of life of the Native communities. Although the Ojibwa community was poor by the standards of the mainstream society, they were self-sufficient and a stable community until 1963 when the government relocated them closer to the town of Kenora. The annual cycle of hunting and fishing created a pattern of gathering and dispersal that drew together family groups and the community in a seasonal cycle. Treaty Day would mark the time all the clans would be together at the reserve for celebrations and to collect the treaty payments from the RCMP. In the spring and summer, the men would trap for muskrat and beaver while gardening would occupy the women. Commercial fishing and guiding tourists would bring in extra money. August would be the time for berry picking and late autumn would signal the time for the wild-rice harvest.

The winter dispersed the community as each family group would leave to tend the winter traplines. In December most of the families would see each other again to sell their furs at the Hudson's Bay Company. They would disperse again until spring when they would all return to the summer community to repeat the cycle. The families looked after their own welfare and the problem of alcoholism, sexual promiscuity and crimes were almost non-existent (Hutchison and Wallace, 1977; Shkilnyk, 1985; Zeitlin and Brym, 1991).

In 1963 the department of Indian Affairs decided that they would "improve" this community's living standards and "help" the people assimilate easier into the mainstream society. The residents were told to move to a new location. They were told they would have better access to the improved housing, electricity and sewage, the improved medical services, the on-reserve school and the social-welfare programs. In particular, the road to Kenora was emphasised as the link in which the community would have better contact with the non-native communities. All these things, they were told, would help improve and modernize their living conditions.

The Ojibwa did not want to move, as they had made a life for themselves at that location. The government countered with financial reprisals; and they promised jobs and welfare payments. The people reluctantly moved; the last family moved out in 1972.

The new location proved to be not only inappropriate for gardening because of the poor soil conditions, but also the proximity to the neighbouring communities reduced the game caught due to the increased disturbance and competition from the non-native hunters. The school on the reserve established a year-round sedentary community. While the women stayed in the community with the children, the men had to leave their families for hunting. The separation of the men from their families made it difficult for them to engage in hunting for extended periods. Therefore, they began to look for work nearby the reserve or go on welfare.

The placing of the new houses were built without taking into account the residence patterns of the Ojibwa people. The Ojibwa are clan based and the residence pattern respects certain groupings to avoid friction. Space and privacy assured the respect. As well, the houses were built too close for effective gardening, even if the soil had been good. The relocation eventually diminished all aspects of a physically challenging and mentally stimulating way of life. The normal social interactions which were part of a vibrant community were replaced by inactivity and lassitude (Hutchison and Wallace, 1977; Shkilnyk, 1985; Zeitlin and Brym, 1991).

The final strain came in 1970 when it was discovered that methyl mercury had been dumped into the surrounding lakes and rivers polluting virtually everything in it. Fishing, which had been a major activity, became impossible. By the 1970s, the new Grassy

Narrows Reserve was the site of substandard housing, absence of running water and proper sewage. Most residents suffered from poor health, unemployment and alcohol abuse. Three out of four persons died a violent death that was drug or alcohol related. Three out every four children were removed from their families by welfare agencies because of neglect or abuse. Nearly a fifth of eleven to nineteen year olds tried to commit suicide. Most Canadians attribute these problems to the inability of Indians themselves to adapt to mainstream society or that the Indians are inherently too lazy or irresponsible to change their present circumstances (Zeitlin and Brym, 1991:164).

Grassy Narrows reserve was a "dry" town at the beginning. But the people of Kenora—the neighbouring town to the reserve—soon discovered that there was money to be made on the reserve. Some taxi drivers became bootleggers. The low morale of the people of the reserve combined with the easy access to alcohol destroyed the community. By giving up their own way of life for new housing, schools, and medical treatment they became more dependent on government handouts. The people of the reserve were subjected to prejudice on the grounds that they were receiving free handouts from the government, and were not working for a living. The Indians were accused of not living up to their own cultural standards of self-sufficiency. The anticipated assimilation of Indians to the mainstream society by the relocation of Ojibwa community was not materialized because the officials of the Department of Indian Affairs did not have any understanding of the cultural and community values of Indians. The project was undertaken without proper consent of the whole community. The end result of the ill-fated assimilation project was the greater animosity between the two communities (Shkilnyk, 1985; Zeitlin and Brym, 1991).

Aboriginal people over the last two centuries have been fighting to keep their right to choose how their culture should develop and how they should live. Either they were removed from the land by force or if they wanted to assimilate into the mainstream society they were prevented by prejudice and discrimination. They were marginalized by the government policy itself that did not recognize the cultural and social values of the people. The attribution of social and economic problems of the aboriginal people to their culture by many Canadians obscure the actual cause of their problems and undermine amicable solutions to the problems of aboriginal people (Zeitlin and Brym, 1991).

Reclaiming Aboriginal Rights

As a result of the long frustration with the way governments handled Native issues, the aboriginal people are now seeking to re-negotiate the terms of older contracts. They want the right to self-govern their own affairs, land and people. As the aboriginal communities across the country are united at this time, the conflict will no doubt continue for many years to come unless the government is willing to accommodate their demands. The current constitutional debate in Canada is an important opportunity for the leaders of this country to resolve the century old claims of the aboriginal people once and for all.

Most of the native demands involve the following issues:

1. Aboriginal rights arise in areas where no treaties were ever signed and the Indians, therefore, state that they never ceded their rights to any government,

2. Treaty rights concern those Indians who believe that their treaty promises were ignored or broken by governments and
3. Specific band claims are usually in reference to lost reserve land or the control of the administration of Band money and affairs (Barber, 1978).

The demand for the re-interpretation of treaties is a complex legal issue that involves both federal and provincial jurisdictions. Already, a number of provincial political leaders have indicated how far they are willing to compromise on these matters. The federal government's involvement is particularly necessary to resolve the land claim issue because the existing laws are inadequate to deal with these issues. For example, after almost twenty years of court battle with the Ontario government, the Teme-Augama Anishnabai band lost its claim to the 9,800 square kilometres of mineral rich forest land in Northern Ontario. According to the Supreme Court of Canada, the band had forfeited their claim when they signed the Robinson-Huron Treaty in 1850. However, the court also noted that the Ontario government has not complied with the terms of the treaty. The court specifically mentioned that "The Crown has failed to comply with some of its obligations under this agreement, and thereby breached its fiduciary obligations to the Indians" (*The Globe and Mail,* August 16, 1991).

In 1984, Gitksan and Wet'suwet'en bands filed a suit in the British Columbia Supreme Court to force the province to recognize the existing band's title to their traditional territories. Claiming a territory of 22,000 square miles, Gitksan and Wet'suwet'en bands argued that not only were they seeking the recognition of title to their land, but also the right to self-government within their territory. The process of settling these complicated land claim issues take a long time even if all parties agree to negotiate in good faith. However, the province of British Columbia had been arguing all along that it would not discuss these issues because they believe that it is within the jurisdiction of the federal government (Wa and Uukw, 1989).

A similar situation exists in the province of Alberta where the Lubicon Lake Indians have been trying to resolve their land claim issue with provincial government for many years. The Lubicons claim about 25,000 square miles of land and 900 million US dollars for damages done to their territory during the period of illegal Canadian occupancy. Initially, the government ridiculed the Lubicon claim and refused to deal with the issue at all. In the meantime, the Lubicons took their case to the public through a province wide educational campaign during the period of 1983 to 1984. To the government's surprise, the public reaction to this campaign was so favourable, the government had to take certain measures to contain the situation. The government ordered an independent investigation in 1984 by Dr. Randall Ivany, Ombudsman of Alberta. The Ombudsman report predictably supported the governments assertion that the Lubicon claim had no factual basis. The official outcome was intended to undercut the rising tide of public sentiment in support of the Lubicon. It is important for the government to maintain that the land does not belong to the Lubicons because a large amount of oil reserves are located within this territory (Churchill, 1989).

The federal government has indicated in recent months that it wants to resolve land claim issues outside the court system. However, the two parties are still far apart on their interpretations of what the treaties mean to them. Particularly, much of the land under dispute are rich in natural resources. On the one hand, the federal government does not want to antagonize the provincial leadership, especially at the present time, when the federal government has been engaged in constitutional reform. And on the other hand, with the failure of the Meech Lake Accord in 1990, the federal government realized that it has no alternative but to deal with Native issues in order to resolve the constitutional crisis. Therefore, both the aboriginal people and the government are fully aware of each other's agendas and they may work towards satisfactory solutions to their concerns.

The Ethnic Canadians

The ethnic Canadians who are neither English nor French comprise almost one-third of the population. These people come from many different ethno-cultural backgrounds. At the beginning, most immigrants arriving in Canada were English, Scots, Welsh and Irish. The French mainly settled in Quebec. Immigration policies were established by the British to encourage Europeans with agricultural knowledge to settle in the prairie provinces. In particular, those from northwestern Europe were encouraged to come, non-Europeans were outright rejected. Germans, Dutch and later on Ukrainians, who although they were from eastern Europe, had considerable agricultural knowledge, made their home on the prairies (Troper, 1972). As the west developed, the number of immigrants grew, but the immigration policy established favoured those of Anglo-Celtic background to live in the cities while the new immigrants settled in rural areas.

This pattern of immigration did not change until World War II. During the period of 1945 and 1962 a large influx of Italians and others from southern and eastern Europe changed the Canadian ethnic population. After 1962 a new component to the Canadian mosaic was added. Although it was not officially stated, the Canadian immigration policy before this time "encouraged" only whites to immigrate to Canada (Richmond, 1976). The new liberal policy opened the doors to immigrants from Asia and Caribbeans who by 1980's represented the majority of immigrants coming into Canada. The majority of these new immigrants settled in urban centres such as Montreal, Toronto and Vancouver.

This sharp increase of immigrants from non-European countries since the World War 11, have considerably changed the structure of the Canadian population. The new immigrants with industrial and economic skills have been able to secure a wide range of positions which were traditionally dominated by the British and the French. Asians, in particular, have risen rapidly into positions of status and income (Marger, 1985). Although a tiny community of Blacks lived in Canada long before the liberalization of the Canadian immigration policy, since the 1960s their number has been steadily increasing. However, political and economic standing of the Black population across Canada has not improved. Although the increase of immigrants who are physically and culturally quite different from the norm, e.g., Anglo-Celtic, has increased racism in Canada, the discrimination against visible minorities existed in Canada long before the increase of their proportion in the population.

When the Chinese workers finished the construction of the Canadian Railway in the late 19th century, they became surplus labour which was seen as a threat to the economic interest of white labourers. This even resulted in communal violence between the two communities. The government soon established policies preventing their entry and by 1923 had completely denied their immigration.

Those of Japanese descent in Canada during World War II, were forcefully removed from their homes and businesses and were incarcerated during the war. East Indians, in the first part of this century, were denied access to some jobs, the right to vote and hold citizenship (Marger, 1985).

In 1976, the study of national attitudes toward multiculturalism by John Berry, Rudolf Kalin and D. M. Taylor found that those who were most like white Anglo Saxons were accepted more readily than those who were different. This relegated most Asiatics and Blacks to the least favourable standing. The French, generally were shown to be more prejudiced than the English but both groups were equally prejudiced against Blacks. The level of acceptance of the groups in Canada can be seen in the following chart.

Attitude and Stereotypes Attributed to Some Nominated Groups

The Stereotypes and Attitudes Attributed:

1. Important
2. Canadian
3. Clean
4. Similar to me
5. Likeable
6. Wealthy
7. Well known to me
8. Interesting
9 Stick together
10. Hardworking

Canadian Groups	Considered to be an Attribute	Considered not to be an Attribute
English	1,2,3,4,5,6,7	9
French	1,2,3,4,5,7	
Native Indians	2,9	3,4,6,7,10
German	3,10	
Chinese		2,4,7
Ukrainian		7
Jews	6,9	
Italians	(not higher or lower on any attribute)	
Belgian	3,4,5,7,8	
Czech	3	2
Dutch	3,4,5,7,10	9
East Indian	9	1,2,3,5,7,10
Greek		2,4,5
Hungarian	3,4	
Irish	3,4,5,7	9
Japanese	10	4
Negro		1,3,4,6,8,10
Polish	(not higher or lower on any attribute)	
Portuguese		1,2,6
Russian	10	1
Scandinavian	3,4,5,7,10	9
Scottish	2,3,4,5,7	9
Spanish		1,2,6,10
West Indian		2,6
Yugoslavian		2

Adapted from Tables 5.4 and 5.5 of the Multicultural and Ethnic Attitudes in Canada Report (1977: 103–105).

The authors concluded, that although there was a scale of acceptance of different groups, Canadians could not be seen as openly racist. However, recent events concerning police treatment of Haitians in Montreal, East Indians in Toronto and Natives in Winnipeg indicate that Canadians continue to foster racist attitudes. As Canada becomes increasingly multi-ethnic these problems can be expected to increase. Despite the introduction of legislations in 1971 to encourage multiculturalism within a bilingual framework, most groups felt that they nonetheless were compelled to conform to one of the Charter groups. The French Canadians, on the other hand, saw themselves relegated to be just another ethnic group (Rocher, 1976). The policy, it has been argued, does not address the problems of inequality, discrimination and racism (Marger, 1985). John Porter (1975, 1979), likewise argues that the encouraging of ethnic pluralism will only hinder some groups in aspiring to positions of higher status. The French, Native people and different ethnic groups will continue to defend their rights to practice their language and customs in the English dominant society.

Conclusions

Canada is a plural society with many ethnic groups and two official languages. Canadian ethnic hierarchy is dominated by the two charter groups—British and French—who control more than seventy-five percent of key economic and political institutions of the country (Porter, 1965; Kelner, 1970; Newman, 1975, 1979; Presthus, 1973). It has been shown that nearly all the business elite are either of British or American origin. Although French Canadians make up nearly one third of the Canadian population they only compose 6.7 percent of the elite. The groups most under represented are ethnic Canadians and the aboriginal people. This domination of one group does not reflect the multi-ethnic character of the Canadian society and can be seen as a potential source of social conflicts.

The French and English conflict that stems from the 18th century wars between the two colonial powers is a struggle for power and autonomy. The current separatist movement in Quebec can be seen as the culmination of the power struggle. For the French, the protection of language and culture is a symbol of their autonomy within the territory of Quebec.

The Native groups, which make up about 2 percent of the population have the least representation in education, employment and political office. The long history of oppression of the aboriginal people have resulted in a bitter struggle for basic human rights. Now they demand nothing less than a form of self government within the Canadian geo-political system. They also claim large tracts of land rich in natural resources. Conflicts concerning the rights of the indigenous population to occupy the land on their own terms and the intention of the Canadian government to exploit these natural resources are growing concerns (Cumming, 1977).

Although the other ethnic groups comprise nearly one third of the Canadian population and have contributed greatly to the development of Canada, many still encounter discrimination and prejudice. Europeans have been generally more successful in achieving significant upward mobility than non-European ethnic minorities. The length of stay in Canada, age and the level of education are important elements that determine social and economic mobility of new immigrants.

The various groups that make up Canada are stratified in a complex system of hierarchy. The unequal distribution of economic and political power among different groups at present provides a greater possibility for social conflicts than a peaceful coexistence. The conflict is inevitable in pluralistic societies when one group or a few controls a disproportionate share of power and wealth. Accordingly, one can argue that the conflicts Canada is currently experiencing may bring about a fundamental redistribution of political and economic power.

References

Ashmore, R. D. and F. D. Del Boca
1981 "Conceptual Approaches to Stereotypes and Stereotyping." in David L. Hamilton ed. *Cognitive Processes in Stereotyping and Intergroup Behavior.* New Jersey: Lawrence Erlbaum Associates.

Barber, L.
1978 "The Nature of Indian Claims," in Martin L. Kovacs ed. *Ethnic Canadians, Culture and Education.* (Canadian Plains Studies 8). Saskatoon: Modern Press.

Berry, J. W., R. Kalin and D. M. Taylor
1977 *Multiculturalism and Ethnic Attitudes in Canada.* Ottawa: Minister of Supply and Services.

Bolaria, B. S. and P. S. Lee
1988 *Racial Oppression in Canada.* Toronto: Garamond Press.

Churchill, W.
1989 "Last Stand at Lubicon Lake, An Assertion of Indigenous Sovereignty in North America," in Ward Churchill ed. *Critical Issues in Native North America.* IWGIA Doc. No. 62, Dec. 1988/Jan. 1989. IWGIA (International Work Group for Indigenous Affairs).

Cumming, P. A.
1977 *Canada: Native Land Rights and Northern Development.* Copenhagen: IWGIA (International Work Group for Indigenous Affairs).

Dyer, R.
1977 "Stereotyping," in *Gays in Films.* London: British Film Institute.

Frideres, J. S.
1988 "Institutional Structures and Economic Deprivation: Native People in Canada," in B. Singh Bolaria and Peter S. Lee eds. *Racial Oppression in Canada.* Toronto: Garamond Press.

Hutchison, George and Dick Wallace
1977 *Grassy Narrows.* Toronto: Van Nostrand Reinhold, Ltd.

Isajiw, W. W.
1985 "Definitions of Ethnicity," in Rita M. Bienvenue and Jay E. Goldstein eds. *Ethnicity and Ethnic Relations in Canada.* Toronto: Butterworths.

Juteau Lee, D
1979 "The Evolution of Nationalism in Quebec," in J. L. Elliott ed. *Two Nations, Many Cultures.* Scarborough, Ont.: Prentice-Hall of Canada.

Kelner, M.
1970 "Ethnic Penetration into Toronto's Elite Structure." *Canadian Review of Sociology and Anthropology.* 7(May): 128–137.

Lambert, C.
1978 "To Be or Not To Be Indian, A Question Concerning Cultural Identity in Whitehorse, Yukon," in Martin L. Kovacs ed. *Ethnic Canadians, Culture and Eduction.* (Canadian Plains Studies 8). Saskatoon: Modern Press.

Lippmann, W.
1922 *Public Opinion.* New York: Harcourt, Brace, Jovanovich.

Manyoni, J. R.
1978 "Ethnics and Non-Ethnics: Facts and Fads in the Study of Intergroup Relations," in Martin L. Kovacs ed. *Ethnic Canadians, Culture and Education.* (Canadian Plains Studies 8). Saskatoon: Modern Press.

Marger, M. N.
1985 *Race and Ethnic Relations American and Global Perspectives.* California: Wadsworth Publishing Co.

McMillan, A. D.
1988 *Native Peoples and Cultures of Canada.* British Columbia: Douglas & McIntyre Ltd.

Morrison, R. B. and C. R. Wilson, eds.
1988 *Native Peoples: The Canadian Experience.* Toronto: McClelland and Stewart.

Newman, P. C.
1975 *The Canadian Establishment.* Vol. 1. Toronto: McClelland and Stewart.
1979 *The Canadian Establishment.* Vol. 2. Toronto: McClelland and Stewart.

Porter, J.
1965 *The Vertical Mosaic: An Analysis of Social Class and Power in Canada.*
Toronto: University of Toronto Press.
1975 "Ethnic Pluralism in Canadian Perspective." Pp. 267–304 in Nathan Glazer and Daniel P. Moynihan eds. *Ethnicity: Theory and Experience.* Cambridge, Mass.: Harvard University Press.
1979 *The Measure of Canadian Society.* Toronto: Gage.

Presthus, R.
1973 *Elite Accommodations in Canadian Politics.* Toronto: MacMillan of Canada.

Redfield, R.
1958 M "Race as a Social Phenomenon," in E. T. Thompson and E. C. Hughes eds. *Race: Individual and Collective Behavior,* Glencoe, Ill.: Free Press.

Richmond, A. H.
1976 "Immigration, Population, and the Canadian Future." *Sociological Focus* 9 (April):125–136.

Rioux, M. and Y. Martin
1978 *French Canadian Society.* Toronto: MacMillan of Canada.

Robertson, H.
1970 *Reservations Are for Indians.* Toronto: James Lewis & Samuel.

Rocher, G.
1976 "Multiculturalism: The Doubts of a Francophone." in *Second Canadian Conference on Multiculturalism.* Ottawa: Minister of Supply and Services.

Royal Commission on Bilingualism and Biculturalism.
1969 *Report.* Vol. 3, *The Work World.* Ottawa: Queen's Printer.

Sealey, B. D. and A. S. Lussier
1975 *The Metis: Canada's Forgotten People.* Winnipeg: Pemmican.

Seiter, E.
1986 "Stereotypes and the Media: A Re-evaluation." *Communications.* Spring.

Shkilnyk, A. M.
1985 *A Poison Stronger Than Love: The Destruction of an Ojibwa Community.* New Haven: Yale University Press.

The Globe and Mail.
1991 August 16, "Temagami band loses land claim."

Smooha, S.
1985 "Ethnicity," in Kuper, A. and J. Kuper, eds. *The Social Science Encyclopedia.* London: Routledge & Kegan Paul.

Troper, H.M.
1972 *Only Farmers Need to Apply.* Toronto: Griffen House.

van denBerghe, P.
1985 "Race and Ethnicity: A Sociological Perspective," in Rita M. Bienvenue and Jay E. Goldstein eds. *Ethnicity and Ethnic Relations in Canada.* Toronto: Butterworths.

Venne, S. H.
1989 "Treaty and Constitution in Canada, A View From Treaty Six," in Ward Churchill ed. *Critical Issues in Native North America.* IWGIA Doc. No. 62 Dec. 1988/Jan 1989, IWGIA (International Work Group for Indigenous Affairs).

Wa, G. and D. Uukw
1989 *The Spirit in the Land.* Gabriola, British Columbia: Reflections.

Weber, M.
1978 *Economy & Society.* Vol. 1. Guenther Roth and Claus Wittich eds. Berkeley: University of California Press.

Zeitlin, I. M. and R. J. Brym
1991 *The Social Condition of Humanity (Canadian Edition).* Toronto: Oxford University Press.

7

Gender Relations

Gisele Marie Thibault

The goal of this chapter is to provide the reader with an introductory understanding of the sociology of gender—how men and women are structured in society because of social definitions of biological sexual differences that structure how men and women relate to each other in personal, collective, economic and political ways. The chapter extends our understanding of how social life is structured in context of the various networks of relationships that we are embedded within. Many of these networks are interpersonal but many are also forged into linkages within geographical regions, economic sectors, and political institutions.

The chapter begins with a look at how the sociology of gender relationships emerged in Canadian sociology and then continues to outline the basic concepts of sex and gender. The chapter proceeds to present a theoretical understanding of gender, and then presents the various kinds of feminism: liberal, radical and socialist. The chapter concludes with the linkages between gender and a number of social institutions.

What Is the Sociology of Gender Relations?

The Background

In order to derive a systematic basis for understanding gender relations as an academic study, it is necessary to ask how the field emerged in sociology. While it is impossible to provide an entire analysis of the evolution of gender studies or the women's movement in the scope of this chapter, some general background information enables one to better appreciate the implications that gender analyses have had on the discipline as a whole.

The recognition of sexual divisions within sociology, and the development of gender relations as a distinct field of study; both owe an enormous debt to the ideas and political activism of the women's movement. The sociology of gender relations has its origins in the grass-roots feminist movement. The feminist movement (or women's movement) has a long history stemming from the nineteenth century in Canada, but took on a more vocal, visible and collective presence in the general ferment of the late 1960s and early 1970s, or what has been referred to as "the second wave" (Thibault, 1987).

The social context of the late 1960s affected women's consciousness in a number of significant ways. First, the period was one of social and political change in the United States and Canada, and in many other parts of the world. The continuing movement for civil rights, protests against the war in Southeast Asia, the women's movement, and somewhat later the gay movement, were principal events that called into question the authority and values of Canadian and American institutions. Since a significant segment of the participants in these movements were students and faculty at universities across the continent, the educational establishment itself became subject to scrutiny and challenge (DuBoise et al., 1987). Both students and faculty began to politicize a number of issues including gender, race, and class. The time period also affected middle-class women in two ways: the growth and composition of universities had changed to include more women and industry was booming which brought about a rapid increase in the percentage of women working outside (Hole and Levine, 1971).

Those social movements most active during this time were demanding a reallocation of societal power, and argued for equitable treatment for blacks, native Canadians, the poor, students, and women (Wilson, 1991). The "New Left" protested the Vietnam war, the alienation of humans and their labour, the dehumanization of an automated and technocratic society, and the appropriation of identity by mass consumerism and the world of the corporate elite (Marcuse, 1972; Miles, 1982). Coupled with these issues was a concern for identity and freedom which became reflected in a criticism of all social institutions. Radical groups began to criticize the "establishment" for attempting to restrict radical political activity to a separate and narrow political sphere—a sphere that would be less threatening to the existing social structure or status quo.

Within the context of these struggles, feminist radicalism emerged (Hole and Levine, 1971). For feminists, the question of male dominance and an essentially masculine "humanity" was addressed as women realized that what they were experiencing as "personal" was political. While sexist practices in other radical movements were a powerful cause for anger and disillusionment among women, their critique of male dominated institutions was generally applauded by feminists. However, they came to view their subordinate position in these movements as indicative of a general failure to create an independent statement about women and for women (Wine and Ristock, 1991).

Concurrent with the political movements that led women and men to reexamine patriarchal society were political movements that challenged hierarchies of academe. These movements set out to demystify the illusion that the university, as an institution, could be isolated from the mainstream of national power. The problems of education on all levels were connected to the perpetuation of social class inequalities. For many faculty and students, the ivory tower of academe reflected the interests of government, corporations, and military political machines (Rozak, 1967). At the same time there were charges that scientific and technological research ultimately served the military rather than the progress of human knowledge. Further, scholarship in the social sciences was criticized for its neglect of urgent social issues, the working class, minority groups, and of most importance to this discussion, women (DuBoise et al., 1987).

The first women's campus groups to emerge in the late 1960s were those composed of students and faculty who began organizing to confront and challenge the inequities they were experiencing in academe (Freeman, 1973). Their criticisms were directed at both the structure of university and the practices and content of scholarly research. Feminists complained that as a subject of research in all disciplines, women were being neglected, overlooked, or distorted by existing scholarship.

It was at this juncture that sociology "discovered women" (Mackie, 1991). Women showed that biases existed in the way women were researched and analyzed. Research did not focus on the myriad examples of sexual divisions in society, nor did it center on gender as an organizing feature of social life. "Gendering" was not seen as an essential feature of what role all our social institutions play in society—the school, the medical system, the family, the judicial system, and the economy. In terms of the subject matter of sociology, women as a topic of research were "confined to a special section" (Mackie, 1986:15) or "appeared in male related roles" (Huber, 1976). Similarly, it was demonstrated that women had been systematically omitted or presented in distorted and pejorative ways in both theoretical models and in the interpretation of research studies (Thibault, 1987;1988). As Mackie (1991) points out,

> What had been accepted, until then, as the sociology of human behaviour was consequently discovered to be the sociology of male behaviour. Research had been conducted primarily on males (and females who had been socialized to accept the masculine ruling ideas), on topics that interested men, using methods congenial to men. (1991:20)

Since sociological theories had also been developed with reference to males alone, women's experiences had been left out and misrepresented.

The recognition of these problems, in turn led to what Hesse and Ferree (1987) refer to as a "feminist revolution in the social sciences." From this revolution arose a struggle to restructure the various academic disciplines in ways that more readily permitted the study of women and their experiences. Mackie (1991) suggests that as a result of the rapidly expanding post-secondary education system in the 1970s, and the increasing numbers of women in academia (particularly in sociology), gender and the study of gender relations became a component of the sociological curriculum.

The Current Status

The popularization of the term "gender relations" in the current sense is associated with feminist research. A more precise designation is the specific form of sociopsychological behaviourism linked originally with women scholars working in psychology and sociology—influenced heavily by radical sociologists and the growth of women's studies as an academic discipline (Bowles and Duelli-Klein, 1977).

Today, the term gender studies has assumed various distinctive forms. This diversity has provoked numerous efforts at developing a definition. One definition that seems to provide a satisfactory starting point is Mackie (1991), where she proposes that gender relations applies to the study of the causes and consequences of the cultural identification of emotional, attitudinal, intellectual, and behaviourial traits as either masculine or feminine. The causes and consequences, she explains, are examined from the point of view of individuals, groups, and society as a whole. The term relations emphasizes the interdependence among individuals, groups, and societal institutions. Consequently, the field of gender relations attempts to encompass the situation and experiences of women and men, both individually and in relation to one another. Due to the fact the women have generally been neglected in the sociological account of the social world, more emphasis is placed on the position of women.

Since the late 1970s, major transformations have taken place in sociology, of which the emergence of gender studies has been a vital part. The last decade, in particular, has seen considerable shifts both within the organization of the discipline itself and the structure of the profession. These changes are the result of a greater awareness of gender issues brought about by the women's movement and through the work of gender theorists.

Studying gender from a sociological perspective involves examining both the social differences between men and women as well as the resulting inequalities that these differences entail. Women and men in most societies are socialized differently, assume different roles, and have different experiences of the social world. They live out their lives in a social environment that is separate at some junctures and overlapping in others. Accordingly, some questions that feminist sociologists may ask include: What are gender roles and what purpose do they serve? How is gender part of the very fabric of Canadian institutions? What assumptions are behind the assignment of gender roles, tasks, and behaviours? How and in what ways are women placed in a disadvantaged position in comparison to men? What forms does this inequality take?

To address these questions, the sociology of gender relations, first and foremost, attempts to provide theoretical explanations by critically examining social patterns of inequality. This is accomplished by carefully reevaluating existing theories and providing an alternative knowledge base that includes the experiences of women. As a distinct field of study, it seeks to investigate the consequences of the gender system with respect to the division of labour in societies and the marginalization of women.

Conceptualizing Gender Relations: Some Basic Concepts

In order to fully grasp the importance of feminist research to sociology, it is necessary to define some of the basic concepts used to explain and analyze gender inequality. The following are the most fundamental concepts that must be clearly understood, as they represent the building blocks of gender analyses; sex, gender, role, stereotype, feminism, and patriarchy.

Sex is a term used by social scientists and biologists to refer to certain biological categories—female and male. In the biological sense, a "woman" is thought to be a person whose chromosomes, internal and external organs, and hormonal chemistry come together to make them "female"—a label which is prescribed to them at birth. Overall, the term sex is considered to represent the biological aspects of a person which differentiates females and males using anatomical, reproductive, hormonal, and other physiological characteristics (Lindsey, 1990). Generally, a person's sex cannot be changed—the anatomical differences of males and females cannot be denied. However, the rich variety of social arrangements that exist in North American cultures and others, suggests that biological sex differences cannot, by themselves, explain the social patterns of inequality that exist between men and women in virtually all societies. There is much more than biological or physiological differences that determine who is a man and who is a woman.

Gender is a social not a biological concept. It refers to neither a "natural" nor innate characteristic—people are not born with a gender. Rather, gender is a social construct, which involves a set of cultural and psychological traits linked to females and males in particular social contexts. Femininity and masculinity, terms used to denote a person's gender, refer to a complex set of characteristics and behaviours that are prescribed for a particular sex by a society and learned through socialization. For example, femininity for certain groups of women in various cultures refers to those qualities associated with passivity, fragility, and the inclination toward nurturing behaviours. Consequently, a little girl is given a doll to play with, dressed in frilly or constrictive clothing, and rebuked for so-called unladylike behaviour. These serve to reinforce behaviour patterns thought to be feminine, and learns to be passive, dependent, and nurturing. Thus, gender refers to what is socially recognized as femininity or masculinity and can therefore be seen as socially created or constructed.

The cultural norms of a particular society at a certain point in time identify ways of thinking, behaving, and feeling as "appropriate" for females and other ways of thinking, feeling and behaving as "appropriate" for males (Mackie, 1986). Furthermore, as Mackie argues, "The momentous impact of gender stems from the direct translation of the greater social prestige enjoyed by males into a monopoly of **power** [emphasis mine] at both institutional and interpersonal levels" (1990:7). In this sense, a "woman" and a "man" are social constructs. An important part of this social definition is the fact that a "woman" is capable of bearing children (or that most women are capable of bearing children). Consequently, in order to fulfill personal and societal expectations, a woman must bear a child. Even though many women never marry, bear children, or nurse them, we are socially defined by our capacity to do so and by the social expectation that this capacity is an intrinsic, "natural" characteristic of our existence.

Similarly, social definitions of "man" include many physical, psychological, and behavioral characteristics, the sum of which, for any one society, represents the gender label "man" for that group. To understand the social definition of men, one must untangle men's biological "manhood" or their sex with their "historically specific, socially constructed and personally embodied notions of masculinity" (Kaufman, 1987a:xiv).

Roles are composed of a pattern of behaviours prescribed for individuals playing a certain part in the "drama of life" (Lindsey, 1990). Roles can also be defined as the "organized actions of a person in a given position" (Sarbin, 1954:225). For example, the role of a teacher in our society requires actions such as imparting knowledge to the student, attending classes, advising students, or grading papers.

In almost every society, females and males are assigned separate and specific roles on the basis of their sex. These roles are referred to as gender roles. Varying from culture to culture, and within a culture by a variety of factors (class, religion, age, sexual orientation and so on), gender roles are made up of a set of expected behaviours with accompanying gender traits. The role of a middle-class white female in our society typically includes playing with dolls, helping mother, getting married, having children, doing the housekeeping work, striving to be attractive as defined by a male dominated society, and so on. Many of these behaviours in their turn form other role configurations or role sets. Thus, the role of a woman may include several subroles such as daughter, wife, mother, and grandmother to name a few. A key point here is that gender roles refer to the specific attitudes and behaviours that women and men are expected to adopt. There is nothing biological about the roles people play. The role concept places the reference squarely on the sociocultural level.

On a final note, the nomenclature commonly including "sex roles" or "gender roles" is now considered unsatisfactory (Mackie, 1991). Since objections have been raised to the concepts of "role" and "sex" both have fallen into disuse. We will go into further elaboration on this point in the section on analyzing gender.

Stereotype is a concept related to role. Simply put, a stereotype is a composite image of traits and expectations pertaining to a group—an image that is persistent in the social mind though it is inaccurate or built upon prejudicial beliefs. Or as one author suggests, it is a "picture in our heads." Typically, the stereotype is an over-generalization of characteristics that may or may not have any basis in reality.

Not all stereotypes are pejorative, but many become images that are tinged with negative connotations—connotations that are often reinforced through the media. For example, a stereotypical image of a "women's libber" or more recently a "feminist" often involves viewing these women as incapable of fulfilling the traditional gender role requirements for "proper" femininity, or that all are "man-haters" who are generally homely, dirty, aggressive, strident, shrill, sexually promiscuous (or frigid, or a lesbian, or all three) making speeches, carrying banners, and burning underwear. The fact that many feminists are not middle class or white or college educated, that feminists wear a variety of dress and have differing sexual codes and identities are pieces of reality that do little to change media-produced images (Ruth, 1980). Stereotypes, often born and maintained in ignorance and fear, can and do have wide-reaching effects on both the stereotyped group and those with whom the members of the group interact. Stereotypes can and do dictate gender behaviour to a great extent.

In order to further clarify the nature of gender relations and how it is analyzed, it is vital to de-mystify the preconceived notions about who or what is a feminist. First, **feminism** is not a monolith, but rather it represents a collection of ideas, theories, and divergent approaches which can be loosely defined as a movement and an ideology, and insofar as many have engaged in extended philosophic, sociological analyses, it gives rise to theories about the way gende—masculinity and femininity—are constructed and socially produced in our society (Pierson and Prentice, 1982). Second, intrinsic to feminism is the understanding of social inequality and polarity between women and men imposed not by individual men, but by an institutional and state system of masculine dominance. This system of power and domination is referred to as **patriarchy**.

The concept of **patriarchy**, or "rule of the fathers" is usually used to mean all systems of male dominance (Jaggar, 1983:103). Instead of seeing patriarchy as a trait of one or several individuals, feminist scholars insist that it is a system in which both men and women are exploited—albeit in differing forms. Kaufman (1987a) explains patriarchy as something that involves "Domination by men based on, and perpetuated by, a wide range of social structures, from the most intimate of sexual relations to the organization of economic and political life" (1987a:xiv).

While feminism has been defined in various ways, feminists share an ideal of a world in which men and women could be different without these differences becoming value laden and sources of inequality. In general, feminist scholarship proposes that to attain this ideal, patriarchy must be dismantled. From a feminist perspective, patriarchy is a system and an ideology that is reflected in all social institutions. While some women maintain some power, influence, and autonomy in society, the majority are subject to the authority of men. Patriarchy does not refer so much to the specific activities of men and women but rather the value society attaches to particular activities—primarily the greater value attached to activities performed by men. Such is the nature of patriarchy according to feminist thinking, and therein lies its importance to understanding the organization of gender inequalities.

Finally, fundamental to feminists' work in sociology is the analysis of how political, economic and social systems, and their accompanying ideologies, work to perpetuate women's subordinate status. However, feminist research argues that an exclusive preoccupation with the exploitation of women can lead to a purely negative picture of women as passive victims. Therefore, feminist scholars emphasize that women should be viewed as active agents who can resist domination individually and collectively.

All of these concepts are involved in the analyses of gender relations and in explaining the social positions of women and men. In the next section, a short synopsis of various feminist theories used in sociology is presented to help explain gender oppression and the relations of domination and subordination which they create.

Feminist Scholarship

As part of the challenge to mainstream research in sociology, feminist scholarship has made it clear that traditional sociological theories assume an androcentric view of the world where women are seen as the deviation from the norm, the exception to the rule, or the "other." This represents a critique of traditional scholarship and forms the basis for the emergence of new modes of analysis. Feminists have attempted to both modify existing sociological paradigms to include women and an analysis of gender inequality, and focus attention on forging new theoretical models which differ from sociological theories in several ways.

Traditionally, sociology has studied social behaviour and the connections between individual experience to the social organization of society. It has analyzed how individual experiences are created and transformed through social, political, and economic institutions. Consequently, the impact of sociology proper on feminist insights cannot be denied. As Epstein (1984) proposes:

> The methodological and theoretical perspectives offered in ethnomethodology, structural-functional analysis (with its focus on systematic analysis), conflict analysis and other sociological approaches are not **intrinsically** [emphasis mine] unsuited for analyzing

women in society. Rather the problem has been that most social scientists of diverse conceptual persuasions have not considered women to be important or interesting subjects of study. (Epstein, 1984:153)

While not all would necessarily agree with Epstein, feminist sociologists have found many established theories and methodologies helpful in understanding gender relations. For example, feminists have utilized theories of gender socialization or social psychological perspectives to establish the significance of learning in the acquisition of gender (Mackie, 1991). As most of the psychosocial differences between men and women are not innate, theories of learning grounded in psychology, have helped explain how gender relations are acquired through our culture and through agents of socialization such as the family, the school, the media.

In general, socialization theorists have relied on three explanatory models which delineate the way in which cultural expectations about gender are transmitted to the individuals in a society. These models are: the identification model; the social learning model; and the cognitive-development model.[1]

It is important to note that socialization takes place in the context of social institutions and these institutions pass on gender expectations that are consistent with institutional needs (Anderson, 1983). Both Anderson (1983) and Mackie (1991) emphasize that understanding the influence of socialization on the development of our gender identities encourages us to perceive how gender roles contour our behaviour and our beliefs (Anderson, 1983:70). It is equally important, however, to recognize that socialization cannot fully account for all of the complexities of gender inequalities. As Anderson (1983) writes,

If we limit our understanding of gender relations to a perspective on sex roles, we tend to downplay the significance of gender in the social-institutional framework of society. To illustrate this point, consider how absurd it would be to explain racism in society in terms of a role perspective. No one uses the term race roles to describe patterns of inequality between blacks and whites, although surely it is true that, because of racism, blacks and whites establish expectations of each other. Similarly, to assume that roles are the only appropriate framework for studying gender is to assume that consciousness, not structured inequality, is the sole basis for women's subordination. (1983:71)

The "sex role" perspective neglects the institutional basis for gender inequality and tends to view women and men as the "passive victims" of social messages, rather than active agents in their social relations. As a result, gender theorists have looked to other theoretical and methodological approaches to aid them in explaining gender relations. One cluster of approaches, coined "micro-sociological" perspectives, have proven to be useful in this regard.

The use of symbolic interactionism or symbolic interaction theory has provided feminist research with a conceptual framework that facilitates a deeper understanding of the socialization process involved in psycho-sociological theory. This approach explores the reflexive character of all interaction as people respond to their interpretation of the meanings of others (Hale, 1991:33). Generally, advocates of this perspective argue that behaviour is symbolic. Consequently, roles such as gender roles are not adopted uncritically as taught to them by various socialization agents but rather they are actively created by the participants—women and men. According to the symbolic interactionist perspective, the process of socialization rests on the ability of people to take the role of others. It is suggested that through a reflective process of envisioning oneself from the perspective of others, that people form their self-concepts (Anderson, 1983).

While the symbolic interactionist perspective has been helpful in the study of gender identity formation, it tends to remain within the confines of sex role socialization paradigms created by men. Consequently, it still fails to explain the motivation people have to comply to socially prescribed roles, "or how the world, made up of mundane typifications, actually exerts itself upon the perceptions, actions, and interactions of people" (Hale, 1991:37). As a result, feminists have turned to ethnomethodology and ethnomethodological research because it reveals the way in which sociologists and others actively work at creating their versions of reality that they claim to be studying "objectively." For example, some feminist scholars argue that much of the research data on male-female differences succeeds only in identifying patterns already built into the way the research was conducted. When the findings are reported as "scientific evidence," they come to represent authoritative fact and become the basis for organizing people's expectations, where "people who do not fit such experiences come to consider themselves deviant" (Hale, 1991:39).

Put simply, ethnomethodology focuses on the ways in which women and men, in their everyday lives, use their "common sense" knowledge and understandings to make sense of themselves and the world around them. Hale (1991) proposes that the central contribution of ethnomethodology is its focus on the practices by which people actively create a sense of what is happening in their interactions and how they actively construct their own actions to make them sensible to others (1991:101). However, this method does not take into account how larger social structures are created and simultaneously shape the experiences of women and men. Feminist theorists have recently turned their attention to examining how society is socially created to explain this process.

The social construction of reality, as a conceptual framework, begins with the premise that ideas emerge from particular social and historical settings and that this social structural context shapes—not determines—human consciousness and interpretations of reality (Anderson, 1983). Rooted in the ideas of Karl Marx and Karl Mannheim, the social world and how it is experienced in the form of ideas and consciousness, is related to the social structure, social institutions, and human culture—how experience is socially located. Feminist sociologists have used this framework to criticize sociology on the grounds that knowledge varies according to the social location of the "knower," and because one's social experience and consciousness are conditioned by the social location of one's existence, males (who have generally been the dominant figures in sociology) have developed a different view of the social world than women. To the extent that their situations or "locations" differ, their culture, consciousness, ideas, and conceptions of the world are also different.

By examining the social construction of reality, it is possible to recognize that what people come to know and experience as women and men is not just a product of social learning, but rather something that is actually socially produced by the practices and processes of institutions and the people working in them. Dorothy Smith (1974a; 1974b;

1975; 1977a; 1977b; 1987), who insists that knowledge and the social production of knowledge be socially located, argues that men and women live in worlds that are subjectively and objectively different. These insights question the whole notion of "objective truth" as an abstraction from reality. From this perspective, "truth" is in fact, constituted by real people in their everyday lives. However, as Smith (1977b) points out, this does not dismiss the centrality of macro social structures and their interaction with social consciousness. She suggests that people's everyday worlds are shaped by macro structures (social, political, and economic institutions) which are in themselves configured by socio-historical specifics.

To summarize, feminists have found axioms and postulates of several existing sociological models useful for considering new problems and incorporating women with their unique experiences to the study of gender inequality. The feminist dialogue with sociology has enabled scholars to examine the emergence and persistence of unequal and problematic gender relations in novel ways. There are currently several distinctive features of feminist theory and practice which can be summarized as follows:

> Feminist theory is that part of the new scholarship on women that implicitly or formally presents a generalized, wide-ranging system of ideas about the basic features of social life and of human experience as these can be understood from a women-centered perspective. (Lengermann and Niebrugge-Brantley, 1988:282).

Feminist theory is woman-centered in three ways. First, the starting point of investigation is always the situation and position of women in society. Second, women are treated as "subjects" not objects of research. Third, feminist theory is critical of existing gender relations and the inequalities they entail and works to produce not only better explanatory systems of the social world but to bring about changes in the social structure of society. Consequently, feminist theory is inextricably linked to practice.

The Feminist Perspective

It is important to recognize that just as there is no one sociological interpretation of the social world, there is no single feminist perspective. Within feminist thought, different assumptions and observations have created rich and varied analyses of women. For example, differences can be found "in political strategy, in visions about what constitutes women's liberation, in attitudes toward men, in understanding the roots of women's oppression, in setting priorities, in identifying constituencies and allies" (Adamson et al., 1988:9). Differences also exist in the theoretical explanations of how and why contemporary gender relations take their current forms.

Although it is not possible to present every feminist theory or political philosophy here, the following section outlines three particular currents of feminist theory that can be found in the literature.[2] They are as follows: liberal feminism, radical feminism, and socialist feminism. Each current represents a different interpretation of gender inequality and gender oppression though they share some common themes. This review provides an overview of the variety of interpretations found in feminist theory as to how social institutions reproduce gender and actually sustain gender inequality.

Liberal Feminism

Liberal feminism's explanations of gender inequality begins with the identification of the sexual division of labour, the existence of private and public spheres of social activity, the primary location of women in the private sphere and men in the public sphere, and the systematic socialization of children into adult roles and spheres appropriate to their gender (Lengermann and Niebrugge-Brantley, 1988:296).

The central theme of liberal feminism, or the cluster of writings and ideas categorized as "liberal feminism," is "equality of opportunity" which proposes that

> each individual in society should have an equal chance to compete for the resources of that society in order to rise within it as far as talents permit, unhindered by law and custom; wealth, position, and power should not be distributed on the basis of inherited qualities such as race and sex. (Adamson et al., 1988:9)

Liberal feminists are generally considered to be the more moderate feminists and base their philosophy on the proposition that all people are created equal and should not be denied equality of opportunity because of gender. Rooted in the tenets of the liberal political philosophies of John Locke and Thomas Hobbes, liberal feminism shares a belief that women and men have the same rational faculties, a belief that education is the best means to change and modify society, and a belief in the doctrine of natural rights.

Liberal feminist thinking has been called "mainstream thinking" because of its conviction that the existing social system is not problematic requiring revolutionary changes, but rather requires some modification and reform. In general, liberal feminism accepts the existing social framework (Adamson et al., 1988:190). Unlike their counterparts, liberal feminists do not regard the oppression of women as an inherent problem of the capitalist economic system. They believe that it is possible to eliminate sources of inequality by working within the system. By working within the existing social framework, liberal feminists have pressed for important reforms to benefit women. Such things as equal pay for work of equal value, maternity leave, provisions for daycare, and services for abused and battered women all represent improvements to the current system, brought about by the efforts of liberal feminists working on the inside (Mackie, 1991:257).

Contemporary liberal feminists, while tolerant of the existing system, are particularly critical of women's relegation to the private sphere. Betty Friedan's classic book, *The Feminine Mystique* (1963), was one of the first liberal feminist critiques of the ideology which defined women as primarily wives and mothers. Friedan argued that such an ideology was oppressive to women because it prevented them from developing their own identities. As a liberal feminist, she is critical of motherhood, marriage, and housework, but does not include in her analysis the possibility of structural factors involved in the oppression of women. Instead, Friedan examines the individual character of gender inequality.

As a result of their philosophical orientation, liberal feminist strategies for ending unequal gender relations often include the following: mobilizing women using the existing political and legal channels to initiate change (including having equal numbers of women in positions of power and authority); lobbying for equal economic opportunities; and introducing changes to the major socialization agents such as the family, the school, and the mass media to break the rigid gender roles in society. Those critical of liberal feminism suggest that these reforms only serve to make women a part of the existing structure, and do little to abolish gender inequality. It is argued that liberal feminists do not recognize the ways in which the patriarchal social structure, in and of itself, promotes inequality of opportunity.

Radical Feminism

Radical feminism is the antithesis of liberal feminist theory. As mentioned above, the liberal feminist framework emphasizes the enactment of sex role, the socialization process, and the denial of opportunities as central to the existence of gender inequalities. The radical feminists focus attention on how gender develops and persists as a social, political, and economic category in a particular social structure. The radical analysis of gender relations goes beyond the method of "adding women and stirring" proposed by liberal feminism (Bunch, 1977). Radical feminism argues that all dominant social institutions are characterized by gender, race, and class oppression, and therefore, reforming the existing cannot and will not eliminate inequality (Anderson, 1983:264). Furthermore, radical feminists view the social structure as something that is dominated by men, and used to systematically exploit, control, and suppress women (Hartman, 1981). This is in sharp contrast to liberal feminist thinking which views individual attitudes, not the social structure, as the primary factor that governs gender relations.

Radical feminist thinking begins by identifying women's unique capacity to give birth to children and how this is central to both their life experiences and their oppression (Adamson et al., 1987:10). Put simply, radical feminists argue that the social relations that determine the fate of women are the relations of reproduction. Central to the theory of radical feminism is the primacy of sexual, rather than economic power, and the power which men, or patriarchal society has over women.

This has allowed feminist research to move beyond studying the biological basis of the sexual division of labour and examine the larger issue of female sexuality and the issue of violence against women. In addition, radical feminism has been instrumental in identifying the emotional, social, and political differences between women and men. Finally, and perhaps its most significant contribution to the study of gender, lies in its analysis of power and power relationships. Patriarchy rather than capitalism is viewed as the main system of power, where it is defined as "a sexual system of power in which males have more power and privileges than females" (Lacombe, 1988:27). By adopting this explanation of power, radical feminists suggest that "the personal is political," or that there can be no separation between the private and public. Sex moves from the private to the public, where sex becomes part of the political landscape where women come to share in their oppression based on the expropriation of their sexuality as women.

In sum, radical feminists see all of society as characterized by oppression. Every institution, even society's most basic structures, are assumed to be systems by which some people dominate others. They suggest that their is a continual pattern of domination and submission between classes, castes, racial and ethnic groups, religious groups, and age and gender categories (Lengermann and Niebrugge-Brantley, 1988:306). The existing arrangements are said to benefit men—sexually, economically and politically—at the expense of women.

However, as mentioned previously, patriarchy is a pervasive and ubiquitous source of domination. Patriarchy shapes socialization practices and is embedded in institutional practices and ideologies. Consequently, radical feminists posit that it is often the least noticed and the most significant structure of oppression. To alter and transform the unequal relations between women and men, or break the pattern of domination and submission, radical feminists suggest that only by making women aware of the inherent inequalities of the existing social structure can they be free from the present patriarchal rule. They propose consciousness-raising groups to provide women with new opportunities to gain a sense of who they are and what are their rolcs—a process based less on adapting to or imitating current role models and more on recognizing the unique potential of being a liberated woman through interaction with women who share common experiences. Then together, women can create a new social structure, as opposed to adopting a new role in the old social system.

Socialist Feminism

A third current found in feminist writings has been coined "socialist feminism." This position represents a synthesis of traditional marxism and radical feminism "unified more by a theoretical agenda and less by substantive theoretical conclusions" (Lengermann and Niebrugge-Brantley, 1988:307). According to Adamson et al. (1988), the basic tenets of the socialist feminist position can be summed up as follows. First, socialist feminism is concerned with transforming the relations of domination between men and women and redistributing political and economic power more equitably across class and racial lines. In addition, this form of feminist thinking assumes that there are fundamental interconnections between the structures of political and economic power—capitalism and the organization of male power—which require a dramatic reorganization of all social institutions that perpetuate unequal social relations. Further, it is posited that because the domination of men over women is not biologically based but rather rooted in the social and economic structures, resistance and conflict are very real means through which social change can be brought about. Finally, socialist feminism values cooperation over competition, need over profit, and emphasizes the need for collective rather than individual action. In this way, socialist feminist analyses put forward a view in which the relations of power inherent in gender, class, race, and sexual orientation are not prioritized, but rather examined in terms of how they are interrelated, and how they reinforce and contradict each other.

Recent development in socialist feminism have been instrumental in distinguishing between the everyday gendered lives of women and men and the larger socio-economic, political, and ideological structures that are at once shaping and are shaped by human action. For example, socialist feminists contend that the sexual division of labour is a major organizing principle of capitalist patriarchies. The sexual division, in simple terms, refers to the processes of social, political, and economic activity which separates and divides the world into two seeming different spheres—the private (or the domestic) and the public (the political world of economics, business, and commerce). Or as Luxton

(1980) puts it, the sexual division of labour is "a distinct separation between workplace and home, between workers and family and between work and leisure." What makes the sexual division of labour important to socialist feminist analyses is the fact the women are often regulated to the private sphere and men to the public sphere, which works to place women in a disadvantage position. The following excerpt from Adamson et al. (1988) illustrates this where they write:

> Inside the workplace women are segregated [from men] in a few occupational classifications (in particular, clerical, sales and service work) where the wages, degree of unionization, extent of benefits, and chances for promotion are low. The current sexual division of labour between the household and the workplace in Canada means, for example, that the care of young infants is generally located inside the household and is a form of unpaid labour performed mostly by women. Finally, the sexual division of labour inside the household assigns women disproportionate responsibility for housework, despite the fact that increasing numbers of women are working for wages [outside the home]. (1988:110-111)

As feminists, theorists who have adopted this position oppose the conventional gender (or sexual) division of labour which places women in the home and thus excludes them from being full participants in the economic system (most of their work is unpaid labour) and the political system (reflected in the inferior legal status of women). The socialist feminists have played a vital role in focusing attention on the various aspects of women's work. For example, the fact that women's labour in the home is devalued, not respected, and generally not recognized as work because it is unpaid labour are just a few of the concerns raised by these feminist scholars (Luxton, 1980; Adamson et al., 1988).

In addition, socialist feminism has contributed significantly to understanding how gender relation are perpetuated by focusing attention on bow the state—as a source of patriarchy capitalist domination—affects the power relationships in other social institutions. They argue that the state (the government) is not politically neutral, but rather grants privileges to men over women, whites over people of colour, middleclass over working-class, and heterosexuals over lesbians and gay men. Further, these biases are said to exist at the very foundation of government policies, legislation, and institutional practices. Consequently, the state is posited to affect virtually every facet of people's lives, from welfare benefits to educational funding, immigration, housing, the administration of justice. All of which, they suggest actively produce gender, as well as class and race inequalities.

In short, socialist feminism develops an analysis of the social world in which the oppression stemming from patriarchy and capitalism is seen as an integrated whole that forms a set of unequal relations between genders, classes, races, and people with different sexual orientations. Further, the sexual division of labour, both inside the home and outside the home is considered to be detrimental to women because their work and the contribution it makes to the functioning of society is diminished. Finally, the functioning of the state is viewed as a process by which inequality is actively produced by intruding into people's lives and determining their fate through discriminatory policies, procedures, and practices. The socialist feminist solution to abolish inequality calls for the complete restructuring of all social institutions to eliminate barriers to opportunity, whether it be gender, race, ethnicity, religion, or sexual orientation.

In concluding this overview of the various currents of feminist thinking, two key issues must be addressed. First, as Mackie (1991) points out, "a fine line must be drawn between appreciating the ideological and tactical distinction we have just made, and exaggerating the divisive forces within the Canadian women's movement" (1991:260). In other words, students of gender relations should not rely on these arbitrary categories to define feminism, categories that tend to stress the differences between feminist ideas at the expense of thinking about the common concerns that have been brought to light through their collective efforts. Rather, students should focus attention on how these concerns have propelled women of all political persuasions and theoretical orientations to organize and actively seek the elimination of gender inequality.

A second, equally important issue, is the apparent neglect of ethnic differences and inequality in much of the predominantly white feminist writings (Hooks, 1984; Moraga and Anzaldua, 1981; Rollins, 1985). In general, feminist theory is representative of white, middle-class, heterosexual interests and therefore is subject to criticism for being inherently biased towards this population of women. All three currents of feminist thought are increasingly cognizant of this problem and are taking steps to deal with the experiences of Third World women, women of various racial and ethnic groups, and lesbian women.

Gender and Social Institutions

Feminist sociologists have used the varying theories and concepts discussed earlier in this chapter to examine the institutional structuring of gender that occurs in the many social institutions that make up any given society. All social institutions establish and organize patterns of gender relations that often result in gender inequalities. An analysis of gender relations in one of the most central institutions in contemporary society—namely the education system—illustrates this process.

Education is a pivotal social institution in modern societies. It plays a crucial role in gender socialization and the reproduction of gender inequality and oppression. Paradoxically, education is seen as one of the most equitable and progressive institutions—as the path to upward mobility in an ever increasing "credentials oriented" society. At the same time, however, it has been the sight of resistance and rebellion against the status quo as evidenced by the emergence of radical social movements on university campuses (Thibault, 1987). In this "most equitable" and progressive social institution, the gender of a child continues to be a key determinant of his or her educational experience and future life chances (Lindsey, 1990). The following discussion examines gender development and reproduction within the context of this apparent contraction.

First, the education system is one of the most significant sources of gender stereotypes and gender "consciousness" in modern society, beginning in kindergarten and ending in graduate school. The feminist critique of the education system has centered on socialization issues and structural issues. Conventional wisdom suggests that the business of education is the "teaching and learning" of knowledge, norms, and the dominant beliefs of a particular culture-that is socialization. Feminists argue that what is taught and the values that are imparted to students represent patriarchal, capitalist interests. Consequently, they propose that what is taught and learned in the education system is "man made" (Spender, 1985). Or as Gaskell (1988) and McLaren (1988) suggest, school curricula is not socially and politically neutral, nor is knowledge merely unbiased information presented in such a way that meets the needs of all students. Instead, curricula and knowledge tend to exclude women altogether and portray them in a stereotypical manner.

Evidence has generally supported this view. A number of studies have shown that the illustrations, language and the depiction of gender roles in textbooks provide children with explicitly differentiated gender imagery (Mackie, 1991). Other related empirical findings suggest that textbooks which teach reading skills, social studies, and even mathematics consistently reinforce the idea that females are less important (Spender, 1985). Research that has examined school readers has revealed that stories about females are rare in comparison to those about males. Further, the contributions of females in history, science, or government are rarely included in school readers. Finally, where female characters are present, they tend to reflect the stereotypical views of women—they are generally portrayed in nurturing—caregiving roles such as mothers, nurses, and teachers.

The curriculum involves what is officially taught but also what education theorists have called "the hidden curriculum." A considerable body of literature exists that suggests that the inequalities between the sexes is related to the hidden as well as official school curricula.

For example, little girls "learn" through their texts and the teacher's treatment of the material to be nurturant, passive, and dependent. They are encouraged, through the content of the course and the usage of certain language (i.e. mankind), and by example, to assume a subordinate role in a patriarchal society. In particular, women are taught that physical beauty, domestic competency, and their future roles as mothers and wives are of utmost importance to their future well being. Consequently, feminists argue that education is central to the perpetuation of the present inequalities that exist between men and women. Through the preferential treatment of boys found in the reading material and the presentation of course material, teachers' differential expectations of performance, the role of guidance counsellors in streaming boys and girls into sex-segregated programs, the pressures of peer cultures to conform, the gender inequality which places men in a superior position and women in a subordinate position is maintained (Frank, 1990).

To summarize, the education system plays an important part in stereotyping men and women into very static roles. Through the differential allocation of resources, differential curricula (both official and hidden), and the actual formation of educational settings, gender is used to both manage and regulate childhood socialization processes. At all levels of education, higher valuation is placed upon the male gender, by both females and males.

Notes

1. See Mackie (1991) for a thorough discussion of these models.

2. To find a good overview of the various feminist theories and political philosophies see Jaggar (1983) and Walby (1990).

References

Adamson, Nancy, Linda Briskin, and Margaret McPhail
1988 *Feminist Organizing for Change: The Contemporary Women's Movement in Canada*. Toronto: Oxford University Press.

Anderson, Margaret
1983 *Thinking About Women: Sociological and Feminist Perspectives*. New York: Macmillan.

Bowles, G. and Renata Duelli-Klein, eds.
1977 *Theories of Women's Studies*. Berkeley: University Press.

Bunch, Charlotte
1977 "Beyond Either/Or: Feminist Options." *Quest: A Feminist Quarterly*. 3(1): 2-17.

DuBoise, Ellen and Gail Kelley, et al., eds.
1987 *Feminist Scholarship: Kindling in the Groves of Academe*. Chicago: University of Illinois Press.

Epstein, C. F.
1984 "Ideal Images and Real Roles." *Dissent*. 31: 441–447.

Frank, Blye.
1990 "Hegemonic Heterosexual Masculinity." *Studies in Political Economy*. 24 (Autumn): 159–170.

Freeman, Jo
1973 "The Origins of the Women's Liberation Movement," *American Journal of Sociology*. 78: 792–811.

Friedan, Betty
1963 *The Feminine Mystique*. New York: Laurel.

Gaskell, Jane
1988 "The Reproduction of Family Life: Perspectives of Male and Female Adolescents," in *Gender and Society: Creating a Canadian Women's Sociology*, edited by Arlene Tigar McLaren. Toronto: Copp Clark Pitman

Hale, Sylvia
1991 *Controversies in Sociology: A Canadian Introduction*. Toronto: Copp Clark Pitman.

Hartman, Heidi
1981 "The Family as the Focus of Gender, Class and Political Struggle: The Example of Housework." *Signs* 6: 366–394.

Hess, Beth B. and Myra Marx Ferree, eds.
1987 *Analyzing Gender: A Handbook of Social Science Research*. Newbury: Sage Publications.

Hole, J. and E. Levine
1971 *The Rebirth of Feminism*. New York: Quandrangle Books.

Hooks, Bell
1984 *Feminist Theory: From Margin to Center.* Boston: South End Press.

Huber, Joan, ed.
1976 "Sociology." *Signs.* 1: 685–697.

Jaggar, Alison
1983 *Feminist Politics and Human Nature.* Totowa: Rowman and Allanheld.

Kaufman, Michael
1987a "The Construction of Masculinity and the Triad of Men's Violence," in *Beyond Patriarchy: Essays by Men on Pleasure, Power and Change,* edited by Michael Kaufman. Toronto: Oxford University Press.

Kaufman, Michael, ed.
1987b *Beyond Patriarchy: Essays by Men on Pleasure, Power and Change.* Toronto: Oxford University Press.

LaCombe, Dany
1988 *Ideology and Public Policy: The Case Against Pornography.* Toronto: Garamond Press.

Lengermann, Patricia Madoo and Jill Niebrugge-Brantley
1988 "Contemporary Feminist Theory," in *Contemporary Sociological Theory,* by George Ritzer. New York: Alfred A. Knopf.

Lindsey, Linda
1990 *Gender Roles: A Sociological Perspective.* Toronto: Prentice-Hall.

Luxton, Meg
1980 *More Than a Labour of Love: Three Generations of Women's Work in the Home.* Toronto: The Women's Press.

Mackie, Marlene
1986 *Exploring Gender Relations: A Canadian Perspective,* Second Edition. Toronto: Butterworths.

Mackie, Marlene
1991 *Gender Relations in Canada: Further Explorations.* Toronto: Butterworths.

Marcuse, Herbert
1972 *Counterrevolution and Revolt.* Boston: Beacon Press.

McLaren, Arlene Tigar, ed.
1988 *Gender and Society: Creating a Canadian Women's Sociology.* Toronto: Copp Clark Pitman.

Miles, Angela
1982 "Ideological Hegemony in Political Discourse: Women's Specificity and Equality," in *Feminism in Canada: From Pressure to Politics,* edited by A.Miles and G. Finn. Montreal: Black Rose Books.

Moraga, Cherrie and Gloria Anzaldua
1981 *This Bridge Called My Back: Writings by Radical Women of Colour.* Watertown: Persephone Press.

Pierson, Ruth and Alison Prentice
1982 "Feminism and the Writing and Teaching of History," in *Feminism in Canada,* edited by Miles and Finn. Montreal: Black Rose Books.

Rollins, Judith
1985 *Between Women: Domestics and Their Employees.* Philadelphia: Temple University Press,

Rozak, Theodore, ed.
1967 *The Dissenting Academy.* New York: Pantheon Books.

Ruth, S., ed.
1980 *Issues in Feminism: A First Course in Women's Studies.* Boston: Houghton Mifflin.

Sarbin, R. T.
1954 "Role Theory," in *Handbook of Social Psychology,* edited by Gardner Lindzey. Reading: Addison-Wesley.

Smith, Dorothy E.
1974a "The Social Construction of Documentary Reality." *Sociological Inquiry.* 44(4): 257–268.

1974b "Women's Perspectives as a Radical Critique of Sociology." *Sociological Inquiry.* 44(1): 7-13.

Smith, Dorothy E.
1975 "An Analysis of Ideological Structures and How Women Are Excluded: Considerations for Academic Women." *Canadian Review of Sociology and Anthopology.* 12 (Part I): 353–369.

1977a *Feminism and Marxism—A Place to Begin, A Way to Go.* Vancouver: New Star Books.

1977b "Some Implications of a Sociology for Women," in *Woman in a Man-Made World,* edited by N. Glazer and H. Y. Waehrer. Chicago: Rand McNally.

1987 *The Everyday World as Problematic: A Feminist Sociology.* Toronto: University of Toronto Press.

Spender, Dale
1985 *Man Made Language,* Second Edition. London: Routledge and Kegan Paul.

Thibault, Gisele
1987 *This Dissenting Feminist Academy: A History of the Barriers to Feminist Scholarship.* New York: Peter Lang Publishing.

1988 "Women and Education: On Being Female in Male Places," in *Gender Bias in Scholarship: The Pervasive Prejudice,* edited by Winnifred Tomm and Gordon Hamilton. Waterloo: Wilfred Laurier University Press.

Walby, Sylvia
1990 *Theorizing Patriarchy.* Oxford: Basil Blackwell.

Wilson, S. J.
1991 *Women, Families, and Work*, Third Edition. Toronto: McGraw-Hill Ryerson.

Wine, Jeri Dawn and Janice L. Ristock
1991 *Women and Social Change: Feminist Activism in Canada.* Toronto: James Lorimer.

Deviance and Social Control

Behavior that departs from group or societal expectations and/or violates social norms is usually considered to be deviant behavior. Common images of deviant behavior that usually come to mind are acts of crime. However, criminal acts as deviant behavior account for only a portion of all deviant acts. For example, a homicidal act is both a criminal and a deviant act, while getting drunk at home every morning can be considered a deviant act but not a criminal act since it only violates socially acceptable conduct, not legally sanctioned rules.

Deviance is often defined as a breach of trust, ignoring or defying social expectations that society defines for its members. We all are expected to play by the rules. Those who cut corners may be considered as deviants. In any given society, most people conform to the fair play of social normative system. However, some people, in every society, do not adhere to, and play by, the rules. They are the rule breakers; they are the deviant ones.

Nonconformity to social norms can result in either severe or minor consequences depending on a number of factors and circumstances. If a deviant form of behavior is considered dangerous, societal reaction may be severe. This is particularly true for acts that are premeditated. On the other hand, acts that are not considered to be dangerous or straying too far from societal expectations result in only minor reactions from others. In Canada, for example, picking your nose as you walk down the street may result in strange and disgusting looks from others. But this type of reaction is different from robbing an elderly woman or trafficking drugs to young children. Therefore, relatively minor deviations from social norms do not cause special concern to society, while significant deviations result in societal intervention to control the behavior and to punish the rule breaker.

It is not a simple matter for any society to divide its people into conformists and nonconformists. Most people, at any given time, are considered as conformists not necessarily because they have never deviated from any specific norm considered important by their society, but because their deviant acts have not been detected. Some people have more means to hide, or to defend, their violations of norms. Consequently, they do not become part of the statistics. It is asserted that those who violate social standards, or legal norms for that matter, and are able either to hide their violations or defend themselves successfully, are not considered, or defined, as nonconformists, deviants, or criminal persons, but their behaviors are deviant or criminal depending on the definition of the norm in question. For example, if a person smokes marijuana or commits adultery and does not get caught or proven guilty, the person is not a criminal or a deviant, but his or her behavior is criminal or deviant.

Social control is to maintain conformity and to prevent and reduce nonconformity in society.

Society will do anything to induce its members to live up to its standards whether they are social or legal norms. Every society tries to help its members to learn, internalize and obey its rules. Social control is easier and more effective if and when people internalize voluntarily the important norms of their society. Once internalized, the norms and values are considered as personal standards and as personal codes of conduct. In this case, they become part of one's conscience and morality. If they are not internalized, and enforced externally, some individuals may not feel bad about violating them.

Social control is applied formally as well as informally. The presence of police, courts, prisons, remand centres, and halfway houses, to mention a few, reminds us to conform to important and written rules. Socialization in the family, school, church, and peer groups, to mention a few, provides us with social persuasion and moral influence to obey social norms. Some people will argue that social control takes many different forms such as socio-legal attempts at preventing deviance, or threatening the deviants with punishment to deter them from deviance. Some may argue that, especially in Canada, the emphasis of social control is on punishment more than it is on reform. Some even go as far as suggesting that the agencies of social control are bent upon revenge, and not on justice. Whatever the argument, social control is to keep things under control.

Socialization, not coercion, is considered to be an integral part of social control. We learn and teach what is considered to be right in our society. Coercion may turn people off from conformity. But socialization, formal as well as informal, can persuade people to conform to socio-legal norms. It is considered to be one of the most effective ways to help people to internalize society's norms, rules and expectations. Learning from others in warm and close relationships such as a family situation, school and church organizations may help us to internalize society's norms more than the threat of retaliation from the police, courts and prisons. However, one must remember that the process of socialization is never complete: it is an ongoing process that starts at birth and ends with death. Nevertheless, Socialization sometimes is defective. In that case, people become confused and lose their sense of direction. That may result in some kind of deviance. Also what is deviant in one culture, or subculture, is not in another. The differential expectation of proper demeanor may, therefore, create confusion, especially for new immigrants, for they are sometimes perceived as acting in deviant ways because their behavior is based on code of conduct acceptable in their culture of origin.

Social control cannot function without sanctions. The positive sanction is rewards and approval, where as the negative sanction is punishment and disapproval. Conformity is rewarded and nonconformity is punished in every society. Sanctions can be used formally as well as informally. The spontaneous reaction of people can be used as an informal sanction just as imprisonment is used as formal sanction. A pat on the back or applauding one's good behavior is an informal positive sanction just as disassociation from the offender is an informal negative sanction. A presentation of an award, a medal, a degree, is a formal positive sanction and convicting an offender is a formal negative sanction.

In our teaching experience, quite a few students have tried to do research and write essays mainly in the field of general deviance and crime in society. We have, therefore, included in this section two chapters on Deviance and Crimes and Punishment in Canada.

In chapter eight, Bernard Schissel explains what constitutes deviant behavior and what the associated sanctions are. He also discusses variations; who is more deviant—the drunk driver or the automobile business executive who knowingly sells a defective product. Schissel introduces various theories of deviance as he refers to some of the pioneers such as Emile Durkheim. He provides a very good explanation and the review of related literature, as well as a systematic critique of various points of view in this area. He makes it easier for the reader to understand the relativity of defining deviant behavior. In this regard, the discussion on the labelling theory and ethnomethodology is very useful for our readers. Also discussed in this chapter is the social dimensions of deviant behavior. This includes mental disorder, substance abuse, alcohol related deviance, youth deviance and sex related deviance.

Finally, in chapter nine, John Winterdyk treats crime as a serious social phenomenon. He debates the issue of crime being equated with social control, and defines punishment for crime as he discusses functional and dysfunctional aspects of crime. Winterdyk Provides details on society's justification for sentencing that may lead to deterrence, rehabilitation, or retribution. He also discusses statistics and keeping track of crimes and punishment. As it was reported in the media (CBC The National, March 26, 1992 and the

Calgary Herald, March 27, 1992), violent crimes in particular and other crimes in general rose sharply in Canada during the last ten years. This chapter provides a timely discussion on violent crime trends in Canada. Also discussed are property crime trends, the risk of criminal victimization and the patterns of punishment in Canada. Winterdyk further explains the characteristics of adult and young offenders, women and crime, and the sociological causes of crime.

8

Deviance

Bernard Schissel

In the introduction to sociology, we found that the concept of culture was central to understanding society. To remind ourselves again, in our relationships with others, we interact with them channelled or framed by social structures. In addition to that, however, we are thinking persons who view our social behaviours through world views and mental maps. Within these world views, we have a sense of what we consider to be "right" behaviour and what is "wrong" behaviour. This helps us to "map" our relationships with others according to some predefined codes that are constructed both by ourselves and cultural systems.

However, we all know so well that, because we are free agents, we have freedom, at least relative freedom, to follow these codes or not. It is thus that we meet the concept of deviance which may be generally defined as deviation from cultural codes.

Then, in the chapter on culture, we were introduced into what McGuigan calls "cultural as code," which is the normative element of a culture. They are, again, codes which direct people to what is considered good or bad, normal or abnormal, acceptable or unacceptable, and desirable or undesirable. Deviance, then, is understood to be the breaking of society's rules or codes of behaviour.

Introduction

We know that social life involves people breaking society's rules. Some people violate the formal rules by assaulting others while some violate the informal rules by persistent staring in elevators or by chronically arriving late to class. Both types of **norm violation** are considered as **deviance** and have penalties attached to them.

As we will come to see, however, the issues of what constitutes deviant behaviour and what are the associated penalties are difficult to define. The degree of consensus regarding what is acceptable behaviour is highly variable. Who is more deviant, for example, the intoxicated driver who threatens the lives of pedestrians or the automobile business executive who knowingly neglects to rectify defects in a new product.

Variations, then, as to what is defined as deviant occur over time, over social group, and over society. For Durkheim (original 1897, 1964), for example, deviance depends on the characteristics of the individual, the social context, and the historical period. Others, such as Stanley Cohen (1985) and Michel Foucault (1979), argue that the definition of deviance is closely associated with social control—society's need or tendency to categorize and control the behaviour of certain types of individuals. Historical studies of conditions such as mental illness and homosexuality illustrate that definitions of abnormal behaviour have ranged from sin, to sickness to lifestyle, coinciding with the influences of religion, science, and the law.

The theoretical or philosophical approaches to deviant behavior are premised on one of two basic ways of viewing such behaviour: the **absolutist** and the **relativist.** The absolutist stance assumes that morality, and the rules that prescribe the morality, are inherent and unchangeable. Furthermore, the rules of conduct—definitions of good and evil, right and wrong—are assumed to be shared by most people. The basic problem facing the society, from this perspective, is the rule breaker herself and the focus of social control, then, is on either punishing or reforming the violator. As we will see in subsequent discussions, the absolutist explanations of deviant behavior are encompassed by a general category of theories called **consensus theories** and the focus of attention is on deviance **as norm violation.**

The relativist perspective challenges the absolutist. This approach, which is held by many contemporary sociologists, argues that because societies are complex, definitions of right and wrong are not generally shared, but arise from one group exerting its power over another, or arise from accommodation resulting from unequal groups in conflict. Morality is not a given but changes relative to time, place, context, social standing, political power, economic influence, etc. The basic problem facing the society is not the rule breaker but the rule itself. Relativist theories can generally be subsumed under the general category of theories called **conflict theory.** The focus is on deviance as **social constructed.**

The **interactionist** perspectives can include both relativist and absolutist perspectives. The interactionist perspective, however, is less concerned with the structure of the society and the origins of rules and more concerned with how individuals come to accept or reject rules. The focus is on shared meanings and values and the interchanges between people that result in deviance behaviour. This perspective is micro-sociological in that the object of study is primarily the individual, while consensus and conflict theories which are macro-sociological, concentrate on the structure of the society. As we will see in subsequent discussions, interactionist theories, like the macro theories, fall into absolutist or relativist categories based on assumptions about origins of rules.

Theories of Deviant Behaviour

Although the primary focus in this chapter is on sociological explanations of deviant behaviour, it is important to realize that there are other levels of explanation that are characteristic of other scientific disciplines. The basic levels of explanation other than the social, are the biological and the psychological.

Biological Theories

Biological theories fall into the general category of consensus theories. The underlying assumption in this general body of theories is that certain biological conditions cause bad behaviour and that certain types of deviant behaviour can be "cured" through medical intervention.

The original research using a biological perspective is typified by the work of Cesare Lombroso (1911) who argued that criminal behaviour was a symptom of a lower position on the evolutionary scale. Based on comparison of a sample of inmates and a sample of Italian soldiers, Lombroso found that, relative to the soldiers, inmates were typified by physical anomalies, such as high cheekbones, protruding foreheads, eye defects, poor dentition, and bodily malformations such as excessively long arms. Deviants were viewed as evolutionary throwbacks (atavists) which could be identified by bodily characteristics. The flaws in this type of logic can be readily seen when we consider the effects that prison may have on the physical body, and especially when we consider that the physiological traits that Lombroso identified may be stigmatized and may prevent individuals from leading a normal productive life or that poverty and malnutrition may produce both physical abnormalities and a need to engage in criminal activity. Lombroso's faulty logic and poor research design coupled with future research that failed to support his findings, discredited these particular types of biotheories and Lombroso's work is only of historical interest today. Despite this, we will see that altered versions of the biological approach continued to flourish.

The work of William Sheldon (1949) is one of the most noteworthy extensions of biological theories. In the 1940s Sheldon attempted to link body type to criminal and deviant behaviour arguing that certain body types—the ectomorph who is skinny and fragile, the mesomorph who is muscular, stocky and athletic, and the endomorph who is soft, round and fat—are associated with temperament and behavior. An excessively high percentage of criminals, especially juvenile gang members, were found to be mesomorphs which led Sheldon to argue that there was a cause and effect relationship between physiology and behaviour. Again, faulty logic seems to be at play; mesomorphs are more likely to be recruited to delinquent gangs, or judges may see strong athletic boys as more of a threat than other types. Like Lombroso's theories, the supporting evidence was weak.

Later, research into genetic abnormalities, created excitement in the medical and crime control communities with the claim that deviants were more characterized by genetic abnormalities than non-deviants. Specifically, Klinefelter's Syndrome was identified as a genetic abnormality where an extra Y chromosome is present. Where ordinary men have a typical XY chromosome composition; violent criminals were argued to have an abnormal XYY combination, and this defect was manifested in aggressive behaviour, large (excessively tall) body types, and mental deficiency. The resulting argument was that there must be a casual connection between the genetic abnormality and criminal behaviour (Shah and Roth, 1974). Once again, the subsequent evidence has suggested that the research and the casual logic underpinning these studies may be faulty. Even if the association between chromosome composition and deviant tendencies can be made, it does not suggest how or why the abnormality leads to deviance. It may be that the physical difference isolates individuals and restricts them from conventional society. If

XYY individuals have lower mental capacities, for example, it may be that they find it impossible to engage in conventional social and economic activities and that they are "driven" into the world of deviance. The underlying assumption is that the stigmatizing effects of an intolerant world may force deviant behaviour.

Despite the flaws in earlier bio-studies, biological research has currently gained a new life. Current sociobiological research in alcoholism concentrates on identifying the neurological or genetic traits of individuals with high risk propensities to alcoholism (Pollock et. al., 1986; Goodwin, 1986). As well, recent work on male predispositions to violence attempts to link evolutionary concepts, such as reproductive competition—which are characteristics of our lower primate ancestors—and status competition, with homicidal behaviour in male gangs (Wilson and Daly 1985). An interest in biological phenomena is also seen in recent twin studies comparing identical (monozygotic) and non-identical (dizygotic) twins. The basic research question in these studies is the degree to which twins of different types share criminal or deviant tendencies (Mednick and Volavka, 1980), and the overall findings suggest a greater similarity in deviant behaviour for identical compared to non-identical twins.

Although biological studies are compelling and persistent, they have gained little favour in sociological research primarily because the research has failed to control psychological and social factors which interact with biology, and, most importantly, because the implications of such research appear to be rather frightening. Certain policy implications such as genetic engineering and selective abortions of defective foetuses are considered objectionable goals by many people.

Psychological Theories

Psychological explanations of deviant behaviour, like biological theories, adopt the absolutist view of deviant behaviour and focus on the causes of the violation as originating within the individual. Unlike biological theories, however, psychological theories argue that character and personality is acquired in early life and is not primarily biologically inherited; the emphasis is on the mind and not the body.

For example, psychoanalytical theories concentrate on the improper development of conscience. Sigmund Freud suggested that personality is comprised of the id, the ego, and the superego. The id was envisioned as a part of the personality that all people had and that led us to aggressive, self-destructive, and antisocial tendencies, the more animalistic side of human nature. The ego, or the social self, and the superego (the conscience) were the dimensions of personality that held the id in check. Deviants, then were those whose ego and superego development was impaired. For Freud, this impairment starts at the earliest stages of infant development and is influenced by degree and type of parental training.

Some psychological theories suggest that deviance results from the frustration that results from unmet needs. According to the frustration-aggression hypothesis (Berkowitz, 1969), frustration leads to aggressive behaviour that may be manifested in outward deviant behaviour or in self-destructive behaviour. Bandura and Walters (1963) extended this explanation of aggression in a **theory of social learning** which suggested that people come to behave aggressively through a process called modelling, whereby individuals who observe the behaviour of others being rewarded, are prone to internalize the rewarded behaviour as acceptable. For example, much of this research focused on the influence that violence on television has on deviant behaviour. Simply put, if the viewer is exposed to depictions of deviance that are socially acceptable, then he or she may become insensitive to the deviance and may no longer see acts of violence, for example, as negative.

The types of vicarious conditioning that social learning theorists discussed were seen to be fundamental to the **theory of behaviourism**. Beginning with the work of B. F. Skinner (1953), behaviourism assumed that behaviour was instilled through reward and punishment and that, because behaviour is learned, bad behaviour can be unlearned. Eysenck (1977) argued that immoral behaviour is the result of improper conditioning; children never learn to associate fear and pain with bad conduct. Eysenck considered this conditioned fear as the basis of conscience. In this general arena of psychological research which stressed the effect of fear and punishment on moral development, the **theory of cognitive development** focused on how moral development coincides with stages of psychological and physical maturity. For psychologists like Jean Piaget (1932) and Lawrence Kohlberg (1969), the individual is the source of "badness' and as in psychoanalytic theories, deviants are characterized by deficits in moral reasoning. These deficits occur at certain stages of psychic development and deviant tendencies can be rectified by redirecting the individual through the appropriate stages of development.

Psychological theories have maintained their appeal in the study and control of deviance primarily because the emphasis on the individual permits the development of a treatment program based on psychotherapy. Therapies such as behaviour modification are still used in prison to establish conformist behaviour. The main criticism of psychological theories, however, is that they ignore the relative nature of deviance, that definitions and reactions to deviant behaviour depend on social power, social context, etc. As well, psychological theories have been criticized for ignoring certain major forms of deviant behaviour including violations committed by organizations (corporate crime), political crimes, and certain types of rational individual crimes such as credit card fraud. The sociological theories, some of which include elements of biology and psychology, tend to consider factors other than the act and the actor.

Sociological Theories

As mentioned previously, sociological theories of deviant behaviour can be broadly categorized into consensus (absolutist) and relativist (conflict) paradigms. This distinction, however, tends to ignore the **interactionist** tradition in sociology which is concerned less with the structure of the society and more with how the individual interacts with others in creating his or her "reality." Nonetheless, interactionist theories can be associated with the broad categories of either consensus or conflict theory and, in the following discussion I will locate the interactionist theories under these two categories.

Consensus Theories of Deviance

Consensus theories concentrate primarily on deviant behaviour and make the assumption that the rules and norms by which we conduct ourselves are shared and therefore correct. Morality is a given, and as such, the basic problem facing society is that certain people fail to conform.

Structural Theories

Structural Functionalism

Structural functionalist theories can be traced to the tradition of Emile Durkheim. For Durkheim and successive functionalists, deviance stems from lack of conformity and societies with a low level of social cohesion are characterized by high rates of deviance. According to Durkheim, suicide is a deviant activity that can be attributed primarily to lack of social integration and conformity. Societies which experience rapid social change are less likely to integrate and regulate their citizens, and will, as a consequence, experience high rates of deviance. The psychological state that disrupted societies engender is *anomie* or normlessness. Anomic conditions exist when value consensus is low and when societies fail to regulate or control their members.

Robert Merton (1938) extended Durkheim's work by emphasizing the influence that social pressures have on certain relatively vulnerable people. This more contemporary body of research has been discussed under the label of **anomie** or **strain theory.** Merton argued that anomic societies do not provide adequate legitimate means for people to achieve the culturally defined and accepted goals. The discrepancy between goals and the actual means to achieve those goals creates strain, and this strain, in turn, produces various non-legitimate innovations for circumventing **blocked opportunity.** Merton categorized five types of responses to the strain of blocked opportunity: conformity, innovation, ritualism, retreatism, and rebellion. Conformity is the only non-deviant response and requires no further discussion. Innovation, however, involves the acceptance of shared goals but not acceptance of the legitimate means of achievement. For example, an unsuccessful student may cheat on an exam or a fired corporate executive may decide to defraud his company. Most types of criminal behaviour fall into the category of innovation. Ritualism identifies activity wherein the means are accepted and the goals are rejected or altered. For example, Merton considered individuals who simply show up for work but do not accomplish as much as they can as deviant in industrial societies. This type of goal de-escalation is considered somewhat harmless and has received very little attention in research. Retreatism, on the other hand, as a response to blocked opportunity, has received considerable attention in research on deviance. Retreatists reject the goals and the means of achieving by "dropping out" of society. Mental illness, substance abuse, and compulsive gambling may all be forms of retreatist behaviour, and as we will see further on in this chapter, retreatist forms of deviance are highly visible in studies on social control and deviance, despite the likelihood that these forms of deviance are primarily victimless activities. Lastly, rebellion signifies a form of deviance much like retreatism wherein the goals and mean are rejected. Rebellion, however, constitutes behaviour which advocates new forms of achievement. Merton might argue that political rebellion, for example, is born of blocked opportunity, and that revolutionary activity on university campuses or the activities of the Black Panther civil rights organization typify forms of rebellion in response to blocked opportunity.

Social Control Theory

Like structural functionalism, **social control** or **deterrence theory** assumes that norms are shared by everyone, and, as a consequence, the proper subject for study is the investigating of why some people violate norms and others do not. Unlike other consensus theories, however, social control theory assumes that norm violations are attractive and that most people are motivated to engage in deviant behaviour. Simply put, man is a rational, calculating being, and he will choose to deviate if it is in his best interests to do so. This theory, then, is concerned with why so few people engage in illegal or abnormal behaviour, given that such behaviour has high utility.

The answer to this question lies in two forms of social control: inner and outer control. The former refers to the internalization of the rules and norms that are shared and valued by a majority in society. The acceptance of such rules controls behaviour because people experience guilt and remorse when they act in a deviant manner. Deviance results from a lack of moral socialization, a lack of conscience. Psychopathology, for example, may result from a complete lack of morality or conscience—the deviant is not moral nor immoral, but rather amoral.

Travis Hirschi (1969) focused on the degree of bonding to conventional society as a general determinant of inner control and moral conduct. He introduced the dimensions of attachment, involvement, commitment, and belief as components of bonding—as they relate to family, education and peer group. Hirschi's theoretical model suggests a behavioural as well as an attitudinal component to bonding, and measures elements of inner control, tapping the strength of conscience/morality and outer control by measuring the degree to which individuals respond to social pressure and proscription. Attachment is defined in terms of attraction to parents, school, and peers. Commitment involves an attitude to conventional aspirations in terms of occupation and education. Involvement is viewed as participation in conventional goal-oriented activities. The belief component involves an attitude toward consensual moral values, values which are perceived as generated by society as a whole, in essence, a measure of morality or conscience. For Hirschi, then, the greater the degree of bonding—as measured by the four dimensions——he less likely is youth deviance.

Outer control involves the various types of positive and negative sanctions that encourage normal behaviour and discourage or deter deviant behaviour. From this perspective, people who deviate forego social rewards like job promotion and respect from peers and may also suffer punishment, such as fines and imprisonment. Deterrence theory is a special case of outer control theory which looks at how people are constrained by official, state-administered punishment. For example, deterrence theory investigates the degree to which a certain form of punishment will inhibit (a) the individual violator (specific deterrence), and (b) the general public (general deterrence) from engaging in a targeted behaviour. Punishment is a concrete event and individuals are aware that it can happen to them—this information is taken into account when individuals rationally choose to commit or refrain from deviant behaviour. One of the basic premises of our system of law and punishment is the principle of deterrence/cost-benefit.

Socio-Cultural Theory

Socio-cultural theories of deviant behaviour focus on the processes by which individuals learn deviant behaviour. Cultures and sub-cultures are targeted as the "transmitters" of deviant values. This body of research originated with the ecological theories of crime and deviance attributed to the Chicago School of sociology. This approach concentrated on the spatial or geographical patterns of urban areas, and how these patterns were associated with levels of deviant activity. *Cultural transmission theory,* otherwise known as subcultural theory, arose from Chicago sociology and argued that deviance and crime were concentrated in certain urban areas and that deviance becomes part of the culture of urban areas. The deviant values that were attributed primarily to inner city subcultures, were said to be passed on from generation to generation and deviance was, then, based on conformity to subcultural norms. *Social disorganization theory* explained urban patterns with high deviancy rates as a consequence of poorly organized communities which resulted from disruptions associated with rapid in- and out-migration. Unstable populations contributed to inner city areas, for example, that had unstable cultural values and poorly defined mechanisms of inner and outer control.

Interactionist Theories

Differential Association Theory

Differential association theory extended both social disorganization and cultural transmission theories to explain how deviant values become part of certain subcultures. Sutherland (1939) maintained that criminal and deviant behaviour was learned in intimate association, and that if an individual is exposed to deviant influences that are viewed as favourable, then deviant behaviour is likely—the higher the ratio of exposure to deviant versus non-deviant definitions the more likely deviant behaviour will be exhibited. This theory then stresses the psychological process of socialization into a deviant lifestyle, and focuses attentions on the process of learning and evaluating moral definitions.

Neutralization Theory

Neutralization theory, which drew on the premises of social control theory argued that norms are not as rigid and well-defined as most sociologists have perceived. Sykes and Matza (1957) defined neutralization as a psychological technique whereby individuals use justifications for engaging in deviant behaviour that remove guilt and shame. These individuals do not lack inner control, but they do use certain techniques to neutralize inner controls. Deviance is not the result of attitudes and values that stand in contrast to those of conventional society; deviance occurs because of learned justifications which temporarily neutralize the restraints of conscience. Young offenders typify this type of behaviour, and were viewed by Sykes and Matza as characterizing justifications for typical kinds of deviance in youths, such as vandalism, substance abuse, and truancy.

Conflict Theories of Deviance

Conflict theories stand in contrast to consensus theories by arguing that society does not necessarily share a single set of values. Conflict theory can be traced to the works of Karl Marx and Max Weber (1969); Marx (original 1848, 1964) for his arguments that social inequality is part and parcel of the capitalist economic system, that conflict between social classes is the basic social process in society, and that deviant definitions are determined largely by the dominant class; and, Weber for his insistence that conflict can arise from sources other than class, sources such as political, organizational and professional groups. Nonetheless, Weberian conflict theory maintains that deviance and the corresponding mechanisms of social control are the result of conflict and compromise.

Structural Theories

Conventional **Marxist** theories of deviance argue that social conflict exists between those who control the means of production and those who do not. Those in control constitute a ruling class which controls relationships in arenas other than economy. This class is responsible for defining, identifying and sanctioning those whom it defines as unacceptable. Richard Quinney (1977), for example, argues that the ruling class uses the law to define certain types of activity such as prostitution and theft as deviant, while tolerating or at least minimizing the seriousness of corporate and organizational deviances, including price-fixing, safety violations, and workplace safety violations. The law, then, as determined by ruling class interests, can be selectively applied to maintain advantage for wealthy, powerful people. Chambliss (1969) has argued that we punish those people who can be tried and convicted with the least difficulty, namely, the socially and economically disadvantaged.

Pluralistic conflict theorists, like Marxist theorists, suggest that deviance and crime result from the use and abuse of power. Unlike Marxist theorists, however, pluralists see conflict and accommodation stemming from other than economic bases. Status groups, as defined by Weber, may gain power and privilege because of wealth, status, political power, occupational authority, etc. These multi-dimensions of power and inequality are the bases on which groups are formed and on which privileged or powerful groups try to influence the content and application of our systems of laws. The drama that is played out is one of constant struggle for influence.

Austin Turk (1969) argued that the law, rather than being an impartial arbiter of disputes, is a mechanism for expressing power and influence. Turk viewed status groups as dichotomized into authority and subject groups, and maintained that conflict arises when cultural, educational, and political differences between authorities and subjects are so vast that conflict inevitably results. Ultimately, in the struggle for influence, authority groups are most successful in influencing the type and direction of social control. For example, medical practitioners and researchers command a good deal of authority and respect, but they have, as well, a vested interest in ensuring that certain forms of deviant behaviour are defined as medical problems in need of medical intervention or control. The security of this status group depends on the successful definition and control of certain forms of deviant behaviour, exemplified by the increasing intervention of medicine into problems of the workplace; problems stemming from poor work environments are redefined as individual medical problems.

Interactionist Theories

Labelling Theory

Labelling theory, although microsociological in nature, accepts the conflict premise that social inequality is a primary condition when studying the definition and control of abnormal behaviour. Labelling theory, however, takes the notion of social inequality and the abuse of power, and searches for the process by which individuals come to see themselves as deviant or criminal. Central to the process of the *internalization* of deviant definitions is the argument that deviance is not naturally bad behaviour but that the deviant is one to whom the deviant label has been successfully applied. Howard Becker (1963) has suggested that "social groups create deviance by making the rules whose infraction constitutes deviance . . . deviance is not a quality of the act the person commits, but rather a consequence of the application by others of rule and sanctions to an offender" (Becker 1963:9).

Edwin Lemert (1951) has expanded this perspective by suggesting that initial acts of deviant behaviour, **primary deviance** comes from diverse sources which may include biology, psychology or social circumstance. For Lemert, however, such inconsequential and fleeting acts become important only when they are defined as abnormal. *Secondary deviance* is internalized behaviour which results in response to societal identification. As Lemert argues, "When a person begins to employ his deviant behaviour or role based upon it as a means of defense, attack or adjustment to the overt and covert problems created by the consequent societal reaction to him, his deviation is secondary" (Lemert 1951:76). Edwin Schur (1971) has extended this argument by suggesting that the process of becoming a secondary deviant is determined by negotiation, and that some people who so are labelled successfully defend themselves against negative labels. For Schur, the power to negotiate positive labels is based on individual self-concept rather than on social status or social power.

The social policy implications of labelling theory can be seen in Canada's Young Offenders Act of 1984. This legal reform stressed that the law must not contribute to the negative labelling especially of first time young offenders, for fear that legal identification was the first step on the road to a criminal career. The act, as a result, contains provisions for diverting youth from the formal justice system, and also specifies that the names and identities of youth must be confidential. The premise of this legal approach is that the police, lawyers, judges, court workers, and society in general, by identifying and publicizing the names and identities of young offenders who are relatively powerless, may contribute to further criminal involvement.

Ethnomethodology

The second conflict-based interactionist approach is similar in many respects to labelling theory but makes few assumptions about social inequality and the rightness or wrongness of definitions of deviance. **Ethnomethodology**, like labelling theory, is concerned with the social construction of deviance: abnormal behaviour is neither right nor wrong, but is defined by different people in different contexts. Ethnomethodologists study how we come to create typifications (stereotypes), and how these collective images of deviance are applied in specific situations.

D. L. Rosenhan (1973) and a group of research colleagues gained admission to mental hospitals as false patients whose false claim was that they heard voices. None of the pseudopatients was detected as a liar; all gained admittance to the hospitals. Rosenhan reported that although they all conducted themselves normally, they were diagnosed and treated as mental patients. Rosenhan illustrated how the hospital behaviour of the pseudopatients was reinterpreted by hospital staff to conform to the original diagnoses, and was further confirmed when the patients were released with their illnesses defined as "in remission." Such research illustrates how images of deviance, like mental illness, are held in common by people in authority, like doctors, who used these predefined images to reinterpret and reinforce initial labels or definitions. Although ethnomethodological research in theory does not concentrate on power and inequality, much of the research stresses the effectiveness of people in authority—psychiatrists, police, judges—in judging and typifying people of lower status, and as a result, falls under the general category of conflict theory.

Whatever theoretical perspective we choose to study deviance, the reality is that some rules are just while others are unfair, some rules are applied without prejudice while others discriminate against the underprivileged, and, certain types of deviance are more prevalent amongst certain categories of people than others. In this next section, we will discuss the social dimensions of rules and behaviours.

The Social Dimensions of Deviant Behaviour

Mental Disorders

Defining mental disorder is not as straightforward as we might think. Mental disorder is a condition which is exhibited in a wide range of behaviours. The DSM III-R diagnostic manual for psychiatry covers a wide range of diagnoses from the extreme **psychoses** of psychopathy or schizophrenia to the much less severe neuroses of phobias and anxiety. These disorders range from biologically based—mental impairment, organic brain disorders, schizophrenia—to the socially determined—alcohol dependence, traumatic shock disorder, hypochondria. Although I have implied that the origins of these disorders are either biological or social, there is a continuing controversy whether, for example, alcoholism is triggered by a biological intolerance or whether alcohol consumption is a learned behaviour that results in physical dependency.

Despite the ongoing nature/nurture debate in the field of mental health, we can show that incidence of certain types of disorder occur more often in some groups than others. For example, mental illness occurs most often in the 30-40 age group and then declines until the advanced years when age-related mental disorders occur. Social class also appears to be related to certain forms of mental illness—psychoses or the more serious forms of mental disorder are more prevalent amongst lower class individuals while the less serious types of neuroses are more prevalent in the higher classes. We might argue that poverty may lead to mental illness—through lack of health care, poor nutrition, physical injury—or we could claim that mental illness causes poverty by blocking legitimate channels for success. A third possibility might be that low status individuals are more likely to come to the attention of public psychiatric practitioners and are more likely to be recorded as mentally ill. Simply put, wealthier individuals can provide alternatives to institutional psychiatry, including private psychiatrists, private clinics and personal caregivers, and as a consequence, more financially solvent individuals seldom show up in official statistics.

An historical analysis of mental illness shows quite clearly that all societies and historical epochs are characterized by some type of mental deviance, and that the social control of the mentally disordered differs across time periods. The historical "development" might be best described as a transformation from sin to sickness to lifestyle and back to sickness. Szasz (1970) discusses the dominance of religion in the Middle Ages and the predominance of the belief that disease was a form of sin. The famous Inquisition and the organized witch-hunts that resulted sought out the mad and eradicated the evils of madness by eradicating witches. Many historians hold that witches were really the mentally ill of the Middle Ages, and that when science took over from religion during the Renaissance, medicine took over the control of the mad (Szasz, 1970). Szasz, like many others envisions the growth of the psychiatric profession as a social control agent; mental illness thus became the new concept to explain certain types of behaviour. From a typical relativist position, medical historians argue that scientific conceptions of madness are invented at certain historical junctures and that science and the needs of industry demand that unproductive and threatening people be controlled. The mental health industry thus developed as a rational response to the scientific orientation of the time, and asylums were to be the utopian "hospital" for sick minds (Foucault, 1965). As the science of mental illness developed, physicians increasingly looked to the organic brain and nervous system for the origins of madness. For Szasz (1970) the incorporation of science into the control of madness was a deliberate attempt by psychiatry to take and maintain control over the mad; psychiatry's purpose, he says, was to define and seek out new types of mentally ill people.

With the popularization of Freudianism, the scientific method gained new respectability in relation to madness. Freud and the whole psychoanalysis movement introduced the assumption that psychiatric symptoms arose from conflicts between biological impulses and socio-cultural forces. These conflicts were either resolved in the context of family socialization or exacerbated by improper child rearing. Freud was successful, as a result, in introducing the psycho-social into the arena of madness. The resulting "psychotherapy" model attempted to meld the medical/scientific model with the conception that medical illness not only resulted from bio-genetic causes but also from "lifestyle."

Conrad and Schneider (1980) argue that since the 1950s, there has been a resurgence of the medical model of mental illness. These authors suggest that the involvement of drug companies in the cure and control of mental disorder has ushered in a new era of mental health control that once again stresses the biological disorder and the curative/pharmaceutical response. Despite the decline of the asylum/mental hospital and the rise of community methods of help for the mentally sick, psychiatry has persisted in its search for the genetic origins of madness.

The historical research on mental disorder illustrates quite clearly that what we consider sick or deviant is not necessarily absolute, that institutional, political and social influences help determine the definition of madness as well as the acceptable means of its control. As this body of critical literature suggests, like the typical witch—women, the poor, the homeless—people most often diagnosed as suffering from mental health problems exist at the margins of society.

Substance Abuse

Deviance and Drug Use

The concern about the use of illegal drugs has become one of the prominent political issues of our time. Election campaign rhetoric brims with fear and panic regarding street drugs and moral decay. As we will see, however, the abhorrence of drugs such as heroine, cocaine, and marijuana is specific to this historical period and to our typical first-world, industrial society. As well, the definition of dangerous drugs is very closely tied to the medical/pharmaceutical definition of legal drugs, substances claimed to have medical usefulness.

An historical analysis of Canadian drug legislation illustrates quite clearly that at one time in Canada drugs like opium were accepted as part of cultural and medical practice. Comack (1986) shows that up until 1908, there were no restrictions in Canada regarding the manufacture, sale, or use of opium. Furthermore, opium was used primarily by the Chinese community and medicine. The prohibition of this drug, however, did not occur until Chinese immigration came to be seen as a threat to employment opportunities. Simply put, Comack argues that the Canadian state "created" the opium problem (which was directed against the Chinese immigrant and was facilitated by racist sentiments) as a means of diverting attention away from problems of unemployment and labour unrest. A similar history of the Marijuana Tax Act of 1937 in the United States shows that marijuana use was defined as a problem only at a certain historical juncture, coinciding with increased Latin American immigration and the expansion of the Federal Bureau of Narcotics (Schaller 1970).

While certain drugs seem to be targeted for control at certain times in history, other drugs seem to be immune from being labeled dangerous, and so remain part of the "legal drug trade" despite addictive qualities and harmful side effects. The pharmaceutical industry is responsible for dispensing medicinal remedies that alter moods and behaviour as much as illegal drugs do. Legal drugs, however, have worked their way into mainstream use and suffer very little prohibition despite their potential harmful qualities. Some of these drugs are abused through improper usage by patients and doctors, through attempts by pharmaceutical companies to find and market a pill for all human problems, and through the redirection of prescription drugs into underground drug trade. Stuart Hills (1980) reveals that legitimate drugs, because they are used primarily by mainstream society and are given legitimacy by medicine, are a real social problem but they remain uncondemned.

Alcohol and Deviance

Probably the most dangerous of abused substances in our society is alcohol. More deaths occur as a direct or indirect result of excessive drinking, more work hours are lost because of alcohol abuse, and more money is spent on curing alcohol addiction than any other type of substance addiction. Why, then, do we tolerate and perpetuate this social problem by advocating drinking as normal and acceptable and condemning excessive drinking as sickness? The answer may lie in one or more of the following. Firstly, the powerful brewing industry has a large influence on definitions of acceptable behaviour; through advertising and the corporate sponsorship of athletics, social drinking is associated with the good life. The brewing industry is a major player in the corporate world and much of the marketing of alcohol is based on advertising alcohol consumption as a means to popularity and social enjoyment. In essence, through the media and cultural socialization we are taught that drinking is a preferred activity. Secondly, the medical model of substance abuse suggests that the individual is responsible for excessive drinking because of his/her weak will or genetic predisposition. Overall, the medical model of alcoholism is based on excessive drinking as a disease and the therapeutic response is treatment of the individual. Psychiatric medicine, for example, treats alcoholism as a psychiatric illness that is treatable by drug or psycho therapy. So, despite the influence of socialization and media campaigns to encourage drinking, our society has decided that excessive drinking is solely an individual pathology. This is not to say, though, that individual cures are not effective. Alcoholics Anonymous has been very successful in treating the individual alcoholic. Thirdly, in western culture "taking time out" has become a social convention that is tied to success in the business, social, and occupational worlds. Lastly, alcohol consumption creates tremendous amounts of revenue for governments. In light of the aforementioned reasons for the tolerance of alcohol, little has been done to resolve the contradiction between society's encouraging of drinking on the one hand, and its branding people who drink excessively as sick or weak-willed on the other.

Youth Deviance

To understand the nature of youth misconduct and societal reactions to such conduct, we must first recognize that the types of deviance that create fear and revulsion in society are not typical of youth deviance. We must also recognize that rule-breaking behaviour amongst youth is quite universal, especially non-serious types of behaviour. Reports of a 93 percent delinquency rate in Sweden (Elmhorn, 1965, quoted in Corrado, LeBlanc, and Trepanier, 1983:33), an 88 percent rate for a national sample of 13-16 year olds in the United States (Williams and Gold, 1972), and a 96 percent rate for working class adolescents in England (Farrington, 1979) illustrate the point. In Canada, Frechette and LeBlanc (1978) have determined that 92.8 percent of adolescents between the ages of 12 and 18 had committed one deviant act and that 81.8 percent had contravened the criminal code. From a labelling theory perspective, inconsequential types of behaviour become important only when the violator is isolated for punishment and public degradation. Such treatment may affect the individual's self-concept and foster the internalization of a criminal self-image.

The assumption of universality must not, however, ignore the fact that certain types of deviance, such as murder, sexual assault, and gang violence are of considerable concern and importance to society. What is more important however, is that most acts of deviance, especially those committed by juveniles, are relatively inconsequential and transitory. Such a statement gains credibility when one realizes that most juveniles at one time or another, violate drug and alcohol abuse laws and vandalism laws. In fact, in certain contexts such as high school peer groups, types of norm-violating behaviour are outwardly condoned as acceptable. Most important, then, to any discussion of youth deviance is the concern that only certain types of deviance and certain types of youth are isolated for detection and punishment. To this end, we must realize that relativist views like labelling theory offer great insight into youth deviance because they suggest that underprivileged or marginalized youth come under the severest labeling and control. The mechanism of such discrimination is best illustrated by the landmark research of Chambliss (1973).

As we observe the historical development of juvenile delinquency we gain further insight into the changing and discriminatory definition and control of youth deviance and the changing nature of the causal origins ascribed to juvenile delinquency. Prior to the nineteenth century, no legal distinctions were made between juveniles and adults. Most historical accounts of pre-modern, pre-nineteenth century society, reveal the absence of an acknowledged stage of adolescence in human development. Simply put, teenagers did not exist. As Aries (1962) suggests, the family in pre-industrial life, especially the lower-class family, was much more community-centred than the modern family. As a consequence, childhood autonomy and independence fostered a rapid transformation from childhood to adult responsibility: "lower class children were mixed with adults ... They immediately went straight into the great community of men, sharing in the work and play of their companions, old and young alike" (1962:411).

With the onset of the Industrial Revolution, exploitation of children became commonplace. It is likely that the initial motivation to create a juvenile justice system was based on generally humanitarian and philanthropic concerns directed against child exploitation and that the concept of adolescence arose as a result of the "Child Saving Movement" (Platt, 1969) which was based on the principle of *patens patriae* the state was the ultimate guardian of the child. The Juvenile Delinquency Act of 1908 in Canada gave the state the absolute authority to intervene forcibly in family life, denying the family's right to due process in the law. Blame for juvenile deviance was placed squarely on the shoulders of families, and the reasons thought to cause bad behaviour were defective intelligence, uncaring parents, and poor home environments. The defective families were assumed by people with political influence to predominate in poor, working class and immigrant families. The juvenile justice system came to determine delinquency on the basis of unclear definitions such as truancy, immoral behaviour, and incorrigibility—definitions which served to provide the system with a wide range of discretionary power. A rather large body of research shows quite clearly that this discretionary power was used against poorer, marginalized youth and their families.

The Civil Rights Movement, coupled with the whole social reform era of the 1960s, gradually led to a reform of the juvenile system, the seminal stages of which have now been determined by the Young Offenders Act in Canada, passed by parliament in 1982.

The Young Offenders Act was implemented to correct the inequities of the Juvenile Delinquency Act which were responsible for discrimination against the powerless. Specifically, the new act addressed the problems of lack of access to legal resources and knowledge for certain people. In the spirit of the new act, implemented in 1985, young offenders were to have the same legal rights as adults. As well, in response to labelling theory, trivial acts of deviance (status offences) which were covered by the Juvenile Delinquency Act were no longer under the purview of the youth court. In essence, the new act melded the best of the due process model of justice, which was characteristic of the adult system, with the child welfare model, which was retained from the former juvenile court system. The underlying philosophy of our current approach to youth deviance is that young people are like adults; they are responsible for their behaviour and they should receive the legal rights that are accorded to adults. Our definition of adolescence has historically come full circle to a pre-industrial revolution view of youth as accountable citizens.

Sexuality and Deviance

The legal status of homosexuality is rather straightforward in Canada. As of 1968 when sexual activities between consenting adults were excepted from the Criminal Code, the Canadian state has had no legal right to intervene in the private lives of individuals. In the United States, the same trends toward legal tolerance are evident except that in some states, making love to someone of the same sex still carries criminal penalties. The historical trends toward legal tolerance, however, have not been accompanied by social acceptance or institutional tolerance. As we will see, the history of the social control of homosexuality is similar to histories of other forms of deviance such as mental disorder and drug abuse. Fear and loathing and state intervention have been based on ideas regarding the causal origins ascribed to the deviant behaviour and to the assumed dangerousness of such behaviour to society.

The history of homosexuality in the Western world is best described as the transformation from normal to sinful to sick to lifestyle difference. In pre-biblical time in ancient Greece, bisexuality was commonplace and homosexual behaviour was considered quite normal. With the onset of Judeo-Christianity, however, homosexuality was condemned as a crime against God. This redefinition and re-moralization of sexuality resulted in extreme forms of punishment from the burning of homosexual witches in the Middle Ages to the execution of a quarter million homosexuals in Nazi Germany—justified mostly by biblical teachings.

The institution of medicine is currently active in the search for the causes of and the "cure" for homosexuality. The origins of the medical model of sexuality dates back to the turn of the century when physicians addressed the problem of same-sex conduct from a genetic perspective. Homosexuality as a genetic phenomenon, was originally viewed as biological degeneration; it is currently viewed as a neurological difference (Time, 1991). Despite our view of homosexuality being somewhat less harsh than it was in the past, the search for its cause still implies a persistent belief that homosexuality is abnormal conduct. The medical assumption of disease/abnormality is best illustrated in psychiatric medicine which has only recently shifted its view of homosexuality from sickness to lifestyle variation. In 1973, the American Psychiatric Association endorsed changing the DSM-III diagnostic manual for psychiatry by removing the designation of homosexuality as a disease and replacing it with the designation of lifestyle. "Sexual orientation disturbance" was to be diagnosed only to those who were dissatisfied with their sexual orientation. Despite this enlightened transformation, subsequent studies reveal that psychiatrists persist in viewing homosexuality as a sickness.

The research of Alfred Kinsey has had a substantial impact on society's perceptions of sexual conduct. Kinsey's work in 1948 and 1953, and subsequent studies, startled North American society with evidence that 1) a considerable proportion of men, and a smaller proportion of women, had some form of homosexual experience (Kinsey reports 37% from men), 2) a substantial portion of those who experience homosexuality engage actively in the behaviour for a continued period, and 3) homosexual orientation is not fixed and may change. From these results, Kinsey and subsequent researchers have concluded that sexual behaviour is not an either/or orientation but rather a continuum on which most people fall not at either extreme but somewhere in the middle.

Perhaps most important in understanding sexuality in a North American context is the extreme prejudice against homosexuality and the tolerated acts of violence against gays and lesbians. The legacy left by religion and medicine has provided the legitimacy that has resulted in the persistence of a mythology surrounding homosexuality that has permitted discrimination and violence against it to exist. Homosexual men, for example, are not typically effeminate (they cannot be identified by their physical appearance, are not typically sexually active or passive, and pose no particular threat to young children—in fact, child molestation is more common amongst heterosexuals (Bell and Weinberg, 1978). Despite this kind of evidence, homosexual men and women have faced official discrimination within social institutions: during World War II men caught engaging in homosexual activity were classified as "psychopathic" and were given a dishonourable discharge (Conrad and Schneider, 1980); sexual orientation may be used as reason for dismissal or prohibition from teaching positions; and homosexuals are still denied access to hierarchical positions in churches, especially ministerial appointments.

Continued discrimination has led to politicization of homosexuality by gay rights advocates. The Gay Pride Movement, which started in the late 1960s and continues to the present, was a product of the political activism of the sixties coupled with an increasing awareness that homosexuality, as defined by medicine and religion, was a label that prohibited gays and lesbians from leading normal, discrimination-free lives.

Summary

In the first part of this chapter, I have described the numerous theories that exist to explain deviant behaviour. As numerous and as varied as absolutist theories are, they are held together by the common thread that morality is shared and that the rule breaker presents a threat to social order. For the various relativist theories, the common denominator is social inequality and the basic problem facing society is that the rules themselves are unfair. As we have seen from our discussions on mental illness, substance abuse, youth deviance, and sexuality, rules regarding normal conduct change over time and place. As social investigators, our task is to try and unravel the changeability of definitions and the changeability of punishments and mechanisms of control: if our morality is shared, why, for example, are some addictive drugs considered dangerous while others are considered therapeutic?

We might look, then, to the influences that people in positions of authority have had on social control. Historical research has shown that major institutions like religion and medicine, and the attendant authority that we have given to religious leaders and doctors, have had a substantial impact at certain points in history on the explanations for deviance and on the methods of controlling or curing rule-breakers. While we have shown that the power of religion historically gave way to the power of science in defining and controlling deviant behaviour, it is apparent that the influences of religion remain in many areas of deviance control, and that medicine, in spite of the criticism surrounding biological explanations, has persisted as a major mechanism in social control.

Finally, we must mention the power of knowledge production and the power of words in the study of deviance. The term deviance, itself, implies something negative and even in this chapter, when we study homosexuality as deviance, for example, we implicity assign a negative label to a type of sexual conduct. Similarly, when deviance is defined as sin, the implication is something wicked; when defined as a medical problem, the implication is sickness. The sensitivity and objectivity that sociologists struggle to maintain in studying deviance must be based on the realization that research in this area of human behaviour, however important, can be misused and misrepresented to the detriment of certain people.

References

Aries, Philipe
1962 *Centuries of Childhood.* New York: Random House.

Bandura, A. and R. H. Walters
1963 *Social Learning and Personality Development.* New York: Holt, Rinehart and Winston.

Becker, Howard
1963 *Outsiders: Studies in the Sociology of Deviance.* New York: Free Press.

Bell, Alan P. and Martin S. Weinberg
1978 *Homosexualities: A Study in Diversity among Men and Women.* New York: Simon and Schuster.

Berkowitz, L.
1969 *Roots of Aggression: A Re-examination of the Frustration-Aggression Hypothesis.* New York: Atherton Press.

Chambliss, William
1973 "The Saints and the Roughnecks." Society. Nov.: 24–31.

Chambliss, William
1969 *Crime and Legal Process.* New York: McGraw-Hill.

Cohen, Stanley
1985 *Visions of Social Control.* Cambridge: Polity Press.

Comack, Elizabeth
1986 "'We Will Get Some Good Out of This Riot Yet': The Canadian State, Drug Legislation and Class Conflict," in Stephen Brickey and Elizabeth Comack eds. *The Social Basis of Law: Critical Readings in the Sociology of Law.* Halifax: Garamond Press.

Conrad, Peter and Joseph W. Schneider
1980 *Deviance and Medicalization: From Badness to Sickness.* St. Louis: C. V. Mosby Co.

Corrado, Raymond, Marc LeBlanc, and Jean Trepanier
1983 *Current Issues in Juvenile Justice.* Toronto:

Durkheim, Emile
1897 *1951 Suicide.* Translated by John A. Spaulding and George Simpson. New York: Free Press.

Eysenck, H. J.
1977 *Crime and Personality.* London: Routledge and Kegan Paul.

Foucault, Michel
1965 *Madness and Civilization: A History of Insanity in the Age of Reason.* New York: Vintage Books.

Foucault, Michel
1979 *Discipline and Punish: The Birth of the Prison.* New York: Vintage Books.

Goodwin, Donald W.
1986 "Studies of Familial Alcoholism: A Growth Industry." in Donald W. Goodwin, Katherin Teilman Van Dusen, and Sarnoff A. Mednick (eds) *Longitudinal Research in Alcoholism.* Boston: Kluwer Academic Publishing Group.

Hills, Stuart
1980 *Demystifying Social Deviance.* New York: McGraw-Hill.

Hirschi, Travis
1969 *Causes of Delinquency.* Los Angeles: University of California Press.

Kohlberg, Lawrence
1969 "Stage and Sequence: The Cognitive-Developmental Approach," in David A. Goslin ed. *Handbook of Socialization Theory and Research.* Chicago: Rand McNally.

Lemert, Edwin
1951 *Social Pathology.* New York: McGraw-Hill.

Lombroso, Cesare
1911 *Crime: Its Causes and Remedies.* Boston: Little, Boston,

Marx, Karl
orginal 1948 *1964 Selected Writings in Sociology and Social Philosophy.* T. B. Bottomore and M. Rubel eds. Baltimore: Penguin.

Mednick, S. A. and J. Volavka
1980 "Biology and Crime," in N. Morris and N. Tonry eds. Chicago: University of Chicago Press.

Merton, Robert K.
1938 "Social Structure and Anomie." *American Sociological Review.* 3: 672–82.

Piaget, Jean
1932 *The Moral Judgement of the Child.* New York. Harcourt.

Platt, Anthony
1963 *The Child Savers: The Invention of Delinquency.* Chicago: University of Chicago Press.

Pollock, V. E., T. W. Teasdale, W. F. Gabrielli and J. Knop
1986 "Subjective and Objective Measures of Response to Alcohol among Young Men at Risk for Alcoholism." *Journal of Studies on Alcohol.* 47: 297–304.

Quinney, Richard
1977 *Class, State and Crime.* New York: David McKay.

Rosenhan, D. L.
1973 "On Being Sane in Insane Places." *Science.* 179: 250–258.

Schaller, M.
1970 "The Federal Prohibition of Marijuana." *Journal of Social History.* 4: 61–74.

Schur, Edwin
1971 *Labeling Deviant Behaviour.* New York: Harper and Row.

Shah, Saleem A. and Loren H. Roth
1974 "Biological and Psycbophysiological Factors in Criminology," in Daniel Glaser ed. *Handbook of Criminology.* Chicago: Rand McNally.

Sheldon, William
1949 *Varieties of Delinquent Youth: An Introduction to Constitutional Psychiatry.* New York: Harper and Row.

Skinner, B. F.
1953 *Science and Human Behaviour.* New York: MacMillan.

Sykes, Gresham and David Matza
1957 "Techniques of Neutralization: A Theory of Delinquency." *American Sociological Review.* 22: 664–70.

Sutherland, Edwin
1939 *Criminology.* Philadelphia: J. B. Lippincott.

Szasz, Thomas
1970 *The Manufacture of Madness.* New York: Harper and Row.

Turk, Austin
1969 *Criminality and the Legal Order.* Chicago: Rand McNally.

Weber, Max
1947 *The Theory of Social and Economic Organization.* New York: Free Press.

Wilson, Margo and Martin Daly
1985 "Competitiveness, Risk Taking, and Violence: The Young Male Syndrome." *Ethology and Sociobiology.* 6: 59–73.

9

Crimes and Punishment in Canada

John Winterdyk

Perhaps our worst crime is our ignorance about crime.
K. Menninger (1968:3)

The chapter on crime continues the discussion on deviance. What we said about deviance in the beginning of chapter seven can be applied to crime with the following proviso: when speaking of crime, we are focusing on one sub-division of deviance. Crime is the deviation from a norm that has been defined in a particular society as being a law. When we look at crime, then, we are necessarily including the state as a central player which is designated to act on behalf of members of society to protect their interests.

If one can believe media reports in Canada, then crime is a serious social phenomenon. Some recent headlines from a local Calgary daily newspaper include: "Calgary murders shoot homicide ranking higher" (Feb. 27, 1991), "Jail for youths too lenient, say ex-inmates" (Feb. 26, 1991), "Ferocious teens mob stuns cops" (April 2, 1991), "City police lay blame on weak juvenile law" (April 2, 1991). The picture portrayed by the media in many respects may only be the tip of the iceberg. Results from the 1981 Canadian Urban Victimization Survey show that based on the seven cities surveyed, 81% of the respondents said "they believed that crime had increased in their city in the year or two prior to the survey." A poll published by Maclean's magazine of Canada in January 1991 shows that compared to July 1989 more Canadians own a handgun and are now more afraid to walk the streets of their community alone at night. As John Hagan (1985), a Canadian sociologist noted, crime and criminality is a "hot topic" and whether the phenomena is real or apparent, there is no denying that it receives a great deal of attention these days.

The response of the Canadian Criminal Justice System (i.e., police, courts, & corrections) to this apparent increase in crime has met with varying degrees of success. Recent figures suggest that our criminal justice system is becoming 11 percent more costly each year, nine percent less efficient, and 8.5% less effective (Menard, 1987). Demars (1984) notes that Canadians pay nearly four times as much to maintain our system than in 1960 (adjusted to Implicit Price Index). Some interesting observations from a selection of Statistics Canada "Juristat Service Bulletins" include:

1. Policing in 1989 cost $4.68 billion. This represents an increase of 6.7% over 1988. This represents a per capita cost of $179 for every Canadian.
2. For 1988–89, a total of $639.9 million was spent in the Canadian court system. This represents a 5.8% increase over the 87–88 level and a per capita cost of $424.45 to Canadians.
3. As for adult correctional services during the fiscal year 1989–1990, total federal and provincial government operating expenditures were $1.7 billion. After adjusting for inflation, this represents a 10% increase from 1988–1989 and a 22% increase from 1985–1986. It cost over $115 per day to house an inmate in 1989 (an increase of 1% over 1988).
4. Legal Aid services are funded by three main sources. For 1989–90, governments contributed 81%, the legal profession 12%, clients 4%, and other miscellaneous sources 4%. Excluding Newfoundland, legal aid cost $338.9 million, an increase of 8% over the previous year.

It seems increasingly evident that social control of crime and deviance is becoming increasingly more costly and less effective. The implications of such a trend from a sociological perspective are numerous. It would appear that we are justified in viewing crime and our societal response as a serious social issue.

In this chapter we will explore some of the trends and patterns in crime and punishment in Canada. First, however, a brief overview of the concepts of crime and punishment will be presented so that the reader can better appreciate some of the issues raised.

What Is Crime?

> ...the inescapable conclusion is that society secretly wants crime, needs crime, and gains satisfaction from the present mishandling of it.
>
> Karl Menninger, 1968

As Rick Linden (1987), from the University of Manitoba, has noted everyone seems to know what we mean by crime but no one understands it. The dilemma stems from the fact that its definition allows for ambiguity. Hagan (1991:6–12) and Silverman, Teevan, and Sacco (1991:1–9) offer five basic definitions of crime which include: the lexical (dictionary), economic, psychological, political, and sociological. Each definition allows for a different frame of reference and perspective as to the nature of crime and its causes. In North America, however, we have historically favoured a sociological perspective which asserts that crime reflects some antisocial behaviour that is injurious to those social interests which rules of behaviour (e.g., criminal code) are designed to support. Another common sociological definition comes from the work of Emile Durkheim (1933). Durkheim argued that punishment is the defining characteristic of crime and that social harm is its corollary.

Regardless of one's frame of reference, the underlying theme appears to be one of (social) control. That is, laws are intended to encourage or force potential offenders to control their criminal intent in order to maintain harmony within society. In a recent book by Stanley Cohen (1985), he talks about crime control as representing a vision of control by those in control of power; Jason Ditton (1979) in his discussion of what crime is uses the term "controlology." This notion implies that crime is synonymous with control, or the lack thereof.

The issue of crime being equated with control has spawned considerable debate. Among sociologists, these debates evolve around critical or radical based theories. These theories tend to focus on the crime problem by examining society's social structures (e.g., institutions, certain relevant professions) and its control systems (i.e., criminal justice system). For example, why do some crimes such as computer crimes, embezzlement, insider trading, and political corruption, which are sometimes referred to as nonconventional crimes, appear to go relatively undetected? (see Goff & Reasons, 1986). And why are crimes like murder, treason, robbery and assault, sometimes referred to as conventional crimes, considered more serious than others? (Wilson, 1985). One explanation that has been offered argues that the likelihood of detection is related to the fact that conventional crimes represent those offenses recorded by the police and non-conventional crimes are those which are not officially recorded by the police. Also conventional crimes are those crimes most often committed by the lower and middle class members of society who make-up the majority of any society but have the least amount of political power. Furthermore, the differences in detection reflect the relative and evolutive nature of crime. By relative we mean that crime is not absolute. That is, what a crime is varies with time and place. For example, murder during times of war is often considered "acceptable," gambling is legal in some States and not others; and prostitution is tolerated in some European countries and considered illegal in Canada. Crimes which are described as evolutive refer to those behaviours/acts which at one time were not considered deviant or criminal but later become defined as such (e.g., environmental pollution, wearing of seat belts, smoking in public places, etc.).

In summary, the above description of crime reflects that there are very few (antisocial) behaviours which reflect unanimity. Kennedy (1989:11) refers to this principle as "a sea of conflict." Hence, defining the boundaries of crime depends on many social factors such as social harmony, economic stability, morality and ethical standards.

Space does not permit a detailed discussion of the pros and cons of the definition of crime and its various theories but suffice it to note that the subject of crime remains an enigmatic phenomenon worthy of investigation.

What Is Punishment?

The concept of crime and deviance seems to connote a negative stereotype, hence we generally view crime as being synonymous with punishment. But, as will be discussed shortly, not all crimes are punished nor are all behaviours which are punishable by law necessarily crimes. In fact, for some crimes it may NOT be to our advantage to punish the individual.

The French sociologist Emile Durkheim once noted that crime can be either functional or dysfunctional. That is, some recurrent activity (e.g., crime) or established institution (e.g., law) may actually benefit society or certain social groups within it. This perspective in sociology is referred to as a functionalism. One of the key contributors to this perspective was the American sociologist Robert Merton who is perhaps best known for his theory of Anomie (see Hagan, 1991).

The functional perspective, one of two dominant sociological paradigms of crime and punishment, has been instrumental in advancing the notion that anti-social behaviour is best corrected through neutralization processes involving counselling, guidance, and therapy. In criminology this perspective corresponds with the positivist school of thought (to be discussed shortly). The positivist or functional approach tends to downplay the notion of "punishment" in lieu of "treatment" and resocialization. This perspective sometimes takes the form of sentencing and incarceration—the backbone to our judicial and correctional elements of the criminal justice system.

Some of the key principles concerning societies justification for sentencing and/or incarcerating an offender include:

1. Deterrence: general and specific. General deterrence occurs when a punishment for a crime is seen as a deterrent by a potential offender while specific deterrence is the punishment of the offender.
2. Rehabilitation: when someone commits a crime, it is sometimes believed the individual was 'misguided' somehow and can be resocialized.
3. Retribution: Weihofen (1956) believed that we all, at some level, want to see an offender suffer for their crime and since the law will not allow us to administer punishment, we expect and want the State to do this for us. Denunciation: as noted in Griffiths and Verdun-Jones (1989), denunciation as a goal of sentencing is becoming increasingly common. By punishing/sentencing an individual for their crime, society (via the Court) is openly denouncing the act. Hence, the behaviour is meant to be viewed as an unacceptable conduct.
4. Just deserts: Andrew Von Hirsch in 1976 was among the first to actively promote this notion. Similar to Becarria's principles of punishment in 1764, Von Hirsch was more concerned about the punishment being proportionate to the gravity of the crime as opposed to its simple imposition. Although a noble idea, Blumstein (1982) points out that the notion of just deserts is somewhat ideal when trying to account for all the mitigating circumstances surrounding an offence.

The second dominant paradigm of crime and punishment, according to Chambliss (1976), is the conflict perspective. The work of Karl Marx and Fredrick Engels (1947) formed the basis of conflict theory. In essence, this perspective assumes that society represents an arena of struggles over a limited amount of resources between those who have and those who do not. Since it is believed that crime is more common among the lower classes, it is left to the ruling class to define crime as behaviour that disrupts the economic and political power of those in control or who retain authoritative positions within society. Hence, violators should be punished or have their liberties restricted as such behaviour would violate class structure and "social contract."

During the mid 1700s, the French philosopher Jean Jacques Rousseau supported a number of views which have provided justification for the punishment of offenders. In his monumental work, "The Social Contract," be argued that law and government were needed to ensure social and legal equality.

Rousseau believed that in accordance with the social contract the government had an obligation to protect the public by enforcing laws which control those actions which threaten the life, liberty, and freedom of society. In turn the public is to understand that any violation (i.e., crime) would be subject to punishment.

Philosophers like Rousseau (1712–1778), Thomas Hobbes (1588–1679), John Locke, (1632–1704), and François Voltair (1694–1778) have been referred to as the "enlightment philosophers" because of their concerns for social reform and their humanistic concern over societal issues. Their ideas for social reform and humanitarian principles spread throughout Europe and in Italy. Another reformer was Cesare Beccaria (1738–1794) who in his prophetic book entitled "Essay on Crimes and Punishments" incorporated the principles of social reform and humanitarian treatment of criminals. Beccaria is credited with having founded the Classical School of criminology. In his doctrine, he spoke against unreasonable and excessive punishment. He did believe, however, that anyone (i.e., criminal) who derives benefits without paying the price of obedience deserves some deprivation inflicted upon them in order to maintain equality—hence punishment is justified as a form of retribution. Some of his views on punishment still prevail today. For example, he proposed that:

1. Punishment should fit the crime. Crime should be measured in accordance to its material gravity. "For a punishment to be just it should consist of only such graduations of intensity as suffice to deter man from committing crimes" (P. 47–48). Man will obey the law because the penalty will outweigh the pleasure of the crime.
2. Punishment should be certain and prompt, not necessarily severe. Severity he argued would defeat the utilitarian purpose of punishment. "When a crime is of such a nature that it must frequently go unpunished, the penalty assigned becomes an incentive" (p. 85).
3. Punishment should be specific and fixed by the legislature.
4. The death penalty "cannot be useful, because of the example of barbarity it gives man...it seems absurd that the laws, which are an expression of the public will, which detest and punish homicide, should themselves commit it. (p. 50).

Many of these punishment principles have been embraced by our current criminal justice system. But, as is evident today, the principles do not always appear to work well. This is in-part due to the fact that as humans we are not as rational and logical as Beccaria would have us believe. His notion of free-will in choice is unverifiable, and the principle of punishment being certain and swift seems but an abberation today.

Therefore, when discussing the notion of crime and punishment, the two opposing perspectives should be considered. Should we punish in a punitive, retributive sense or should we view criminal behaviour as an unfortunate by-product of social stressors, mental deficiency, a consequence of poor diet which may affect our attention span or ability to reason, etc.? How do we deal with the fact that new crimes may evolve or others become relative? As with crime, the notion of crime and punishment is not an easy issue to resolve. But, it is a fact that in Canada, as in most Western countries, we continue to punish people who violate the laws of the land whether they be Municipal, Provincial, or Federal. An understanding of this basic dilemma should help one to appreciate some of the issues confronting our system of justice and what crime and punishment "really" mean.

We can now move onto looking at some of the trends and patterns of crimes and punishment in Canada.

Keeping Track of Crimes and Punishment

The most common source of statistical information on crimes and punishment are official statistics as collected by the police, Courts, and Corrections. Before examining these statistics, however, some pitfalls of these sources need to be identified.

When using any type of official data to study crime trends either at a regional, national or international level, they have to be viewed with some degree of caution. Chambliss (1889:32) goes so far as to suggest that anyone who uses official data is "making erroneous assumptions based on unbelievable data." He further argues that cross-cultural (e.g., comparing provinces or countries) studies are even more limiting in value because of a variety of problems such as ethnocentric bias, crime definitions, recording techniques, etc. By contrast, Brantingham and Brantingham (1984) argue that while official data may have its limitations, so does any other source of data collection (e.g., self-report studies and victimization surveys) and that despite some technical problems, official statistics provide our largest source of information and can provide "a large quantity of useful information about spatial and temporal patterns of crime" (p. 57).

Leslie Wilkins (1980) astutely noted that official crime data are not, strictly speaking, statistics of criminal events per se. Rather, they reflect police responses to social behaviour with respect to a particular set of offence categories defined by the Criminal Code and of political success. Therefore, as Linden (1987) notes, the study or use of any statistical accounts of crime need to be viewed in a social, political, environmental, and demographic context. Although it is beyond the scope of the Chapter to discuss these factors in detail, the reader should be aware of them when drawing conclusions or impressions.

The next section will explore the extent of violent and property related crimes as well as examine some facts about criminal victimization. Before you begin, try to answer the following questions:

(1) Is violent crime increasing in Canada? (2) Is car vandalism a serious problem in Canada? (3) Who is most likely to be victimized in Canada and why? The fourth section

will review the patterns of punishment for the major crime categories and examine how various social variables may affect police, judicial, and correctional practices.

Violent Crime Trends in Canada

Statistics Canada classifies eight crimes as being violent crimes (i.e., murder, attempted murder, manslaughter, rape, other sex offences, wounding, assault, and robbery). Since 1962, Statistics Canada has been using the Uniform Crime Reporting system for the definition and classification of offences. As Chappell and Hatch (1986) note in their review, over the years, due to various legal, social, and legislative factors, the definitions and classifications have varied somewhat. However, when studying anything involving a protracted time period variations are to be expected, especially given the relative nature of crime. For example, in 1983, Bill C-127 replaced rape with three levels of sexual assault (e.g., aggravated sexual assault, sexual assault with weapon, & sexual assault). Such changes have been even more pronounced for murder. Boyd (1988) presents an interesting chronological overview of how the definition and classification of murder has changed since our first Criminal Code in 1892. As recently as 1987, this crime and its punishment were being debated with great energy. Due to economic changes and the devaluation of the dollar, the crime of theft has been changed from theft over/under $200 to $1000 in recent years.

Notwithstanding these limitations, the violent crime rate in Canada offers some interesting patterns worth noting.

Aside from looking at the overall picture of violent crime in Canada, which admittedly is not "alarming" in the sense that it has not grown exponentially over the years, from a sociological perspective it is interesting to see if there have been any changes at a micro or individual level among the violent crime categories. Here we see that aside from a slight decline in the mid-1970s, the rate of violent crime recorded has increased steadily over the past three decades—46% over the past decade alone (Juristat, 1990, vol. 10, no. 15).

Figures 9:1 to 9:4 and Table 9:1 illustrate some evidence of violent crime.

Figure 9:1. Females/Males Code Offenses Canada 1962–1989

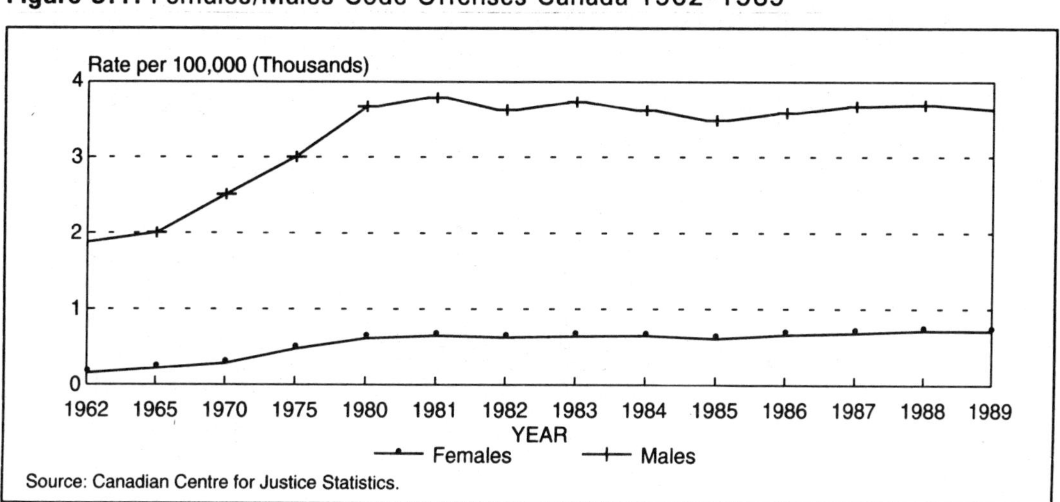

Figure 9:2. Females/Males Charged All Offenses, Canada 1962–1989

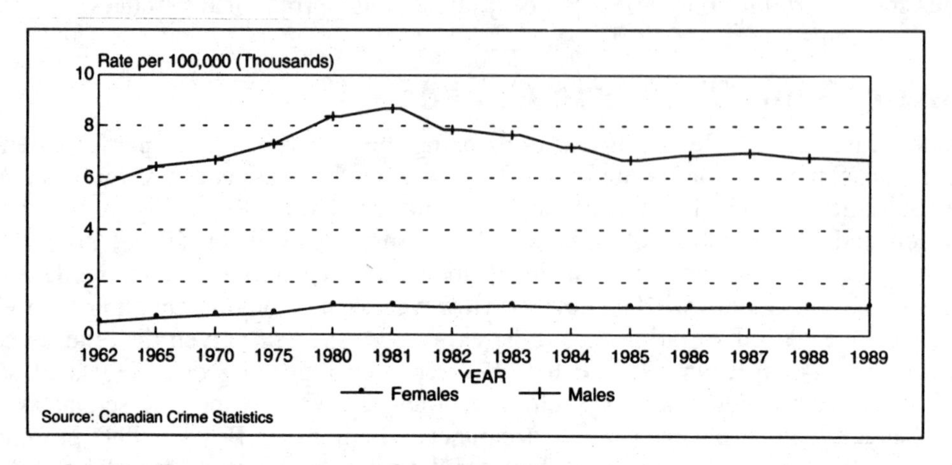

Figure 9:3. Homicide Rate in Canada 1961–1989

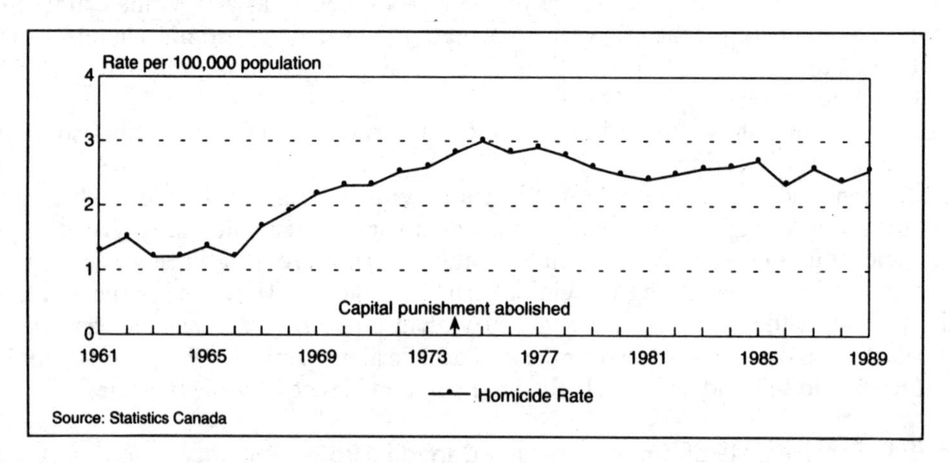

Figure 9:4. Violent Crime in Canada 1962–1989

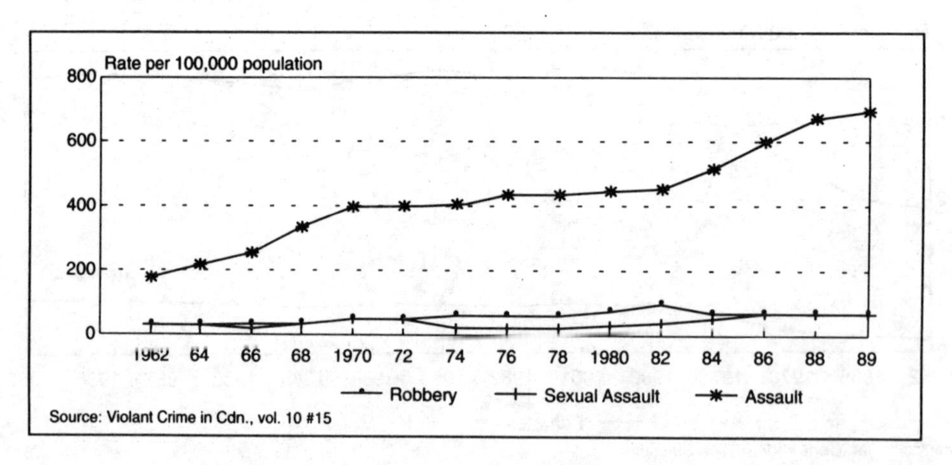

Table 9:1
Violent and Property Crime Categories

Crimes of Violence

a. Homicide
- murder 1st and 2nd degree
- manslaughter
- infanticide

b. Attempted murder

c. Assault
- assault level 1
- assault with weapon or causing bodily harm level 2
- aggravated assault level 3
- unlawfully causing bodily harm
- discharge firearm with intent
- police
- other peace public officers
- other assaults

d. Abduction
- abduction of person under 14
- abduction of person under 16
- abduction contravening custody order
- abduction no custody order

e. Sexual offenses
- aggravated sexual assault
- sexual assault with weapon
- sexual assault
- other sexual offenses
- other robbery

f. Robbery
- firearms
- other offensive

Property Crimes

a. Breaking and entering
- business premises & residence
- other break and enter

b. Theft motor vehicles
-automobiles, trucks, etc.

c. Theft over $200

d. Theft $200 and under

e. Frauds
- cheques
- credit cards
- other fraud

Other Criminal Code Offenses

- prostitution
- gaming and betting
- offensive weapons
- arson

Note: In addition to there being over several hundred criminal code offences, there are also several Federal Statutes which come under criminal justice jurisdiction (e.g., Restricted Drugs, Young Offenders Act, Liquor Act, Customs Act, Admiralty Act, etc.). Then there are Provincial Statutes such as the Highway Traffic Act, Fish and Wildlife Act and Municipal By-Laws ranging from cat laws to the use of firewood. It should come as no surprise then that the laws controlling social behaviour permeate virtually every level of our life.

Figure 9:5. Crimes of Violence, Canada 1985

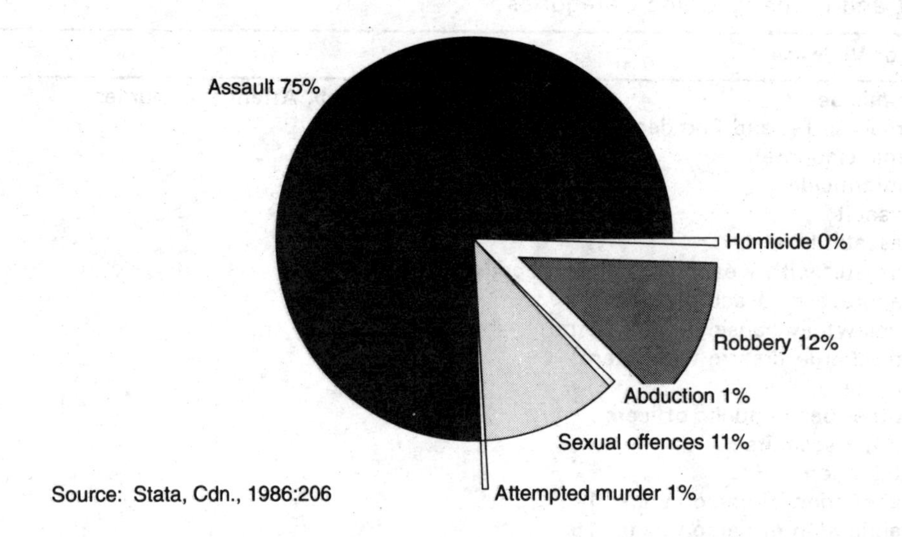

For example, in 1965 the rate of violent incidents per 100,000 population was 299 while in 1985 it was 749. However, according to the Uniform Crime Reports, crimes of violence have remained constant between 8%-10% of the total for all Criminal Code offences.

As can be seen in Figure 9:5, assault not involving a weapon or serious injury to the victim represent over half of all crimes of violence in 1989. Robberies with firearms have been declining since the early 1980s. But, the rate of sexual assault more than doubled in the '80s.

Contrary to what some people may be lead to believe, homicide has remained relatively stable between 1962 and 1989. It has ranged from slightly over one per hundred thousand inhabitants to a high of three per hundred thousand. In 1990 the rate was 2.40 per 100,000. By contrast, the homicide rate in the United States in 1989 (8.7) was three and one-half times higher than the rate in Canada.

Regina had the highest homicide rate in 1990 (4.72 per 100,000 population—see Figure 9:6), and the four Western provinces have had the most consistent high rate throughout the 1980s. Provincially, Manitoba has the distinction of reporting the highest homicide rate (3.86) from 1985–1989. At the other end of the spectrum, St. John's, Newfoundland, has shown the lowest rate for metropolitan areas (rate 1.02 per 100,000). It might be interesting to note that until quite recently, the St. John's police were the only Canadian metropolitan police force who did NOT carry firearms for protection (see Cdn police college journal).

Since capital punishment was abolished in 1976, there has been a slight decline in the national homicide rate but it is still above the rates of the sixties and early seventies. (see Figure 9:3).

Figure 9:6. Homicide Rates for 20 Cities 1990

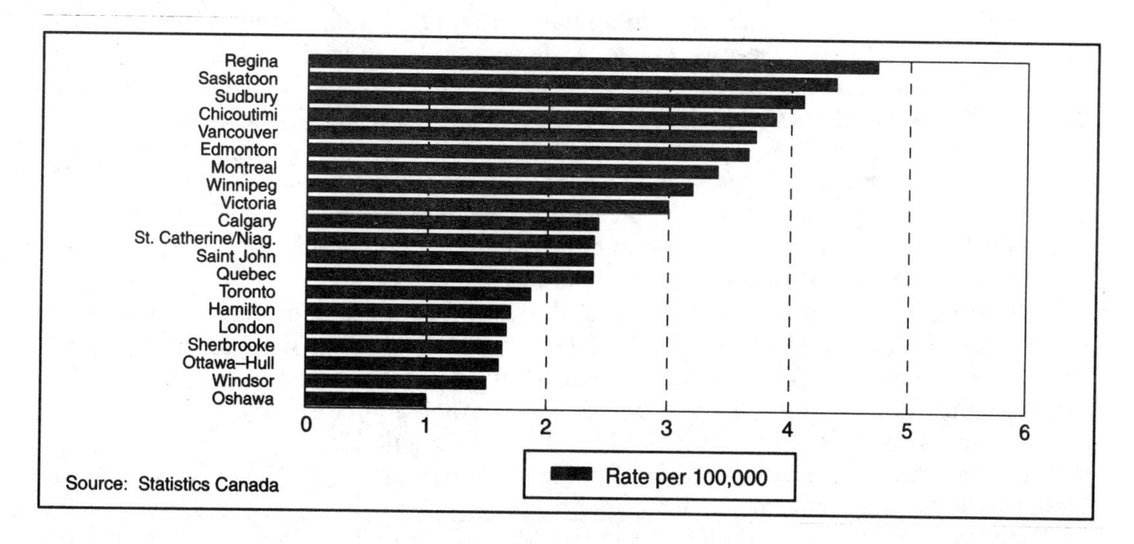

Homicide appears to be somewhat predictable in the sense that nearly 80% of solved homicides were committed by someone who previously knew the victim either in a domestic relationship (37%) or was involved as an acquaintance (41%). Not surprising perhaps is the fact that in 1989, one-half of all homicide victims (majority being women—64%) were killed in their own residences!

As with most crime categories, the age group 19–29 accounted for a higher percentage of suspects (48%) and victims (29) in 1989 than any other age group.

Perhaps because of its perceived seriousness within society, police annually typically clear 80% of known homicides. Of particular interest, as reported in "Homicide in Canada, 1989," of those homicides cleared, the accused committed suicide immediately following the incident in 46 of 657 (7%) cases, the highest number of murder-suicides ever recorded.

With respect to other types of violent crime and of particular interest to criminal justice administrators and sociology or criminology researchers is the fact that young males and adult women have increased as a proportion of all violent suspects since the early 60s. Conversely, adult males show a corresponding decline.

As with homicide, the majority of other violent incidents occur in a private residence and between victims and offenders known to each other.

Property Crime Trends in Canada

Although most people seem more interested in violent crime rates (e.g., read any newspaper for a few days), it is property related crimes which occur the most frequently in Canada. Based on 1989 statistics, a property crime occurs approximately every 4 seconds while violent crimes occur every few minutes.

The time figure for property crimes is conservative because it is a well documented fact that property related crimes tend to go unreported more often than violent crimes for a variety of the following reasons. (1) never detected, (2) too trivial to report, (3) police cannot do anything about it, (4) fear of reprisal, etc. Priority in occurrence is also reflected in how Statistics Canada records such crimes. While all violent crimes known to the police are recorded, for property related crimes only those crimes for which a charge/conviction has been made are recorded. Hence, for those studying crime patterns and trends, it is important to have a sense of the "dark figure" or hidden amount of criminality, that is, the amount of crime which goes unreported and hence officially unknown to the police and the rest of the criminal justice system.

Depending on which source one reads, the dark figure problem may or may not be problematic. As Brantingham and Brantingham (1984) noted, the dispute remains unresolved. Anyone using official crime statistics should be aware of the dilemma and if it is necessary they can employ other sources to enhance the validity of the data (e.g., self-report and victimization survey). This is referred to as triangulation and helps researchers to obtain a more realistic or valid picture of crime. (However, researchers studying non-conventional crimes may require a different approach).

Based on data available in the Juristat Bulletin, the following is a sampling of some recent property related crime trends:

1. In 1989, more than 100,000 vehicles were reported stolen. This represents approximately one in every 183 registered vehicles. Quebec reported the highest proportion of nonrecoveries. Compared to 13 other Western countries, Canada ranks 10th behind countries like France, Australia, England in the number of vehicles stolen.
2. In 1989, over 300,000 incidents of theft of radio/stereos, etc. occurred. It is estimated that such thefts alone account for three-quarter of a billion dollars annually! According to the International Victimization Survey, Canada ranks third behind Spain and the United States.
3. As for car vandalism (the wilful destruction or damage of a motor vehicle), Canada had the highest rate of the fourteen countries at 11.0% followed by Germany and Holland.
4. Since 1962, the rate of break and enter has increased from 442 to 1509 in 1981, after which we have witnessed a small decline (e.g., 1427 in 1986). And while being the most prevalent property crime, the solution rate by police has hovered around 24% for business premises and 20% for residential dwellings. Nearly half of the break and enters are committed by young males (2% by adult females).

Before we look at patterns of punishment of crimes in Canada, a few observations need to be made about the risk of criminal (violent & property) victimization. Until recently, victims received little attention in the literature. But today there are numerous Studies on crime victims and Canada has been one of the leaders with its Canadian Urban

Victimization Study and the work of people at the University of Montreal and Simon Fraser University in Burnaby, British Columbia.

Risk of Criminal Victimization

During the early 1980s, the Solicitor General of Canada funded a massive national victimization survey involving seven major cities and over 70,000 telephone interviews.

The purpose was to examine the extent to which Canadians are at risk of becoming a victim of a crime and under what conditions does victimization occur. Such information can be invaluable to criminal justice agencies in helping to determine who is at risk, the type of programs which might be required, and how to best educate the public as to their real as opposed to perceive level of risk.

The Study has resulted in a series of ten bulletins beginning in 1983 (i.e., Victims and Crime) to 1988 (Multiple Victimization). Some of the highlights include:

1. An estimated 4,8 million Canadians, 15 years and over, were victimized in 1987.
2. Approximately 31% were violent victimizations.
3. Forty percent involved crimes against households, motor vehicle theft, and vandalism.
4. The rate of victimization was 143 per 1,000 Canadians over the age of 15. However, the range is age and gender specific. For example, for single or divorced persons, the rate was 274 as compared to 88 for those who are married.
5. The rate of household victimization was 216 incidents per 1,000 households.
6. While British Columbia had the highest risk of personal victimization, Quebec had the lowest rate per 1,000 at 60. The results show that as one moves West, one's risk of personal victimization increases.
7. In terms of the type of person most at risk, it would appear that males between the ages of 15–24 with some postsecondary education, being single, living in cities, still going to school, and enjoying regular outings and drinking are most at risk.
8. Approximately 25% of Canadians, in 1988, stated they felt unsafe walking alone in their own neighborhood at night.
9. Women are more fearful of being victimized then men. Around 55% of the elderly women and 40% of women expressed feeling unsafe alone in their homes.
10. Urban dwellers tend to feel "somewhat" to "very" unsafe more frequently than rural dwellers regardless of age or gender.
11. Canadians generally have a more positive perception of the police in their communities than they do of the criminal courts.

12. Sixty percent of those victimized fail to report the incident to police because they do not believe the police could do anything.

While Johnson and Sacco (1991:98) suggest that an accurate assessment of the way in which lifestyle, exposure, and target suitability and guardianship affect victimization is still not possible, it is apparent that social and demographic factors play a major role in one's risk of victimization.

Now that you have a sense of how serious crime is in Canada, who is committing these crimes and how does the criminal justice system respond to criminal offenders? We will explore some of these issues in the following section.

Patterns of Punishment and Descriptive Characteristics

Under the British North America Act (1867), criminal law is a federal responsibility. That is, the federal government in accordance with Section 91(27) of the Act has the power to legislate all criminal law for the country. However, under Section 92(14), the provinces are empowered to administer justice. The result being that Canada has a three tier system for administering justice throughout the country (see Figure 9:7).

Figure 9:7. Administration of Justice in Canada: Governmental Agencies

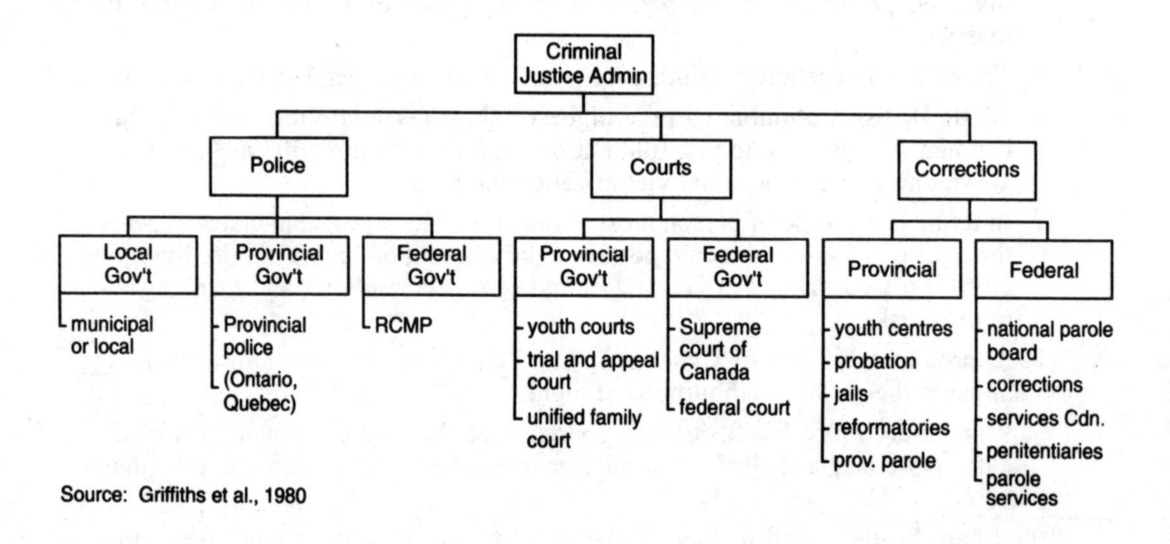

Source: Griffiths et al., 1980

Each year Statistics Canada produces justice statistics for the country which are available to the public and will serve as the primary source of information for the trends and patterns of punishment in Canada.

Characteristics of Adult Offenders

While Canada borders on the United States, its crime and punishment trends and patterns do not necessarily mirror those of its neighbor. For example, Canada does not have the death penalty, parole is still used across the country, trial by jury is less frequently used, and violent and property crime rates are considerably lower than in the United States. But according to Linden (1987), among others, Canada still has a comparatively high crime rate and is considered one of the more punitive of the western nations. For example, Corrections Service of Canada recently (1990) released some figures comparing the imprisonment rate for adults from fifteen different countries. While the United States had the rate of 413 per 100,000 inhabitants, Canada's is 106, the United Kingdom's is 97.4, for Sweden it is 56, and the lowest being The Netherlands at 40 per 100,000 inhabitants. According to the same report, the typical Canadian federal male inmate is:

- age 20–34	64.5%
- single	49.0
- common law spouse	26.0
- married	13.2
- serving his first penitentiary term	60.7
- serving a sentence for break and enter, robbery or murder	52.0

The typical federal female inmate is:

- age 20–34	58.9
- single	45.0
- common law spouse	16.1
- married	15.0
- serving her first penitentiary term	83.1
- serving a sentence for murder, manslaughter, or robbery	51.2

With respect to racial background, in 1989, 84% of the male inmate population was Caucasian while 10.6% was Native. As for the female inmate population, 75% were Caucasian and 14.4% Native.

Women and Crime

Criminologists have become increasingly interested in female offenders. Today there are journals dedicated to the study of female offenders (e.g., Canadian Journal of Women and the Law), a growing number of textbooks (e.g., *Too few to count: Canadian women in conflict with the law,* E. Adelberg and C. Currie (eds.), 1987). Even the feminist movement has had an impact on theories used to describe crime and female criminality (see Daly & Chesney-Lind, 1988). Perhaps one of the more progressive theories to acknowledge the work and ideas of women is the British Left Realism school (see Thomas & O'Maolchatha, 1989).

Whereas in the past women were perceived as victims of crime, we are increasingly recognizing their involvement in criminal activity (Chunn & Gavigan, 1991). In 1989, one woman in 100 was charged with a crime compared to seven in 100 men (Juristat, 1990, vol. 10, no. 20). And while women still account for a relatively small percentage of all adult crime (15% in 1989), their rate of involvement has almost tripled since 1962 (476 vs. 1,092 in 1989). Needless to say this increase has further added to an already burdened criminal justice system.

Since 1962 women's overall involvement in violent crime went from 4% to 10%, and for property offences from 7% to 23%. According to the Juristat Bulletin, since 1962, the rate of women involved in violent and property crime increased dramatically when compared to men. For example, for violent crime, the female rate went up 527% in nearly thirty years compared to 207% for men over the same period of time.

Not surprising, given social attitudes towards women, statistics on sentencing practices reveal that for 1989–90 young females received sentences one-third the length of those of young males. No information is available as of yet on proceedings involving adults. However, for adult women the data shows that probation is being more widely used than either federal or provincial corrections. And while the admission rates to correctional facilities have remained relatively stable since the early 1980s (3% of all admission to federal custody and 8% to provincial custody), the percentage change for women being placed on probation went from 15% in 1979–80 to 17% in 1989–90.

Characteristics of Young Offenders

In 1989/90, 52,432 cases were heard in youth courts according to a special Juristat Bulletin from the Canadian Center for Justice Statistics. About half of the dispositions handed down by the youth courts were terms of probation while 23% of the dispositions involved terms of custody, either secure or open. With regard to custody dispositions, the length of custody was shorter. There was a 33% drop for orders of six months or more and an increase for orders of one month or less (18%).

Since 1986, probation has remained the most frequent disposition order by the courts while fines were the most frequent disposition for cases relating to "Other Federal Statute" offences (e.g., driving under the influence & possession of narcotics).

With these definitions and statistics in mind, the final section of this chapter turns to consider some of the major sociological explanations of crime. Before you begin, on a separate sheet of paper write down some of the factors you consider to be most important in helping to understand the causes of crime. Try to offer a brief explanation as to why you feel this way. For example, does one's education, type of upbringing, one's ability to "fit-in," or watching too much television play any role in crime and delinquency?

Sociological Causes of Crime

Throughout the past several decades researchers have offered many explanations to explain the crime trends and offered numerous recommendations to solve the increasing "headaches" confronting justice administration. But to paraphrase an extremely controversial observation from Robert Martinson in 1974, nothing seems to be working very well. Crime continues to increase and the cost to combat the problem also increases. It would appear to be a losing battle. Such observations are also compounded by the fact that the public appears to be feeling less trusting of the criminal justice system.

One of the reasons why we may not be able to deal with this growing dilemma is because of the varied frames of reference used to tackle the issue. It is all in how you look at it! Recently, the Brantingham's observed that:

> full crime analysis has four dimensions: a legal dimension, an offender dimension, a victim or target dimension, and a spatio-temporal or locational dimension. Moreover, those dimensions must be understood and interpreted against a complex historical and situational backcloth of social, economic, political, biological and physical characteristics that sets the context in which all dimensions of crime are contained. (1991:2)

Hence criminologists, over the years, have developed a variety of theoretical approaches to explain crime and criminality. A summary of some of the leading or key perspectives follows.

Hartnagel and Lee (1990), using Canadian statistics, tested a number of popular urban crime theories: urbanization theory, inequality theory, composition theory, and opportunity theory. The only theory for which they were able to provide strong support based on the statistical analysis was the opportunity theory. The opportunity theory as used by Hartnagel and Lee is based on Cohen and Felson's routine activities model (1979). They argued that routine activity patterns can influence crime rates based on three fundamental factors interacting within a particular time and space. The three factors include: (1) a motivated offender, (2) a suitable target, and (3) the lack of capable guardians of that target. Cohen and Felson argued that any of these elements can potentially increase the opportunity for certain predatory type crimes by allowing the motivated individual to pursue their target with relative minimal risk of detection at the given moment and place. For example, if you leave the garage door open (point #3) with your new mountain bike clearly visible (point #2) and a young person who has been thinking about a new mountain bike walks by alone and unnoticed (point #1) you might well risk losing your bike. Many break-and-enter specialists realize that stolen property is usually replaced by insurance and that over a relative short period of time the owner is likely to let down their guard. Hence, many break and enter victims become repeat victims. This can be explained via the routine activity model.

Based on their results, however, Hartnagel and Lee suggest that further research into refining Cohen and Felson's opportunity model is needed since there appear to be interaction effects the model is not capable of accounting for. But Canadian researchers like Keonig (1987) have found considerable support for the model.

Another interesting approach, which has received considerable attention, has been the work of the Paul and Patricia Brantingham (1991) in the area of environmental criminology. Based loosely on a variation of the opportunity model, they note that in order for a crime to be committed three basic ingredients are necessary. First there must be a motivation to commit a crime, then one must have the basic skill to execute the offence and third the opportunity (time, location, etc.) must be present. They argue that all three ingredients are needed before a criminal act can be committed. For example, if you do not know how to "hot wire" a car, no matter how motivated you might be, you are not likely to be able to steal it. However, all things being equal (i.e., motivation, skill & opportunity) why do some people choose to commit a crime while others do not?

Environmental criminologists acknowledge that crimes occur neither randomly nor uniformly in time and space (see Brantingham & Brantingham, 1989; Cohen & Felson, 1979; Gottfredson & Hirschi, 1990; Kennedy & Ford, 1990). Instead there appears to be a complex interaction between the location, routine movement of victims and offenders, and individual perceptions. Brantingham and Brantingham (1991:240) note that many conventional crimes "reflect patterns of consistent decisions." Therefore, many environmental criminologists argue that many crimes can be understood via this model. For example, research has shown that convenience store robberies are committed in a particular manner by particular offender types.

Knowledge of this has helped reduce the victimization rate considerably over the past number of years. Similar knowledge has helped communities develop effective crime prevention programs. By adding street lights (maximize the chance of being seen) or introducing Block Watch into a community have had dramatic effects on reducing predatory type crimes. More recently we are witnessing the mobilization of community groups in drug infested ghettos who are being very successful at driving the drug gangs out of formally established neighborhoods. These programs are all aimed at trying to reduce, if not, eliminate prior opportunity. Based on a review of the literature they report that property crimes can be understood in terms of the temporal and spatial location. For example, researchers have demonstrated that different types of property crimes reflect different types of behavioral characteristics on behalf of the offender. They note however that the model is limited in terms of the types of behaviors which have been adequately studied. They include such crimes as serial murder, prostitution, and many forms of nuisance crimes.

While the Brantinghams acknowledge that much work still needs to be done in the area of environmental criminology, one of its strongest appeals is the fact that once a crime is "understood," responses by criminal justice agencies can be more proactive than reactive. And as they conclude:

> environmental criminology and related studies should increase in specificity and complexity, they should also begin to find the details of strong patterns that cross types of crimes, a variety of positions on the opportunity backcloth and a variety of motivation factor patterns, and thus return to a conceptually simpler theory. (p. 251)

Space does not permit us to explore the wide range of other sociologically based theories of crime. Therefore, Figure 9:8 presents a summary of a number of traditional and more recent sociological theories being used.

The Role of Prediction Variables in Crime

A final area worth briefly mentioning involves the use of predictor variables to help explain crime and punishment trends. Gabor (1986) identifies four primary information gathering methods to enable the development of prediction models. They include:

1. Official crime data collected by the police, courts, and corrections. And while such data is collected regularly there have been numerous studies showing that certain crimes remain relatively undetected and unreported. Hence, with the exception of a few crimes and certain offender types, such information is of limited predictive value.

Figure 9:8. Sampling of Sociologically Based Theories for Crime

Theory	Theoretical Concerns	Major Contributors
Anomie		
1930s**	Deviance as stress generated by conflict between goals of success and structural means of achievement.	E. Durkheim R.K. Merton
Differential Association 1940s	Due to normative conflict a variety of social phenomena (e.g., subculture, social differentiation, and differential social organization) can account for deviance—behavior is learned.	E. Sutherland
Opportunity Theory 1950s	Blocked opportunities due to limited access to legitimate means of achieving desired economic success.	R. Cloward and L. Ohlin
Control Theory	The importance of bonds (e.g., attachment, commitment, belief, etc.) and how they affect conformity.	T. Hirschi
Power Control 1970s	The distribution of power and prestige among individuals and groups in society.	J. Hagan A. Turk
Labelling 1960s	Focuses on how negative social reactions create stigitization and isolating effects.	K. Erickson E. Lemert H. Becker
"New criminology" 1970s	Similar to Labelling but shifts focus from labelling the individual to society itself (e.g., class conflict, political economy and crime, power and authority).	K. Marx W. Bonger I. Talor, et. al. R. Dahrendorf
British Realist 1980s	Shift from focus on the role of the state to impact of crime on the victim and need to establish realistic social policy.	R. Kinsey, J. Lea, J. Young
Feminism 1970s	Examine how the patriarchal structure has limited the understanding of crime and justice, especially among women.	C. Smart M. Chesney-Lind

**Dates denote the approximate time period during which the theory emerged.

2. One of the techniques used to uncover the extent of unreported crimes involves self-report studies. They represent a second source of predictive information. However, due to a variety of methodological limitations, they too represent a rather limited vein.
3. One of the more recent information sources used to predict crime trends and patterns involve victim surveys. But as with the self-report studies, this source is also limited. Some people do not even know they were victimized, some fear reporting in case of retaliation, some simply forget, and some may even stretch the truth.
4. According to Gabor (1986:25), "direct observation of people in their natural environments" (e.g., ethnography) is potentially a more enriching source of information. Because this approach does not rely on the accuracy of official data collectors but rather on the care and diligence of the researcher it is likely that the information will be complete. This is especially true if the study can be controlled. But, as Gabor notes, few situations would lend themselves ethically to such manipulations. Hence, this source is perhaps as dubious as the others.

However, rather than ignore the value of trying to explain, predict and ultimately control crime, it should be noted that few "good" things fail to involve some degree of risk and so with criminal justice decision-making one must weigh the value of attempting to understand at the expense of leaving crime unchecked.

Summary

Crime is an evolving concept and will likely continue to represent a serious social dilemma for us. As we learn to handle existing crimes, new crimes will evolve to present us with new problems. This is already being witnessed in the area of white collar type of crimes (e.g., computer crimes, stock market frauds, real estate fraud, lawyers embezzlement, medical malpractice, even various forms of terrorism).

Historically, in Canada, our attitudes toward punishment seem to have been somewhat cyclical. As we become less efficient we risk being more conservative and with escalating cost there are fewer programs being initiated for prevention or intervention.

From a theoretical position, our theories of crime and punishment also appear somewhat relative and evolutive. Hence, it is somewhat unclear as to whether we will ever be able to truly control crime. But perhaps as Emile Durkheim once noted, crime can be functional and even necessary. Hence we must continue our search for the answers to the dilemma and hope that through critical thinking and sound research we might someday attain a level of peace and harmony in which few people wish to commit crimes and fewer require being punished. However, to paraphrase a noted Canadian criminologist, Gywn Nettler, society is like a social fabric which can only be mended and rewoven so many times before it is beyond repair or perhaps it is time to release the old social fabric, the old structures, the status quo, our old ways of thinking and conceive a new order! Hence we must move forward with caution and be careful in what we report and believe. The gauntlet has been placed before you!

References

Adelberg, E. and C. Currie (eds.)
1987 *Too Few to Count: Canadian Women in Conflict with the Law.* Vancouver, BC: Press Gang.

Beccaria, C.
1963 *On Crimes and Punishments.* Translated by H. Paolucci. Indianapolis: The Bobbs-Merrill Co., Inc.

Boyd, N.
1988 *The Last Dance: Murder in Canada.* Scarborough: Prentice-Hall Canada Inc.

Blumstein, A.
1982 "Research on Sentencing." *Justice System Journal,* 307–330.

Brantingham, P. and P. Brantingham
1984 *Patterns in Crime.* New York: Macmillan Pub. Co.

Brantingham, P. and P. Brantingham
1988 "Situational Crime Prevention in British Columbia." *J. of Security Administration,* 11(2): 18–27.

Brantingham, P. and P. Brantingham eds.
1991 *Environmental Criminology.* Waveland Press, Inc.

Chambliss, W.
1988 *Exploring Criminology.* New York: Macmillan Pub. Co.

Cohen, L.E. and M. Felson
1979 "Social Change and Crime Rate Trends: A Routine Activity Approach." *American Sociological Review,* (44), 588–608.

Chappell, D. and Hatch, A.
1986 "Violent Crime in Canada: An Assessment of Current Knowledge," in R.A. Silverman and J. J. Teevan Jr., *Crime in Canadian society* (3rd ed.). Toronto: Butterworths. pp. 228–237.

Chunn, D. and S. Gavigan
1991 "Women and Crime." In M. A. Jackson and C. T. Griffiths eds. *Canadian Criminology: Perspectives on Crime and Criminality.* Toronto, Ont.: Harcourt Brace Jovanovich, Cdn.

Cohen, S.
1985 *Visions of Social Control.* Cambridge: Polity Press.

Daly, K. and M. Chesney-Lind
1988 "Feminism and Criminology." *Justice Quarterly,* 5(4): 497–538.

Demers, D. J.
1984 "Criminal Justice Spending in Canada: Recent Trends," in Solicitor General of Canada, *IMPACT—Cost of Criminal Justice,* 4–12. Ottawa: Supply and Services Canada.

Ditton, J.
1979 *Controlology: Beyond the New Criminology.* London: The Macmillan Press, Ltd.

Garbor, T.
1986 *The Prediction of Criminal Behaviour.* Toronto, Ontario: University of Toronto Press.

Goff, C. H. and C. E. Reasons
1986 "Organizational Crimes against Employees, Consumers and the Public," in B. D. MacLean ed. *The Political Economy of Crime.* Scarborough: Prentice-Hall Canada, Inc. pp. 204–231.

Gottfredson, M. and T. Hirschi
1990 *A General Theory of Crime.* Stanford, CA: Stanford University Press.

Griffiths, C. T. and S. N. Verdun-Jones
1989 *Canadian Criminal Justice.* Toronto: Butterworths.

Hagan, J.
1985 *Modern Criminology: Crime, Criminal Behavior, and Its Control.* Toronto: McGraw-Hill Ryerson Ltd.

Hagan, J.
1991 *The disreputable pleasures* (3rd ed.). Toronto: McGraw-Hill Ryerson Ltd.

Hartnagel, T. F. and G. W. Lee
1990 "Urban Crime in Canada." *Canadian Journal of Criminology,* 32(4), 591–606.

Kennedy, L. W.
1989 *On the Borders of Crime.* White Plains, N.Y.: Longman.

Koenig, D. J.
1987 "Conventional Crime," in R. Linden ed. *Criminology: A Canadian Perspective.* Toronto: Holt, Rinehart and Winston of Canada, Ltd. Chpt. 12.

Johnson, H. and V. F. Sacco
1991 "The Risk of Criminal Victimization: Data from a National Survey," in R. A. Silverman, J. J. Teevan, Jr., and V. F. Sacco eds. "Crime in Canadian Society." Butterworths. Chapter 7.

Linden, R. ed.
1987 *Criminology: A Canadian Perspective.* Toronto: Holt, Rinehart and Winston of Canada, Ltd.
Juristat Service Bulletins. Statistics Canada.
Drug offences in Canada 1962–1987. vol 8, #2.
Break and Enter in Canada 1962–1986. vol. 8, #1.
Women and Crime. vol 10, #20.

Court Services in Canada—1989. vol. 11, #3
Police personnel and expenditures—1989. vol. 10, #8.
Police persons in Canada—1988. vol. 9, #3.
Violent crime in Canada—1989. vol. 10, #15.
Youth crime in Canada—1986–1988. vol 10, #12.

Kennedy, L. W. and D. R. Forde
1990 "Routine Activities and Crime: An Analysis of Victimization in Canada." *Criminology,* 28: 137–152.
Maclean's. (Jan. 7, 1991). "High Anxiety." p. 30–38.

Menard, S.
1987 "Short-term Trends in Crime and Delinquency: A Comparison of UCR, NCR, and Self-report Data." *Justice Quarterly,* 4(3): 455–474.

Menninger, K
1968 *The crime of punishment.* New York, NY: Viking Compass Book.

Silverman, R. A., J. Teevan, Jr. and V. F. Sacco (eds.)
1991 *Crime and Canadian Society* 4th ed. Toronto: Butterworths.

Thomas, J. and A. O'Maolchatha
1989 "Reassessing the Critical Metaphor: An Optimistic Revisionist View." *Justice Quarterly,* 6(2):143–172.

Weihofen, H.
1956 *The Urge to Punish.* New York: Farrar, Straus and Giroux, quoted in S. T. Reid, *Crime and Criminology.* (1976). The Dryden Press, P. 495.

Wilkens, L.
1980 "World Crime. To Measure or Not to Measure?" in G. R. Newman ed. *Crime and Deviance: A Comparative Perspective.* Beverly Hill, Calif.: Sage.

Wilson, J. Q.
1985 *Thinking about Crime.* New York: Vintage Books.

The Social Institutions of the Family, Health, Economy and Religion

The social network is an integral part of human society. Perhaps the most important part of the social network is marriage and the family for the creation and the maintenance of the kinship network. There is a wide range of marriage and family relationships in different cultures. Some cultures maintain joint and extended kinship systems that emphasize close cooperation among members, group orientation, sharing resources and mutual aid, to mention a few. The extended family system includes the members of two or more generations who live together. They could be parents, grandparents, aunts, uncles, cousins, brothers, sisters (mostly unmarried), nieces and nephews (mostly brother's children), spouses, siblings, and in some cases even step-siblings. On the other hand, societies such as Canada maintain the nuclear family system which encourages personal freedom, privacy, independence and individualism. The nuclear family normally consists of the husband, the wife and their unmarried children. In recent years, the relatively high rate of divorce in western societies has created the sub-nuclear family system consisting of single parents and their children. Sub-nuclear families can also lead to step-families or blended families, in some cases.

In chapter ten, George Kurian discusses marriage and the family in Canada. He points out that the family system in Canada varies because Canadian society is constituted by people of different ethnic backgrounds. Kurian briefly traces the historical trends of the Canadian family. Although the nuclear family system is the norm in Canada, he acknowledges the diversity of family structure that arises from the ethnic pluralism built into the fabric of Canadian society. Kurian provides a brief history of marriage, its legal framework, intermarriage, marital expectations, marital roles and conjugal power. Further, he highlights the process of communication within the family, marital satisfaction and the recent trends in the Canadian family. Moreover, he provides a timely discussion on the transition of sexual relations in the family system in Canada.

In recent years, most Canadians have become concerned about their health, health care services, and health care cost. However, introductory sociology textbooks in Canada often ignore the importance of health and health care issues. This is partly due to the misunderstanding that medical sociology is a specialized sub-discipline of itself. On the contrary, in chapter eleven of this volume, Harley Dickenson provides an extensive analysis of the causes of death, patterns of morbidity and the distribution of health care in Canada. Further, he examines the historical background of the development of the Canadian health care system and the rising health care cost, with special reference to the shifting emphasis from cure to prevention of illness, and the role of physicians in this regard.

In chapter twelve, Paul Divers examines the emergence of industrialization, the social transformation of work, and the occupational structure in Canada. In the context of the growing mechanization of the workplace and the rising unemployment in Canada, Divers emphasizes the importance of training and the retraining of workers for the future changes at the workplace.

These three authors examine three fundamental areas—family, health and work—of contemporary Canadian society. The changing family structure, the changing patterns of causes of death, rising health care costs, and the changing conditions at the workplace are all important issues in current social and political discussions that Canadian sociologists cannot afford to ignore.

In the last and final chapter of the book, Swenson presents a definition of religion and then structures the chapter according to that definition. In this article, he outlines religion from its essential dimensions: the individual and social experience of the sacred, mythology, ritual, ethos and organizations.

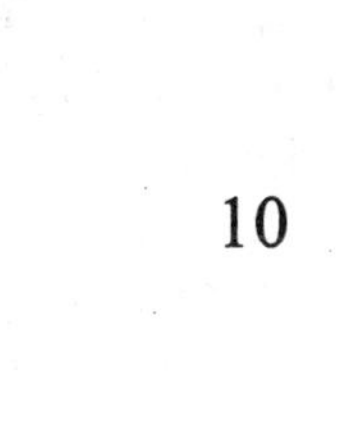

Marriage and Family in Canada

George Kurian

If you recall, the concept of social action was presented in Chapter One of the text. There we found, from Weber, that there were three categories of social action: traditional, affective, and rational. The focus in studying marriage and the family is on the second type: affective social action.

Affective social action is at the heart of the familial relationships. When we think of such family-laden terms as love, affection, nurture, care, trust and compassion, we are thinking of affective social action. As we have seen in the Weberian perspective on the family, we also learned that affective social action can also be negative in such ways as being revengeful, angry, malicious and the like. Research on family dynamics gives evidence for the presence of family violence which is profoundly counter productive to the development of human beings.

We also meant social structure, culture and history in family studies. When we speak of the family as an institution, we are saying that affective social action has become structured where family roles are given to members who are expected to adhere to them. Culture is also useful in the sociology of the family for values, beliefs, attitudes and norms are important ingredients in the successful functioning of family life. In this chapter, the cultural aspect of families will be illustrated in the legal aspects of marriage, changing sexual relationships, and intermarriage between ethnic groups in Canada.

Finally, history is important for sociology in general and also important in family studies. The sections on the history of marriage and changing patterns in the Canadian family illustrate this importance.

Introduction

The Canadian Family is composed of people of various ethnic origins. The policy of the Canadian Government is to maintain the cultural diversity and not to have a homogenous type of family or a melting pot like in the U.S.A. The idea that the Canadian Mosaic is beneficial to the country in the long run is an unresolved debate. What one can do here is to present some of the aspects of diversity in the Canadian Family.

The most dominant groups are the British and the French who were the first immigrants from Europe. The political domination of the British has influenced social institutions as well. Most of the other immigrant groups from Europe eventually spoke English and adjusted to British traditions. While there were people in Canada long before the arrival of Europeans, namely the aboriginal people, they were pushed aside by the colonial powers and are still not part of modern Canadian society. The other ethnic groups began to arrive in Canada in large numbers by the middle of the past century. "In 1871, European settlers other than French and British constituted only about 7 per cent of the population. By 1951 the figure had increased to 18 per cent." (Emily M. Nett, 1988, p. 100).

By the turn of the 20th century non-European immigrants started arriving in Canada. This was a continuation of the process when the Canadian Pacific Railway was built across the Rocky Mountains when Chinese workers were brought in. However, the non-Europeans, who were all Asian immigrants were never welcomed. All kinds of obstacles were placed to prevent them from bringing their families—especially in British Columbia. Legislation, like the Immigration Act of 1910, made it expensive for immigrants to come to Canada. Each person had to pay $200. In the case of the Chinese, a head tax of $500 was imposed between 1885 and 1923.

However, by the end of the Second World War, Canada gradually changed the restrictive immigration laws. In 1962, a major change took place allowing immigrants to come in without quota restrictions. By 1967, the racial bias was removed and immigrants were allowed on the basis of Canadian national needs. With the realization that there was not much interest for Europeans to come to Canada, the Government looked to non-European countries for immigrants. Canada cannot afford the luxury of keeping out non-white immigrants when one looks at the demographic realities. An alarming decline in birthrate occurred from 2.1 children per woman, which is the minimum replacement number, to an average of 1.7 for the country with some provinces like Quebec showing even steeper decline.

Assuming Canada has only 10 per cent of the land as habitable, it has only 26 people per square kilometer. Professor Morton Weinfeld of McGill University compared this to West Germany (247), Britain (231), Japan (318) and Netherlands (422). Canadians also have underestimated the loss through emigration. For example in 1985 though immigration was 84,000 the net growth was only 36,000 due to emigration. Many overlook the fact that immigrants are a bargain with highly qualified people who were educated at no cost to Canada. (Morton Weinfeld, 1987, June 19).

The people of British and French ethnic background are the largest where 34% of the population could trace their origin in Great Britain and Ireland, and 24% representing people of French background, 25% of people belonged to neither British nor French ethnic origins. Of these who are from the continent of Europe were 16% of the population due to increasing level of non-European immigration the Asians form numerically significant representing 4%. Finally, the aboriginal people of Canada including Canadian Indians, Inuits and Metis are about three quarters of a million forming 3% of the population.

(Pamela M. White, 1990, Pp. 3–6). “Canadians were ethnically diverse in 1986 with almost one third of them reporting mixed ethnic roots, Statistics Canada said yesterday.” (Canadian Press, 1989, July 5). The English speaking population in the large urban areas seem to spearhead the social change in Canada as in the U.S.A. The nuclear family is the norm in Canada.

History of Marriage

The history of marriage of the majority of Canadians who are descendants of immigrants from Europe is similar to the traditions that existed in Europe. It seems in the early days of Christianity, marriage was viewed as a civil and private affair based on Roman Civil Law. The church also emphasized the idea of free consent of partners. In the beginning, church encouraged intermarriage with non-Christians to get more converts. Gradually the church felt strong enough to halt intermarriage with non-Christians. By the Middle Ages, the presence of a priest at wedding ceremonies was considered important as a symbol of religiosity. They had a clear definition of the ideal spouse, “The ideal wife was expected always to submit humbly to her lord, raise his bastards if he desired, never utter a word of disapproval and by earnest efforts of love try to win him back from distracting influences.” (Bernard J. Murstein, 1974, p. 145). Women were expected to be virgin before marriage.

In Canada, the early settlers were not influenced by aboriginal people whose social customs, considered pagan, were never respected. The interest of the people were to acquire as much land at the expense of the indigenous people. Eventually, due to war and infectious diseases, Indians were reduced to a fraction of their original numbers which continues to be true even today.

According to studies done by Peter Laslett and others based on the census data of 17th Century England, using family-reconstitution techniques, the nuclear family was the norm rather than the extended family. “According to Laslett, research findings reveal that, except for Japan and possibly Serbia (part of present-day Yugoslavia), household size has not varied to a great extent in the last 300 years. The extended family system is found not to be particularly prevalent.” (Mark Hutter, 1988, p. 85).

“In her ground-breaking study of Canadian families, Emily Nett maintains that the historical record available to us, leaves little doubt that regardless of geographical location or urban or rural setting, most Canadians lived in nuclear simple family households” (Karen L. Anderson, 1988, p. 27).

Family and marriage continued to feel the influence of the Christian churches in Canada till recent times. “The Roman Catholic Church in New France, and the Anglican and Protestant Churches (primarily Presbyterian and Methodist) in the Maritimes and Upper Canada played an important role in early Canadian life” (Emily Nett, 1988, p. 111). However, the influence of church suffered a rapid decline in post Second World War days with a decline in church attendance especially among Anglicans and Roman Catholics. This definitely has an impact on family life with increasing tolerance of premarital and postmarital sexual permissiveness.

Legal Aspects of Marriage

In a society in rapid transition, it becomes increasingly difficult to give an appropriate definition for marriage. From the traditional institutional perspective, the functional aspects are given primary emphasis. These may include sexual rights leading to reproduction and other obligations of spouses. Probably the most crucial role in married life is the rearing of children meaning the learning process from early childhood through the years in school leading them into socially responsible adults. Finally, marriage includes inheritance rights and the responsibility of caring for the old. Family ties preserve and interpret the values of society in general. For the individual, "a sense of self-worth may be generated and nourished through the mutual love, respect and loyalty of members in two, three or four generations" (C. Crysdale & Beattie, 1977, p. 112).

From a historical perspective, only by the mid 19th century, were there clearly defined family laws. "Early laws regulating family relations were embedded in a variety of property laws, devolution of estate statutes, illegitimacy and guardianship acts" (Jane Ursel, 1986, p. 174).

However, family law was never properly regulated. It seems the first significant act reducing patriarchal authority was the Married Women's Property Act of 1872. Before this, husband had complete control on wife's property. To emphasize the male responsibility to the family, the husband was obliged to support wives and children if the marriage broke down. An interesting aspect of the legal position of the husband was that "he never lost access to his wife's sexuality through legal separation, he never lost control in law over that aspect of the woman's reproductive capacity" (Jane Ursel, 1986, p. 176). A further development was Social Welfare legislation to care for dependents who had no means of sustenance.

Legislation recognizing equality is only meaningful if women have equal opportunities especially eliminating discrimination of women in the labour market. "The assumption of primary responsibility for childrearing and homemaking carries with it a unilateral risk of economic deprivation which is inconsistent with the concept of marriage as a partnership of legal equals" (McCall (Marnie) M. L., Joseph P. Hornick and Jean E. Wallace, 1988, p. 40).

Getting married is a legal contract between a man and woman. A number of conditions are expected in marriage. The parties must be male and female as there are not yet provisions for homosexual marriages. At the time of the marriage the person must be single emphasizing monogamous union. One is not allowed to marry within prohibited degrees of consanguinity and affinity to prevent incestuous unions. Both parties must have reached the marriageable age. This varies from province to province with a minimum age of fourteen. "Having recommended eighteen as the appropriate minimum age for marriage in the case of both males and females, the Royal Commission on the status of women saw no further role for the notion of parental consent and advocated its abolition as a legal requirement" (Iwan Saunders, 1975, p. 47). In addition to formal marriages, there are informal alliances like common-law relationships which in effect have legal validity.

The State is concerned about the welfare of the children and peaceful resolution of property rights according to Emily Nett. "Generally speaking, spouses have the right of sexual access to their partners, to respect and kindness and to fidelity or the sexual exclusiveness of their partners" (Emily Nett, 1988, p. 213). However, the rights and duties are difficult to enforce. One of the essential aspects of obligation in marriage is financial responsibility. Women are no longer expected to submit to sex and childbearing today compared to what existed in 19th century laws. Laws regarding property also have variations in provincial laws. A study by the Canadian Research Institute for Law and the Family has mentioned some important points. Historically, at the time of marriage the husband had exclusive rights of property including inherited property. By the turn of the twentieth century women earned the right to own property. "In Canada, legislation permitting married women to own property in their own right was enacted primarily in the 1920's. In Quebec, however, women did not acquire these rights until 1969" (M. L. (Marnie) McCall, Joseph P. Hornick and Jean E. Wallace, 1988, p. 18). As long as marriage remained stable, disputes regarding property ownership was not a serious concern.

The Married Women's Property Act moved towards the concept of partnership of spouses. This was precipitated due to the cases where wives were denied their rights even though they had made major contributions to the material success of their spouses. There are some basic features in the present matrimonial property laws. These include assumption of marital partnership with regard to share of assets and their definition and expectation that these will be shared. However, an equitable division can only be accomplished in some cases by disposing of business which in effect undermines the source of income.

Looking at the development of law, alimony or maintenance was awarded to an innocent wife which means misconduct of wife makes her ineligible for claim of support. Some provinces recognized the concept. "Under the present Canadian divorce legislation, fault is not considered" (M. L. (Marnie) McCall, Joseph P. Hornick and Jean E. Wallace, 1988, p. 24).

Sexual Relations in Transition

The post Second World War period heralded the stage of permissiveness with affection in sex life. This was followed by sexual permissiveness even without affection by the later part of this century. With the availability of contraception, a major shift in sexual freedom developed as premarital pregnancy fear receded to a great extent.

According to Professor Charles Hobart, the emerging new "Double Standard," specified generally that a higher degree of emotional involvement is expected for premarital sex to be acceptable in the case of women, than in the case of men. "For example, this standard would specify that premarital sex is acceptable for women if they are in love with their partner, whereas it is acceptable for men irrespective of relationship considerations. The second possible standard, the Engagement Standard, is a more stringent version of the Love Standard, specifying that premarital sex is acceptable for those who are engaged to their partners, but not otherwise. The occasion for increased support for such a standard could be a growing discovery of what an elusive, transitory, self-delusive, and binding emotion some versions of "love" (sex attraction, pity for the other, needing the other, etc.) may be in the absence of specific and mutually binding commitment" (Charles Hobart, 1984, pp. 231–255).

In one of the most significant studies on teenage pregnancy in industrialized countries, the comments on Canada are worth mentioning especially in view of the greater use of contraceptives compared to the United States. "It seems probable that there is less sexual activity among younger Canadian teenagers than elsewhere and that reduced exposure might be partly responsible for keeping the pregnancy rates of young teenagers low in that country" (Elize F. Jones, 1986, p. 213).

With the increasing and alarming increase of AIDS (Stephen Genius, 1991) virginity is re-emerging as a socially responsible value. "Moreover, since AIDS is an "equal opportunity disease," virginity may come to be considered as important for males as for females" (Jean Veevers, 1990, p. 8).

The following are some of the recent findings of the study of attitudes towards cohabitation and marriage in Canada, industrialization, urbanization, higher education, decline in religiosity, increase in female labour force participation, changes in ethnic and language composition, etc., which affect the norms of marriage and the family. It is hardly surprising that currently married women have a positive attitude towards marriage. Those with positive attitudes are more likely to get married. Besides, those who are married are unlikely to express a negative attitude towards marriage unless they are particularly unhappy with their marriage. In contrast, the women who are never married, separated, divorced or are currently cohabiting are apt to take a liberal attitude towards cohabitation. Women who are residing in rural areas tend to have a more conservative attitude towards cohabitation than women in small towns and cities. These findings support the idea that an urban environment promotes liberal attitudes. Working women are forced to retain more liberal attitudes towards cohabitation than non-working women.

One important finding of this study is the regional effect, namely being a resident of Quebec or residing outside of the province. Quebec residents are more positive towards cohabitation and less so with marriage, a pattern that persists almost unchanged even when other factors are controlled.

Apart from their religious affiliation, the respondents' religiosity is found to be associated with the attitudes as well. As hypothesized, the women who attend church more frequently tend to be more conservative in their attitudes. Finally, a desired number of children shows a clear pattern of both marriage and cohabitation scale. The women who desire no children have the highest deviation score on cohabitation and lowest score on marriage. (Zheng Wu & T. R. Balakrishnan, 1992). "According to the census results 487,000 couples (or 974,000 individuals) were living in common-law partnerships in 1986, 37% gain over 1981, far outpacing the 2.7% rise in the number of married couples. Consequently, common-law unions accounted for 8% of all couples in 1986, up from 6% in 1981" (Pierre Turcotte, 1990, p. 148).

The expectations in all societies, including Canada, are that all adults will eventually get married and have a family. However, the fact is that an increasing and significant minority choose not to get married and are quite content with a single life-style. "An analysis completed in 1985 suggested that, at that time, 17% of men and 14% of women would never marry" (Adams, 1990, p. 143).

"In all age groups except the elderly (65 and over), the proportion of people who were married dropped between 1981 and 1986" (Mary Sue Devareaux, 1990, p. 140). Remarriage rates also show a downward trend especially for the older women. Generally Canadians are delaying their marriage which also affect the reproduction rates. "After reaching a record low of 24.4 years for females in 1968, the mean age of marriage rebound to 27.7 in 1986. The 1986 census results have reinforced the belief that an increasing number of Canadians have recently been delaying getting married" (Bali Ram, 1990, pp. 18–19).

Intermarriage

The issue of intermarriage is now significant in Canada due to an increasing number of immigrants from various cultures who are interacting with each other. The increase of immigration in the 1960's based on the point system rather than national origins have brought to Canada families of professionals who are urban oriented. These people are tolerant towards intermarriage compared to the less educated working class people. The favourable attitude towards intermarriages have become more acceptable in the last 15 years compared to earlier periods. The 1981 census of Canada for the first time acknowledged the growing number of ethnic intermarriages by allowing individuals to specify more than one ethnic origin, and nearly one Canadian in ten indicated multiple origins (Statistics Canada, 1983).

> In popular usage, intermarriage represents at the minimum, the linkage of two people with different cultural and behavioral norms and backgrounds grounded or based on religious, racial or ethnic differences. Intermarriage has implications not only for the couple themselves but also impacts on the linkages of larger family and lineage groups. The consequences of the marriage affects future generations as well as present and past generations. The understanding of the nature and dynamics of intermarriage provides insights into the understanding of religion, race and ethnic group relationships as they separate both within and between societies. (Mark Hutter, 1990, pp. 143–144)

How far ethnic identity can be maintained is a concern in intermarriages for the couples as well as the children who are the product of the mixed cultures. In a study done in Winnipeg, "the impact of intermarriage on ethnic identity of the adult offspring of such marriages has furnished evidence consistent with the proposition that mixed parentage tends to be associated with lower levels of both internal and external dimensions of ethnic identity" (Jay Goldstein and Alexander Segall, 1985, pp. 60–71).

According to the interesting analysis of intermarriage by Cerroni-Long, people can only be tempted to intermarry if potential partners from different religions, racial and ethnic groups are available. (Cerroni-Long, 1985, pp. 25–46). But what do we really mean by "available"? Evidently this is a crucial point and a complex one. Generally speaking we can distinguish three kinds of availability: physical, actual and psychological. Physical availability refers to the sex ratio and numerical size of groups. Actual availability refers to the fact that for people to become potential marital partners they have to be in situations that allow or favour this potentiality. Finally, psychological availability refers to the fact that intermarriage between two members of endogamous groups is directly proportional to the ratio of "compatibility" between the groups.

The most obvious rationalization is of course provided by real exceptional circumstances. Among these the most typical is created by residence abroad in situations in which the only potential marital partners available are to be found outside one's immediate group and the ties with this group are themselves felt to be looser than normal. The whole "war brides" phenomenon is created by a situation of this kind and of course this can also be the case when the sex ratio of an immigrant group is totally imbalanced.

One more situation in which the prescriptive value of the endogamous norm is downplayed or even outright disregarded can happen when an individual willingly rescinds or alternates the ties with his/her primary group of affiliation. This most typically takes place when, because of conversion or loss of faith, a person parts with his/her original religious community. It can also be observed when a minority group is in an advanced stage of acculturation and assimilation. At this stage the group as a whole still maintains its endogamous norm but some individuals, in increasingly identifying with the majority group and in accepting their values, end up considering intermarriage as a most desirable strategy leading to quicker integration. Of course, as said before, if the process of assimilation of the group as a whole proceeds successfully it could well happen that in the long run the endogamous norm is abandoned in *toto* (E. L. Cerroni-Long, 1985, pp. 25–46).

According to a fairly recent study in Canada, the interreligious marriage pattern was similar for most of the groups. In most cases, the highest proportion of those who outmarried tended to marry into the largest religious groups: Anglicans, Roman Catholics, and the United Church. Religious intermarriage continues to be the highest (60+ percent) among Jews, followed in rank order by non-Christians, Pentecostals and Mennonites (Larsen & Munro, 1990, pp. 239–250).

One of the communities most concerned about intermarriages are people of the Jewish faith. An observer at the Canadian Jewish Congress in 1989 expressed his concern "citing an intermarriage rate of 40 percent, he believes that assimilation of Jews in Canada is a more pressing concern than the situation in Israel or the State of Soviet Jewry" (John Allemang, 1989). In the United States, "Virtually none of the immigrant generation intermarried, but 10 percent of their children did, and so did almost 18 percent of their grandchildren. Exposure to higher education pushed rates up even more: 37 percent of college graduates in that third generation intermarried. These findings, coming at a time when other data indicated a falling Jewish birthrate, evoked great concern among Jewish leaders" (The William Petschek National Jewish Family Center, 1986).

In a recent study of Jewish intermarriage in the Denver area some interesting conclusions emerged. The intermarriage rate here may not be the highest among World Jewry but in an estimated one to two-thirds of all marriages involving an American Jew the partner is a non-Jew. Modern Jewish women are more likely to intermarry than their mothers were but they are nearly as likely to raise their children Jewish.

It may be that due to the increased Jewish educational opportunities available to women, they are now better prepared to raise Jewish children although the father is not a Jew. Intermarriage appears to be a function of the changing role of Jews in the American social structure. Despite barriers erected by the parts of the Jewish community designed to exclude non-Jewish spouses from participating in religious and communal activities, there is outreach to the mixed married and many are responding. The traditional Jewish community fears that actions taken to ease the entrance of mixed married into the community will only serve to encourage more intermarriage. Most Jews will continue to consider intermarriage an option as long as ethnic tensions are at a tolerable level and it remains acceptable to identify with one's ethnic heritage. While intermarriage does not necessarily lead to assimilation, assimilation can lead to intermarriage. (Eleanore Parelman Judd, 1990, pp. 251–265)

Intermarriage has lasting implications for the immigrants in Canada from non-European cultures. In spite of the fear of loss of ethnic and cultural identity changes are inevitable. Immigrants who came in the 1960's onwards are educated as the point system favour them. Most of them are already exposed to urban oriented lifestyles prior to immigrating to Canada. Therefore, they are well disposed to accepting changes. Now, there is already a generation of youth born and brought up here and their heterosexual interactions are with people of all types of cultural backgrounds outside their own communities. While parents would like to get involved in marital choice decisions, they are at a disadvantage in a society with relatively free premarital heterosexual relations.

The parents who came as immigrants in the early sixties are faced with the reality of dealing with twenty year old sons and daughters who want to associate freely with the opposite sex. For example, for South Asians, there are not sufficient numbers of people in their communities to develop heterosexual friendships. It is inevitable that quite a few of them have friends from other ethnic groups and some of them wish to get married. Some of the parents are accepting the seriousness of these relationships leading to inter-ethnic marriages. Those parents who are keen to get their children to marry within the communities try to place advertisements in matrimonial columns in ethnic newspapers. On the whole, time is not on the side of these reluctant parents.

In a thought provoking and well written article, the conflicts between immigrants and their children were discussed. "Most parents try to provide an antidote by forcing their kids to adopt what they consider 'Indian' culture. The children are torn between their parents and their friends, and since the desire for peer approval is so strong, they rebel when forced to adopt values they hold in scorn" (Badrinath Krishna Rao, 1991, May 7, p. A17).

Sometimes one finds rather strong reactions among the South Asian youth in Canada regarding the question of arranged marriage. A rebellious young Canadian born girl, who married a non-Indian despite her parents' objections, remarked that, "by the time my sister and I were ready to go out we would never have permitted our parents to arrange a marriage. My brother let himself be bribed into an arranged marriage. He is dumb enough for that" (Joy Inglis and Michael M. Ames, 1967).

The present author made an interesting observation regarding South Asian immigrant families in Australia. Among the number of families familiar to the author all their grown up children married non-South Asians who are of European descent. Most of them are their classmates. This seems to be partly as a result of a lack of available partners in their own community which encourage the South Asian youth to interact frequently with non-South Asians. To a lesser extent, this is true in Canada as well.

In a major study undertaken in Great Britain of 5140 married couples 1% were intermarried. The female spouses in most intermarriages were white (62%). There was a tendency for intermarried couples to be living in urban areas, to be younger, to be more recently married and to have achieved a higher level of education than their intra ethnically married counterparts (Gary A. Cretser, 1990, pp. 227–238). It is likely that intermarriages in Canada will follow a similar pattern.

Marital Expectations

The expectations in marriage can vary depending on the attitudes of individuals who enter into marital relationship. In a society like Canada where free choice is the norm for most people, the level of expectations in marriage determine the success of the marriage. If a person has high unrealistic expectations and if these don't work out, he or she is not satisfied with the relationship. On the other hand those with low expectations have greater possibility of satisfaction. In most successful marriages, people have realistic expectations based on experience of interacting with many individuals which help them to develop certain level of maturity.

One way of looking at expectations in marriage is to compare modern marriages to traditional arranged marriages which has meaning for many of immigrants in Canada who are from non-western societies. A question that is often asked by people who have accepted self-choice as the normal form of mate selection is about the adjustment process in arranged marriages, since the couple are in a sense strangers compared to modern urban couples. The assumption is that if a young man and woman know each other in a dating situation for at least one year, the adjustment is easy. However, in actual practice, when the two meet each other for several hours a day, they are primarily concerned about close emotional ties. Even those who tried living together before marriage, the emotional aspect of their relationship become dominant. However, once they formalize their relationship in marriage, and live in the same residence, life moves gradually away from the early romantic situation. One has to face many practical aspects of life like reasonable efficiency of household management with the limited financial resources and allied responsibilities.

The difference between self-choice marriages and arranged marriages is the relative emphasis of expectations in marriage. In self-choice marriages, however, one might claim that love that precedes marriage in modern urban industrial society is not abstract love but is influenced by practical considerations of compatibility, the young couple do tend to idealize each other to a great extent. This is very important to maintain their emotional ties. Therefore, when they get married, they have very high expectations of each other. But when they start living together facing the many issues of daily life in a family, problems might arise. These problems can precipitate some amount of disillusionment which is inevitable because both have the maximum of expectations of each other, which are unlikely to be realized in daily life. The majority of the couples are able to overcome the transition from the ideal to the practical without much strain because they have adequate, mature personalities enabling them to make adjustments in the early stages of married life. On the other hand, there are many who are not able to make proper adjustments. This is the beginning of serious strain in their relationships. At times, the strain builds up and reaches a point at which it is impossible to make adequate adjustments.

During these periods of strain, the young couples themselves are primarily responsible for making adjustments without seeking advice from parents, kin and friends. The very nature of self-choice implies a high value on individuality in which the relationship between the parents, siblings, and friends is one of mutual respect for each others' individuality. It is not easy to accept advice at the first sign of trouble, and also it is difficult for others to initiate help without being accused of some kind of interference. In addition to these problems, the survival of self-choice marriages depends to a most significant degree on the continuation of love and common interests. Once these conditions are weakened, the couple will seriously consider the possibility of separation or divorce. This follows the logic of structural functionalists.

In modern urban industrial society like Canada in which marriage is more a civil contract than a sacrament, divorce is accepted as an alternative to unhappy marriages. Therefore, the social stigma against divorce is less and less relevant, especially in view of the tendency toward liberalizing divorce laws. Religion in western societies is fighting a losing battle against liberalizing divorce laws.

In arranged marriages, the young men and women are married only after the parents and close relatives have made adequate enquiries about their compatibility of each other and also in relation to the two families. In the absence of emotional commitments, it is possible for the parents and close kin to make an objective appraisal of the qualities of the young men and women and they are informed of each others' qualities. At the time of marriage, they have only the minimum of expectations but it is no exaggeration to claim that in arranged marriages most of the couples get much more than the minimum from the marriage. One also has to consider the fact that these young people do not meet a number of people before getting married. They, therefore, become less critical of each other. In modern self-choice marriages the fact that young people have had the opportunity to meet many of the opposite sex has not necessarily made these marriages more successful. The saying that in self-choice marriages you fall in love and then get married while in arranged marriages you get married and then fall in love, seems significant. In arranged marriages the strengthening of the relationships between the couples who might fall in love, in addition to the objective criteria of compatibility, contributes to maximum possible adjustments.

In addition, the sacramental nature of marriage is still dominant in cultures in which the arranged marriage continues to exist. This means that marriage is viewed as a permanent tie, and very little consideration is given to the possibility of separation. Therefore, the couple develops a greater sense of tolerance with give-and-take. After all, no two people can be ideally compatible and, therefore, the greater one's willingness to see the other person's point of view, the more chance there will be significant chance of success of such a marriage. If there are serious problems in a marriage, other family members will do all they can to help solve them. This is not considered interference because the good relationship between the two families is most important, and, therefore, those people who have taken an interest in arranging the marriage are willing to help the couple in their emotional and financial difficulties. This discussion about the adjustment in arranged marriages is not an attempt to claim that all such marriages are successful. In the past, when family interests were more important than those of the individuals who were getting married, it was difficult to assess the success of such marriages. However, in modern arranged marriages, the increasing possibility of expressing individual wishes has weakened the extreme authoritarianism of the families. On the other hand, the role of the family members in providing advice and help continues to be highly valued. This type of arranged marriage definitely contributes a lot to marital happiness and stability (G. Kurian, 1975, pp. 71–75).

Marital Roles and Conjugal Power

In the Canadian society, one expects that men and women enter into the role of spouses with some knowledge of marital roles. Sometimes, it is surprising to find that people have no clear idea of their roles in a culture moving away from tradition to modernity. The spouses need to have some basic understanding between marital role expectations and personality needs. As experience in marriage increases, role adjustment changes depending on the circumstances of reactions between them and in relation to others. For example, the initial excitement of managing the household for the wife, might turn out to be routine and not all that interesting. The socialization process in the family can influence the future marital roles.

"An important quality of role playing is the ability to take the role of the other so as to understand and predict the other's behaviour and to relate it to one's own behaviour—in short, having one's behaviour influenced in part by the desires of the significant other" (Bell, 1979, p. 233). Some frustration is inevitable in trying to reach the role expectations which can be a likely experience in a great number of individuals. However, this does not necessarily mean that such marriages are unsatisfactory. Robert Bell has suggested some general theoretical criteria of successful marriages. (1) Satisfaction is achieved in one's marriage role and that of the mate. (2) Each partner in the marriage has some opportunity to express his own personality. (3) Each marriage partner is an important focus of affection for the other. (4) Each partner derives some pleasures and satisfactions from the marriage role relationship. While these may not be universal, these patterns can be considered ingredients for successful marriage (Robert Bell, 1979, pp. 234–238).

The roles can be traditional at one extreme and fully egalitarian at the other end. Most of the traditional roles involve inflexible division of labour based on sex differences with the man as the bread earner and playing only a minimal role in household management and the woman shouldering most household chores and childrearing responsibilities. Ideally speaking, egalitarianism is based on sex-role equality. Canada has no typical family form, but have variations in ethnic, religious and regional differences. 'Most attitudinal sex-role studies demonstrate a clear trend toward more equalitarian perception of gender roles" (Nancy Mandell, 1989, pp. 239-243).

One of the most important conditions for successful marital adjustment is the exercise of conjugal power. This subject has interested many scholars. One of the significant contributors to the study of marital power is the Canadian sociologist, Hyman Rodman. The following are some aspects of his ideas. A finding that is common to many studies of marital power is that the husband's status is positively associated with the husband's powcr. Several studies have examined marital power in relation to the wife's working status. The findings in most of these studies indicate that working wives have more marital power than non-working wives. When wives work, their husbands are more likely to do more of the housework, although this may be by and large true, some men are still not willing to help in the house. One interesting finding with regard to change of conjugal power is a study done in Greece and Yugoslavia. Although most of the data show a positive correlation between the husband's status and the husband's power, the data for Greece and Yugoslavia show a negative correlation. From the perspective of the developed societies education, income, and occupational status are resources and the comparative amount of such resources possessed by husband and wife are important in determining the distribution of power. But the reversal of the relationships for the Greek and Yugoslavian data forces one to reconsider the view of education, income and occupation. This is particularly true of education. The more highly educated the Greek man, the likelier he is to hold attitudes that would lead to a more egalitarian status for his wife (Safrilios-Rothschild, 1967).

Interestingly, it is equally true of many immigrants in Canada from traditional cultures. To the extent that it operates to place the man in a patriarchal society in closer touch with equalitarian norms, it decreases his marital power (Hyman, Rodman, 1972, pp. 50–69).

It is of special significance to look at the husband's participation in the household duties. In all traditional cultures there is a clear division of labour of men and women. Men are not expected to participate in household duties and even women are quite willing to support this role. One might hope that in economically developed countries where egalitarian ideology is well entrenched, men will do their equal share of household chores. Not much changes have taken place. "Men are claiming credits for more housework than their mates say they actually do," says Homemaker's Magazine editor Jane Gale. According to research conducted for her magazine, Gale said "men report greater participation in household tasks than women attribute to them" (Bob Bragg, 1984).

A fairly recent study done in Calgary of 562 dual earning and dual career couples, it was found that irrespective of the wives' work outside the home, and even if they had children, the men's contribution to housework does not differ significantly. Further, as expected, the father's proportionate share is consistently less than the mother's in both comparison groups. "This pattern persists on weekends: though fathers increase their help with housework, mothers increase their share of housework even more" (Eugen Lupri, 1988, p. 288). The same pattern of unfairness is reported in American studies. Arlie Hoschchild, a sociologist at the University of California, Berkley found that wives typically come home from work to another shift doing 75% of the household tasks. "Men are trying to have it both ways" she claims. "They're trying to have their wives' salaries and still have the traditional roles at home" (Claudia, Wallis, 1989). In a report released called Women and the Labour Force, Stats Canada reported that "In addition to their work in the labour force, married women continue to be responsible for child care and household work," said the report's authors, Patricia Connelly and Martha MacDonald of St. Mary's University in Halifax (Vivian Smith, 1990).

Communication

Successful marriages and good communication go hand in hand. Many scholars agree on the special significance of effective communication in marriage. This is something which has to develop before marriage in the dating period. Premarital courses now put emphasis on the development of communication skills. One of the most successful organizations providing premarital counselling is the Pastoral Institute in Calgary. This is an inter-denominational organization started by United Church in 1962. Dr. Rev. Ed Mullen was instrumental in the establishment of the Institute. They have individual as well as group sessions. The real test of their counselling is the success of the marriage of people who received counselling. Dr. Mullen has some convincing arguments that the tests conducted by the Institute can find people suitable partners. "I guess we have married about 800 people," estimates Mullen, "and I suppose we have introduced about 6000." Not only that, but "the solid figures we have are that one in 22 marriages divorce," says Mullen, "compared to a one-in-2.7 norm for Alberta" (Barton Jacques, 1985).

After marriage, good communication plays a crucial role in success of marriage. There are two aspects of communication which are verbal and non-verbal. It is interesting to note that there is no clear agreement by scholars about the impact of verbal communication on marital quality. However, "research into the non-verbal behaviour of married partners suggests that non-verbal behavior may be more important in predicting marital distress than is verbal behaviour. One interpretation of this research is that non-verbal communication tends to carry more emotional content than does verbal communication" (James White, 1989, p. 205).

The most frustrating thing is wanting to discuss something important, only to find that your mate refuses his or her point of view. Most important, to keep in mind that it is unrealistic to expect either partner to change his or her habits completely to suit the other. "Whatever you do, don't forget to maintain a good sense of humor" (Amy H. Bergen, 1989).

An essential aspect of good communication is honesty. This helps to clarify feelings, avoid misunderstandings, and resentments. Another aspect of marital communication is in sexual communication. "Some couples who report they communicate well in other areas of their lives, may find talking about sex troublesome" (Laswell, 1991, p. 204). There is also no such thing as conflict-free marriage and if anyone claims otherwise, they are either lying or do not really have any individuality. Fortunately, most people can resolve problems in a mature manner of give and take. Another important aspect which can be part of effective communication is insight which helps to smooth out the relationship. "By anticipating more quickly and more accurately, he or she may be able to influence the partner. That power may be used to help both partners and the relationship or it may be used to profit the one partner at the expense of the other" (Leslie & Korman, 1989, pp. 406–407). Finally, "people who marry for the right reasons combine romantic love, attraction and emotional maturity in their relationships" (Barbara Somerville, 1987).

Marital Satisfaction

Marital satisfaction is a combination of many factors. Some of them are already discussed in marital expectations, marital roles, conjugal power and communication. However, there are still other factors as well.

One of the problems influencing marital satisfaction is the problem of shift work. When both spouses are working, they have very little time to relax. Sometimes they are in different shifts and so hardly ever meet each other leisurely. The evenings at home are demanding with cooking, cleaning and care of the children, which is taken for granted as the female's duties.

In a major study in United States involving 1668 married women, it was found that shift work affects marital quality negatively. "Most notably, shift work is associated with significantly lower marital happiness. One reason shift work reduces marital happiness is because it is less satisfying." The study found that while the negative effect of shift work is small, "the negative effects of shift work are real rather than a sampling artifact" (Lynn White & Bruce Keith, 1990, pp. 453–462).

If both spouses have identical interests, especially when they are both educated, there is a mutual understanding of each other. This is generally true about those who are in professions like teaching, medicine, business partnerships, etc. However, if a woman has no direct economic contribution outside the family, she is frustrated when she is educated. A less educated wife in comparison to the husband becomes alienated and has to put up with the husband's impatience.

In the case of South Asian immigrants, the opposite situation occurs when professionally qualified women marry men with inferior qualifications; these marriages are usually arranged by parents in India. The classical example is provided by persons of the medical profession such as laboratory technicians, nurses and doctors. While in India many of them marry men of well known families such as businessmen and land holders. These husbands have no technical education and are incapable of getting a job of comparable status to that of their wives. Some of these men end up in jobs of sales attendants in a store or even as unskilled workers in a factory.

The conflict arises because he asserts himself as the manager of his wife's earnings and tries to be the lord of the household while not sharing her after job household chores. The woman gradually realizes that she is the real bread winner and she has higher status than her husband. So she begins to assert her strength and freedom. After a period of intensive conflict either the husband yields to his wife, or as in a few cases, both break up the relationship. Another problem is stress caused by long distance travel in traffic to places of work. When mothers come home they are busy with household work and care of children leaving little time for leisure (A.K.B. Pilai, 1984).

One of the ingredients of successful adjustment is proper management of finances, sharing expenses, keeping records and communicating with each other about proper use of resources. "As with sexual adjustment, the causes of conflict over finances are often inseparable from the effects. As well, effective communication is very important in dealing with such conflict" (Emily M. Nett, 1988, p. 242).

In a Canadian study, it was indicated that men and women assess their marriages differently "Regardless of family life-cycle stage, women tend to be more satisfied with the extent to which their sexual needs are met, while there is greater male satisfaction with spouse's help at home, spouse's time with the children and friendship" (Darla Rhyme, 1982, p. 953). In a recent study it was noted that, "both men and women with larger families report higher levels of distress. Moreover, men indicate experiencing greater role conflict and time pressure, parental stress, marital stress, and physical distress associated with parenting more children" (Maureen G. Guelzow, Gloria W. Bird and Elizabeth H. Koball, 1991, pp. 151–164.) "Although many men are more involved in child rearing than fathers were in the past, we are a long way from a situation where shared family and domestic responsibilities is the norm" (S. J. Wilson, 1991, p. 61).

According to a Calgary study of marital satisfaction in the life cycle, it was found that satisfaction declines from the beginning of the marriage until the grown up children leave the parents and interestingly, there is a significant increase in marital satisfaction to the point of contributing to considerable improvement in the marital relationship (E. Lupri & J. Frideres, 1981, pp. 283–306).

One of the interesting aspects of modern marriages is the influence of premarital cohabitation on marital stability. The general impression is that premarital cohabitation does not contribute to the quality of marriage. One of the Canadian studies indicates some positive effects of premarital cohabitation on marital stability. In a study of 10,472 married Canadians, positive effects are discussed by James M. White. His study indicated premarital cohabitation with the spouse prior to marriage has a significant positive effect even though difference between co-habitors and non-cohabitors is only 6%. With regard to marital stability the possibility of continuing marriage favours the cohabitants. He also suggests as cohabitation is increasingly accepted in society the factors that contribute to marital disruption could disappear. Finally he observes that it is difficult to make generalization based on U.S. population for the Canadian society. However, "premarital cohabitation appears to be positively associated with marital stability even when the effects of length of marriage and age at marriage have been controlled. The odds for staying married are much better for co-habitors than non-cohabitors" (James M. White, 1987, pp. 641–647).

Crisis in the Family

Everyone expects some amount of tension in family life. However, it is important to know about the high level of violence that is part of significant number of families. Violence in the family is not something new. In almost all societies, male dominance in economic and physical spheres encourages intolerance. In many cases, it may be only at verbal level, but in a large number of cases it is physical. Wife and children are not in a position to prevent it due to their total dependence.

The discussion about family violence was not considered important in family sociology till recent times. For example, the *Journal of Marriage and the Family,* the most important publication in family sociology, only published articles in early 1970s. Now there are a number of well known sociologists actively involved in the study of family violence. Some of them are Richard J. Gelles, Murray Strauss and Suzannc Steinmetz.

The respect for privacy of the family and also assumption that family is a safe haven have all contributed to the lack of interest in the study of family violence.

Family violence affects every member in the family, and includes wife assault, elderly abuse and sexual abuse of children. Violence is not limited to one social class. "When surveyed under circumstances guaranteeing anonymity, Canadian men aged 18 and over reported that they have committed significant amounts of violence against their partners. While abuse of a female partner was reported by men in all income groups, it was more common among those with low incomes" (Eugen Lupri, 1990, pp. 170–172).

Wife assault is more than an isolated event. "Half the incidents involved women who were assaulted more than once. The risk of assault was highest for women who were separated" (Holly Johnson, 1990, pp. 173–176). The violence almost always happens at home. "Women are hit in the head and the face, assaulted with weapons such as stove burner coils, broken bottles, knives and guns. Assaults result in bruises, broken bones, internal injuries and even death" (Janice Drakich and Connie Guberman, 1988, p. 207).

Physical and sexual abuse of children is far more common than one expects. "The violence of incestuous assault can no longer be viewed as a problem that involves only a few particularly disturbed offenders. It reveals an immense trouble in the contemporary family" (Janice Drakich and Connie Guberman, 1988, p. 213). There is so much media reporting of sexual violence making Canadians aware of the serious problem. In addition to family related sexual abuse, there are numerous reports of teachers accused of sexual abuse. A number of them including some religious leaders were charged in court and some are punished in 1991.

Another problem about which Canadians are increasingly concerned is elderly abuse. "More than 100,000 elderly people, many of them women over 75, are subjected to physical, psychological and financial abuse each year in Canada. And those to blame are not necessarily employees of homes for the aged, but frequently the children of those abused" (Zuhair Kashmeri, 1986, March 23).

There are various types of elderly abuse. "It may include financial exploitation, where pension cheques or other monies are taken; physical injury including beatings or restraints; threats, ridicule, insults, humiliation, and imposed isolation (both physical and social); or a forced change in living arrangements" (Janice Drakich and Connie Guberman, 1988, p. 215).

At present, the law enforcement officials are expected to take action in the cases of all types of family violence which hopefully may be a deterrent reducing the incidence of the serious problems facing many people.

Another issue which threatens family stability is marriage breakdown. There is a decline in the number of marriages and an increase in divorces. "The average proportion of life spent married differs for men and women. Men expect to be married close to half (48%) of their lives, compared with 43% for women" (Owen Adams and Dhruva Nagnur, 1990, p. 144). This discrepancy is largely due to the fact that women tend to outlive men.

The Divorce Act of Canada of 1968 granted divorce for marital offence or marriage breakdown. The concept of "no-fault" divorce gradually emerged since marriage breakdown was recognized. "The most recent legislation, the Divorce Act 1985, was followed by a sharp increase in the divorce rate, which reversed a three-year downward trend" (Owen Adams, 1990, p. 146).

"The Divorce Act of 1985 is a social and legal response to changing trends in Canadian society. It shows a secularized interpretation of marriage and divorce, conscious of individual and human rights" (John F. Peters, 1988, p. 153). "The number of divorces in Newfoundland, Manitoba and Prince Edward Island rose substantially between 1986 and 1987, Statistics Canada reported yesterday. Alberta was the only province that saw a decrease" (Canadian Press, 1989, Oct. 7).

According to Professor T. R. Balakrishnan a well known sociologist and demographer at the University of Western Ontario, marriage breakdown by itself is not necessarily a bad thing. He said, "In one sense it may be good. People are not prepared to stay in marriage that's not so good ... what is now happening is that the good marriages stay intact" (Deborah Wilson, 1986, July 21). One also should consider the fact many of the divorced also remarry. "Although divorce is more frequent than in the past, many divorced people remarry. In 1985, for example, at least one partner in 27% of all marriages was divorced" (Owen Adams and Dhruva Nagnur, 1990, p. 144). Most people are pessimistic about the success of remarriages. "However, many people who remarry is evidence that they are not against the institution of marriage, but rather their first was not a good match" (John F. Peters, 1988, p. 160).

Changing Patterns in the Canadian Family

Already there are enough signs of the decline in legal marriages with common-law relationships and also the preference to stay single. Due to the desire to succeed in their chosen careers, many postpone their marriages which also encourages nonmarital cohabitation. "As the forces of modernization and post industrialization intensify, individualism continues to remain a dominant value in our culture. Thus, further gains in alternative sexual unions and other life styles incompatible with long-term commitments to married life will likely to continue in the future" (Frank Travato, 1988, pp. 507–521).

Canadian families are also shrinking in size. "In 1986, 84% of Canadians lived in families, this was down from 85% in 1981. Over the 1981–1986 period, the number of lone-parent and common-law unions increased much faster than traditional husband-wife families. The average size of Canadian families is falling. In 1986, there were an average of 3.1 people in each family, down from 3.3 in 1981 and 3.9 in 1981" (Mary Sue Devereaux, 1990, pp. 135–137).

Canadians also tend to marry late. "In 1986, the average age of first marriage was 28 years for men and 26 years for women. In addition, a growing proportion of Canadians never marry. Overall, the annual number of marriages fell from 200,000 in 1972 to 176,000 in 1986" (Owen Adams & Dhruva Nagnur, 1990, pp. 142–145).

In addition to the fact that Canadians marry late, many women bear their first child later in life. "Almost 25 percent of Canadian babies born in 1982 to women over 30 were first born children—making this the highest rate of older new parents Canada has ever had, a Statistics Canada Study says. Large families have almost disappeared, and most couples are limiting their families to two children" (Dorothy Lipevenko, 1984, July 12).

Along with these bleak statistics, there is increasing unwillingness of Canadians to have large families. "Most Canadians believe there aren't enough people in the country but few are willing to have more children even if they are paid to do so, a national poll says" (Joan Bryden, 1988, June 4).

Another factor which has direct impact on Canadian families is that "about three-quarter of lone parents in Canada in 1984 were female, according to a new statistics Canada survey" (Southam News, 1986, Dec. 5).

Some interesting figures regarding economic well being of Canadian families are also important. "The top 1 percent of Canadian families had an average income $143,061 in 1980 or $212,000 in today's dollars, five times the national average, according to Statistics Canada study conducted last year. And while nearly 50 percent of the income of the country's 63,250 highest-income families came from self-employment and investment, a third of the families would not have been in the highest income bracket had the wife not worked" (Canadian Press, 1986, July 9).

Families continue to improve their standard of living according to Statistics Canada. "Average family incomes in Canada exceeded $50,000 for the first time ever in 1989 as families continued to make up ground lost in the early 1980s" (Alan Freeman, 1990, Nov. 30).

On the other hand, most Canadians are not able to keep up with inflation. According to Terrance Hunsley, Executive Director of the Canadian Council of Social Development, "If we were to rank all Canadian families by income and then divide them into five equal layers, we would find most families—80 percent, in fact—not keep up with inflation between 1981 and 1985" (Thomas M. Hunsley, 1987, Feb. 6). This problem continues even in later years. Alan Mirabelli, Director of Administration and Communication for the Vanier Institute expressed some of his concerns. "Canadian families are earning more than they did 20 years ago, but it's now taking two parents to do so—and after taxes and inflation there's been almost no real income gain in 10 years ago. In a study released this month, the Institute shows that the average family income has risen to almost $50,000 from $16,000 in 1971. So the issue of women working isn't a moral issue, it's an economic issue, said Mirabelli" (Joanne Ramondt, 1991, June 5).

In view of the very high probability of instability in marriages many couples contemplate, as well as take concrete steps to have prenuptial contracts which have no legal validity. Later age marriages mean the potential couples individually must have accumulated considerable wealth. Some of them are entering second marriages and that also provides good reason to protect their wealth. "Although exact figures are not available, lawyers involved in the family and estate fields say that the number of couples entering into prenuptial agreements is up sharply" (March Schagol, 1986). Parents also encourage children to draw up prenuptial agreements so that spouses do not make claim on the assets. Marriage contracts make good sense to those whose previous marriage ended in divorce with attendant financial commitments. "It isn't a romantic notion, but it is a realistic one for those people," says Paul Daltrop, a Vancouver family lawyer. "It is a logical step for them." Typically, the gist of most prenuptial contracts is simple: essentially, the parties keep everything they owned before the marriage, but share everything they acquire as a couple" (Calgary Herald, 1990, May 17). According to Toronto lawyer

Lorne Wolfson, "a majority of people sign these contracts without making a fuss," but warn that discussing the divorce before the ring slides on the finger can destroy the romance. "I'd say that 50% sign the marriage contracts and get married, 25% decided not to sign and get married anyway, while the other 25% break-up" (Michael Salter, 1988).

Another aspect of major change is the fact that for every two Canadian weddings one couple who is already married break-up their marriage per year. This is a dramatic increase and according to Statistics Canada, "in fact, the divorce level in Canada have nearly reached the U.S. level, which 20 years ago was more than twice as high as the Canadian level and 10 years ago was 50 percent higher, the federal agency said." (Sean Fine, 1990, Nov. 16). Thus, the emerging marriage and family patterns have to make adequate adjustments for changing values and lifestyles.

References

Adams, Owen
1990 "Divorce Rates in Canada." *Canadian Social Trends,* edited by Craig Mckie and Keith Thompson. Thompson Educational Publishing, Inc., Toronto, p. 146.

Adams, Owen and Dhruva Nagnar
1990 "Marrying and Divorcing: A Status Report for Canada," in *Canadian Social Trends,* Edited by Craig McKie and Keith Thompson. Toronto, Thompson Educational Publishing, Inc., pp. 142–147.

Allemang, John
1989 "Intermarriage Directions Judaism in Canada, CJC Delegate State." Toronto, *Globe and Mail,* May 9.

Anderson, Karen L.
1988 "Historical Perspectives on the Family," in *Family Matters,* edited by Karen L. Anderson and others. Scarborough, Ontario, Nelson Canada, p. 27.

Bell, Robert R.
1979 *Marriage and Family Interaction,* Fifth Edition. Homewood, Illinois: Dorsey Press.

Berger, Amy H.
1989 "Fatal Detraction—How a Single Flaw Can Kill a Lovely Relationship." *Calgary Herald,* Calgary, July 15.

Bragg, Bob
1984 *Calgary Herald.* Calgary, Nov. 23.

Bryden, Joan
1988 "Children Not Priority, Polls Shows." *Calgary Herald,* Calgary, June 4.

Calgary Herald
1990 Calgary, May 17.

Canadian Press
1989 "Number of Divorces in Canada Rises 11 Percent." *The Globe and Mail,* Toronto, Oct. 7.

1986 "Working Wives Are Key to High Income Families." *The Globe and Mail,* July 9.

Cerroni-Long, E. L.
1985 "Marrying Out: Socio-Cultural and Psychological Implications of Intermarriage." *Journal of Comparative Family Studies,* Spring, Vol. XVI, No. 1, pp. 25–46.

Crester, Gary A.
1990 "Intermarriage between 'White' Britons and Immigrants from the New Commonwealth and Pakistan." *Journal of Comparative Family Studies,* Special Issue, 'Intermarriage,' Summer Vol. XXI, No. 2, pp. 227–238.

Crysdale, Stewart and Christopher Beattie
1977 *Sociology Canada—An Introduction Text.* Toronto, Butterworths and Co. (Canada) Ltd., Toronto, p. 112.

Devereaux, Mary Sue
1990 "Marital Status," in *Canadian Social Trends,* edited by Craig McKie and Keith Thompson. Toronto, Thompson Educational Publishing, Inc., pp. 138–141.

1990 "Changes in Living Arrangements." *Canadian Social Trends,* edited by Craig McKie and Keith Thompson. Thompson Educational Publishing, Inc., Toronto, pp. 135–137.

Downey, Donn
1990 "More Migrating South Than North." *The Globe and Mail*, Toronto, Sept. 20.

Drakich, Janice and Connie Guberman
1988 "Violence in the Family." *Family Matters,* edited by Karen L. Anderson and Others. Butterworths Canada, Toronto, p. 207.

Fine, Sean
1990 "Divorce Level Increases Dramatically, Figures Approximate U.s. Situation, Statistics Canada Indicates," Toronto, *The Globe and Mail,* Nov. 16.

Freeman, Alan
1990 "Family Incomes Clear $50,000." *The Globe and Mail,* Nov. 30.

Genius, Stephen,
1991 "Risky Sex." Edmonton, KEG Publishing, Box 32025, Edmonton, Alberta, Canada.

Goldstein, Jay and Alexander Segall
1985 *Canadian Ethnic Studies.* Vol. 17, pp. 60–71.

Guelzow Maureen, G., Gloria W. Bird and Elizabeth H. Koball
1991 "An Exploratory Path Analysis of the Stress Process for Dual-career Men and Women," *Journal of Marriage and the Family,* Feb., Vol. 53, pp. 151–164.

Hobart, Charles W.
1984 "Changing Profession and Practice of Sexual Standards: A Study of Young Anglophone and Francophone Canadians." *Journal of Comparative Family Studies,* Vol. XV, No. 2, pp. 231–255.

Hunsley, Thomas M.
1987 "Rich Get Rich and the Poor Get Poorer," *Calgary Herald,* Calgary, Feb. 6.

Hutter, Mark
1988 *The Changing Family, Comparative Perspectives,* 2nd edition. New York, Macmillan Publishing Co.

1990 Introduction, Special Issue on Intermarriage, *Journal of Comparative Family Studies,* Summer, Vol. XXI, No. 2.

Hyman, Rodman
1972 "Marital Power and the Theory of Resources in Cultural Context." *Journal of Comparative Family Studies,* Special Issue. "Comparative Perspectives on Marriage and the Family," edited by Eugen Lupri and Günther Lüschen. Spring, Vol. III, No. 1, pp. 50–69.

Inglis, Joy and Michael M. Ames
1967 "Conflict and Change in British Columbia Sikhs, Ideal of Family Life." Unpublished manuscript. Canadian Sociology and Anthropology Association, Ottawa, June 10-11, p. 42.

Jacques, Barton
1985 *Calgary Herald.* Calgary, June 7, P.B. 6.

Johnson, Holly
"Wife Abuse." *Canadian Social Trends,* edited by Craig McKie and Keith Thompson. Thompson Educational Publishing Inc., Toronto, pp. 173–176.

Jones, Elize F.
1986 "Teenage Pregnancy in Industrialized Countries." A study sponsored by the Allan Guttmacher Institute, New Haven and London, Yale University Press.

Judd, Eleanore Parelman
1990 "Intermarriage and the Maintenance of Religio-Ethnic Identity: A Case Study: The Denver Jewish Community." *Journal of Comparative Family Studies*, Summer Special Issue, "Intermarriage," Vol. XXI, No. 2, pp. 252–268.

Kashmeri, Zuhair
1986 "100,000 Elderly Canadians Abused a Year, Panel Says." *The Globe and Mail.* Toronto, March 23.

Kurian, George
1975 "Structural Changes in the Family in Kerala, India," in *Socialization and Communication in Primary Groups*, World Anthropology Series, edited by Thomas R. Williams. The Hague, Paris, Mouton Publishers, pp. 59–79.

Larson, Lyle E. and Brenda Munro
1990 "Religious Intermarriage in Canada in the 1980s." *Journal of Comparative Family Studies*, Summer, Special Issue, "Intermarriage," Vol. XXI, No. 2, pp. 238–250.

Laswell, Marcia and Thomas Laswell
1991 *Marriage and the Family*, 3rd Edition. Wadsworth Publishing Co., Belmont, California, pp. 193–208.

Leslie, G.R. and Sheila K. Korman
1989 *Family in Social Context*, 7th Edition. New York, Oxford University Press.

Lipevenko, Dorothy
1984 "First Time Mothers Getting Older." *The Globe and Mail*, July 12.

Lupri, Eugen
1990 "Male Violence in the Home." *Canadian Social Trends*, edited by Craig Mckie and Keith Thompson. Thompson Educational Publishing, Inc., Toronto, pp. 170–172.

1988 "Fathers in Transition." Zeitsukrift für Sozialistions Forschung und Erziehungs-Soziologie, Vol. 8, p. 288.

Lupri, Eugen and J. Frideres
1981 "The Quality of Marriage and the Passage of Time; Marital Satisfaction over the Family Cycle." *Canadian Journal of Sociology*, Vol. 6, pp. 283–306.

Mandell, Nancy
1989 "Marital Roles in Transition." *Family and Marriage, Cross-Cultural Perspectives*, edited by K. Ishwaran. Toronto, Thompson Education Publishing Co. Toronto, pp. 239–243

Murstein, Bernard I.
1974 *Love, Sex and Marriage through the Ages*. New York, Springer Publishing Co., p. 145..

McCall, (Marnie) M. L., Joseph P. Hornick and Jean E. Wallace
1988 "The Process and Economic Consequences of Marriage Breakdown." Calgary, Canadian Research Institute for Law and the Family, July.

Nett, Emily M.
1988 "Canadian Families—Past and Present." Toronto: Butterworths Canada Ltd.

Peters, John F.
1988 "Changing Perspective on Divorce." *Family Matters,* Edited by Karen L. Anderson and Others. Butterworths Canada, Toronto, p. 153.

Pillai, A.K.B.
1984 "Asian Indian Family—Psychological and Cultural Adaptation," in Conference of Family-Bicultural Socialization, edited by B. N. Varma and Jagat-Motwani. National Federation of Asian Indian Organization in America, Washington, D.C., May.

Ram, Bali
1990 "Current Demographic Analysis, New Trends in the Family." Minister of Supplies and Services, Ottawa, Canada.

Ramondt, Joanne
1991 "Two Incomes Not a 'Luxury'." *Calgary Herald,* Calgary, June 5.

Rao, Badrinath Krishna Rao
1991 "The Agony When East Meets West.' *The Globe and Mail.* May 7, p. A17.

Rhyne, Darla
1981 "Bases of Marital Satisfaction among Men and Women." *Journal of Marriage and the Family,* Nov. pp. 941–955.

Saffilios-Rothschild, Constantina
1967 "A Comparison of Power Structure and Marital Satisfaction in Urban Greek and French Families." *Journal of Marriage and the Family*, May, Vol. 29, pp. 345–352.

Salter, Michael
1988 "The High Cost of Leaving." Report on Business. Toronto, *The Globe and Mail,* Oct., pp. 113–119.

Saunders, Iwan
1975 "Canadian Law and Marriage," in *Marriage, Family and Society, Canadian Perspectives.* Toronto: Butterworths Canada, Ltd., p. 47.

Schogol, Marc
1986 "Marriage Contracts Fast Becoming Fact of Life." *Calgary Herald,* Calgary, June 7.

Smith, Vivian
1990 "Woman's Occupations Still Lowest Paying, Statistics Canada Study Says." Toronto, *The Globe and Mail,* March 10.

Somerville, Barbara
1987 *Calgary Herald,* Calgary, May 7.

Southam News
1986 "Single Mothers Top Survey." *Calgary Herald,* Calgary, Dec. 5.

Statistics Canada
1983 Update from 1981 Census: Highlight Information on Ethnicity, Language, etc. Ottawa, Supply and Services, Canada.

The William Petschek National Jewish Family Center of the American Jewish Committee, New York, Spring, Vol. 6, No. 1.
1988

Travato, Frank
1988 "A Macro-Sociological Analysis of Change in the Marriage Rate: Canadian Women, 1921–25 to 1981–85." *Journal of Marriage and the Family*, May, Vol. 50, No. 2, pp. 507–521.

Turcotte, Pierre
1991 "Common-law Unions-Nearly Half a Million in 1986," in *Canadian Social Trends,* edited by Craig McKie and Keith Thompson. Toronto: Thompson Education Publishing Inc., pp. 148–152.

Ursel, Jane
1986 "The State and the Maintenance of Patriarchy: A Case Study of Family, Labour and Welfare Legislation in Canada." Garamond Press, pp. 150–191.

Veevers, Jean E.
1990 "Continuity and Change in Marriage and Family." Toronto: Holt, Rinehart and Winston of Canada, Ltd.

Wallis, Claudia
1989 "Onward Women." *Time*, Dec. 4, 1960.

Weinfeld, Morton
1987 "Immigrants Are Key to the Future." *The Globe and Mail*, Toronto, June 19.

White, James M.
1989 "Marriage A Developing Process in Family and Marriage: Cross-Cultural Perspectives," edited by K Oshwaran. Toronto, Thompson Education Publishing Inc., p. 205.

1987 "Premarital Cohabitation and Marital Stability in Canada." *Journal of Marriage and the Family*, Aug., Vol. 44, No. 3, pp. 641–647.

White, Lynn and Bruce Keith
1990 "The Effect of Shift Work on the Quality and Stability of Marital Relations.' *Journal of Marriage and the Family,* May, Vol. 52, No. 2, pp. 453–462.

White, Pamela M.
1990 "Ethnic Origins of the Canadian Population." *Canadian Social Trends,* Edited by Craig McKie and Keith Thompson. Thompson Educational Publishing, Inc., Toronto, pp. 3–6.

Wilson, Deborah
1986 "Family Life in 'Crisis' State, Study Finds," *The Globe and Mail,* Toronto, July 21.

Wilson, S. *J.*
1991 *Women, Families and Work.* Toronto: McGraw-Hill Ryerson Ltd., p. 6.

Wu, Thengand T. R. Balakrishan
1992 "Attitudes Towards Cohabitation and Marriage in Canada." *Journal of Comparative Family Studies,* Vol. XXIII, No. 1.

11

Health and Health Care in Canada

Harley D. Dickinson

As will be presented in the introduction to this chapter, the sociology of health and health care in Canada is twofold: the sociology of heath and the sociology of medicine and health care. Both are tied significantly to the basic concepts of social structure and culture.

In the first instance, how our society is organized and structured will enable us to understand the distribution of health, illness, injury and death. In the subsequent topic of the sociology of medicine and health care, the focus will be on the social institutions of health care. In the section about reducing the number of contacts that people have with the health institutions, we see that this is framed, in part, by culture. Health is seen to be a valuable resource that Canadians desire. In addition, health care in Canada is built into the code of human rights in our nation, which is a reflection of Canadian culture.

Introduction

Sociology can be defined as the study of both the nature and consequences of society-individual relations (Dickinson, forthcoming; Brym with Fox, 1989). Within that general analytical project there are a number of substantive specializations, including medical sociology. Medical sociology consists of two interrelated parts; a sociology of health and illness, and a sociology of medicine and health care. A sociology of health and illness is concerned with the relationship between the nature and organization of society and the differential distribution of health, illness, injury and death among individuals and various categories of individuals differentially situated within society. A sociology of medicine and health care, includes the study of both individual and institutional definitions of, and responses to, illness and injury.

This chapter outlines selected topics within a sociology of health and illness and a sociology of medicine and health care in Canada. It is divided into two main sections. In the first, selected aspects of the differential distribution of mortality (death) are presented. The second consists of a brief overview of the Canadian health care system. It includes a

Table 11:1
Average Life Expectancy at Birth, by Sex, Canada, Selected Years, 1931–1986[1]

Year	Female	Gain	Male	Gain	Female-male difference in life expectancy
1931	62.1		60.0		2.1
1941	66.3	4.2	63.0	2.3	3.3
1951	70.8	4.5	66.3	3.3	4.5
1961	74.2	1.3	68.3	0.7	5.9
1971	76.4	1.2	69.3	0.6	7.1
1976	77.5	1.1	70.2	0.9	7.3
1981	79.0	1.5	71.9	1.7	7.1
1984–86	79.8	0.8	73.0	2.1	6.8

Sources: Statistics Canada, 1976: Deaths vital statistics, vol. III, Statistics Canada, 1983: Mortality Summary list of causes vital statistics vol. III, 1981, Statistics Canada, 1988: Mortality Summary list of causes vital statistics vol. III, 1986. Reproduced with permission of the Minister of Industry, Science and Technology, 1992.

discussion of some factors contributing to the current crisis in health care, and an overview of key cost containment strategies.

Sociology of Health and Illness in Canada

The fact that the incidence and distribution of injury, illness and death is related to the nature and organization of societies is well known. Rosen (1963: 44), for example, identified four ways in which social conditions are causally related to disease: (1) they may cause disease directly, (2) they may create predispositions among particular categories of individuals for certain diseases, (3) they may facilitate the transmission of the causes of diseases, and (4) they may influence the course and outcome of diseases.

The nature and organization of societies are also causally related to the achievement and preservation of health (Northcott 1991). Different categories of individuals within society, of course, are differentially integrated into structured social relations that either impede or facilitate the promotion and preservation of health. One would expect, therefore, a differential distribution of health and illness between groups and over time. That is precisely what is found.

Canada, like other advanced capitalist societies during the past several decades, has experienced increased life expectancies at birth and increased average age at death. These general trends hold for both males and females. A traditional female advantage in terms of life expectancy, although decreasing in recent years, persists. Table 11:1 shows the average life expectancy for females at birth in Canada in 1931 was 62.1 years, for males it was 60.0 years, for a difference, at birth, of 2.1 additional years of life for women compared to males. By 1984–86 the average life expectancy for females had increased to 79.8 years. For males it had increased to 73 years. This represented a difference of 6.8

additional years of life expected for females compared to males. The gap between females and males has been declining since 1976 when it had reached a high of 7.3 additional years of life. Since that time, although both females and males have continued to achieve gains in life expectancy, for the first time since 1931 the gains for males have exceeded those for females.

Part of the reason for increased life expectancy at birth is the dramatic decline in infant mortality rates. The greatest decline in infant mortality, for both males and females, occurred between 1931 and 1951. The main reason for the decline in infant mortality rates up to 1951 were the result of decreased mortality from various infectious diseases such as whooping cough, influenza, bronchitis, pneumonia, enteritis and diarrhoea (Dominion Bureau of Statistics, 1967:9). In 1986, for infants under one year of age, almost three quarters of all the deaths that did occur were caused by congenital anomalies and other causes specific to the perinatal period. Although the infant mortality rate has continued to decline since 1951 the rate of decrease has slowed. This slowing is associated with the above mentioned shift in the primary causes of death among that age group. Even so, the infant mortality rate per 1,000 live births decreased to 8 in 1986 from about 42 in 1950 (Statistics Canada, 1988 a:9, Figure III). The mortality rate for all age groups has tended to be steady or decline over the 1950–1986 time period as shown in Figure 11:1.

Figure 11.1. Trends in Age Specific Death Rates Canada, 1950–1986
(Reproduced with the permission of the Minister of Industry, Science and Technology, 1992.)

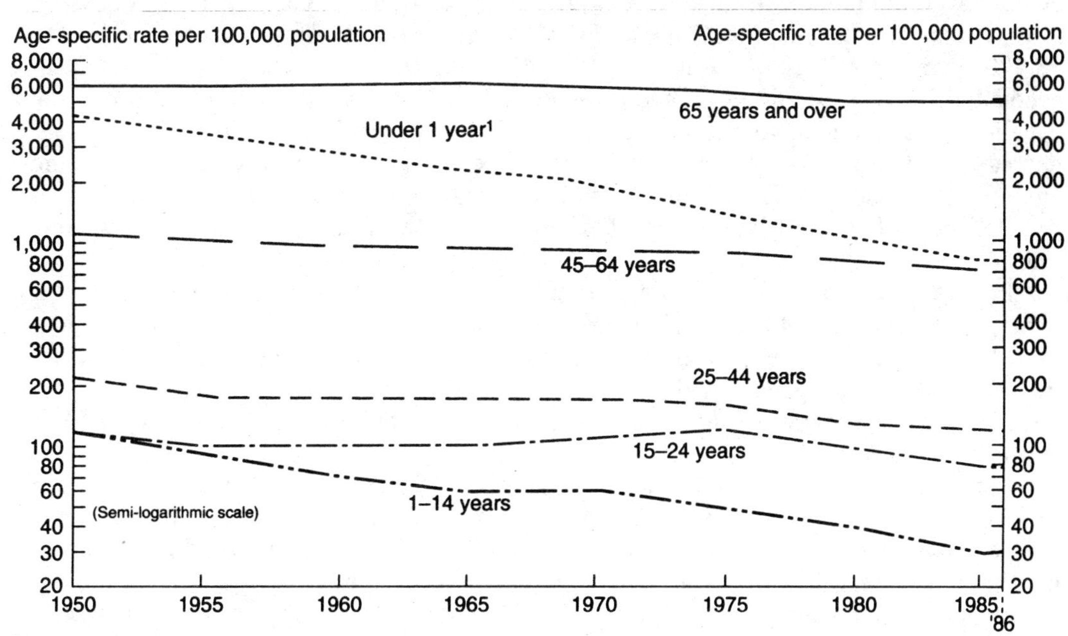

[1]Rate per 100,000 live births.
Source: Statistics Canada, 1988: Mortality Summary list of causes vital statistics vol. III 1986, Figure II p. 8.

Table 11:2
Percentage of All Deaths by Age Groups, Both Sexes, Canada, Selected Years, 1951–1986

	1951	1961	1971	1981	1986
Under 1 year	11.7	9.2	4.0	2.1	1.6
1–24 years	5.7	4.5	4.9	3.8	2.7
25–44 years	7.0	5.8	5.8	5.5	5.2
45–64 years	22.0	21.4	23.0	21.6	20.0
65 years and over	53.6	59.1	62.3	67.0	71.0
Total deaths (000s)	125.8	141.0	157.3	171.0	184.2

Sources: Statistics Canada, 1976: General Mortality 1950 to 1972, Statistics Canada, 1982: Causes of death 1981, Statistics Canada, 1988: Mortality, summary list of causes, vital statistics, vol. III, 1986. Reproduced with permission of the Minister Of Industry, Science and Technology, 1992.

As shown in Table 11:2, however, the percentage of all deaths accounted for by those under one year of age and those 65 years and older has changed dramatically. Deaths in the under one year age group dropped from 11.7 per cent of all deaths in Canada in 1951 to 1.6 per cent in 1986. In absolute numbers this corresponds to a decline of about 11,772 deaths; from around 14,719 in 1951 to 2,947 in 1986. That decrease was achieved despite the fact that the total number of deaths in Canada, regardless of age, increased by about 58,400; from around 125,800 in 1951 to 184,224 in 1986. The percentage of all deaths accounted for by those 65 years and older during that time period increased from 53.6 to 71. That corresponded to 67,429 deaths in 1951 and 130,782 in 1986. In addition to decreased infant mortality, the increased number and proportion of deaths among those aged 65 years and over is a result of a shift in the demographic structure of the Canadian population; in both absolute and proportional terms the Canadian population is getting older.

Part of the reason for this demographic shift is the fact that the infectious and contagious diseases that previously were principal causes of deaths have been eliminated, or at least greatly reduced, as causes of death in contemporary Canadian society. Consequently, individuals generally live longer. Various chronic and degenerative diseases have become the leading causes of morbidity and death in Canadian society since the Second World War.

Figure 11:2 shows the trends in age-adjusted death rates for selected causes of death in Canada between 1950 and 1986. The rate of death per 100,000 population has decreased steadily over that time period, even though, as mentioned above, the total number of deaths has steadily increased. The declining death rate reflects a greater rate of total population growth compared to growth in the death rate, even though both rates increased.

Cardiovascular disease, both heart diseases and stroke, remained the leading cause of death for both males and females over the entire 1950 to 1986 period. In 1950 it accounted for 45 per cent of all deaths, this rose to 50 per cent in 1970, and it had fallen to

Figure 11.2. Trends in Age-adjusted Rates for Selected Causes Canada, 1950–1986
(Reproduced with permission of the Minister of Industry, Science and technology, 1992.)

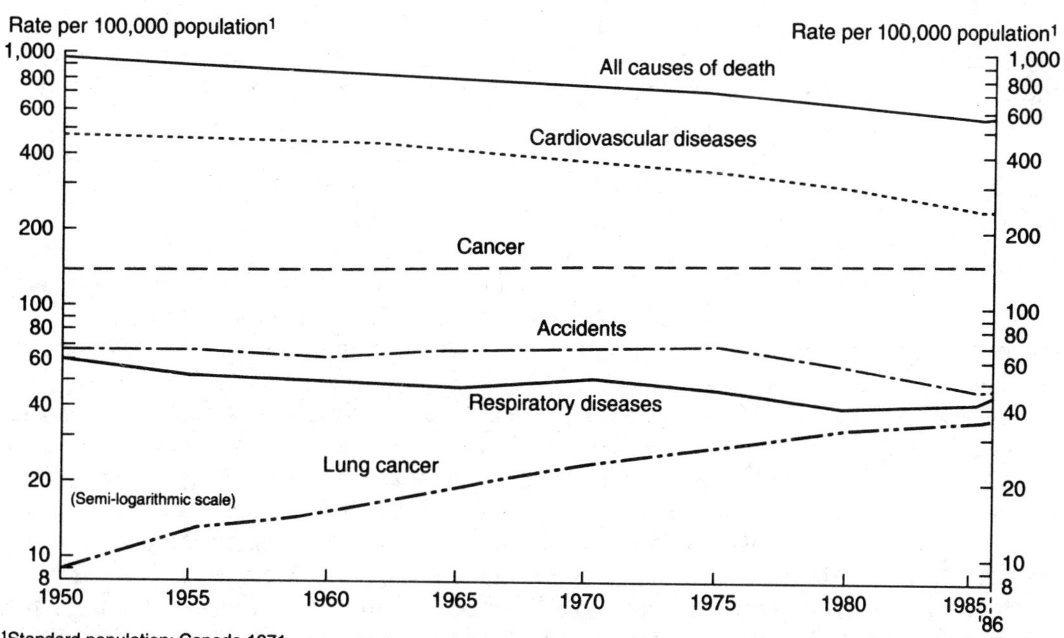

[1]Standard population: Canada 1971.
Source: Statistics Canada, 1988: Mortality Summary list of causes vital statistics vol. III 1986, Figure IV p. 11.

43 per cent in 1986. A slight gender difference existed in 1986 when cardiovascular diseases accounted for 44.9 per cent of all female deaths and 41.4 per cent of all male deaths (Statistics Canada, 1988b:7). Current attempts to explain the observed decline focus on a number of factors, including (1) a reduction in risk producing behaviors and characteristics, such as cigarette smoking, obesity, high cholesterol diets, and high blood pressure; (2) an increase in preventative behaviors, such as higher levels of physical activity; (3) a reduction in the severity of diseases; and (4) improved treatments (Statistics Canada, 1988a:9).

The second leading cause of death, for both men and women, is cancer. The death rate from all cancers has been rising steadily for both males and females so that by 1986 it accounted for 25 per cent of all deaths in Canada. Death from lung cancer accounted for one third of all male cancer deaths in 1986, while breast cancer caused one fifth of all female cancer deaths that year. These two cancers predominated as the leading causes of cancer caused deaths (Statistics Canada, 1988a:9)

Among males, lung cancer death rates levelled off after 1984 following decades of increases. Among women, lung cancer death rates are still rising steeply, particularly for those over 65 years of age. It is generally thought after a lag of at least twenty years, that increased female death rates from lung cancer followed increased cigarette smoking

(Statistics Canada, 1988b:10). Reduced lung cancer death rates among males in Canada, as well as in a number of other countries, is thought to be the result of decreased cigarette smoking among men. There is also some evidence that filter and lower tar cigarettes may have contributed to reduced risk of lung cancer (Statistics Canada, 1988b:1). The age adjusted death rates for women as a result of breast cancer remained steady between 1950 and 1984. Between 1984 and 1986 there was a slight increase in breast cancer death rates.

The third and fourth leading causes of death in Canada are respiratory diseases and accidents. The rank order for these two causes of death are different for males and females. Death by accident, which includes all external causes of injury and poisoning, was the third leading cause of death for males, accounting for 9.4 per cent of all male deaths in 1986. Accidental death was the fourth leading cause of death for females in Canada that year representing 5.1 per cent of all female deaths. Respiratory diseases represented a greater proportion of women's deaths (7.3 per cent) than accidents, while, for men respiratory disease ranked fourth as a cause of death accounting for 8.8 per cent of all male deaths in 1986 (Statistics Canada, 1988 b:11).

Between 1981 and 1986 the age adjusted death rates for respiratory disease rose by 17 percent over all age groups. Most of the observed increase, however, was among those 65 years and over. The rates for persons under 65 years of age were generally stable. This is similar to the age related trends observed for cancer death rates.

In the case of accident related deaths there has been a decrease in the age adjusted rates since the mid-1970s, with a levelling off in the mid-1980s. Motor vehicle death rates continued a steady downward trend that has been attributed to reduced speed limits established in 1976–77, and the introduction of mandatory seat belt use in most provinces between 1976 and 1986.

Although these figures on rates and causes of death reveal important information, they also obscure some significant facts concerning age specific death rates and causes of death. We have already seen that among Canadian infants less than one year old the two leading causes of death in 1986 were those specific to the perinatal period, and congenital anomalies.

Table 11:3 shows, that for the those aged 1 to 24 years the leading causes of death for both males and females were accidents and adverse effects of medical treatments, and cancer. For males accidents and adverse effects accounted for almost 74 per cent of all deaths, while cancer, the second leading cause, represented 7.3 per cent of male deaths. For females 53.2 per cent of all deaths were caused by accidents and 11.9 per cent by cancers.

A similar pattern was evident among those 25 to 44 years of age. In 1986, 50.6 percent of all deaths among males were the result of accidents and adverse effects. Sixteen per cent of all male deaths were caused by cardiovascular disease and almost 15 per cent were the result of cancers. For females, 29.7 per cent of deaths were the result of accidents and adverse effects; 38.7 per cent were caused by cancers, and 11.3 per cent were the result of cardiovascular disease. The substantial gender differences in proportional distribution and absolute numbers of deaths characteristics of the 1 to 24 year age group continued to exist for the 25 to 44 year age group.

Table 11:3
Leading Causes of Death at Different Ages, Canada, 1986[1]

Causes of death	Male Number	Male Percent	Female Number	Female Percent	Total Number	Total Percent
Under 1 year old						
Causes of perinatal mortality	704	42.4	510	39.9	1214	41.3
- Respiratory distress syndrome	183	11.0	105	8.2	288	9.8
- Other respiratory conditions	144	8.7	99	7.7	243	8.3
Contenital anomalies	500	30.1	424	33.2	924	31.4
- Circulatory system	197	11.9	174	13.6	371	12.6
- Nervous system	76	4.6	86	6.7	154	5.2
Sudden infant death syndrome	222	13.4	151	11.8	373	12.7
All other causes	234	14.1	193	15.1	427	14.5
All causes	1660	100.0	1278	100.0	2938	100.0
Ages 1 to 24 years						
Accidents and adverse effects	2528	73.6	775	53.2	3303	67.5
Cancer	250	7.3	173	11.9	423	8.6
Congenital anomalies	125	3.6	115	7.9	240	4.9
Disease of the nervous system	139	4.0	78	5.4	217	4.4
Cardiovascular disease	97	2.8	71	4.9	168	3.4
All other causes	296	8.6	245	16.8	541	11.1
All causes	3435	100.0	1457	100.0	4892	100.0
Ages 25 to 44 years						
Accidents and adverse effects	3272	50.6	931	29.7	4203	43.7
Cancer	968	14.8	1214	38.7	2170	22.6
Cardiovascular disease	1036	16.0	355	11.3	1391	14.5
Endocrine, nutritional and metabolic diseases	328	5.1	65	2.1	393	4.1
Diseases of the digestive system	212	3.3	126	4.0	338	3.5
All other causes	668	10.3	444	14.2	1112	11.6
All causes	6472	100.0	3135	100.0	9607	100.0
Ages 45 to 64 years						
Cancer	8011	34.9	6404	50.4	14415	40.4
Cardiovascular disease	9110	39.7	3264	25.7	12374	34.7
Accidents and adverse effects	1912	8.3	761	6.0	2673	7.5
Disease of the digestive system	1150	5.0	595	4.7	1745	4.9
Respiratory diseases	971	4.2	526	4.1	1497	4.2
All other causes	1810	7.9	1152	9.1	2962	8.3
All causes	22964	100.0	12702	100.0	35666	100.0
Ages 65 years and over						
Cardiovascular disease	31577	47.5	33722	52.1	65299	49.8
Cancer	16959	25.5	13467	20.8	30426	23.2
Respiratory disease	7635	11.5	5384	8.3	13019	9.9
Disease of the digestive system	2210	3.3	2497	3.9	4707	3.6
Endocrine, nutritional and metabolic diseases	1607	2.4	2249	2.5	3856	2.9
All other causes	6447	9.7	7361	11.4	13808	10.5
All causes	66435	100.0	64680	100.0	131115	100.0
All ages all causes	100969	100.0	83255	100.0	185224	100.0

Source: Statistics Canada, 1988: Mortality Summary list of causes vital statistics vol. III 1986, pp. 14. reproduced with permission of the Minister of Industry, Science and Technology, 1992.

The pattern changed for the next age group. For those between the ages of 45 and 64 years the three leading causes of death were cancer, cardiovascular diseases and accidents and adverse effects corresponding to 40.4, 34.7 and 7.5 per cent respectively of all deaths regardless of gender. There were also significant gender differences in that age group. The leading cause of death for males was cardiovascular diseases at 39.7 per cent, followed by cancer at 34.9 per cent, with accidents and adverse effects coming third at 8.3 per cent of all deaths. The leading cause of death for females was cancers which accounted for 50.4 per cent of all deaths, cardiovascular diseases was the second leading cause of death at 25.7 per cent.

The three leading causes of death for those in the 65 years and older age group for both males and females were cardiovascular diseases, cancers and respiratory diseases. About 50 per cent of deaths among males and females over age 65 were the result of cardiovascular diseases, 25.5 per cent of male deaths and 20.8 per cent of female deaths were caused by cancers and 11.5 and 8.3 per cent of male and female deaths respectively were the result of respiratory diseases. Accidents and adverse effects that play so prominent a role in the deaths of the younger age groups are much less significant as relative causes of death among Canada's elderly population. It is important to note, however, that accidents account for a large number of deaths among that age group.

Age and gender are not the only sources of variation in morbidity and mortality rates. Indeed, it is probably the case that observed age and gender differences in mortality rates and causes of death, in many instances, are influenced by the different socio-economic statuses and social positions of men and women, the young and the old. Support for this notion is provided when one examines the distribution of morbidity and mortality by income. Table 11:4 shows that in the late 1970s men in the first quintile of income earners, that is, men in the lowest 20 per cent of income earners in Canada, at birth could expect to live for 67.1 years. This compared to a life expectancy at birth of 76.6 years for women in the first quintile of income earners. This amounted to a difference of 9.5 additional years of life for women compared to men among the lowest 20 per cent of income earners.

Table 11:4

Income Level by Quintiles, and Life Expectancy at Birth, by Sex, Canada, Late 1970s[1]

	Life expectancy at birth	
Income	**Female**	**Male**
First quintile	76.6	67.1
Second quintile	77.6	70.1
Third quintile	78.5	70.9
Fourth quintile	79.0	72.0
Fifth quintile	79.4	73.4
Total	78.3	70.8

Source: Hay (1988) adapted from Wilkins and Adams (1983: 1078, Table 11:3). Reproduced with permission of the Minister of Industry, Science and Technology, 1992.

Comparing high income earning men to low income earning men reveals a similar pattern (Wolfson, Rowe and Gentleman, 1990). Men in the fifth quintile of income earners, that is, in the top 20 percent of income earners, in the late 1970s, could expect 73.4 years of life at birth compared to the 67.1 years expected for men among the lowest 20 per cent of income earners. High income earning men, thus, could expect an additional 6.3 years of life compared to low income earning men. In addition to greater life expectancy, high income earning men could expect about 14 more years of disability free life compared to men with low incomes. For women the difference is eight years (Epp, 1986:4).

Income level is also directly related to life expectancy at birth for women, although as shown in Table 11:4, differences between low income women and high income women is not as great as for men. High income women could expect 79.4 years of life at birth compared to 73.4 years for men for a difference of six additional years of life for high income earning women compared to high income earning men. The difference in life expectancy at birth for high income earning women compared to low income men is the most dramatic amounting to 12.3 additional years of life.

We have observed increased life expectancy at birth for both males and females over the course of most of this century. Associated with that is an increased average age at death, and a transition in the major causes of mortality away from infectious and contagious diseases towards more chronic, degenerative diseases and accidents. Although the major sources of morbidity are not exactly congruent with major sources of mortality, there is substantial overlap (Blishen, 1991).

A good indicator of the main sources of morbidity is reason for hospitalization. The main reasons for hospitalizations generally correspond to the main causes of death discussed above (Blishen, 1991:38). Blishen does not include in his list of the main reasons for hospitalization the rate of patient days for cancers which, as we have seen, is a leading cause of death. This omission appears to be an oversight. According to Blishen's data, the leading causes of hospitalization in Canada in 1969, expressed as age-standardized rates of in-patient days per 1,000 population, were heart diseases (181.76), other cerebrovascular diseases (104.92), accidents (152.84), respiratory diseases (129.01), and mental disorders (102.50). By 1982, although the leading causes of hospitalization expressed in those terms remained the same, the rank order had changed: mental disorders had become the leading cause of hospitalization at 157.33 age-standardized in-patient days per 1,000 population, followed by heart diseases at 146.77, cerebrovascular diseases at 137.94, accidents at 123.68, and respiratory diseases at 115.57 (Blishen, 1991:37).

An exception to the observation that the leading causes of death and hospitalization correspond, is mental disorders. Mental disorders in themselves are not causes of death. Following the invention and introduction of psychotropic drugs in the early 1950s, and especially since the introduction of hospitalization insurance and medical care insurance in the 1950s and 1960s respectively, the old mental hospital system of treatment has declined and most in-patient treatment has been shifted to general hospitals (Dickinson, 1989; Dickinson and Andre, 1988). Given the current crisis in health care costs in general and acute care hospital costs in particular, one might anticipate renewed efforts to find less expensive alternatives to general hospital inpatient treatment and care for those diagnosed with mental disorders or illnesses. It is interesting to note in light of various cost containment strategies and efforts to reduce utilization rates of health care services discussed below, that there has been a decline in hospitalizations measured as age-standardized rates of in-patient days per 1 000 population for all causes since mid-1970s (Blishen, 1991:37).

Despite variations in the main causes of both of morbidity and mortality along gender, age and income lines, it is widely expected that observed trends will continue, perhaps even at an accelerated rate, because of the demographic shift in the nature and composition of the Canadian population. The Canadian population, like that of most other advanced industrial nations, for some time now has been characterized by declining birth rates and increased longevity of the population. In combination, these two factors have resulted in a situation where the elderly constitute a larger proportion of the population in both relative and absolute terms. This will continue to have a profound impact on the level and nature of health care needs, service utilization patterns, and costs.

Anticipation of increased need, utilization, and costs of health care has contributed to the perception of a growing crisis in health care costs (Blomquvist 1979; Weller and Manga, 1983; Evans, 1984; York, 1987; Brown, 1987; Dickinson and Hay, 1988). Much effort is currently being directed to an analysis of the nature and organization of the existing health care system to determine if it is effective and appropriate given changing health care needs. Attention is also directed towards determining if necessary and effective health care services are being provided in the most cost efficient method possible. It is to an exploration of these issues that we turn in the following section.

Sociology of Medicine and Health Care

The present health care system in Canada, both in terms of its prevention activities and its treatment responses, developed largely as a solution to the problems of infectious and contagious diseases. Despite its effectiveness in contributing to the cure and control of certain types of illness and injuries, the dominant biomedical model of medical practice, has been widely criticized for its shortcomings. Most commonly critics point out the tendency for those employing the bio-medical model, founded as it is on the twin pillars of "germ theory" and the insights of pathology (Shorter, 1985), to individualize the explanation and treatment of illness and injury and, consequently, to fail adequately to recognize the social, economic, political and cultural determinants of health and illness (Illich, 1976; Navarro, 1976; Powles, 1973: Bolaria, 1983; Foss and Rothenberg, 1987; Hewa and Hetherington, 1990b).

This criticism has gained increased cogency in recent years as the major sources of illness and death have shifted from those caused by a single biological organism to those that are thought to be the result of complex interactions between genetic, psychological, social and other environmental factors and processes. The application of the biomedical model to explanations and treatments of mental disorders, heart diseases, cancers and accidents, for example, is often inappropriate. These, however, are the health problems that the system is increasingly being asked to solve. The dominant bio-medical model and related forms of health care and promotion are the wrong tools for the main job at hand (Foss and Rothenberg, 1987).

This does not mean that the maintenance of an effective and efficient prevention and treatment system for infectious and contagious diseases is unnecessary. Although most diseases of that sort have been controlled within the context of advanced industrial countries, changing economic conditions, alterations in international population movements, variations in the virulence of illness producing organisms, and changes in host resistance, require continual vigilance in the areas of prevention and treatment of these diseases (Gellert, Neumann and Gordon, 1989). Resurgences in polio, cholera and malaria in recent years are examples. In addition, new infectious and contagious diseases emerge as the nature of social and individual behavior changes in the context of structural transformations in the social, economic, political and cultural sub-systems of society. The most well known contemporary example is the HIV virus and AIDS. Thus, changes in the nature of the primary health problems facing Canadian society cannot be solved simply by transferring resources from one set of health problems to another. The system must both expand and change. This has implications for the level and allocation of health resources.

Financing and Cost Containment in the Health Care Sector

Under the Canadian constitution health care is a provincial responsibility. Thus, one cannot speak of a national health care system in any meaningful sense until after the Second World War. Even then, however, the role of the federal government was, and is, restricted to setting standards and contributing money to, or withholding money from, provincial and territorial governments as an incentive to adopt, or as a sanction for not adopting, federal standards. This jurisdictional situation has resulted in protracted negotiations over the last several decades directed towards the establishment of mutually agreeable funding arrangements. One consequence of this feature of the Canadian polity is that the development of a national health care system has proceeded slowly and in stages. Indeed, in many respects it might be argued that a national health care system does not exist at all, but rather, there are several more or less congruent provincial and territorial systems that, taken together, constitute the Canadian national health care system.

The first step towards a national health care system was the 1948 hospital construction grants. This was followed with the 1958 Hospital Insurance and Diagnostic Services Act which established a national system of hospitalization insurance cost-shared between the federal and provincial/territorial governments. The final step was the introduction of the 1968 Medical Care Services Act.

The Medical Services Act established a national medical care insurance plan, Medicare, on a cost-shared basis. Under its terms provinces and territories were eligible for federal funds to pay for all necessary physician services if the following principles were adopted: (1) universality, virtually all Canadian citizens were covered, (2) comprehensiveness, all necessary medical services were included, (3) accessibility, no financial or other barriers to treatment were imposed, (4) portability, eligible residents who are temporarily absent from their province of residence were covered, and (5) public administration on a non-profit basis, which is self explanatory. By 1972 all provinces and territories had instituted these principles and joined Medicare.

Table 11:5 provides a breakdown of national health care expenditures over time. For 1986 it is estimated that the federal and the provincial/territorial governments combined spent about $33.1 billion on health care services (Statistics Canada, 1986c; 1987). The proportional distributions by function are probably not much different than indicated in Table 11:5.

Table 11:5

Total Health Expenditures in Millions of Dollars, by Category, Canada, Selected Years 1971, 1976, 1982 and 1987[1]

Category	1971	1976	1982	1987
TOTAL HEALTH EXPENDITURES	7118.7	14119.9	31150.2	47934.8
PERSONAL HEALTH CARE	6206.2	12360.9	27044.0	42136.2
INSTITUTIONS	3674.6	7893.8	16974.1	24547.4
Hospitals	3149.9	6349.8	13036.4	18808.8
Other institutions	516.0	1424.5	3535.7	4945.6
Home Care	~	51.5	183.5	377.5
Ambulances	8.7	67.9	218.5	415.4
PROFESSIONAL SERVICES	1666.7	3019.1	6731.9	10933.3
Physicians	1250.4	2165.7	4649.8	7678.8
Dentists	311.5	699.8	1702.4	2609.6
Chiropractors	39.3	77.4	209.9	356.7
Optomitrists	49.1	39.0	83.5	141.8
Podiatrists	4.2	14.6	27.6	36.3
Osteopaths	2.1	1.4	1.6	1.4
Private duty nurses	10.1	13.5	16.9	26.0
Physiotherapists	~	7.8	40.3	82.8
DRUGS AND APPLIANCES	865.0	1447.9	3338.0	6655.5
OTHER HEALTH CARE COSTS	912.4	1759.0	4106.2	5798.7
Prepayment Administration	122.6	209.1	403.0	578.3
Public health	214.7	631.3	1325.8	2130.8
Capital expenditures	420.2	649.6	1712.6	2132.6
Health research	78.3	113.3	273.6	411.3
Miscellaneous health costs	76.7	155.7	391.2	545.7

Sources: National Health Expenditures in Canada databank, Health Information Division, Health and Welfare Canada. September 1992. Reproduced with the permission of the Minister of Supplies and Services Canada 1992.

Since the introduction of Medicare, three interrelated strategies have been used to control health care costs: (1) reductions in the episodes of illness requiring medical or hospital care; (2) reductions in the frequency and duration of care required for any episode of illness; and (3) reductions in the cost per contact (Task Force, 1970). Recently a fourth strategy, which consists of reducing the amount budgeted for health care, has been adopted. Selected aspects of these strategies are examined below.

Reductions in the Episodes of Illness

Reducing the episodes of illness requiring medical or hospital treatment can be achieved in two ways; first, by improving the health of the population, that is, by reducing the amount of illness and injury in society, and second, by modifying illness behaviors so that individuals seek less medical assistance and provide more self-care. In this section critical attention is focused on aspects of the first strategy. Attempts to alter illness behaviors are looked at in the next section.

The health status of the population can be improved by preventing illness and promoting healthy lifestyles. Illness prevention techniques are determined by a number of factors. including the causes and nature of illness and injury. It is generally thought that the new public health problems facing Canadians are caused by a number of interacting factors, including, biological/genetic, psychological/behavioural and social/environmental. Effective prevention, therefore, requires interventions and modifications in all three causal factors.

Current medical research suggests that for many, if not most, contemporary illnesses, including cerebrovascular diseases, cancers, mental disorders, as well as congenital abnormalities, genetic predispositions play a large role. Drawing upon the art and the science of animal husbandry it has long been known that selective breeding and natural selection are mechanisms that can increase or decrease a species' resistance to certain illnesses. Historically, the eugenics movement has advocated selective human breeding so as to control the intergenerational transmission of both positive and negative physical and mental characteristics and predispositions for and against various diseases thought to be hereditable. The main strategies adopted in the name of the genetic improvement of a race or nation have been controlled immigration, and controlled reproduction of those considered unfit. Controlled reproduction has included compulsory sterilization, restricted marriage of the "unfit" through a system of marriage licences, and the encouragement of fertility among those deemed to have desirable traits (McLaren, 1990).

The eugenical improvement of the stock of the nation was actively encouraged in the name of preventive medicine and mental hygiene by certain sectors of the medical profession, and other emerging "helping professions," in Canada throughout most of the first half of this century, and particularly during the interwar years. The eugenics movement was not restricted to Canada. It was an international movement most fully developed and institutionalized in Nazi Germany. The brutal genocidal policies of the Nazis, carried out in the name of racial and social improvement, and legitimated as medical science, led to the collapse of the movement by the end of the Second World War.

McLaren (1990:170) points out, however, that after World War II, "just as the crude social engineering policies campaigned for by the traditional eugenicists were being consigned to the dustbin of history, geneticists were making important breakthroughs that established the basis for a 'new eugenics.'" These breakthroughs made it possible, for the first time, to know the genetic make up of an individual before birth. The expansion of genetics screening techniques and fetal diagnostic technologies, have resulted in greatly increased capacity to diagnose a range of disorders, defects and disabilities such as Downs Syndrome, spina bifida and others. Combined with genetic counselling services, these screening and diagnostic services have enabled the prevention of much illness and misery through therapeutic abortions.

This has helped entrench individual level strategies of prevention based upon genetic intervention. Combined with an increasing consensus that more resources must be devoted to prevention efforts, it seems likely that as a society we will increasingly be faced with the questions who is to live, who is to die, and who is to decide? Current debates over reproductive rights and technologies, euthanasia, and quality of life concerns, are harbingers of social and cultural changes. As the history of the eugenics movement has shown, the application of individual level solutions to social problems, regardless of intentions and motives, can set us on an undesirable path to an equally undesirable destination.

Strategies and practices for the prevention of illness and the promotion of health must recognise that health and illness are related not only to what we "are" genetically or physiologically, but also to what we "do" and how we do it, individually and socially. Consequently, substantial effort is directed towards the encouragement or enforcement of what are thought to be health producing and illness preventing behaviors. It is to a brief discussion of these efforts that attention is now turned.

It is a self evident truth that individuals' lifestyles are related both to health and illness. What is often obscured by this self evident truth is the less evident, but no less truthful fact, that individual lifestyles are themselves largely shaped, influenced or perhaps even determined, by the structured set of institutionalized social relationships within which, and through which, we live our lives. Thus, attempts to modify individual behaviors must be based upon an adequate theoretical understanding of the nature of the social, economic, political and cultural structures within which individuals work, rest and struggle (Dickinson and Stobbe, 1988). Indeed, health promotion and illness prevention and treatment policies and practices are part of those structured social relations.

Individual illness preventing and health promoting behaviors fall at various points on a continuum between voluntary and compulsory compliance. Different approaches are taken with respect to different health problems and in different institutional contexts. For example, we all more or less accept the requirement of compulsory vaccination against a wide range of infectious and contagious diseases. It is interesting to point out, however, that acceptance of vaccination has not always existed (Bator, 1983). Its continued acceptance requires constant reproduction both through public health education campaigns and vigilance in enforcing existing legislation.

Other examples of illness and injury prevention behaviors that are legislated would include mandatory seat belt use in motor vehicles, the requirement for motor cyclists to wear safety helmets, motor vehicle speed limits, and the criminalization of impaired driving, as well as a number of other road safety laws and regulations. Usually the legislation of behavior is accompanied by public health education campaigns intended to encourage people to do on a voluntary basis that which is legally required or deemed desirable from a public health perspective. Included would be educational campaigns to encourage people to not smoke, to exercise more, to adopt good nutritional habits, to abstain from drug abuse, to encourage "responsible" alcohol use, and, to engage in "safe" sex, to name a few.

The government also claims that it attempts to encourage people to give up health damaging behaviors such as tobacco smoking and alcohol abuse through the imposition of heavy consumption taxes on those products. Insurance companies use financial incentives/sanctions in the form of differential insurance premiums that are lower for non-smokers and higher for smokers.

Although few would deny that health promotion and illness prevention initiatives play an important role in a comprehensive health policy, critics argue too much effort is directed towards individual behavior modification strategies and too little towards altering the social, economic, political and cultural structures which serve as impediments to health and the choice of healthy lifestyles. Policy makers, of course, are aware of the fact that policy decisions in a large number of areas have health consequences. There is also an awareness of the fact that the health dimension of various policy decisions may not, and often does not, have top priority (Epp, 1986:10).

This is an important insight. To suggest, however, that the problem can be solved by making "health matters attractive to other sectors in much the same way that we try to make healthy choices attractive to people" (Epp, 1986:10), appears to reduce the problem, and the solution, to the individual level. Presented in this way the problem appears to be a lack of understanding or inappropriate attitudes, that can be corrected by providing information to individuals. Such an approach, although undoubtedly appropriate in some respects, fails to adequately recognize that various, structured impediments, imperatives and interests may prevent the realization of health priorities even if they are attractive to individuals who recognize their importance.

The sociological study of the nature and consequences of society-individual relationships has demonstrated that individuals' interests, goals, motives and capacities to achieve them are influenced, if not determined, by the patterned sets of social relationships within which, and through which they live. We have already seen, for example, how social characteristics are related to health and illness patterns among individuals who belong to various social categories and whose lives reflect the different social relationships related to age, gender and income. In particular, the structured inequalities of age, gender, race, and class repeatedly have been linked to differential morbidity and mortality patterns. It is also important to point out that in societies where individuals are characterized by structurally determined and differentiated interests, and structurally and individually differentiated capacities to realize those interests, it may not be easy, or even possible, for individuals, acting as individual, to fundamentally change their behaviors.

It has been argued, for example, that in societies where capitalism is the dominant mode of economic production and circulation an irresolvable contradiction exists between the need for profits and the goal of healthy workplaces and safe consumer products. The structurally determined imperative of economic growth and expanded profits impedes the capacity of both government and business to adopt policies and practices that give priority to health (Renaud, 1977). This is true whether or not any individual business person or policy-maker as an individual would like to put health before profits.

The health promotion and illness and injury prevention efforts discussed above have in common the goal of improving health and reducing the level of injury and illness. It is reasoned that it will reduce the need for, and hence utilization of, health care services. Reduced utilization will reduce health care costs. Two other methods for reducing utilization and costs, which do not require reductions in need levels, exist. These are reductions in the range and number of services provided, and modifications to illness behaviors intended to reduce utilization rates without necessarily reducing the incidence of illness and injury. Attention is turned to an examination of these points below.

Reducing the Number of Contacts with the Health Care System

Conceptually illness behavior must be distinguished from illness. Illness refers to a physiological condition or state of the individual. Illness behavior refers to the actions taken by individuals when they are ill, or when they consider themselves to be ill. Illness behavior is learned behavior that is historically and culturally specific and, therefore, subject to change. Related to the concept of illness behavior is the concept of care giver behavior, or more specifically physician behavior. Alterations in both illness behavior and physician behavior are important ways to reduce the number of contacts with the health care system, and thereby, to reduce costs.

Changing Illness Behaviors

Containing health care costs by reducing service utilization may be in contradiction with well established health promotion principles and treatment practices. In particular, regular check ups and screening programs intended to enable early diagnosis and treatment, in some cases, may be seen as an ineffective and inefficient use of health care resources. Thus, individual health care consumers receive conflicting messages concerning what currently is considered appropriate illness behavior. Within the modern health promotion framework, self-care and mutual aid are advocated as preferred forms of illness behavior (Epp, 1986).

Self-care refers to actions taken by individuals to achieve and protect their health. "Simply put," the Epp (1986:7) report states, "encouraging self-care means encouraging healthy choice." Closely related to self-care is the notion of mutual aid, or self-help. Self-help differs from self-care. It refers to a pooling and sharing of resources and information to create socially supportive relations of interdependence that will foster increased capacity of individuals for independent, community-based living. That is, it refers to positive attempts to reduce utilization of the formal health care system.

The goal of reduced service utilization is sensitive because access to necessary medical and hospital services has been a right of Canadian citizenship since the introduction of Medicare (Taylor, 1978; York, 1987; Begin, 1988). Not only is universal access to a comprehensive medical care services system currently a right of citizenship, it also has a broad base of popular support. Consequently few politicians, even if they were so inclined, have been willing to suggest that Canadians be denied access to necessary medical services without proposing an acceptable alternative, such as that outlined in the Epp report, or without justifying proposed restrictions of access and utilization as fair and just because of some alleged characteristics of service users themselves. In terms of this second situation, the strategy adopted has been to attack alleged abusers of health care services.

Historically, those who have claimed that overutilization of medical and hospital services was a major factor contributing to the crisis of rising costs, have proposed or imposed various forms of "deterent," or user fees. These take the form of direct, out-of-pocket payments by service users for doctor's and/or hospital services. User fees, in their several manifestations, however, are charged to all service users. They are not targeted at the alleged service abusers. Such fees, therefore, have the effect of deterring both alleged abusers and legitimate users, particularly low income users (Beck, 1973). By creating a financial barrier to low income Canadians, deterrent fees undermine one of the foundations of Medicare, the principle of equality of access (Grant, 1988).

Proponents of user pay schemes point out that low income users could be identified through a means test and exempted from payment of user fees on that basis. Means testing would violate the principle of universality and would facilitate the development of a two tier health care system, one for the rich and one for the poor. If individuals must be officially designated as paupers to receive health care services, they may delay or avoid seeking those services. This is because, in societies like ours, where individual self sufficiency and independence are highly valued, receiving charity is a degrading and humiliating experience. The humiliation and degradation of means testing can be as real a barrier to health care services as lack of money. As we have seen previously, the poor have higher mortality and morbidity rates, therefore, they presumably have the greatest need for health care services. If, as stated in the Epp Report, a goal of health policy is to eliminate health status inequities from Canadian society, then deterent fees, user charges or whatever they may be called, by creating barriers to accessibility, are likely to be counterproductive.

The cost of administering means tests also would probably exceed intended savings Canada-U.S. comparisons of the proportion of health care dollars devoted to administrative expenses, rather than direct service provision, support this claim. In 1983 in the U.S., where the state health insurance sector of the health care system is targeted to the elderly and the poor, rather than being universally available as in Canada, administrative costs were estimated to be sixty per cent higher (Woolhandler and Himmelstein, 1991).

Another reason altering illness behaviors and reducing utilization rates among certain categories of the population through user fees is unlikely to be effective in reducing costs is because, given the fee-for-service system of remuneration, physicians are able to offset service utilization reductions among one group by generating higher levels of utilization among others. Since doctors, after an initial contact has been made, are the primary gatekeepers into the health care system, they largely determine, through their diagnostic and treatment practices, service utilization patterns and costs. Although physician incomes account for only about 15 per cent of total health care costs, it has been estimated that physician decisions concerning service utilization account for 80 per cent of total health care costs (Chappel, Strain and Blandford, 1986).

Doctors, however, are often reluctant to acknowledge that the crisis in Medicare may be largely a result of a system from which they derive considerable benefit. They are more likely to see the problem as one of inappropriate or unnecessary utilization patterns by a public that has "unrealistic expectations" of the health care system in general, and doctors in particular. If unrealistic expectations exist it is partly because of both the accomplishments and promises of the medical profession itself (Illich, 1976; Dubos, 1979). Defining the problem in this way leads to the solution of better educating the public on when, how or if, to use physician's and other health care services (Webb, 1991; Barale, 1991). An adequate resolution of the health care crisis, however, requires alterations to both illness behaviors of patients and the patterns of practice of physicians.

The notion that expectations and hence utilization rates are too high also gives rise to various policing strategies intended both to identify abusers and to provide information and incentive for them to change their allegedly inappropriate health and illness behaviors. In Alberta, for example, it has been proposed that frequent service users and abusers be identified and visited by Department of Health officials. The purpose of these proposed visits will be to find out why they are wasting their doctor's time, and the taxpayers' money, and to determine more appropriate ways to help them with their problems (Walker, 1991). Although this form of policing patients has not yet been acted upon, other ways of educating service users and changing their illness behavior patterns have been, or are being considered.

In Saskatchewan, for example, every family is sent an annual itemized and priced statement showing the cost of their medical services utilization patterns for the year. This education strategy is based on the assumption that because there are no direct costs for using physician's services, that is, because they appear to be free to the user, there is no constraint on their use. By educating people concerning the true costs of their service utilization patterns it is hoped that they will cut down on inappropriate and unnecessary visits to the doctor. The problem with this type of education strategy is that few people will acknowledge that they use doctor or hospital services unnecessarily, although many are willing to acknowledge that such is certainly the case with regards to other people's utilization patterns.

In Quebec it is currently being suggested that a $5.00 deterrent fee be charged to those who use hospital emergency services unnecessarily. In addition to generating revenues it is thought that such a fee will discourage the inappropriate use of expensive hospital services and encourage greater use of less expensive community health center services (Seguin, 1991b). Financial incentives/disincentives such as these are intended to modify illness behavior and to have an educational effect on health care service users.

While it may be true that high expectations are producing a crisis of overutilization, those same expectations, coupled with the fact that the biomedical model has proven to be ineffective in curing the principal diseases of modern life, have contributed to a growing legitimation crisis for the medical profession. A growing number of people are unwilling to assume that "doctor knows best," or to unquestioningly follow doctor's orders. Indeed, in many cases people are turning to alternative health care providers and by-passing doctors entirely, or relegating them to a more marginal position in the definition of the problem and the determination of the most appropriate solution. This process is referred to as demedicalization.

Several reasons for this change in the nature of the doctor-patient relationship have been suggested, including a reduction in the education gap between doctors and patients, the growth of individual and civil rights consciousness, the challenges of other health care occupations to medical dominance, the growth of medical technology (Blishen, 1991) and, as we have seen, the relative ineffectiveness of medicine, and the bio-medical model upon which it is based to cure, the maladies of the post-modern age.

The changing distribution of knowledge and hence power, between doctors and patients, is related to the fact that with many of the chronic and degenerative diseases "patients," or other non-medical health care providers, probably know as much about the nature of the problem, and more about the long-term management of it, than do doctors. This shift in knowledge and power towards the "patient" contributes to the transformation of the doctor-patient relationship into one that is more similar to a producer-consumer relationship (Frankel, 1988). In the ideal typical producer-consumer market relationship the consumer is "always right." This is the antithesis of the traditional doctor-patient relationship wherein the doctor is "always right."

These types of relationships can be considered poles on a continuum. The shift in knowledge and power towards the patient-consumer, although by no means absolute, contributes to the growing legitimation crisis of medicine and contributes to the displacement of the medical profession from an unambiguous position of dominance within the health care system. Certain statutory rights and privileges historically granted to the organized medical profession presently prevent the complete marginalization of medicine, or demedicalization of health care. These include control over training, licencing, and the prescription of drugs. It must be remembered though that these rights and privileges are not absolute. They were legislatively established and they can be eliminated in the same way.

It seems reasonable to argue that certain aspects of the health care system stand as obstacles to the establishment and institutionalization of new forms of illness behavior and health care delivery. These include, but are not restricted to, various legislatively provided rights and privileges of doctors. Thus, only limited changes to illness behaviors and health care service utilization patterns can be achieved by "educating" individuals. The crisis of health care in Canada is not primarily a problem of individual ignorance and, therefore, it cannot be resolved at that level. This is equally true of efforts to understand and change physician behavior and patterns of practice. Any effort to contain health care costs must adequately understand the nature and organization of medical practice and its relationship to patterns of service utilization and costs.

Changing Physician Behavior

Several factors determine physician patterns of practice, including the nature of presented health problems, the form and content of medical education, licencing and other laws that define who can do what to whom, where, when, and how, the system of remuneration, and the practices of others with interests in the health care system, among others. We will look at the nature and effects of the fee-for-service remuneration systems and the interests and activities of the pharmaceutical industry below. Included also is brief discussion of selected forms of resistance to cost containment efforts aimed at altering physician behavior.

The majority of physicians in Canada derive their incomes from fee-for-service practices (Naylor, 1986). Within a fee-for-service system incomes depend upon at least two factors: (1) the level of fees, and (2) the number of services provided. Cost containment strategies, given this system of remuneration, include attempts to "cap" fees, that is, set upper limits on the dollar amount paid for each type of service provided, attempts to limit the number of services provided or reimbursed, and attempts to limit the number of doctors. Less directly, there are also efforts to alter the form and content of medical education so as to create new expectations among future generations of doctors concerning appropriate forms of medical practice in relation to both patients and other health care occupations.

The fee-for-service remuneration system has a built-in incentive for doctors to increase to the maximum the number of services they provide. This is because every billable service provided contributes directly to physician incomes. Thus, there is no financial incentive for doctors to reduce the number of patients they see, or to reduce the number of services they provide to any given patient. Altered practice patterns, therefore, are more likely to be externally initiated. Placing an upper limit on the total amount of money available for medical services, or capping fees paid for each type of medical service provided, are obvious ways to contain rising health care costs. Given the fact that the containment of health care costs has potentially negative consequences for incomes of individual physicians it is not surprising that doctors have sought ways to counteract the income containing consequences of fee capping. One such strategy is for individual physicians to specialize.

Under the existing system of remuneration specialist fees are higher than General Practitioner (GP) fees, therefore, incomes of individual specialists are higher than incomes of GPs at a given intensity of work. There has been a marked trend towards specialization for several decades. In 1984 there were 49,916 practicing doctors in Canada. Of those about 44 per cent were primary contact physicians. This was down from about 54 per cent in 1968 and 67 per cent in 1955 (Dickinson and Hay, 1988: 56). Although the decision to specialize is undoubtedly rational from the perspective of the individual physician, it may be irrational from the societal perspective, at least insofar as it contributes to the maldistribution of medical resources and the perpetuation of inequities of access.

Maldistribution of resources and resultant inequities of access are unintended consequences of the nature, organization and spatial dimensions of specialist medical practice. Most medical specialties are hospital-based and dependent for patients upon referrals from other physicians, consequently, they are concentrated in larger urban centers. This urban concentration results in rural and remote areas of the country being under served relative to urban areas, and in this way specialization contributes to continued inequities of access to medical services among certain segments of the population.

Another strategy adopted by physicians to offset fees considered to be too low is extra-billing (Northcott, 1988). This is the practice of directly charging patients a fee for services rendered that is additional to that paid to the physician by Medicare. The "right" to extra-bill was one of the concessions the government made to the medical profession in order to quiet their opposition to Medicare (Badgely and Wolfe, 1967; Blishen, 1970). By re-introducing a direct charge to patients, however, extra-billing created an obstacle to access to necessary medical services, particularly for the poor.

Concern about the negative effects of extra-billing increased throughout the 1970s and early 1980s. In 1984 the Federal government passed the Canada Health Act which, among other things, banned extra-billing. This was achieved by instating a dollar-for-dollar reduction in Federal cash transfers to the provinces for every dollar they allowed doctors to extra-bill. Many doctors were vigorously opposed to the ban on extra-billing, claiming it was an illegitimate infringement of medical prerogative and a violation of the sanctity of the doctor-patient relationship.

In Ontario, medical opposition to the ban culminated in a 25 day doctor's strike in 1986. This was the longest strike by doctors in Canadian history. Support for the strike, even among doctors, however, was not complete, and it dwindled as the strike continued. By the date set by the Canada Health Act extra-billing had been eliminated. Whether that continues to be the case remains to be seen.

As suggested above medical patterns of practice are influenced by the activities of other interested actors in the health care sector, including the pharmaceutical and the medical supply and technology industries. The nature and consequences of the for-profit pharmaceutical industry on physician drug prescription practices has been of concern for some time (May, 1961; Lexchin, 1984, 1988; Kleinman and Cohen, 1991).

The pharmaceutical industry exists to make a profit. This is not to say that it has not contributed significantly to improved health care and health. One would be hard pressed to imagine life without the products of the modem pharmaceutical industry. Having said that, however, one must not be blinded to the fact that the primary goal of capitalist businesses is the maximization of profits, not the creation of health. If both can be achieved concurrently then everyone is happy, if not, evidence suggests priority is given to profits, not health (Lexchin, 1984; 1988). In the pursuit of profits the drug companies are in perpetual competition with each other for increased market shares. This is especially true with reference to patent protected, brand name drugs with high profit margins.

In order to expand the number of high profit drugs the industry is perpetually involved in "Research and Development." The objective of "R and D" is to discover new drugs and/or to improve already existing drugs. On balance most "R and D" results in minor changes in the qualities and characteristics of existing drugs (May, 1961). These are often patented and renamed, however, with a view towards capturing a larger market share by presenting them to physicians as "new and improved" therapeutic agents.

The number of these insignificant changes generated each year is so great that it is impossible for practicing physicians to be adequately informed concerning which drugs are actually new and which are retreads. Into this gap step the drug company "detail" persons. These are drug company employees whose primary mission is to educate physicians concerning their company's products in order to persuade them to prescribe their high priced, patent protected, profit generating brand name over those of competitors.

To the extent that the detail persons are successful they contribute to increased costs of health care and they have the effect of influencing physician prescribing behaviors to such an extent that doctors may become little more than "pushers" of unnecessarily expensive and, perhaps, even harmful drugs. This close association of physicians with the drug companies also contributes to the legitimation crisis of medicine insofar as it can be suggested that an overly heavy reliance on drug companies for information about drugs and their use throws doubt on the objectivity of doctors judgments and prescribing patterns. The crisis of professional credibility is exacerbated by critiques of other aspects of medical practice and malpractice. Included here are revelations about simple medical incompetence as well as accounts of sexual abuse of patients.

Another aspect of the critique of medicine is the condemnation of what has been argued to be an inappropriate medicalization of various "problems with living" and prescribing drugs, often mood modifying drugs, as the treatment (Harding, 1987; Cooperstock and Lennard, 1987). In many cases, critics point out, the medicalization of life's problems and one's discontents has the undesirable effect of perpetuating unhealthy and oppressive social relationships that are at the root of what appear as personal health problems (Cloward and Piven, 1979). Furthermore, the drugs themselves have serious side effects that are often as bad as, or worse than, the conditions they were prescribed to treat. At the social level this imputed pattern of inappropriate medical diagnosis and treatment contributes to deteriorating health and the rising costs of health care.

Although modern medicine has been unsuccessful in curing many chronic and degenerative diseases, it has been remarkably successful in prolonging life. We saw earlier that life expectancy and average age at death have been increasing throughout this century. A good deal of the success in extending the average age at death may be related to the development and application of new medical diagnostic and treatment technologies in the hospital setting.

The development and application of life prolonging medical technologies has a number of far reaching consequences, some of which are forcing re-evaluation of fundamental societal values and creating new problems for medical ethics (Roy, 1988). In many cases individuals who previously would have died now can be kept alive because of new medical technologies. Of course, sustaining life through various heroic medical interventions is an expensive proposition that has prompted some to ask is it worth it? Should we be using the considerable power of modern medical science and technology to prolong life at all costs? Should the decision to prolong life be taken independently of considerations of the quality of life being prolonged? If the answers to these questions is "no," then who should have the right and duty to decide whose life will be prolonged and who will be allowed, or assisted, to die? If the answer is "yes," all life should be prolonged at all costs, then who should be required to pay—the individuals and their families, or the state? It is in answers to questions like this that the morality and economics of health care converge. Any attempt to deal with these questions in a one dimensional way is inadequate.

Reducing the Cost per Service

The third cost containment strategy includes various efforts directed towards reducing the costs per service provided. This strategy, although applicable in any sector of the health care system, is most apparent in hospital settings. As is evident in Table 11:5 hospitals account for the greatest proportion of health care expenditures. Therefore, any efforts to contain health care costs must focus on hospitals. Within hospitals the greatest proportion of costs are accounted for by salaries and wages. Attempts to contain hospital costs, therefore, have focused on wages.

Wages can be reduced absolutely or relatively. Absolute reductions in wage bills can also be achieved in two ways. The first is to pay those who provide the services less. The second is to reduce the number of workers, or the number of hours worked per worker, without reducing the number of services provided. Both strategies are used by employers to achieve absolute reductions in wage bills. Relative reductions are achieved by increasing the productivity of service providers at a rate greater than the rate of increase of wages. This entails having workers provide more services per time period for the same amount or less money. Practically this is accomplished through organizational means, often in the form of extensions to the occupational division of labor, or technical means, which involves development and application of productivity enhancing and labor replacing technologies (Braverman, 1974). Again, both strategies have been, and are being, used.

The capacity of employers to reduce wages is limited by various labor market considerations, including the supply of, and demand for, individuals with requisites skills and credentials. Generally, when demand is high and supply is low, wage reductions are difficult, if not impossible, to achieve. Indeed, under such conditions the norm is rising wages. This is because the relative scarcity of workers to fill available positions is manifest as increased bargaining power for workers, and a relative decrease in power for employers who must offer wage and other incentives to recruit and retain needed workers.

Throughout the post-World War II period until the mid-to-late 1970s, this was generally the situation that existed in Canada, and other nations in the advanced capitalist world, so that real incomes increased. It is interesting to note that despite income gains for nurses during that time period they were never able to raise incomes to the level of the average industrial wage in Canada (Wotherspoon, 1988).

The imposition of wage controls in the mid-1970s had the effect of creating a real wage reduction for nurses and other hospital workers (White, 1990). In fact, government policy since that time has resulted in a real reduction of incomes for many categories of workers in both the public and private sectors (Myles, Picot and Wannell, 1988).

In addition to reducing wages, absolute reductions in the cost per health care service provided have been achieved by transforming the nature and conditions of work. A major element of this strategy involves the replacement of full-time with part-time workers. Part-time workers are less expensive than full-time workers for a number of reasons. First, because they tend not to be unionized they tend to be paid less per hour than full-time, unionized workers. A second cost reduction effect of the shift towards part-time workers is derived from the fact that part-time workers are not covered by many of the employee plans and programs to which employers are required by law to make contributions. This fact alone results in a lowered wage bill, even if part-time workers are paid at the same hourly rate as full-time workers, which, of course, they usually are not. Savings to employers from this source alone can be as high as 10 or 12 percent per employee. Third, part-time workers are called in to work only at times of peak demand. This enables employers to ensure that they are working at peak intensity the whole time they are at work. In this way "dead time" is reduced. That is, employers are not paying workers for that time when there is little or no work to do (Dickinson, 1991).

Relative reductions in the cost per health care service can be achieved, as indicated above, by having workers produce more in a given time period. This usually takes the form of increasing the intensity of work (Dickinson and Brady, 1984). There are a number of ways in which work is intensified. The two most common are extensions to the occupational division of labor and the application of labor saving technologies.

Labor saving technologies, or what might be more accurately termed productivity enhancing or labor replacing technologies, tend to be developed to replace workers who perform routine, standardized and repetitive functions. In the hospital setting, although still quite rare because of the generally low wages, it is not unheard of to have robots perform certain functions. It has been reported, for example, that in the US, where hospitals are more often run for profit, robots are being tested to perform tasks such as "the pickup and delivery of medical supplies, lab specimens, meals and linens." The same source also reported that Toronto's Hospital for Sick Children had acquired a robot for lab specimen preparation (Robertson, 1985).

From the point of view of nurses, and many other waged hospital workers, such strategies result in a deterioration of their working conditions and a reduction in their capacity to provide the personal care that is generally thought to be the hall mark of good quality nursing (Warburton and Carroll, 1988). From the patient's perspective the rationalization of nursing work in the unrelenting pursuit of efficiency and cost containment is often experienced as a lack of caring, compassion and understanding. There is agreement that currently these conditions constitute a crisis in nursing (Hewa and Hetherington, 1990a). This crisis manifests itself in numerous ways, including, difficulty in recruiting and retaining nurses because of job dissatisfaction, job created stress, and frustration and disappointment which results from a disjuncture between expectations created in the professional socialization process and the realities of the alienating, oppressive and exploitative conditions within which they work (Stroud, 1983; Armstrong, 1988; Campbell, 1988).

Strikes in and of themselves are unlikely to be an adequate solution to the problems confronting the health care system. Nurses strikes however sensitize the general public to the crisis in health care and the need for change. Unlike recent doctors strikes, however, nurses strikes seem to have generated substantial public support. Doctors strikes, particularly the 1986 Ontario strike may well have contributed to a declining social support and respect for doctors who seemed only to be concerned with protecting their right to extra-bill patients. During that strike doctors were unsuccessful in linking their narrow professional interests with broader public interests. Nurses on the other hand have been much more successful in making such a linkage by emphasizing their goal of putting the "care" back in health care. Whether nurses will be successful remains to be seen.

Reducing Health Care Budgets

The cost containment strategies we have looked at so far are all based on the assumption that a universal, comprehensive, accessible, portable and state administered health care insurance program exists, and currently, of course, it does. There is no reason to assume, however, that it will continue to exist, at least in its present form. There are several contemporary developments which suggest that profound changes are imminent.

The most obvious of these is changes to the system of federal government financing of health care services. Many feel that past and present reductions in federal funds foretell the erosion of Medicare as we know it. Before we briefly examine possible consequences of current and proposed changes let us look at the nature of the funding changes that have taken place and that are proposed for the future.

The original federal-provincial cost sharing arrangements entered into with the introduction of hospital insurance and medical care insurance tied federal contributions directly to provincial government expenditures. The federal government had no control over its own health care spending because it was determined by what each province spent. From the federal government point of view this was an undesirable situation. From the perspective of the provinces the original cost sharing arrangement was too inflexible. In order to be eligible for federal funds the provinces were required to spend their health care dollars on medical care (doctor's) services and hospital services. Initiatives in cost containment and the development of alternative forms of health care were discouraged by that arrangement. Every reduction in the cost of hospital services made by the provinces resulted in a reduction of federal government money transferred to them. Thus, the cost sharing arrangement discouraged the provinces from attempting to make hospital services more efficient. Similarly, because of the fact that only hospital and physician services were eligible for federal cost sharing the provinces had little incentive to pursue other avenues of health expenditures such as health promotion and illness prevention or non-hospital forms of institutional treatment and care. Thus, both federal and provincial governments were interested in changing the structure of the cost sharing arrangement (Soderstrom, 1978).

This was done in 1977 with passage of the Established Programs Financing Act (EPF). The arrangement negotiated at that time reduced federal contributions to health care from approximately 50, to 25 percent, uncoupled them from provincial expenditures, and limited future direct federal increases to growth in the Gross National Product (GNP). In order to make this change attractive to the provinces the federal government reduced its level of income taxation and transferred "tax points" to the provinces so that they could increase their tax rates to make up for the reduced direct federal cash transfers.

Under the terms of the 1977 arrangement any provincial increases over the rate of increase of the GNP were met entirely out of provincial government revenues; increased health care expenditures over that amount did not result in increased federal cash transfers. Clearly this arrangement gave the provinces increased incentive to contain costs in the medical care and hospital sectors (Vayda, Evans and Mindell, 1979).

In 1986 the federal government further limited its financial contributions to the provinces for health care by limiting annual transfers to a rate 2 percent *below* the rate of increase in the GNP.

Currently proposed amendments to the federal-provincial cost sharing arrangements, in the form of Bills C-20 and C-69, will further reduce the level of federal government cash transfers to the provinces for health care, post-secondary education and other social programs. The proposed formula will hold federal transfers to the provinces for health care and post-secondary education in 1990–91 and 1991–92 to 1989–90 levels. In 1992–93 federal transfers will be allowed to increase at the rate of GNP growth *less* 3 percent. Under the terms of that legislation, federal cash transfers to the provinces may be completely eliminated by about the year 2004.

The reduction and possible elimination of federal cash transfers to the provinces for health care and other social services has critics gravely concerned. Some have gone so far as to claim that these actions of the federal government presage the death of Medicare. It is reasoned that because a national health care insurance system was established in part by the lure of federal government money, reductions in the amount of that money reduces the federal government's ability to encourage provincial compliance with the national standards upon which Medicare is built; universality, comprehensiveness, portability, non-profit public administration, and accessibility. How is it thought that this dismantling of Medicare will occur?

The argument generally goes as follows. Since federal cash transfers were contingent upon the provinces meeting the five standards mentioned above reduction of those cash transfer payments will enable provinces if they so desire to disregard any or all of them as they attempt to pay for the provision of health care services. In order to make up for the reduction in federal payments the provinces will have a limited number of options. They include (1) development of alternative sources of revenue, (2) cutback on the number and/or type of services provided, and (3) change the type or reduce the cost of services being provided. Each of these three possible options have a number of variations that could be pursued and in many cases have been proposed or already implemented.

Alternative Sources of Financing. As we have seen, one aspect of the changing nature of federal-provincial cost sharing arrangements in the area of health care has been to cut back federal cash transfers and, in exchange, also to transfer tax points to the provinces. This means, of course, that the provinces could in principle increase provincial taxes to pay for health care services. In practice, however, this may be politically dangerous insofar as many people already feel that they are being unfairly taxed and may not support a government that proposes new tax increases. Governments can also borrow money to pay for services. The difficulty with this option is that such a strategy contributes to increased debt and deficits which are one of the main reasons given for cutbacks in the first place.

Another strategy used is to generate revenues by instituting "voluntary" taxes. An example of this strategy can be seen in Manitoba where in 1989 the provincial government announced plans to open a full-scale, full-time gambling casino in Winnipeg at the Fort Gary Hotel. The Department of Health was identified as the recipient of the estimated $10 million profits from that operation.

At about the same time the government of Saskatchewan announced plans to allow the use of electronic gambling machines in the province as a source of revenue. It was suggested that at least some proportion of the anticipated funds raised would be directed towards the health care system (Greenshields, 1989).

Critics of this approach to funding government programs point out that it is an unstable and unreliable source of revenues from which to finance essential services such as health care. It is also noted that organized gambling tends to be associated with various social problems and increased crime. Some also feel that gambling tends to be attractive to the poor who are desperate to find a "quick fix" to their financial woes. As such governments raising revenues through casinos or other forms of gambling are effectively taxing the poor and thereby contributing to intensified problems of poverty, including poor health.

Other, more direct, methods of generating revenues for health care are also possible. These include things like user fees, extra-billing and other types of charges to those who use health care services. Under the terms of the 1984 Canada Health Act the federal government effectively eliminated extra-billing and user fees by imposing a dollar-for-dollar reduction in federal cash transfers on those provinces that allowed additional charges to be made to health care service users. This financial penalty effectively eliminated the practice in all provinces. With the current reductions of federal cash transfers, and their projected elimination in the next few years, there may no longer be any way to prevent provinces from re-establishing user fees or extra-billing as they attempt to generate revenues to pay for health care services.

As is well known, the introduction of user fees differentially affects people depending on their level of wealth. User fees discourage those with low incomes from using health care services. In this way the possibility of the reintroduction of user fees threatens the principles of universality and accessibility, at least insofar as it would introduce an additional financial barrier to health care for the poor. With increasing levels of poverty in Canada, especially among the elderly, children and women, such a development threatens to contribute to a worsening of the inequities in health status that already characterize Canadian society (Bolaria and Wotherspoon, 1991).

A further strategy of dealing with reduced federal government cash transfers for health care takes the form of demands for the re-privatization of health care and medical services. Although privatization has a number of interrelated meanings, with references to the Canadian health care sector, it primarily refers to the processes of shifting financial responsibility for health care services from the government back onto individuals directly and/or through private health care insurance (Weller and Manga, 1983).

There already exists a number of benefits and services not covered by state run health care insurance plans. These include private and semi-private hospital rooms, certain drugs, dental services, and various aids such as wheel chairs and crutches. Proponents of privatization are in favor of reducing the range of benefits and services covered by state health care insurance and increasing the range paid for by individuals directly or through private health care insurance. Critics of this aspect of privatization point out that expanding the private sector of the health care system at the expense of the public sector erodes Medicare and undermines the principles of comprehensiveness, universality and accessibility. Although privatization clearly shifts the costs of health care, and in that sense provides alternative sources of financing, it does so by eroding the system itself.

Cutback the Number/Type of Services Provided. This response to reduced revenues for health care is simply a more direct way of scaling down the scope of state health care insurance. It has been suggested, for example, that certain health care services and benefits currently covered under state health care insurance plans be rationed or even removed from the list of eligible services. In 1989, for example, the President of the Canadian Medical Association suggested that various health screening procedures such as cholesterol level testing or AIDS testing be de-insured or insured only in limited quantities (Saskatoon Star Phoenix, 1989a).

Given the emphasis on certain lifestyle behaviors as risk factors in many sorts of injury and illness some have proposed that heavy smokers, drug addicts and alcoholics should be treated last. The rationale being that because these, and other categories of individuals, have engaged in behaviors which put them at risk for developing certain health problems, they are individually responsible for their illnesses and injuries and, therefore, they should be punished by limiting or barring their access to publicly financed health care services (Saskatoon Star Phoenix, 1989b).

The reasoning behind such suggestions is deceptively persuasive. It can also be extended to expanded categories of individuals; those who have sexually transmitted diseases because they did not practice safe sex, those who are injured in accidents while under the influence of alcohol, those who suffer from cardiovascular diseases because they have not exercised sufficiently and/or because they consume too much high fat food. The list could go on, but the point is clear. Given the fact that some lifestyle factors might be implicated in many, if not most, forms of injury and illness where does one stop blaming and punishing the victims of ill health and injury?

The logical fallacy underpinning the suggestion that those people who are responsible for their own health problems because of lifestyles that include known or suspected risk factors is based upon a confusion of risk factors and causes. Risk factors are not causes. Risk factors are simply factors that are correlated with the risk of developing certain illnesses. They do not by themselves cause the illnesses, and in many cases the relationship between the risky behavior and the illness is non-existent (Marantz, 1990).

The possibility exists within this line of thought to establish two categories of people; the deserving sick and the undeserving sick. The deserving sick will be eligible for publicly funded health care services, the undeserving sick will not be eligible, or will have limited entitlement. For many this creation of a human hierarchy, where some people's lives are considered more valuable than others, is unacceptable. Proponents of this, and some other forms of rationing, retort that making decisions concerning the most effective and efficient allocation of scarce health care resources is not only rational but essential (Mickleburgh, 1991). Not to do so threatens the viability of the entire health care system.

At a more general level, this same argument is used to critique the principle of universality, not only with regard to health care services but also in reference to the whole array of social, and possibly educational, services. From one perspective, universality is seen as a non-affordable relic of the past, a crushing monument to an archaic idealism that has long since become unsupportable. Critics of universality argue, again in a deceptively convincing way, that not only is universal access to comprehensive, publicly financed health care services simply too expensive to sustain, but maintenance of such a system is irrational and renders the health care system ineffective and inefficient. Some health care services, both preventative and treatment service, it can be argued, are simply not necessary or efficiently applied to all individuals or categories of individuals.

An apparent case in point is mammogram screening of women for breast cancer. Recent evidence suggests that early detection of breast cancers among women who are less than fifty years of age does little or nothing in terms of increasing survival rates and saving lives. The situation is different, however, with respect to women over the age of fifty. For that category of women there is evidence to show that survival rates and longevity can be significantly increased by mammogram screening and early detection.

Some have suggested on the basis of this evidence that screening be made available only to those women in the age group where there is a demonstrated statistically significant chance of a positive outcome. Younger women should not have free access to mammogram screening for breast cancer. Others, particularly those who have a vested interest in the production and marketing of the equipment required for mammography, or who have an interest in providing the services for their own financial gain, or who have an interest in fanning the cancer hysteria for fund raising purposes, argue that all women regardless of age should be regularly screened through the mammogram technique.

Other examples can be provided. Some argue that AIDS education efforts should not be aimed at the whole population. Such efforts should be targeted to those groups of individuals most at risk, particularly homosexual males, prostitutes and IV drug users. As we have seen above, others take the position that individuals who engage in lifestyle behaviors known or thought to be risk factors in the contraction of certain diseases should be exempted from, or restricted in terms of their access to, health care services.

Despite these debates over service rationing and cutbacks, the most obvious area of straight forward cutbacks in the health care system is currently occurring in the hospital sector. Virtually every province has cutback or intends to cutback the number of acute care hospital beds available. The recently released BC Royal Commission report on that province's health care system, for example, recommended that the province reduce the number of hospital beds by 25 percent, or what amounts to about 2000 acute care beds over the next three years. This recommendation was accompanied by others, including a reduction in the number of physicians and caps on the amount of money available for physician and hospital services.

The money which is expected to be saved by cutting back on expenditures for hospital and doctors' services is to be used to further develop alternative forms of health care services.

Change the Types of Services Provided. It has been agreed for some time that the future of health care lies in a more co-ordinated approach between acute care hospital and physician services and other kinds of institutional and community-based types of care. A concomitant of this recognition is a commitment to de-centralization and regionalization which involves a transfer of planning and service development and co-ordination to the local level where it is argued assessments of needs and appropriate responses can be best undertaken.

The growth of various kinds of Home-Care programs and special care institutions is indicated by increased expenditures for such purposes in recent years (see Table 11:5). Planners and policy makers agree that further moves in that direction are required. This is not to say that physician and acute care hospital services will be replaced altogether, obviously that is both undesirable and impossible. Rather, the intention is to better co-ordinate social and health care services within a health promotion framework to ensure that institutionalization does not occur when more appropriate, less expensive and independence sustaining alternatives are available. The challenge is to create the conditions whereby it is possible to make the innovations considered necessary to meet the changing health care and social support needs of a changing population.

One widely cited example of such an undertaking is the Extra-Mural Hospital of New Brunswick (Adams, 1987; Ferguson, 1987). It is not possible to provide a detailed description of this innovation in health care here. Suffice it to note that the Extra-Mural Hospital provides a wide range of health care services to patients in their homes who otherwise would be required to stay in more expensive acute care hospital beds as they recuperate or to be admitted to those beds in the first place because previously that was the only place to receive the services now provided by the staff of the Extra-Mural Hospital. According to the director of the hospital about half the patients are early discharges from acute care hospitals and about half are admitted directly from the community thus delaying or preventing their admission to acute care hospital beds.

Although the budget of the Extra-Mural Hospital in New Brunswick is in addition to the budgets of the existing acute care hospitals, so that in the short run no immediate savings are realized, it is thought that in the long run and within the framework of a more co-ordinated health and social services system that such a facility will result in the more effective and efficient use of health care and social service dollars. Indeed, it is thought that the Extra-Mural Hospital will itself be the master institution from which a more integrated and co-ordinated system will develop (Ferguson, 1987).

Conclusions

It seems clear that in the current situation of changing health care needs and scarcity of health care resources, whether real or fabricated, the allocation and utilization of health care resources becomes highly politicized. Given the magnitude of resources involved much is at stake and this ensures the existence of powerful actors intent on protecting and enhancing their self-interests. Within this political and economic arena. possibly the weakest contenders are individuals, particularly the young, the elderly, the poor, and members of other marginalized groups, who are not well organized politically and who, therefore, may not be able to protect their interests, or even to have them clearly articulated.

On the other hand, changed circumstances bring about new conditions, including new political alliances and forms of organization that may contribute to the further empowerment of otherwise marginalized categories of individuals. This, however, won't just happen. It will take considerable political will and organizational effort to ensure that one's interests are considered in the allocation and distribution of health care resources.

The burgeoning of various self-help and advocacy groups in and around the health care sector testifies to the fact that many are actively engaged in attempts to protect and achieve their interests in this and other areas of social life.

Note

1. This information provided through the cooperation of Statistics Canada. Leaders wishing further information may obtain copies of related publications by mail from Publications Sales, Statistics Canada, Ottawa, Ontario KIA 0T6, or by phone at 1-613-951-7277 or national toll free 1-800-267-6677. You may also facsimile your order by dialing 1-613-951-1584.

References

Adams, O.
1987 "Hospital without Walls: Is New Brunswick's Extra-Mural Hospital the Way of the Future? Interview with Gordon Ferguson." *Canadian Medical Association Journal,* 136 (April 15): 861–864.

Armstrong, P.
1988 "Where Have All the Nurses Gone?" *Healthsharing,* (Summer): 17–19.

Badgely, R.F. and S. Wolfe
1967 *Doctors' Strike: Medical Care and Conflict in Saskatchewan.* Toronoto: McMillan.

Barale, A. E.
1991 "Patients Have Unrealistic Expectations of System." *Saskatoon Star Phoenix,* 16 September: A5.

Bator, P. A.
1983 "The Health Reformers versus the Common Canadian: The Controversy over Compulsory Vaccination against Small-pox in Toronto and Ontario, 1900–1920.' *Ontario History,* 75: 348–373.

Beck, R. G.
1973 "Economic Class and Access to Physician Services under Public Medical Care Insurance." *International Journal of Health Services,* 3: 341–55.

Begin, M.
1988 *Medicare: Canada's Right to Health.* Montreal: Optimum Publishing International.

Blishen, B. R.
1991 *Doctors in Canada: the Changing World of Medical Practice.* Toronto: Statistics Canada in association with The University of Toronto Press.

_____.
1970 "Social Change and Institutional Resistance: The Case of Medicare," in *Social and Cultural Change in Canada, Volume II,* edited by W. E. Mann. Vancouver Toronto Montreal: Copp Clark: 223–29.

Blomquist, A.
1979 *The Health Care Business: International Evidence on Private versus Public Health Care Systems.* Vancouver: The Fraser Institute.

Bolaria, B. Singh and T. Wotherspoon
1991 "Income Inequality, Poverty, and Hunger," in *Social Issues and Contradictions in Canadian Society,* edited by B. Singh Bolaria Toronto: Harcourt Brace Jovanovich: 464–80.

_____.
1988 "Sociology, Medicine, Health, and Illness," in *Sociology of Health and Health Care in Canada.,* edited by B. Singh Bolaria and Harley D. Dickinson. Toronto: Harcourt Brace Jovanovich: 1–14.

Braverman, H.
1974 *Labor and Monopoly Capital: The Degradation of Work in the Twentieth Century.* New York: Monthly Review Press.

Brown, M. C.
1987 *Caring for Profit: Economic Dimensions of Canada's Health Industry.* Vancouver: The Fraser Institute.

Brym. R. with B. Fox
1989 *From Culture to Power: The Sociology of English Canada.* Toronto: Oxford University Press.

Campbell, M. L.
1988 "The Structure of Stress in Nurses' Work," in *Sociology of Health* and *Health Care* in *Canada,* edited by B. Singh Bolaria and Harley D. Dickinson. Toronto: Harcourt Brace Jovanovich: 393–406.

Chappell, N. L., L. A. Strain, and A. A. Blandford
1986 *Aging and Health Care: A Social Perspective.* Toronto: Holt, Rinehart and Winston.

Cloward, R. A. and F. F. Piven
1979 "Hidden Protest: The Channeling of Female Innovation and Protest." *Signs,* 4.

Cooperstock, R. and H. L. Lennard
1987 "Role Strains and Tranquillizer Use," in *Health and Canadian Society: Sociological Perspectives, Second edition,* edited by D. Coburn, C. D'Arcy, G. Torrance and P. New. Toronto: Fitzhenry and Whiteside: 314–32.

Dickinson, H. D.
"The Domain of Sociology," in *Sociology,* edited by Peter S. Li and B. Singh Bolaria. Toronto: Copp Clark Pittman, forthcoming.

_____.
1991 "Work and Unemployment as Social Issues," in *Social Issues and Contradictions* in Canadian *Society,* edited by B. Singh Bolaria. Toronto: Harcourt Brace Jovanovich: 278–99.

_____.
1989 *The Two Psychiatries: The Transformation of Psychiatric Work in Saskatchewan, 1905–1984.* Regina: Canadian Plains Research Center.

_____ and G. Andre.
1988 "Community Psychiatry: The Institutional Transformation of Psychiatric Practice," in *Sociology of Health and Health Care in Canada.,* edited by B. Singh Bolaria and Harley D. Dickinson. Toronto: Harcourt Brace Jovanovich: 295–308.

_____ and M. Stobbe
1988 "Occupational Health and Safety in Canada," in *Sociology of Health and Health Care in Canada,* edited by B. Singh Bolaria and Harley D. Dickinson. Toronto: Harcourt Brace Jovanovich: 426–38.

_____ and D. Hay
1988 "The Structure and Cost of Health Care in Canada," in *Sociology of Health and Health Care in Canada,* edited by B. Singh Bolaria and Harley D. Dickinson. Toronto: Harcourt Brace Jovanovich: 51–73.

_____ and P. D. Brady
1984 "The Labour Process and the Transformation of Health Care Delivery," in *Contradictions in Canadian Society: Readings in Introductory Sociology,* edited by John A. Fry. Toronto: John Wiley and Sons: 194–206.

Dominion Bureau of Statistics
1967 *Life Expectancy Trends 1930–1932 to 1960–1962.* Ottawa: Minister of Trade and Commerce.

Dubos, R.
1979 *Mirage of Health: Utopias, Progress, and Biological Change.* New York: Harper Colophon Books: [1953].

Epp, J.
1986 *Achieving Health for All: a Framework for Health Promotion.* Ottawa: Health and Welfare Canada.

Evans, R. G.
1984 *Strained Mercy: The Economics of Canadian Health Care.* Toronto: Butterworths.

Ferguson, G.
1987 "The New Brunswick Extra-Mural Hospital: A Canadian Hospital-at-Home." *Journal of Public Health Policy,* 8(4):561–70.

Frankel, B. G.
1988 "Patient-physician Relationships: Changing Modes of Interaction," in *Sociology of Health and Health Care in Canada,* edited by B. Singh Bolaria and Harley D. Dickinson. Toronto: Harcourt Brace Jovanovich: 104–14.

Foss, L. and K Rothenberg
1987 *The Second Medical Revolution: from Biomedicine to Infomedicine*. Boston: Shambhala Publications.

Gellert, G. A., A. K. Neumann, and R. S. Gordon
1989 "The Obsolescence of Distinct Domestic and International Health Sectors." *Journal of Public Health Policy,* 10: 421–24.

Grant, K. R.
1988 "The 'Inverse Care Law' in Canada: Differential Access Under Universal Free Health Insurance," in *Sociology of Health and Health Care in Canada,* edited by B. Singh Bolaria and Harley D. Dickinson. Toronto: Harcourt Brace Jovanovich: 118–34.

Greenshields, V.
1989 "Don't Rely on Gambling Funds: NDP." *Saskatoon Star Phoenix,* 23 February: B11.

Harding, J.
1987 "The Pharmaceutical Industry as a Public Health Hazard and as an Institution of Social Control," in *Health and Canadian Society: SocioloGical Perspectives, Second edition,* edited by D. Coburn, C. D'Arcy, G. Torrance and P. New. Toronto: Fitzhenry and Whiteside: 545–64.

Hay, D. A.
1988 "Mortality and Health Status Trends in Canada," in *Sociology of Health and Health Care in Canada,* edited by B. Singh Bolaria and Harley D. Dickinson. Toronto: Harcourt Brace Jovanovich: 18–37.

Hewa, S. and R. W. Hetherington
1990a "Specialists without Spirit: Crisis in the Nursing Profession." *Journal Of Medical Ethics,* 16:179–84.

_____.
1990b "Specialists without Spirit: Limitation of the Mechanistic Bio-medical Model." Paper presented at the 25tb Annual Meetings of the Canadian Sociology and Anthropology Association, Victoria, BC.

Illich, I.
1976 *Limits to Medicine, Medical Nemesis: The Expropriation of Health.* London: McClelland and Stewart in association with Marion Boyars.

Kleinman, D. L. and L. J. Cohen
1991 "The Decontextualization of Mental Illness: The Portrayal of Work in Psychiatric Drug Advertisements." *Social Science and Medicine,* 32 (8):867–74.

Lexchin, J.
1988 "Profits First: The Pharmaceutical Industry in Canada," in *Sociology of Health and Health Care in Canada*, edited by B. Singh Bolaria and Harley D. Dickinson. Toronto: Harcourt Brace Jovanovich: 497–513.

_____.
1984 *The Real Pushers: A Critical Analysis of the Canadian Drug Industry.* Vancouver: New Star Books.

Marantz,P. R.
1990 "Blaming the Victim: The Negative Consequences of Preventive Medicine." *American Journal of Public Health,* 80 (10): 1186–87.

May, C. D.
1961 "Selling Drugs by 'Educating' Physicians." *The Journal of Medical Education,* 36 (1): 1–23.

McLaren, A.
1990 *Our Own Master Race: Eugenics in Canada, 1885–1945.* Toronto: McClelland and Stewart.

Mickleburgh, R.
1991 "Plan Ranks Illnesses on Basis of Priority." *The Globe and Mail,* 12 June: A5.

Myles, J., G. Picot and T. Wannell
1988 "The Changing Wages Distribution of Jobs, 1981–1986." *The Labour Force, October 1988.* Ottawa: Supply and Services Canada: 85–129.

Navarro, V.
1976 *Medicine under Capitalism.* New York: Prodist.

Naylor, D. C.
1986 *Private Practice, Public Payment: Canadian Medicine and the Politics of Health Insurance, 1911–1966.* Kingston Montreal: McGill-Queen's University Press.

Northcott, H. C.
1991 "Health Status and Health Care in Canada: Contemporary Issues," in *Social Issues and Contradictions in Canadian Society,* edited by B. Singh Bolaria. Toronto: Harcourt Brace Jovanovich: 178–95.

_____.
1988 "Health Care Resources and Extra-billing: Financing, Allocation, and Utilization." in *Sociology of Health and Health Care in Canada*, edited by B. Singh Bolaria and Harley D. Dickinson. Toronto: Harcourt Brace Jovanovich: 38–50.

Powles, J.
1973 "On the Limitation of Modern Medicine." *Science, Medicine and Man*, 1 (1): 1–30.

Renaud, M.
1977 "On the Structural Constraints to State Intervention in Health." in *Health and Medical Care in the U.S.: A Critical Analysis,* edited by V. Navarro. Farmingdale, NY: Baywood Publishing Company: 135–146.

Robertson, S.
1985 "Check-up." *Saskatoon Star Phoenix,* 25 November: All.

Rosen, G.
1963 "The Evolution of Social Medicine," in *Handbook of Medical Sociology,* edited by H. E. Freeman, S. Levine and L. G. Reeder. Englewood Cliffs, NJ: Prentice Hall: 17–61.

Roy, D. J.
1988 "Decisions and Dying: Questions of Clinical Ethics," in *Sociology of Health and Health Care in Canada,* edited by B. Singh Bolaria and Harley D. Dickinson. Toronto: Harcourt Brace Jovanovich: 527–36.

Saskatoon Star Phoenix
1989 a "Time to Rethink Medicare: CMA." *Saskatoon Star Phoenix,* 9 March: A1.

_____.
1989 b "Smokers, Addicts should be Treated Last: Prof." *Saskatoon Star Phoenix,* 26 October: D10.

Seguin, R.
1991 b "Quebec Liberals Call for Tax on Health Care." *The Globe and Mail,* 31 October: Al.

Shorter, E.
1985 *Bedside Manners: The Troubled History of Doctors and Patients.* New York: Simon and Schuster.

Soderstrom, L.
1978 *The Canadian Health System.* London: Croom Helm.

Statistics Canada
1976 *General Mortality 1950 to 1970.* Ottawa: Minister of Supply and Services.

_____.
1978 *Deaths, Vital Statistics, Volume III, 1976.* Ottawa: Minister of Supply and Services Canada.

_____.
1982 *Causes* of *Death, Vital Statistics, Volume IV, 1981.* Ottawa: Minister of Supply and Services Canada.

_____.
1983 *Mortality Summary List of Causes, Vital Statistics, Volume III, 1981.* Ottawa: Minister of Supply and Services.

_____.
1986 *Provincial Government Finance, Revenue, and Expenditure, 1983 (Fiscal year ended 31 March 1984).* Ottawa: Minister of Supply and Services.

______.
1987 *Federal Government Finance.* Ottawa: Minister of Supply and Services.

______.
1988 a *Mortality Summary List of Causes, Vital Statistics, Volume III, 1986.* Ottawa: Minister of Supply and Services.

______.
1988 b *Causes of Death, Vital Statistics, Volume IV, 1986.* Ottawa: Minister of Supply and Services Canada.

Stroud, C.
1983 "Silent Nightingales." *Quest* (March) 62–8.

Task Force on the Cost of Health Services in Canada
1970 Volumes 1–3. Ottawa: Information Canada.

Taylor, M. G.
1978 *Health Insurance and Canadian Public Policy: The Seven Decisions That Created the Canadian Health Insurance System.* Montreal: McGill-Queen's University Press.

Waitzkin, H.
1983 *The Second Sickness.* New York: The Free Press.

Walker, R.
1991 "Medicare Abuse Targeted." *Calgary Herald,* 14 June: A1.

Warburton, R. and W. Carroll.
1988 "Class and Gender in Nursing," in *Sociology of Health and Health Care in Canada,* edited by B. Singh Bolaria and Harley D. Dickinson. Toronto: Harcourt Brace Jovanovich: 364–75.

Webb, J.
1991 "Education, Not Political Interference Will Fix Medicare." *Saskatoon Star Phoenix,* 6 September: A5.

Weller, G. R. and P. Manga.
1983 "The Push for Re-privatization of Health Care Services in Canada, Britain, and the United States." *Journal of Health Politics and Law,* 8(3): 495–518.

White, J. P.
1990 *Hospital Strike: Women, Unions and Public Sector Conflict.* Toronto: Thompson Educational Publishing.

Wilkins, R. and O. B. Adams
1983 "Health Expectancy in Canada, Late 1970s: Demographic, Regional, and Social Dimensions." *American Journal of Public Health,* 73 (98): 1073–80.

Wolfson, M., G. Rowe and J. F. Gentleman.
1990 "Earnings and Death Effects over a Quarter Century." Research Papers Series, No. 30, Social and Economic Studies Division, Analytical Studies Branch. Ottawa: Statistics Canada.

Woolhandler, S. and D. Himmelstein
1991 "The Deteriorating Administrative Efficiency of the U.S. Health Care System." *New England Journal of Medicine,* 324 (18): 1253–58.

Wotherspoon, T.
1988 "Training and Containing Nurses: The Development of nUrsing Education in Canada," in *Sociology of Health and Health Care in Canada,* edited by B. Singh Bolaria and Harley D. Dickinson. Toronto: Harcourt Brace Jovanovich:178–95375–92.

Vayda, E., R. G. Evans and W. R. Mindell
1979 "Universal Health Insurance in Canada: History, Problems, Trends." *Journal of Community Health,* 4(3): 217–31.

York, G.
1987 *The High Price of Health: A Patient's Guide to the Hazards of Medical Politics*. Toronto: James Lorimer and Company, 1987.

12

The Organization of Work

Paul P. Divers

This chapter continues our series of readings to introduce sociology to students. The two primary organizing concepts that are emphasized in this chapter are social structure and social history.

Of all social structures that frame our lives the most, the places where we work are of the most critical. From the time we enter grade school as children, we are being socialized to be competent, compliant, and faithful people who, it is hoped, will be involved in some way in the economy of Canada. Then after many years of education (averaging now about sixteen years), we are expected to be, again, competent, compliant and faithful workers. In this way, work, as outlined in the introduction, structures our personal identity in major ways. And when we look at the research on the experience of unemployment, we find that it is devastating to our identity as Canadians.

In a word, then, our places of work frame our lives in very real ways. Here, we will find that this framing takes on the face of being industrialized workers, post-industrial employees, and proletarians who constantly need to be aware of what kinds of work are expanding and which ones are declining.

The other central concept that is salient in this chapter is that of history. We will see how our species has adapted to centuries of changes in the way we work from hunting and gathering societies through to post-industrial ones. This historical perspective is important because it enables us to see ourselves in the larger picture and expands our horizons.

Introduction

As long as I kept finding I could do something, I still felt I was able to feel I was in control. The worst times are when you realize that you're done, or you feel that there isn't one more thing you can possibly do. You have made all the phone calls, you've written all

The author would like to express his appreciation to Elaine Grandin and Bradley Zipursky for their editorial comments on earlier draft of this chapter.

the letters, you've sent all the resumes and done absolutely everything: that's when the feeling of hopelessness sets in. Helplessness, too.
So long as I can find even one more thing to do, to help get me out of this situation, I'll do it. It gives me a little more incentive. To go on the next day and not give up.

—an unemployed worker
—(Burman, 1988:16)

You only need to listen to a person who is looking for a job to realize the importance of work in our society. The majority of us throughout our adult lives will work. Work will consume the best part of our days. In general, **work** is often defined as "continuous employment, in the production of goods and services, for remuneration" (Chen and Regan, 1985:5). Or, to put it simply: work refers to paid employment (Jenkins and Sherman, 1979). Yet, work is much more than these definitions suggest. Work remains a critical factor in defining our social existence; including, who we are, how we think, and what we hope to become. Bryant (1972) argues:

> One's standard of living, style of life, political ideology, basic value orientations, choice of friends and spouse, health, daily routine, mode of child rearing, and general satisfaction with life, to name a few considerations, may well be the indirect, if not direct, result of one's work. We are shaped, molded, regulated, even assimilated by our work. Work is our behavioral product, but so, too, are we in many ways the product of our work. (p. xvii)

Once students realize work is more than just earning an income, they are naturally interested in the world of work, how it is changing, and the implications of those changes for themselves and their families.

In this chapter we will explore the world of work, with specific emphasis on Canada. Specifically, we will discuss work in three different, yet intricately related ways: (i) the historical development of industrialization and how it changed the way in which we work today; (ii) the social organization of work in Canada which is commonly known as the societal level *(or structural level)* of analysis since it primarily focuses on large-scale change, trends, and the structuring of work in a society; and, (iii) organizational life or, as it is mainly referred to, the micro-level of analysis since it deals primarily with occupational careers, occupational choices, socialization practice, and so on.

After you have read this chapter, you should have a general understanding of the following key terms and concepts:

Industrialization
Social organization
Division of labour
Technology
Unemployment rate
Primary sector
Secondary sector
Tertiary sector
Labour Force
Labour markets
Occupational choice
Profession
Deprofessionalization
Occupational segregation
Work satisfaction
Deskilling
Skill disruption

The Emergence of Industrialization

The Social Transformation of Work in World History

Since the beginning of time human beings have engaged in work activities to meet their survival needs. To meet these needs, human beings developed and were shaped by the technology and social organization of the society. **Social organization** refers to the relations among those involved in work. For example, is their a division of labour or do people perform all the tasks necessary to meet their subsistence needs? **Technology**, on the other hand, refers to the tools and skills used in the process of work. The technology and social organization at a given stage of history determined the nature of that society, including its degree of social inequality; which set the stage for the next level of development (Marx, 1967 [1887]; Lenski, 1966).

The social organization of work as we know it today, is a relatively recent phenomenon in world history. In fact, the present stage of social organization represents less than one percent of known human existence on this planet. To better understand the present form of social organization, we need to understand the evolution of work throughout history. Figure 12:1 highlights the historical progression of work; we will discuss each stage in turn.

Nomadic Hunting and Gathering Societies

By about 300,000 B.C. the human species, *Homo sapiens,* had evolved to its present form. Human beings lived as nomadic hunters and gatherers, moving from one place to the next as food resources were depleted in an area. Human beings lived as nomadic hunters and gatherers until about 8,000 B.C., accounting for about 97 percent of the history of our species! (Hodson and Sullivan, 1990). Hunting and gathering people did not perceive of "work" as a separate sphere of life. Those activities needed to secure sustenance took place on a daily basis. People did not expend energy collecting a surplus of game, berries, and edible roots because they could not store food nor transport it for future usage.

Figure 12:1. Timeline of the Social Organization of Work

300,000 B.C.	8000 B.C.	2000 B.C.	A.D. 800	1400	1750	1920	1960
Nomadic hunting and gathering societies	Settled agricultural societies	Classical civilizations	Feudal system	Merchant capitalism	Factory system	Mass production	Post-industrial society

Technology was very simple. Most work-related skills were shared in common, so that any single member could do all or most of the tasks required by the group as a whole. There did exist, however, primitive forms of a division of labour based on gender and age. Initially, the division of labour based on gender resulted from biological differences between men and women. However, this division of labour was not strictly based on strength differences nor socially-constructed inequalities. Most women spent much of their adult life, which was short, either pregnant or nursing children. Their primary duties were to pick berries, hunt for small animals, attend to the fire, cook meals, and sew furs together to make clothes for the band. Men, on the other hand, were responsible for hunting big-game, assessing the amount of resources available in an area, and making tools and weapons (i.e., stone cutters and wooden spears). Lee (1981) points out that there is considerable evidence available to suggest that women's small-game hunting and gathering activities were more productive than were men's big-game hunting activities, in both quantity and regularity of contribution.

Settled Agricultural Societies

Early agricultural societies developed independently in several places around the world (including Southeast Asia, the Persian Gulf, and Mesoamerica) from 9,000 B.C. to 3,000 B.C. The major differences between settled and nomadic societies includes (i) settled societies could accumulate a surplus supply of food and other goods since they lived in one area; (ii) technology was more sophisticated in settled societies but still extremely primitive according to our standards; and, (iii) a division of labour became more prominent, but was not restricted to, gender and age based differences.

As these societies matured, improvements in agricultural technology gradually allowed more people to leave agricultural work. These improvements included terracing and irrigation, the increased use of animal and human fertilizers, and advances in metallurgy that led to the proliferation of metal tools (Lenski, 1966). In addition, during the later stages of this societal form, the emergence of political officials, military leaders, artisans and craft specialists were emerging as the economic activity and settled areas expanded.

Classical Civilizations

Large agricultural societies gradually replaced small agricultural societies through military exploitation and subjugation by 2,000 B.C. leading to immense classical empires. For instance, historians estimate that the Inca Empire included about four million people at the time of the Spanish arrival (Lenski, 1966). Other examples of these civilizations include the Mayans and the Aztecs of Central America, the Azande of East Africa, the Phoenicians and the Egyptians of the Mediterranean, and the Imperial Chinese (Lenski, 1966:149). In these cities, several thousand people lived off the agricultural surplus of the subjugated areas. New craft skills were developed in the cities to produce more refined products for the rising tastes of the empires' rulers, officials, and attendants (Hodson and Sullivan, 1990:11).

In the centuries preceding the birth of Christ craftsman formed guilds to regulate standards and to limit the number of skilled craftsman. Membership was restricted almost exclusively to men. Most guild members were the sons of craftsman; rarely did someone gain entry unless they were related by blood to a guild member. Few technological advances occurred in classical civilizations because of the availability of slave labour. Membership in a guild was usually social in nature.

Feudal System

The feudal system was really an extension of simple agricultural societies. The major difference was that peasants in simple agricultural societies only turned over a portion of their crops to support rulers, priests, warriors, and civic officials. In feudal society, however, landlords extracted surplus crops from the peasants, known as *serfs,* to pay for Church taxes, military protection, and for their own personal use. The expropriation of surplus crops forced *serfs* to work continually to meet their sustenance needs. This period of time is probably considered to be one of the most extreme periods of inequality of human history.

Several significant developments occurred in feudal society. Artisans, specialized guilds based on new technologies, and merchants became organized in a more structured manner. The new guilds that were formed controlled not only standards for its members, but also hours of work, and the regulation of prices. These medieval guilds were similar to the guilds of the classical civilizations but they played a much more significant role in organizing the economic and political life of the growing medieval cities.

Many changes led to the passing of feudal society and the transition to modem industrial society. This transition has provided a focus for much of the social history written since that time (Hodson and Sullivan, 1990). This period in the social organization of work was also a central concern of the forerunners of modern sociological thought such as Karl Marx, Max Weber, and Emile Durkheim. In brief, the transition from feudal society to industrial society was brought about by an expansion in trade, markets, and the population base of cities, and the emergence of a factory system of production.

Merchant Capitalism

The period between feudal society and industrial society was one in which increased trade provided the impetus for changes in the social organization of work. This period lasted from the fourteenth century to the advent of the first modern factory in England in the mid-eighteenth century. Merchant capitalism existed not as a way to organize production, but as a means, to organize trade. Prior to this period, craftsmen were responsible for obtaining their own raw materials before they transformed them into finished goods. Under merchant capitalism, merchants took on these roles. Merchants gradually became more powerful since they controlled trade in the market. Eventually craftsmen were required to work for merchants since they had the capital and contacts to obtain the raw products necessary for the craftsmen to perform their trade. These merchants also utilized unskilled non-guild workers to perform simple tasks required for the craftsman to produce his finished product. Essentially, these simple tasks were traditionally performed by the craftsman, but merchants realized if they hired unskilled non-guild workers to perform some of the preparatory and rudimentary tasks for the craftsman, the craftsman would have more time to concentrate on the quality and quantity of finished products. It was under merchant capitalism that we began to see an early form of the division of labour generally associated with industrial society.

Factory System

As the industrial revolution began in 1750, the social organization of work underwent a rapid transformation. A factory system of production emerged with many employees working under one roof for specified periods of time each day. This system of production emerged first in England. The Industrial Revolution in England had begun in the wool industry. The focus shifted quickly, however, as the New World grew and markets for British textiles expanded to Asia and North America. Numerous technological inventions facilitated the rapid growth of the textile industry, including the flying shuttle (1733), the spinning jenny (1767), the water frame (1769), the spinning mule (1779), the power loom (1787), and the cotton gin (1792) (Faunce, 1981:14). The rapid growth of the textile industry quickly spread to other industries since many of the technological inventions in the textile industry required coal to provide steam to operate much of its technology.

These developments not only had a major impact on the economy of England, but also on the social organization of work. Employers began to realize that if they divided all the tasks to manufacture a product into more refined tasks and had certain workers attend to each task separately, they could increase daily production. Adam Smith in 1776 in his book *The Wealth of Nations* (1937), described the advantages of the new division of labour in the manufacturing of pins for the textile industry:

> One man draws out the wire; another straightens it; a third cuts it; a fourth points it; a fifth grinds it at the top for receiving the head; to make the head requires two or three distinct operations; to put it on is a peculiar business; to whiten the pin is another; it is even a trade by itself to put them into the paper; and the important business of making a pin is in the manner divided into about 18 distinct operations, which in some manufactories are all performed by distinct hands, though in others the same man will sometimes perform two or three of them.... Ten persons, therefore, could make among them upwards of 48,000 pins in one day. (p. 4–5)

Prior to this elaborate division of labour, ten men could only produce 20 pins each per day for a total of 200 pins.

Mass Production

The factory system of production continued through to the twentieth century. By 1920, a new system of production emerged . . . mass production. Five characteristics differentiate this system of production from the early factory system of production: (i) scale of industry increased; (ii) ownership of factories fell into the hands of the few; (iii) a bureaucratic structure to organize all facets of production and to control workers emerged; (iv) an assembly-line system of production was instituted; and, (v) shift work over 24 hours periods, seven days a week became the norm of operation (Hodson and Sullivan, 1990). These social inventions changed the way people worked by organizing all work-related activities according to scientific procedures. This new approach became known as *scientific management* and is most often identified with the work of Frederick Winslow Taylor, an American industrial engineer who felt that thinking should be removed from the realm of the worker. Scientific management, or *Taylorism* as it came to be known, involved a detailed study of industrial processes in order to break them down into simple operations that could be precisely timed and organized. Taylor actively studied the work done by workers on shop floors and assembly-lines before redesigning those jobs to increase maximum efficiency for maximum productivity. Taylor's approach was actively resisted by workers because it made them feel like automatons instead of human beings. Nevertheless, controlled output and worker performance strategies were to become commonplace.

Post-Industrial Society

Since 1960 we have seen an increase in technology and a growing service sector (i.e., finance, insurance, and transportation industries, as well as professional and business services). This new trend has brought about a number of occupations that did not exist or employed very few people. We will not describe this stage in the social organization of work at this time since we will return to it in greater detail later in the chapter. Instead, we now turn to how industrialization emerged in the context of Canada.

Industrialization in Canada

The term **industrialization** basically refers to the replacement of human skills in the production of goods and services with machines and the replacement of human or animal energy with inanimate sources of power (Smucker, 1980:1). The course of industrialization in a society is usually unique to that society. In other words, the course of industrialization in Canada has been different from that of England, Germany, Japan and the United States. This may not seem obvious to you until you recognize that the time period of industrialization, the social milieu, and the early manufacturing organizations of each country have been different which inevitably resulted in various courses of development. The historical development of industrialization in each country mentioned above is beyond the scope of this chapter. Instead, we will provide an overview of industrialization in Canada which will allow you to understand the next section on occupational structure.

The economic development of Canada as a colony first of France and later of England was built up around the exploitation and export of natural resources (Rinehart, 1987:25). This economic emphasis persisted well into the nineteenth century. By the mid to late nineteenth century, Canada was primarily known for its trade in furs, timber, and grains. This time period in the development of industrialization can best be considered a pre-industrial period in the Canadian economy since most work done was labour intensive (not aided by machinery) and most exports were not in the form of finished goods. The vast majority of trade was with England and it was there where furs, timber, and grains, were transformed into finished, usable goods.

At the time of Confederation (1867), Canada remained a basically rural nation with 50 percent of the nations labour force employed in agricultural pursuits. Although there were manufacturing in Montreal, steel and railroad car production in Hamilton, and numerous other manufacturing pursuits evident in Toronto, Canada had not yet entered a period of industrialization. Between 1870 and 1890 Canada began to emerge as an industrialized nation stimulated by a protective tariff. Investment in machinery became prevalent resulting in more and larger factories. By 1890 Canada had 70,000 manufacturing firms producing a variety of semi-finished and finished goods; but, by 1920 this number dwindled to 22,000 manufacturing firms (Rinehart, 1987:45). The reduction in the number of manufacturing firms was not a sign of a weakened industrialized nation. On the contrary, it was a sign of a strengthened industrialized nation since one of the signs that Marx so vividly pointed to was a concentration of capital in the hands of the few. In other words, multinational corporations were emerging resulting in greater concentration, centralization, and bureaucratization of production. This process has continued to the present day.

Today, Canada as a society is generally perceived to have the characteristics basic to a member of the fortunate group of advanced industrial nations (Craib, 1986). It has superior levels of modern technological activity in many parts of the country and in some sectors of the economy. The standard of living in Canada is relatively high and most Canadians are able to find work, buy a home, own a car, and periodically take vacations. Canada rates as one of the leading nations in per capita gross national product (GNP). The GNP is the total value of goods and services produced in a country plus the monies earned from foreign investment divided by the number of persons in the country. In 1988, Canada had a GNP per capita of $14,120 U.S., which placed it as the 4th largest in the world behind Norway (3rd), United States (2nd), and Switzerland (1st) (World Bank, *World Development Report,* 1988). The goods produced in this country, however, tend to be based on our natural resources (i.e., oil and natural gas), agricultural products (i.e., wheat and barley), and semi-finished products such as lumber. Our reliance on the exportation of our natural resources, as well as foreign investment in the country, has given rise to two main issues: (i) dependence on foreign trade and (ii) the effects of foreign investors buying Canadian companies and taking the profit out of the country. Presently, close to 50 percent of the mining, petroleum, timber, and manufacturing industries are foreign owned and controlled mostly by American, then German and Japanese investors (Royal Commission on the Economic Union, 1985). The problem with extensive foreign investment, such as that seen in Canada, is that we are unable to be self-sufficient nor are we in a position to reap the profits from our own resources. In addition, economic decisions made within the country and abroad can lead to plant closures outside the control of the workers.

The United States is unquestionably our principal trading partner. Approximately three-quarters of both Canadian exports and imports are with the United States (Royal Commission on the Economic Union, 1985). This trading relationship is expected to strengthen as a result of the Free Trade Agreement between Canada and the United States signed on January 2, 1988 by Prime Minister Brian Mulroney and former President Ronald Reagan. For the Progressive Conservative government, the free-trade agreement represents the centerpiece of its economic strategy for Canada. The agreement is intended to enhance Canada's competitive position, using the American market as a springboard for reaching other international markets. The government argues that Canadian industry needs tariff-free access (that is, the elimination of duties on certain kinds of imports and exports) to the North American market with its 250 million consumers. For the U.S., the economic impact of the pact is small, but not insignificant. A report prepared for the U.S. Trade Representative by the American International Trade Commission showed U.S. industry had little to gain, or lose, from tariff reductions, but the free-trade agreement is still important to Americans. It offers the U.S. nondiscriminatory access to

Canadian natural resources, a significant long-term advantage (Cameron, 1988). At a time when the U.S. is running short of key raw materials, including petroleum, Canada has agreed not to favour Canadian resource users over American users.

The long-term impact of the free-trade agreement has been, and will continue to be, debated for some time. The effects that the pact will have on the Canadian economy and its market, remain unclear. We can only hope as Canadians that the pact will in fact bolster our industries and ensure the economic viability of our markets in the years to come.

In this section we briefly described the emergence of industrialization in Canada. In addition, we explored Canada's economic position vis-a-vis its trading partners. The next section will closely examine Canada's changing occupational structure and the implications of that structure for working Canadians.

Occupational Structure in Canada

Canada's Industrial and Labour Structure

There are several ways in which we can conceptualize the work done in the labour force. One way is to categorize labour force participants by the *industry* in which they work. By convention, there are three major sectors within the labour force: primary, secondary, and tertiary.

1. **Primary sector**—consists of labour force participants who work in agriculture, fishing, logging, hunting, trapping, or mining; with the vast majority working in the farming industry.
2. **Secondary sector**—consists of labour force participants who work in construction and manufacturing.
3. **Tertiary sector**—consists of labour force participants who work in transportation, communications, commerce, finance, health, education, and so on (Hedley, 1988:498).

The occupational categories within the primary sector involves some kind of extraction or harvesting. Generally, there is no transformation of raw products into finished products for consumption. The occupational categories within the secondary sector, by contrast, typically involve manufacturing finished or semi-finished products. Some industries, however, do include both sectors (Hedley, 1988). For example, occupational categories in the fisheries industry includes primary and secondary sector occupations. Individuals who catch the fish are considered to have primary sector occupations since the product is still in its natural state (i.e., a tuna fish). On the other hand, individuals who are employed in fish canning factories are considered to have secondary sector occupations since they transform the raw product into a manufactured good (i.e., canned tuna). According to Daniel Bell in his much acclaimed book, *The Coming of Post-Industrial Society* (1967), when at least half of the labour force works in the *secondary sector* (i.e., a canning factory, an automobile assembly plant, a steel company, etc.), we live in an **industrial society.**

Bell also suggested that when at least half of the labour force works in the *tertiary sector* (i.e., services, communications, health, education, etc.) we live in a **post-industrial society**. Labour Force participation statistics for Canada show that seventy-two percent of the labour force is presently employed in the *tertiary sector,* while six percent are employed in the *primary sector,* and twenty-two percent are employed in the *secondary sector (Statistics Canada, 1990).* This clearly places Canada as a post-industrial society. However, the number of labour force participants in each sector is not necessarily consistent across the provinces. Table 12:1 reveals the percent of labour force participants in each industry by province. For example, we can see that Saskatchewan has a much larger agricultural industry (primary sector) but a much smaller manufacturing based economy (secondary sector) compared to the other provinces in the country. Similarly, in the Maritimes, few labour force participants are involved in agriculture but more are involved in public administration work compared to the other provinces. It is evident, however, that the number of service jobs is most consistently the predominant type of employment for labour force participants.

Recent projections of the occupations expected to contribute most to employment growth in Canada are overwhelmingly *tertiary sector* occupations. Table 12:2 highlights

Table 12:1
Labour Force by Industry and Province, Canada, 1990

				Percent				
Industry	**B.C.**	**Alta.**	**Sask.**	**Man.**	**Ont.**	**Que.**	**Maritimes**	**Total**
Agriculture	2.0	6.5	16.5	7.1	2.2	1.9	0.2	3.2
Other primary	3.3	5.5	3.3	1.7	0.9	1.5	4.8	2.2
Manufacturing	11.5	7.9	5.9	11.8	19.2	18.9	10.7	15.7
Construction	7.4	7.1	4.9	4.5	6.8	5.9	6.9	6.5
Transportation/ communication	8.2	7.3	7.0	8.6	6.5	7.8	8.8	7.4
Trade	18.9	18.8	17.4	18.2	17.8	18.5	19.7	18.3
Finance/insurance/ real estate	6.5	5.4	4.7	5.5	6.8	5.5	3.5	5.4
Service	36.4	35.6	33.5	35.7	33.4	32.7	34.2	34.5
Public administration	5.5	5.7	6.6	6.6	6.0	6.5	8.1	6.4
Unclassified[1]	0.3	_[2]		_	0.4	0.8	_	0.2
Total (%)	100.0	99.8	99.5	99.7	100.0	100.0	97.0	100.0
N, 1000s)	(1,597)	(1,321)	(471)	(532)	(5,227)	(3,328)	(1,033)	(13,509)

1. This category consists of unemployed persons who have never worked for pay and those who have not worked in the last five years.
2. Statistics Canada does not provide provincial estimates of less than 4,000. These omissions lead to total percentages of less than 100 percent.
Source: Calculations based on Statistics Canada, *The Labour Force* (December 1990, #71-001, Table 11), p. B-24.

these occupation categories for the years 1986 to 1995. Most evident from these projections is that most of the occupations expected to contribute to growth tend to be of the low wage, service variety. We will expand this point later in this chapter.

The classification of the labour force by *industry, or what is being produced,* is not the only way that we can come to understand the Canadian labour force. Often, the labour force is categorized by *occupation,* or the *kind of work* that is being performed. Often we differentiate the kind of work that individuals do according to whether they are *white collar* or *blue-collar* occupations. The term **white collar** occupation typically is applied to the work of managers, nurses, lawyers, teachers, salespersons, and office workers. Phrases such as *intellectual* and *mental tasks, working with people,* or *ideas or information* (rather than things) are commonly encountered. In contrast, **blue-collar** occupation typically is applied to work roles involved in manufacturing: the creation of products. It is sometimes presumed to require only manual or labour intensive tasks, usually summarized as "working with the hands." Electricians, carpenters, truck drivers, machine operators, and labourers are considered to have blue-collar occupations. Blue-collar work is often subdivided into two categories: **skilled crafts** and **unskilled work**. *Skilled crafts* are those in which the work requires some degree of manual dexterity combined with a broad

Table 12:2
Occupations Expected to Contribute Most to Employment Growth in Canada, 1986–1995

Occupational Title	New Growth in Employment
Salesperson, commodities	91,000
Food Service	80,000
Bookkeepers	56,000
Secretaries and stenographers	54,000
Chefs and cooks	47,000
Cashiers and Tellers	47,000
Janitors and cleaners	40,000
Truck drivers	33,000
Sales management	26,000
Barbers and hairdressers	26,000
Motor vehicle mechanics	25,000
Nurses	24,000
Financial officers	22,000
Supervisors; food and beverage preparation	19,000
General office clerks	18,000
Labourers, services	17,000
Services management	16,000
Receptionists and information clerks	15,000
Carpenters	15,000

Source: Krahn, J. H. and Lowe, G. S. *Work Industry and Canadian Society.* Scarborough: Nelson Canada, 1988:62
Original Source: Employment and Immigration Canada; based on *COPS 1986 Reference Scenario.*

knowledge of tools, materials, and processes. All craft work combines formal training and certification as well as some experiential knowledge. Skilled crafts include such blue-collar occupations as electricians, plumbers, welders, and masons. *Unskilled work* are those occupations that require no formal training nor certification primarily because the skill level required to perform the task is considered to be minimal. These jobs virtually always consist of routine tasks, require very little training, and are often considered to include tasks that anyone "off the street" can perform. Examples of such jobs include dishwashing, stocking shelves, garbage collection, cleaning offices, and waitressing.

The classification of the labour force by occupation is somewhat misleading since not all white collar jobs are necessarily high paying, provide promotion opportunities, nor are prestigious; conversely, not all blue-collar jobs are low paying, offer few career advancement opportunities, nor have little occupational prestige in the eyes of the general public. For example, selling vacuum cleaners door-to-door is considered to be a white-collar occupation but usually is not well paid and has low occupational prestige. On the other hand, a blue-collar occupation such as being an electrician may include wage benefits that far surpass many white-collar occupations and provides greater occupational prestige; which is often the result of unionization in Canada. These categories, therefore, are only convenient social constructions to classify the kind of work that people perform in the labour force.

As we approach the twenty-first century, it is abundantly clear that the trend toward an ever-increasing *tertiary sector* complemented by a continued growth in *white-collar* occupations is likely to continue for some time. The distribution of males to females in each occupation is still not reflective of the number of females now participating in the labour force (see Table 12:3).

Table 12:3

Labour Force Participation by Sex, Canada, 1901-1990 (Selected Years)

Year	Female	Male	Both Sexes
1901	16.1%	87.8%	53.0%
1911	18.6	90.6	57.4
1921	19.9	89.8	56.2
1931	21.8	87.2	55.9
1941	22.9	85.6	55.2
1951	24.2	84.1	54.3
1961	29.1	80.8	55.1
1971	39.9	75.4	58.0
1976	45.0	75.5	58.0
1981	51.8	78.3	64.8
1986	55.1	76.7	65.7
1990	57.6	74.1	65.7

Note: "Both sexes" category represents the total labour force participation rate for all adults working in each respective year.

Sources: 1901–1981 from Chen, M. and Regan, T. *Work in the Changing Canadian Context.* Toronto: Butterworths, 1985:135; Krahn, J. H. and Lowe, G. S. *Work Industry and Canadian Society.* Scarborough: Nelson Canada, 1988:40; 1990 from Statistics Canada, *The Labour Force* (December 1990, #71-001, Table 1), p. B-5,

As we can see in Table 12:4, in 1990 males were dispersed over a variety of occupations whereas females tended to be more concentrated in lower paying, lower status white-collar occupations. In particular, 29.6 percent of all females in thelabour force were employed in clerical (i.e., secretarial and receptionist jobs), while an additional 16.2 percent were employed in service occupations (i.e., waiting tables and hairdressing). Most of the work that many women do in the labour force is simply an extension of what they have traditionally done in the home (Armstrong and Armstrong, 1984). Hedley (1988) suggests that secretarial and clerical work, cooking, waiting tables, hosting, teaching small children, nursing, cleaning, and sewing are all chores that women have done since time immemorial. The only difference between what most are doing now and what they traditionally did is that they are being paid directly for their labour. Women today, however, are beginning to find entry into traditionally male dominated occupations. This has been a long struggle for women since socialization practices, occupational sex segregation and unequal treatment in the work place has contributed toward female underrepre-

Table 12:4

Labour Force Employment by Occupation and Sex, Canada, 1990

	Number (1000s)			Percent[1]		
Occupation	**Total**	**Female**	**Male**	**Total**	**Female**	**Male**
Managerial/administrative	1,653	661	992	13.5	11.9	14.8
Natural sciences	481	89	392	3.9	1.6	5.9
Social sciences	259	154	104	2.1	2.8	1.6
Religion	33	7	26	0.3	0.1	0.4
Teaching	557	355	203	4.6	6.4	3.0
Medicine and health	655	538	117	5.4	9.7	1.7
Artistic, literary and recreational	230	100	130	1.9	1.8	1.9
Clerical	2,041	1,644	397	16.7	29.6	5.9
Sales	1,259	575	684	10.3	10.3	10.2
Service	1,551	901	650	12.7	16.2	9.7
Farming/horticultural	406	106	299	3.3	1.9	4.5
fishing/hunting/trapping	33	–[2]	31	0.3	–	0.5
Forestry and logging	44	–	43	0.4	–	0.6
Mining and quarrying	57	–	56	0.5	–	0.8
Processing	349	85	264	2.9	1.5	3.9
Machining	209	10	200	1.6	0.2	3.0
Fabricating/assembling/repairing	934	188	746	7.6	3.4	11.4
Construction	651	15	636	5.3	0.3	9.5
Transportation	456	46	410	3.7	0.4	6.1
Materials handling	249	50	199	2.0	0.9	3.0
Other crafts/equipment operating	142	32	110	1.2	0.6	1.6
Total	12,248	5,560	6,688	100.0	99.5	100.0

1. Percentages are calculated by sex, based on the raw numbers in each occupation row divided by the total number employed for each sex.

2. Statistics Canada does not report estimates of less than 4,000 because of concerns about the reliability of small estimates of sample data.

Source: Statistics Canada, *The Labour Force* (December 1990, #71-001. Table 14), p. B-27.

sentation in many higher paying, higher status occupations. We will return to these issues on several occasions in sections dealing with the impact of technology, the barriers to primary labour market entry, and occupational choice.

The degree of inequality can be partly understood by investigating labour market segmentation in Canada. Let us turn to bow labour is segmented in an attempt to explain inequality among the work force.

Labour Market Segmentation in Canada

Labour markets are the structural emphasis that sociologists place on the positions and places where people work. They are, in general, "the economic arenas in which employers seek to purchase labour from potentially qualified employees who themselves are seeking employment suitable to their present education, experience, and preferences" (Krahn and Lowe, 1989:62). What a person dictates as a "good job" or a "bad job" and what an employer dictates as a "good employee" or "bad employee is determined by the rewards and benefits that each exchange for the output that is necessary for the task at hand. Often the two are not commensurate for the jobs and the skills available in the labour market at any give time period. That is, often there are more skilled, experienced, and highly educated people than the number of jobs available to accommodate them. Conversely, those jobs that require fewer skills, education, and experience tend to have a lot of people seeking opportunities for employment. Nevertheless, labour market theories emphasize that it is important to know where individuals and their occupations are located in the labour market if we are to understand career development.

The chief spokesperson for the labour market approach to understanding the types of jobs that people perform, Piore (1969, 1970, 1975), divides the labour market into two sectors: **primary** and **secondary**. The primary labour market is subdivided into upper and lower tiers with the professional (i.e., doctors and lawyers) and technical (i.e., computer programmers) as well as the managerial and administrative groups belonging to the upper tier, and sales (retail outlet employees), clerical, and skilled crafts (i.e., licensed mechanics) comprising the lower tiers. The secondary labour market consists of semi-skilled (i.e., a telephone repairmen) and unskilled nonfarm labourers (i.e., carpenters helpers) and service workers (i.e., gas station attendants). According to Piore (1975):

> The former [primary sector] offers jobs with relatively high wages, good working conditions, chances of advancement, equity and due process in the administration of work rules, and above all, employment stability. Jobs in the secondary sector, by contrast, tend to be low paying, with poorer working conditions and little chance for advancement; to a highly personalized relationship between workers and supervisors which leaves wide latitude for favouritism and is conducive to harsh and impulsive work discipline; and to be characterized by considerable instability in jobs and a high turnover among the labour force. (p. 126)

Jobs that tend to have little remuneration and benefits (the secondary labour market) tend to be occupied primarily by lower educated, female, and visible minority groups. Those jobs with higher pay and benefits (usually in the primary labour market) tend to be occupied by those individuals with higher education, more experience, and skill; typically, but not exclusively, white males. In general, because of low employer investment in updating worker skills and knowledge, the occupations in the secondary market offer little opportunity for career development. Finally, because of the differences in skills and knowledge required by the occupations in the various markets, little mobility occurs between the secondary and primary labour markets. Consequently, an individual who works in the secondary labour market tends to remain in that market throughout their work lives unless they upgrade their skills and knowledge.

Barriers to primary labour market entry are numerous. These include gender discrimination, age discrimination, "contacts" (or the so-called *old "boys" network*), and racial and ethnic discrimination. In most cases, *gender discrimination* as a barrier to primary labour market entry is based on managers and corporations discriminating against women. For years, women have been denied the opportunity to either enter the primary sector or once they move into primary sectors they are denied upward mobility. In a recent study conducted in Calgary, Alberta, Cahoun found that of the private and public sector organizations, surveyed, females represented 47.9 percent of the labour force. Yet, only 13.6 percent were executives, 22.3 percent were middle managers, and 37.4 percent were front-line supervisors (Calgary Herald, January 19, 1991:Fl). In another Canadian study conducted by the Canadian Bankers' Association,women were found in 90.7 percent of all the bank teller and clerking positions, while only 5.7 percent were bank executives (Calgary Herald, February 16, 1991:Fl). Although, women are gaining greater entry into the upper levels of the primary labour market, they still are significantly underepresented. Women are often perceived as less competent than males even though many have similar credentials (i.e., degrees and experience). In addition, many organizations are still hesitant about spending time and money training women for fear that they are not serious about their careers and will leave them for traditional female roles (i.e., childrearing).

Age discrimination has also been considered a barrier to primary labour market entry. Young adults are often discriminated against because they lack the experience and maturity to work in "good jobs." How many times have you thought or said to an employer "how can I get the experience if no one gives me a job?" More recently, age discrimination has worked against middle-aged workers who have lost their jobs. Employers have begun to discriminate against middle-aged people partially because they may expect higher salaries than a younger adult, and partially because they often lack the qualifications that so many younger people who are entering the work force have today. The combination of these two factors detracts from middle-aged workers' ability to effectively compete with the surplus of higher educated younger workers in today's labour market.

Barriers to primary labour market entry also takes the form of job vacancy knowledge. Often, public and private organizations have internal competitions (that is, seeking to fill the vacancy from within the organization) that excludes applications from outside the system. Labour unions also practice this same strategy as a way to provide security and incentives for card carrying members. Research has shown that one-half of all jobholders in this country have found their positions through personal contacts (Anderson and Calzavara, 1986). These findings demonstrate that access to information can act as a barrier to primary labour market access.

Finally, racial and ethnic discrimination can act as a barrier to primary labour market entry. Discrimination of this kind is similar to gender and age discrimination since it is based on physical or socially undesirable characteristics of the individual. The barriers to primary labour market entry discussed here do not entirely account for the difficulties that some groups of individuals face in the labour market today. However, they do provide us with part of the explanation for why some people have "good" jobs and others have "bad" jobs. It should be clear that the structure of our society can have as much influence in this process as individuals themselves do. As these barriers become more pronounced and more people are denied entry into the labour market, unemployment in Canada is likely to rise.

Unemployment

Work is often considered to be a major part of a person's sense of self-identity. The importance of having a job to a strong self-identity is exemplified when you meet a new person in a social encounter where the first question they ask you or you ask them is "What do you do for a living." Most people are able to identify one job or another. What is it like to be without a job? How does it feel to admit being unemployed? How do people react to joblessness? These are important questions in our present society since people are subject to layoffs as a consequence of an unstable economy.

Unemployment Rates

In Canada, an **unemployment rate** is calculated by dividing the number of individuals out of work and who are actively seeking work by the total number of labour force participants (including the unemployed). These rates, however, are only crude estimates since not all people seeking work are known nor do they include those individuals who are **underemployed**—individuals who are presently working in jobs that require less skill than their experience and education would suggest but do so in order to make a living. Unemployment rates vary over time, across regions, and industry in this country.

In Canada, regional differences in unemployment is considerable. These differences are often directly linked to the economic base of the various regions. In particular, provinces with a diverse economic base (economies with primary, secondary, and tertiary sector industries) tend to fare better than others. Table 12.5 breaks down the unemployment rate by province since 1982. As can be seen, the Maritime provinces consistently show the highest rate of unemployment in the country. The unemployment rate of the Maritimes is almost double that of Ontario and the Prairie provinces for any given year.

Unemployment realities in Canada are also differentially distributed across age and sex (see Table 12.6). The percentage of persons, ages 25–44 years, overwhelmingly constitute the bulk of the unemployed in the country. This is alarming since this is the time period in which people begin to develop their careers and have the greatest financial obligations (i.e., childrearing and mortgage payments). Prolonged unemployment has the potential to create irreversible economic hardships and diminish career advancement opportunities. We now turn to the subjective experiences of the unemployed.

Table 12.5
Unemployment Rate by Province, Canada, 1982–1990

					Percent					
Year	NFLD	PEI	NS	NB	QUE	ONT	MAN	SASK	ALTA	B.C.
1982	16.5	12.9	11.9	14.0	12.2	8.5	7.6	5.8	5.6	9.8
1983	19.5	16.7	15.8	16.2	15.3	12.7	10.9	8.9	11.6	16.1
1984	20.5	12.8	13.1	14.9	12.8	9.1	8.3	8.0	11.2	14.7
1985	26.2	16.5	15.3	16.7	13.0	9.9	9.5	9.7	11.9	16.4
1986	21.9	16.3	14.3	16.8	12.3	8.2	8.9	9.1	9.2	14.0
1987	21.4	17.8	15.8	15.0	11.7	7.4	9.0	8.5	11.5	15.3
1988	20.6	17.9	11.7	13.7	10.0	5.0	8.7	8.1	8.3	10.8
1989	16.3	16.4	10.4	13.5	9.7	5.8	8,7	9.1	8.0	10.8
1990	18.5	20.5	12.3	13.2	11.2	6.5	7.5	8.9	7.5	8.5

Source: Statistics Canada, *The Labour Force*, #71-001 (1982, Table 29, p.79; 1983, Table 56, p. 79; 1984, Table 109, p. 145; 1985, Table 54, pp. 94–95; 1986, Table 54, pp. 81–82; 1987, Table 54, pp. 81–82; 1988. Table 54, pp. 81–82; 1989, Table 37. p. B50; 1990, Table 37, p. B53).

Table 12.6
Unemployment Distribution by Age and Sex, Canada, 1990

Age	Male	Female	Total
15–24 years	28.9%	25.2%	27.3%
25–44 years	52.2	55.6	53.7
45–and over	18.9	19.2	19.0
Total	100.0%	100.0%	100.0%

Note: Statistics Canada reports data using the actual (or estimated) numbers of individuals in each category. The data in this table have been converted into percentages. For example, 52.2% of all unemployed males are between the ages of 25–44.
Source: Statistics Canada, *The Labour Force* (December 1990, #71-001, Table 29), p. B-42.

Subjective Experiences of Unemployment

In 1988, *Killing Time, Losing Ground: Experiences of Unemployment* by Patrick Burman was published. The book was based on a study of the unemployed in London, Ontario. Burman showed that the subjective experience of being unemployed was one of fear, insecurity, anger, helplessness, and dismay. Although most of the participants in the research became unemployed involuntarily (i.e., layoffs and plant closures) many believed there was something wrong with them because they could not find immediate employment. Burman's analysis not only provides insight into how individuals feel bout being unemployed, it also shows how the macroinstitutional sphere (i.e., the Unemployment Insurance Commission, Welfare Departments, and Canada Manpower) provide little solace for the circumstances of the jobless. Although these institutions are established to provide a necessary service, they are often seen by their clients as sources of frustration and degradation. The subjective experiences of several respondents are reflected in the following excerpts:

> They really make you feel like you're begging. Their whole attitude is, "You don't deserve this but, out of the goodness of our heart, we're going to give it to you." (p. 69)
>
> They have a real looking-down-on-you attitude, and my back just gets right up. I don't find them very pleasant people. I keep thinking how people less assertive than me deal with that. I bet there's a lot of people that cry. Because they're so negative to you. There's no understanding. It's like, "you quit your job, and you did this just so you could do nothing." (p. 85–86)
>
> There is some sort of thing where you punch in your interests and your education and it comes up with a job or an area that you are suited for.... Well, I went to this and punched in all the stuff and it turned out that I wasn't suited for anything. (p. 72)

According to Burman, the bureaucratic structure of these organizations strips away individuality and the uniqueness of the jobless. Moreover, the longer an individual is unemployed the less assistance these institutions are able to provide which leads to a sense of being trapped in a maze in which the exit seems more and more remote. The interplay among, bureaucratic assistance, loss of occupation, weakening social networks and family hardships, tends to lead to a change in self-identity and individual worth.

From Burman's study of unemployment we can learn so much about employment in our society. By understanding the experiences of the unemployed we are able to comprehend why people often "consent" to *exploitative* and *alienated labour* and why individuals become attached to and express "satisfaction" with jobs that lack intrinsic gratifications. Rinehart (1988) suggests that financial independence, self-respect, and the opportunity to socialize are job-linked elements that are extrinsic to the content of work, but stabilize and give meaning to our lives. Employment insulates us from the abyss of joblessness: a job, any job, is preferable to no job at all.

More recently, researchers have become concerned about the effects of new technologies and their implications for tomorrow's labour force. Will new technologies lead to more unemployment or will they create more job opportunities? And, will technology of the future lead to a more skilled or less skilled work force? It is these questions that we will address in the next section.

Work and Technology

Technology and Its Impact on Skill

The impact of technological change on skill requirements for work is one of the most debated subjects in the study of work and occupations (Form, 1987). This debate has reached new heights with the rapid introduction of microcomputer technology (often referred to as *microelectronic technology*) in the workplace; and is further fueled by the known and unknown potential of future technologies. **Skill level,** can be defined simply as "a complex organization of behaviour (physical or verbal) developed through learning and directed toward a particular goal or centered on a specific activity." Wallace (1989) suggests there are three perspectives on the impact of skill level currently dominating the field: *the upgrading thesis, the downgrading thesis,* and the *mixed effects thesis.*

1. Proponents of the *upgrading thesis* argue that "advanced technologies require that workers take on more responsibility, use more judgment and discretion, and have a broader understanding of the total production process" (Blauner, 1964). This argument is supported by the belief that microelectronic technology will require initial learning and subsequent relearning to keep pace with the advances made in the technology in the future.
2. Proponents of the *downgrading thesis,* however, agree that initially technological change may create a temporary increase in skill requirements for some workers or even that a few workers may experience permanent increase in skill (Bright, 1966). Nevertheless, they argue that the prevailing outcome of technological change for most workers is one of de-skilling, routinization, and closer supervision. This argument was most notably advanced by the neo-marxist Harry Braverman (1974) in his seminal book *Labor and Monopoly Capital: The Degradation of Skill in the Twentieth Century.*
3. The third perspective is the *mixed effects thesis.* Proponents of this perspective argue that both upgrading and downgrading of skill level will result from technological change, but in the long run they tend to balance out resulting in no net change in the skill distribution in the workforce (Wallace, 1989:364–366).

Empirical evidence can be found for each of the perspectives discussed. Blauner (1964) in his work *Alienation and Freedom* provided historical evidence to support the

Figure 12:2. The Relationship between Industrialization and Skill Level

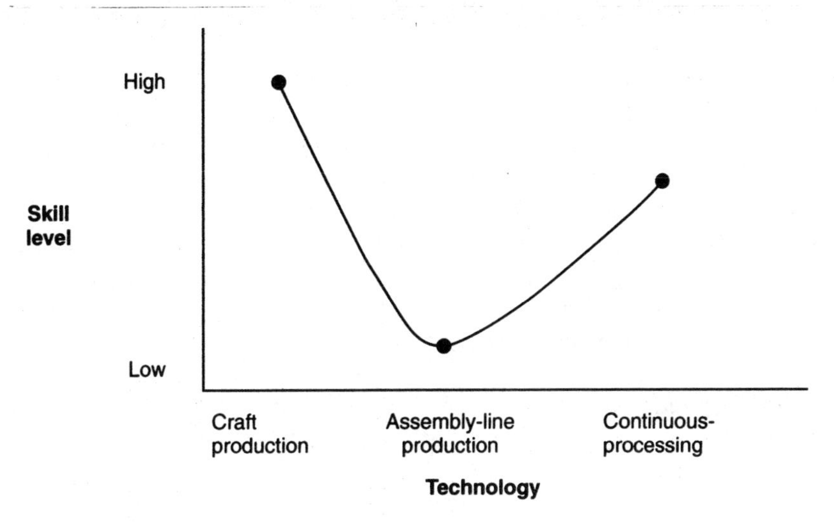

upgrading thesis by showing that industrial societies moved through several stages of development—craft production, assembly-line production, and continuous processing (automation). According to Blauner, skill level was at its highest level during the early years of industrialization, at its lowest during the assembly-line stage, and increases once again due to automation associated with the modern technology available today in corporations and industries (see Figure 12:2). Specifically, long-term occupational trends reveal that industrialization has increased skills by reducing unskilled work and increasing semi-skilled, skilled, clerical, technical, professional, and administrative work. Empirical studies tending to support the upgrading perspective rely primarily on self-reports by workers. For example, Wallace (1988) suggested that the "subjective experiences of workers" is typically one of skill upgrading, since they feel that they are constantly learning new things and tend to disregard the fact that skills previously acquired have fallen into disuse. For example, clerical workers today primarily do most of their daily work on microcomputers. However, most do not recognize that previous skills such as shorthand dictation, filing, and so on are seldom required to the same extent and have been replaced by microcomputers and dictaphones. Today these technological innovations are the new skills of the workplace.

Support for the *downgrading thesis* can be seen in the work of Glenn and Feldberg *Degraded and Deskilled: The Proletarianization of Clerical Work* (1977). Their analysis was based on observations in organizations, discussions with managers and intensive interviews with 30 clerical workers. Glenn and Feldberg concluded that automation of office work was routinized, required fewer skills than were previously needed, and reduced the clerks' control over their job activities because the computer silently monitors every action and has the implicit pressure for greater output. Similarly, Phillip Kraft (1979) in his historical analysis of the changing technology in the computer programming industry suggested that a once highly skilled field has fallen to increasing fragmentation and routinization of the tasks involved in present day software programming. Kraft argues that the skill level of programmers has decreased because once initial programming has been developed, all other software packages can be developed with minor modifications. Kraft concludes that, "programmings transformation into software production shows that even the most complex work can be trivialized, and underscores the self-development in general—that improved machines automatically mean better jobs."

As suggested earlier, proponents of the *mixed effects thesis* note that the distribution of skilled, semi-skilled, and unskilled occupations has remained relatively stable for several decades, despite changes in the particular mix of occupations. Some mixed effect proponents find different effects of technological change of specific workers in an industry. For instance, Baran and Teegarden (1984) found that automation in the insurance industry led to the displacement of many professional occupations, a shift in the burden of work to low-paid clerical workers, and an increase in the supervisory workers, resulting in a net increase in the average skill of the remaining workers. Similarly, Calhoun and Copp (1988) found that computerization of legal work had mixed effects in that the position of elite segments of the law profession (i.e., constitutional and corporate law) was strengthened at the expense of non-elite segments (i.e., wills and trusts and family law), thus reinforcing trends which were already underway.

Irrespective of the position one takes on this debate, it is reasonable to conclude that technological change in the form of microelectronics will at minimum lead to **skill disruption**, whereby a portion of the acquired skills are rendered obsolete and the worker must acquire some new skills to function within the environment created by the new technology. Hodson (1988) argues that the degree of skill disruption will be contingent on the pace of technological change, which is likely to be substantial, the compatibility between old skills and new skills, and the availability of retraining programs to ease the transition from the old technology to the new. As new technology is introduced into most occupations the form of the work force is likely to be rapidly altered. This is the subject of our next section.

Telecommuting Technology and Its Impact on the Workforce

The emphasis on computers and work was fueled in part by Alvin Toffler's notion of the "electronic cottage," presented in his book *The Third Wave.* Toffler argued that as the structure of our economy changed from industrial to information-based, the computer would offer more freedom on the job, including the freedom to take work home to the "electronic cottage." Shortly thereafter, another futurist, Jack Nilles, coined the word "telecommuting" (Christensen, 1988).

The basic idea behind telecommuting is that employees and/or contracted individuals can work at home for an employer via a computer networking system. Several models are compatible with the telecommuting concept, including: full-time telecommuting from home offices, split work weeks, and split work days. Moreover, the potential for telecommuting has also seen the rise of "home entrepreneurs"; persons who use computers to develop their own businesses, which are frequently spin-offs of businesses in which they were previously employed. Telecommuting using personal computers offers benefits for both workers and employers, but it also holds great potential for increasing the exploitation of workers. On the positive side, Christensen (1988) suggests that groups such as the elderly, the handicapped, and working mothers can be employed gainfully in jobs that fit their schedules. Flexibility and autonomy are benefits that are typically mentioned for home workers. Employers argue that working mothers can save on child care by tending children while they work, but others contend that workers who try and tend children while they work cannot do justice to either job. Wallace (1989) points out other drawbacks of this technology:

> Recent experience with some types of "high-tech homework," such as clerical workers who process insurance forms, shows that employers often pay substandard wages and benefits, and do not allow paid vacations, health benefits, workmen's compensation, or unemployment compensation. (p. 380)

Hence, one has to look closely at specific cases to weigh the advantages and disadvantages of working in the home that advanced technology allows.

Educational and Retraining Requirements for New Technologies

In 1981, a report commissioned by the Federal Government of Canada entitled, "*The Task Force Report on Labour Market Development in the 1980s,*" recommended that resources be modestly re-allocated from education, general arts and sciences and social work to engineering, business, economics and technology. The report essentially emphasized that the labour market needs in Canada required a computer literate and technically trained labour force that could lead the country into the twenty-first century.

The recommendations of the Task Force Report are consistent with the pervasiveness and rapidity of technological change in North America. Several studies (Menzies, 1981; Groff, 1983; Abeshouse, 1987) all reach variations of the same conclusion that the de-skilling of jobs in some sectors will be offset by the upgrading of jobs in other sectors, leaving a labour force that, on average, requires the same amount of education and skills. However, whereas workers a generation ago could expect to change jobs two or three times before they retired, today's workers will change jobs six to seven times (Abeshouse, 1987). Consequently, rather than being a straight climb as we have become accustomed to, work careers are likely to entail several detours involving a substantial retooling of job skills.

The disruptive nature of career paths and the de-skilling of many jobs will require further training and retraining of workers throughout their lives. Choate (in Abeshouse, 1987) has suggested that workers will require "regular booster shots of education and training" to keep up with changes in technology.

The basic requirement of a university degree or college diploma will continue to be a prerequisite for most "good jobs" in the workplace, if only because such a degree serves a credentialing function in the job market (Collins, 1979). Nevertheless, it would appear that the content of a post-secondary school education will probably change as suggested by the Task Force Report in 1981. Microelectronic technology will not only be reserved for the technically trained, but also for those seeking liberal arts education. Wallace (1989) clearly identifies this as a necessity:

> People who do not educate themselves—and keep educating themselves—to participate in the new knowledge environment will be the peasants of the *information society.* (p. 381)

Technology and Occupational and Class Structures

Hodson and Parker (1988) found that occupations with projected growth rates of over 50 percent for the decade of the 1990s include data processing mechanics, office machine servicers, and computer operators, analysts, and programmers. However, among similar lists of the fastest-growing occupations in *absolute numbers,* most are "low-tech" jobs that comprise the lower echelon of the white-collar and service sectors. Many of these are relegated to what has come to be known as the "pink-collar ghetto": low-paying, dead-end jobs occupied predominantly by females (e.g., secretaries, cashiers, fast-food workers, and so on). These jobs, naturally will offer little solace or real opportunity to the middle-aged, displaced steel workers whose standard of living is based on an income nearly twice as high. Hodson and Parker (1988) conclude:

> The overall effect of advanced technology appears to be to increase the prevalence of upper-level professional jobs and lower-level operative and service jobs. The demand for middle-range jobs, particularly clerical jobs, will in all likelihood be reduced by high technology developments. The impact of these changes on the distribution of differentially rewarded positions in the economy will be to *increase inequality* [our emphasis] between the top and the bottom of the occupational distribution and to reduce the proportions of middle-range positions. (p. 17)

At the societal level, technological displacement of relatively high-paying jobs in manufacturing and other fields will lead to a phenomenon known as the "declining middle" (Kuttner, 1983). This trend has been occurring during the 1980s and will likely be commonplace in the years to come. Rosenthal (1983) found that between 1978 and 1983, 23.6 percent of households formerly classified as "middle-class" moved out of the middle. Of those displaced from the middle-class, about one-fourth advanced into a higher position, but three-fourths declined. Rosenthal explains this phenomenon by pointing to: (i) the sharp decline in the number of relatively well-paid (often unionized) manufacturing jobs; (ii) accompanied by a rise in low-paid retail and service jobs; and, (iii) the rise of a relatively small layer of well-paid professional and technical jobs. Observations such as these have fueled fears of a two-tiered society in which there are sharper social and political divisions between the "haves" and the "have nots" (see Kuttner, 1983).

Whether or not we believe in the extent of this foreseeable impact at the societal level, it should be recognized that further technological change will have some effect on the socioeconomic status of many individuals; given education, income, and occupational status will likely alter with technological advancement.

Career and Occupational Choice

A basic interest in the study of work is the question of why and how people first enter specific occupations, or types of work. In sociology, we categorize these questions in a broad category, commonly known as *occupational choice.* The term occupational choice has different meanings to different researchers (Chen and Regan, 1985; Ginzberg et al., 1951; Rothman, 1990). The discrepancy of the use of the terminology is based on the fact that the process leading up to entry into the labour force is imperfect. In addition, the term "choice" implies a conscious, logical, rational, decision-making approach to careers. The problem with this implication is that although people do believe that they do make choices, often the choices made are shaped and limited by events and forces that the individual has little, if any, ability to control. It is important to recognize that choices occur in a social context. Often occupational choice begins at an early age but changes as we grow older. You probably remember as a youngster that you wanted to be an astronaut, a doctor, a nurse, a teacher, or an athlete when you grew up. But a combination of factors (i.e., ability, motivation, changing interests, and access to opportunity) made some of your early career choices unattainable.

Numerous theories have been put forth by both sociologists and psychologists for examining the decisions surrounding why and how people make specific occupational choices in their lives. Developmental psychologists, for instance, have concentrated on the *individual-ambition model*, while sociologists have concentrated on the *structure-opportunity model* (Speakman, 1980). A brief discussion of each model should provide you with a general understanding of the approaches taken by the theorists in each discipline.

The Individual-Ambition Model

The developmental theories first appeared during the 1950s in psychology. These theories attempt to explain human behaviour and attitudes in terms of maturation of the individual's innate capacities. Most notably, the work of Eli Ginzberg (1951) represents this model which emphasized viewing a person's occupational choice as a maturational and cumulative process whereby choices change over time and are influenced by previous experiences.

Ginzberg's approach is based on viewing the developmental process of occupational choice as a series of compromises between a person's interests, capacities, opportunities and values. At an early age (six to eleven years of age), children are able to express very specific occupational roles that they identify with through media coverage (i.e., athletes, firefighters, nurses, and cowboys), parents, and people in their immediate environment who are role models. Ginzberg calls this the *fantasy phase* since the occupational choices made by a child is uninformed and not based on a realistic appraisal of their own abilities, the requirements of the work, or the social constraints which will later effectively limit their occupational attainment (Rothman, 1990). The next stage of development, according to Ginzberg, occurs between eleven and seventeen years of age, known as the *tentative choice phase* and can be subdivided into four stages: the interest, capacity, value and transition stages. Basically, this phase typifies the gradual maturation of the self-concept and the growing awareness of the internal and external factors that can influence the choice of a career. During the tentative choice phase adolescents begin to reach an understanding of their interests which is limited by their perceived abilities. This appraisal leads to an evaluation of the possible occupations available to them. The transition stage is usually reached during the last years of high school or the first few years of college when the individual begins to face the constraining effects of external factors that influence their occupational choice (i.e., cost of schooling and the competitiveness of entry into an occupation). The third, and final stage is known as the *realistic choice phase* occurring around age eighteen. This phase is characterized by a realistic appraisal and decision based on a compromise between interests, abilities, and the opportunities available.

Ginzberg's theory has been criticized on several grounds. First, many young adults today do not make occupational choices until after they have finished some post-secondary schooling, while others take a job or travel until they have decided what they would like to do for a career. Today, career choices and decisions are often delayed by young adults compared to young adults of fifty years ago when occupational decisions were forced by educational systems. Secondly, some adolescents leave school at an early age and take a job even before they have moved through the last phase. In particular, Ginzberg has been criticized for not taking into account differences among socioeconomic background, gender, and ethnicity as intervening factors in choosing a career. Finally, occupational choice decisions do not necessarily begin or end during early adulthood. Today, more adults are returning to school at a later age and/or changing occupations throughout their working lives. Ginzberg's theory does not take into account both developmental decisions later in adulthood nor situational and contextual factors (i.e., unemployment and new opportunities to acquire education) that may lead to decisions about career choices.

The Structure-Opportunity Model

The structure-opportunity model has been the focus taken by sociologists to understanding individual decisions about occupational choice. In contrast to the individual ambition model which focuses on the individual's processes of psychological development, the structure-opportunity model stresses the effects of the individual's structural content in influencing occupational choices (Chen and Regan, 1985). In this sociological perspective, the social characteristics of the individual are viewed as "external influences over which the individual has little or no control. In this way they set limits upon and constrain the kinds of occupational choices and decisions that individuals make" (Pavalko, 1971:51). Simply put, sociologists emphasize the social characteristics such as gender, ethnicity, and parental socio-economic status which can have a profound effect on socialization to particular kinds of occupations, access to opportunity, and subsequent decisions about career choices.

Socio-Economic Background

In Canada and the United States, parental socio-economic origin (measured by educational and occupational attainment) is one of the most powerful and pervasive factors in occupational choice. Research over the past 25 years has shown a direct relationship between social origins and educational aspirations. However, even controlling for levels of ability and aspirations, children of higher status parents tend to achieve higher levels of education. In addition, children from higher socio-economic background tend to attain better jobs than children from lower status backgrounds with equivalent levels of education. Rothman (1990) suggests that the continuing impact of socio-economic status reflects the interaction of a combination of factors including the advantage of economic resources, and differential values and orientations, and subsequent experiences in the school system (p. 292). These differences seem to provide part of the answer for determining how and why many individuals make decisions about occupational choices available to them.

Gender

Even from an early age men and women are socialized differently. You will recall the discussion in the chapter on Socialization that whether consciously or not, parents tend to assign household tasks according to the gender of their children. By the time children reach school age they have come to identify with **occupational sex-typing**, that is, a societal view that certain occupations are more appropriate work for one sex than the other. Through an allocative process sex-typing has the effect of limiting perceived occupational choices which channels males and females in different directions. For example, occupational choices among males and females have been influenced by such traditional views as men are doctors and women are nurses; men are managers and women are secretaries. These views have been reinforced through various mass mediums, including television shows, advertising, commercials, and children's storybooks. As we saw earlier in this chapter, women tend to occupy those occupations located in the tertiary sector but of the low pay, low status variety (i.e., clerical and sales). It is true that more women today are entering the traditional male-dominated occupations, but, this trend is not significant enough to suggest that the perceived occupational choices available to women has increased substantially over the last twenty years.

Ethnicity

As suggested in the chapter on Culture, Canada is considered to be a multicultural society. Recent immigration by Asian and Caribbean peoples has reinforced the ethnic diversity in our country. Yet, at the same time, occupations available to many immigrants tend to be those occupations that are less desirable to white Canadians. You only need to walk through a college campus at night time and see who is cleaning offices. Naturally, occupational choice for new immigrants in particular can be limited because of language barriers and education. We must be careful not to suggest that these are the only factors that contribute to the type of work that they perform. Discrimination and prejudice also has contributed to **occupational segregation**, the concentration of members of one sex or ethnic group in relatively few occupations compared to the opposite sex or ethnic groupings. These trends will hopefully change as the second generation gains access to education and fair treatment.

Research in the area of occupational choice and social inequality has contributed to recent legislation at the federal and provincial levels of government, as well as at corporate levels across the country. Recent legislation (i.e., the Canadian Constitution) has encouraged employment equity programs (also known as *affirmative action programs*) designed to increase the number of persons who are not well represented in the professions, management and other upper tertiary sector careers. The groups recognized as under-represented in these occupational groups, include: (i) visible minorities; (ii) aboriginal peoples; (iii) persons with disabilities; and, (iv) women. Once members of these groups gain access to these higher status occupations, it is likely that more members from these groups will have greater occupational choices in the future.

The structure-opportunity model shows that career decisions are sometimes hindered by social characteristics that are beyond the control of the individual. Although this is the view adopted by most sociologists working in this area, it is probably true that the individual developmental model also has an effect on actual occupational choices. Occupational choice, then, is likely based on a constellation of factors that cannot be separated out by theoretical argumentation. Further empirical work still needs to be conducted in this area.

In our next section we will discuss the present state of the professions in our society.

Professions and Professionalization

The use of the term *professional* has several meanings in our society. The term includes those who work for monetary compensation for an activity, differentiating them from those that do not. For example, a professional hockey player versus an amateur hockey player, a professional figure skater with the Ice Capades versus an Olympic figure skater. The term *professional* is also used to identify those individuals with specialized knowledge, talents and/or skills. Examples of this category include doctors, lawyers and professors. Finally, many occupational groups utilize the term *professional* as a form of self-identification to create a positive public image. This category includes occupational groups such as human resource managers, realtors, police, and automobile mechanics.

Sociologists use the term still another way to identify occupations enjoying, or seeking to enjoy, a unique position in the labour force. The use of the term *professional* in this context is reserved for those occupations which have exclusive jurisdiction over certain kinds of services, are able to negotiate freedom from external intervention and have control over the content of their work activities in the delivery of services. In this section, we will emphasize: (i) the identifiable characteristics of a profession; (ii) the debate about whether or not the professions are becoming deprofessionalized or proletarianized; and finally, (iii) the future of the professions.

Characteristics of a Profession

A **profession,** according to Ritzer (1986), can be defined simply as:

> An occupation that has had the power to have undergone a developmental process enabling it to acquire, or convince significant others (for example, clients, the law) that it has acquired a constellation of characteristics we have come to accept as denoting a profession. (p. 62)

This definition alone does not tell us any more about what a profession is unless we identify what are the salient characteristics of a profession. You should be aware before we proceed that the literature on professions and professionalization is voluminous in scope. Obviously, what is presented here is narrow in scope. To begin with, sociologists have suggested that for an occupation to reach the status of a profession, the following characteristics must be met:

1. creation of a full-time occupation;
2. establishment of a training school;
3. establishment of a national governing association;
4. efforts to win legal support; and,
5. establishment of a legal code.

These characteristics were first identified by Wilensky (1964) in his classic article *"The Professionalization of Everyone?"* Numerous authors over the years have identified the same characteristics using different terminology. Wilensky's characteristics however, really have stood the test of time.

Most of you will undoubtedly say that you can identify numerous occupations that meet these criteria. What you must keep in mind, however, is that most occupations lack one, two, or three key criteria. In addition, most occupations lack the autonomy (*or self-regulation*) that most professions have. For example, a complaint against the competency of a medical practitioner is usually dealt with by the provincial medical association. Seldom are external authorities able to determine whether or not the medical treatment provided by the medical practitioner is of the nature that would question their competency. Occupations that are designated as professions usually have a specialized and theoretically-based knowledge beyond a layperson's general understanding. It should be clear to you from this discussion that those occupational groups that proclaim themselves to be *professionals* (i.e., taxi drivers, bartenders, etc.) are using the term inappropriately.

Ritzer and Walzcak (1986) have identified a classification continuum for occupations that either are, or aspire to be, a profession. Accordingly, the continuum is based on how well occupations meet the identified characteristics of a profession. The continuum consists of the following:

1. *Old Established Professions*: occupations in this category on the continuum consist of those professions that are well-established and have control over their knowledge. These include, physicians, lawyers, and university professors.
2. *New Professions*: occupations here include the natural and social scientists with Ph.D's.
3. *Semi-Professions*: although they are professionalized to some degree and have made great effort to make it to the professional end of the continuum, this group of occupations has lacked the power to win widespread recognition as professions. Included in the semi-professions are school teachers, nurses, social workers, and librarians.
4. *Would-be Professions:* these are occupations that have sought or are actively aspiring to professional status, but which, for a variety of reasons, have had even less power than the semi-professions and have had less success in convincing the relevant audiences that they have acquired the needed characteristics. Examples include personnel managers and funeral directors.
5. *Marginal Professions:* included here are a variety of occupations that work 'hand in hand' with the professions, perform many of the same functions, but lack the capacity to acquire professional status in their own right, partly because they very often labour in the shadow of the established professions. Occupations in this category include laboratory and scientific technicians as well as various paraprofessionals. (p. 63)

Although many occupations attempt to seek the status of the professions, many do not. More recently, some sociologists have expressed that we are now moving into a period of deprofessionalization, while others argue that the professions are becoming proletarianized. Let us briefly turn to the arguments supporting these views.

Deprofessionalization or the Proletarianization of the Professions

The process of **deprofessionalization** may be described as the erosion of autonomy and monopolistic privileges of the professions. Figure 12.3 shows that occupations must move from left-to-right along the continuum in order to reach professional status. Movement right-to-left toward the status of most occupations would be suggestive of the deprofessionalization process.

This perspective on the professions is based on the notion that clients are revolting against the authority and decision making powers of the professional. Sociologists (Haug, 1975; Toren, 1975) have argued that the general public is much more educated today than they were 30 years ago and are now in a position to question the judgment of professionals. Deprofessionalization in this form, according to Hodson and Sullivan (1990), is a result of *demystifying the esoteric knowledge* of the professions and *empowering the consumer* (p. 276). You only need to think about all the "do-it-yourself" kits for legal matters, home medical screening kits, and the wealth of information disseminated in the popular press. Much of the knowledge in the public domain today was once exclusive to and protected by many of the professions. Secondly, professionals are now working in large bureaucratic organizations (i.e., universities, hospitals, and corporations) which have financial bottom lines that they must meet. Bureaucratic organizations require professionals to conduct themselves in a certain way which weakens their professional sovereignty. Thirdly, allied professionals are able to do many of the tasks that were traditionally reserved for the professional. In the legal field, for instance, paralegals are filing claims, presenting cases in court, and assisting clients with court documents. Similarly, dentists are no longer cleaning teeth nor taking x-rays, instead a dental hygienist or dental assistant performs these tasks. Finally, recent concerns over professional abuses has diminished the credibility of many professional groups. For example, extra billing, cases of fee-splitting and other complaints about the performance of medical practitioners are rarely made available to the general public by provincial medical associations.

A second perspective on the professions is known as the **proletarianization** of the professions. This perspective differs from the deprofessionalization thesis because it argues that the professions are losing total control over the conditions of work and are

Figure 12.3. A Schematic Diagram of Professionalization and Deprofessionalization

professionalization ————>

Occupation ———————————————————— **Profession**

<———— deprofessionalization

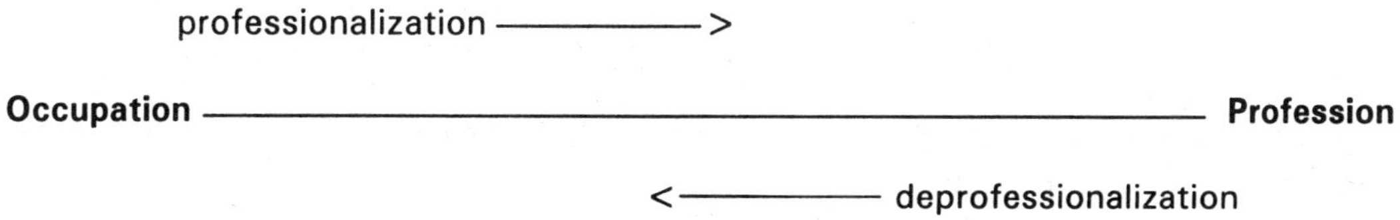

experiencing a serious reduction in compensation. The proletarianization perspective is based on a Marxist orientation (Derber, 1982; Oppenheimer, 1973). Basically, sociologists working with this perspective suggest that white-collar bureaucrats have control over the professional and dictate the nature of the workplace and how professional technology will be used. In addition, the division of labour (*or specializations*) in the professions results in an ever-narrower range of tasks in the delivery of services. The evidence provided for this perspective includes: (i) today hospitals are administered by managers not medical practitioners which diminishes their self-regulation and control over medical practices; (ii) task specialization implies that the medical practitioner is not responsible for the complete treatment nor recovery of the patient; and, (iii) hospital administrators determine what medical technology will be purchased and which drugs will be made available for their patients.

The two views discussed in this section both suggest that the professions are losing ground in maintaining their status and control over their work. The difference between the two is that the deprofessionalization view foresees a modest decline in the status of the professions, while the proletarianization view suggests that the professions will continue to decline and lose most of the control and autonomy that they now have. Whether or not either view is correct is difficult to determine at this time. Further studies will be required to follow the changes, if any, in the professions.

The Future of the Professions

The professions have become significant models for other occupations, because they have achieved so much autonomy, authority, and status. Membership in a profession confers considerable prestige and usually higher income. Today, many of these individuals are considered members of the "new middle-class," which achieves its position based on knowledge and achievement. The future of the professions may take several forms. The positive outlook for the professions is based on the notion that as knowledge expands, specialization within the professions multiplies, and as the economy is transformed by knowledge and service sector industries, the collective prestige of the professions is likely to grow.

The dimmer view stresses the two perspectives described in the last section: deprofessionalization and the proletarianization of the professions. These processes not only threaten the professions but also those occupations that strive to emulate them. It is likely that many professions will lose some authority and control over their practices in the future since many professionals work in large-scale bureaucratic organizations. Whether or not the professions lose the amount of autonomy and control over their activities to the extent suggested by the deprofessionalization and the proletarianization perspectives is really dependent on how fast their knowledge base and specializations grow relative to the empowerment of the consumer. It is likely that the professions will need to be more responsive to consumer needs. Conversely, the consumer of professional services will need to recognize that knowledge is power and they will be unable to keep pace with the knowledge explosion of the future.

Work Satisfaction

One of the most researched areas in the study of work since the 1940s is that of work satisfaction. **Work satisfaction** (*or job satisfaction*) typically refers to a summary attitude of favourable or unfavourable feelings that people experience about their work. Hodson and Sullivan (1990) suggest that work satisfaction is "the result of job tasks, characteristics of the organization in which people work, and the individual differences in needs and values" (p. 97). When workers join an organization, they bring with them a set of wants, needs, desires, and past experiences that combine to form work expectations. Work satisfaction expresses the amount of agreement between one's emerging expectations and the rewards that the work provides.

Organizations have been concerned with work satisfaction because they assume that productivity is affected when workers are dissatisfied. In most studies, the general question that is asked of people is "In general, are you satisfied with your job?" Research has shown that individuals with high occupational levels compared to those from low occupational levels, report higher levels of satisfaction. The result is that professionals and upper-tier administrators usually are more satisfied than skilled workers, who tend to be more satisfied than semi-skilled and unskilled workers. In addition, as workers grow older, they tend to be slightly more satisfied with their work. There are a number of reasons, such as lowered expectations and better adjustment to their work situation because of greater work experience. Younger workers, on the other hand, tend to be less satisfied because of higher expectations, lower adjustment, and other factors (see Figure 12.4). Gender differences, however, are infrequently found in work satisfaction surveys (Northcott and Lowe, 1987).

Early studies on work satisfaction tended to concentrate on interpersonal relationships and the work environment. Over time the research has clearly shown that the sources of

Figure 12:4. The Relationship of Work Satisfaction to Age and Occupational Level

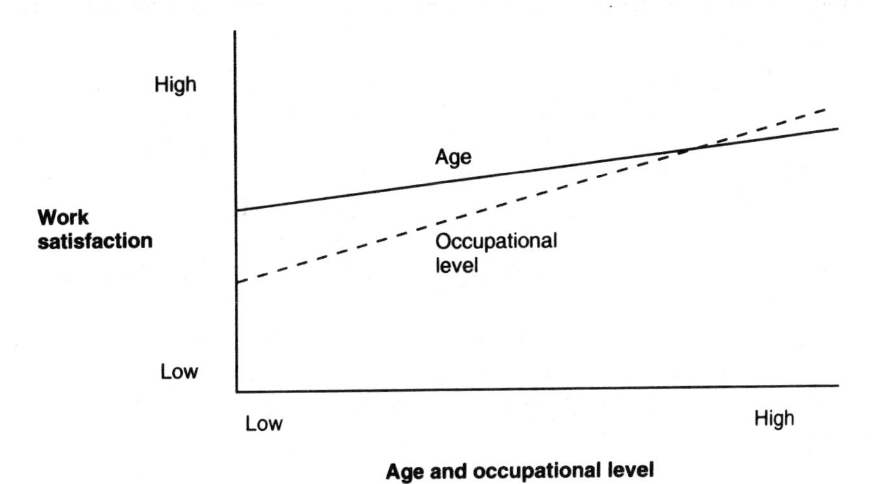

work satisfaction lie beyond positive interpersonal relationships on the job but include the structural components of work itself. Specifically, surveys show that higher satisfaction tends to be associated with such factors as intrinsic interest in the work (it is interesting and meaningful), level of control (the ability to make decisions), level of pay and economic security, and opportunities for social interaction (Scott, 1989). These factors seem to be predominant and consistent across all occupational and professional groups today.

In surveys that address the satisfaction level of employees, however, satisfaction rates among workers tend to be fairly high (approximately 80%). However, researchers have come to realize that at the best of times work satisfaction surveys are suspect. The reason for this is that the response rates of surveys (that is, the number of individuals who complete the questionnaire and return it) tends to be between 35 and 50 percent. The question we should ask ourselves as sociologists is: Are those who do not return the questionnaire satisfied or are they so dissatisfied that they refuse to complete the questionnaire? This is difficult to determine since the anonymity guaranteed to respondents prevents researchers from contacting those individuals who do not complete the questionnaire. Work satisfaction surveys are also subject to criticism because work satisfaction is closely linked to *life satisfaction.* The nature of an individual's environment off the job is bound to influence their feelings on the job. Similarly, since work is an important part of life, work satisfaction influences an individual's general life satisfaction. The result is that there is a spillover effect that occurs in both directions between work and life satisfaction. Consequently, in order to address work satisfaction in a comprehensive way we need to study the overall life satisfaction of workers.

Summary

In this chapter, we introduced the world of work with a specific emphasis on work in the Canadian context As stated in our introduction, work is more than earning an income since it permeates all other aspects of our social existence. After reading this chapter you should make sure that you have an understanding of the following points discussed:

1. Since the beginning of time human beings have engaged in work activities to meet their survival needs. To meet these needs, human beings developed and were shaped by the technology and social organization of the society. **Social organization** refers to the relations among those involved in work. **Technology**, on the other hand, refers to the tools and skills used in the process of production. The social organization of work as we know it today (i.e., advanced industrial society), constitutes less than one percent of known human existence on this planet.
2. **Industrialization** refers to the replacement of labour-intensive skills in the production of goods and services with capital-intensive technology (i.e., machinery and computers), accompanied with an elaboration of the **division of labour** (a functionally integrated system of occupational roles or specializations within a society). Early signs of the growth of industrialization in

Canada did not emerge until 1870–1890. Today, Canada is perceived to have the characteristics basic to a member of the fortunate group of advanced industrial nations (Craib, 1986). In 1988, Canada had a Gross National Product per capita of $14,120 U.S., which placed it as the 4th largest in the world behind Norway (3rd), United States (2nd), and Switzerland (1st). The goods produced in the country, however, tend to be based on our natural resources (i.e., oil and gas).

3. Presently, close to 50 percent of the mining, petroleum, timber, and manufacturing industries are foreign owned and controlled mostly by American multinational corporations. Approximately, three-quarters of both Canadian exports and imports are with the Untied States. The free trade agreement between Canada and the U.S. signed on January 2, 1988 was intended to provide a tariff-free North American trading partnership. The long term effects of this arrangement on our own markets and industries will not be known for some time.

4. The labour force structure in Canada can be categorized by the *industry* in which participants work. By convention, there are three major sectors within the labour force: **primary**, **secondary**, and **tertiary**. At the turn of the century, most Canadians worked in the *primary sector* (i.e., agriculture). By 1920, most Canadians were working in the *secondary sector* (i.e., manufacturing). Presently, labour force participation statistics for Canada show that 72 percent of the labour force is employed in the *tertiary sector* (mostly service industries), while 6 percent are employed in the *primary sector,* and 22 percent in the *secondary sector.* For this reason, Canada is known as a *post-industrial society.*

5. A second way in which the labour force structure in Canada can be categorized is by *occupation,* or the kind of work that is being performed. Often we differentiate the kind of work that individuals do according to whether they are **white-collar** or **blue-collar** occupations. The term *white-collar* typically is applied to the work of managers, nurses, teachers, salespersons, and office workers since these occupations involve working with people and ideas. The term *blue-collar* typically is applied to work roles involved in manufacturing. *Blue-collar* work is often subdivided into two categories: **skilled crafts** and **unskilled work**. *Skilled crafts* are those in which the work requires some degree of manual dexterity combined with a broad knowledge of tools, materials, and processes (i.e., welders and plumbers). *Unskilled work* includes those occupations that require no formal training nor certification primarily because the skill required to perform the task is considered to be minimal (i.e., waitressing and dishwashing).

6. **Labour markets** are the economic arenas in which employers seek to purchase labour from potentially qualified individuals who themselves are seeking employment suitable to their present education, experience, and preferences. (Krahn and Lowe, 1989). Labour markets are often divided into

two sectors: **primary labour markets** and **secondary labour markets**. The *primary labour* market usually offers jobs with relatively high wages, good working conditions, chance of advancement, and employment stability. Jobs that are in the *secondary labour market,* by contrast, tend to be low paying, with poorer working conditions and little chance of advancement. Studies have shown that barriers to *primary labour market* entry include gender discrimination, age discrimination, "contacts" (or the so-called *old "boys" network),* and racial and ethnic discrimination.

7. Unemployment in Canada varies by region, type of industry, age, and gender. **Unemployment rates** are calculated by dividing the number of individuals out of work and who are actively seeking work by the total number in the labour force (including the unemployed). In 1990, the percentage of persons, ages 25–44 years, overwhelmingly constituted the bulk of the unemployed in the country. The subjective experiences of those who are unemployed are ones of fear, insecurity, anger, helplessness, and dismay. Often they feel that the various governmental institutions are not helping them and appear to blame them for their circumstances.
8. The impact of technological change on skill requirements for work is one of the most debated subjects in the study of work and occupations. There are currently three general perspectives on the impact of skill currently dominating the field: *the upgrading thesis, the downgrading thesis,* and *the mixed effects thesis.* The impact of microelectronic technology seems to have fueled this debate.
9. A basic interest in the study of work is the question of why and how people first enter specific occupations, or types of work. In sociology, we categorize these questions in a broad category, commonly known as *occupational choice.* Two models on how individuals make particular career choices were discussed. The **individual-ambition model** viewed occupational choice as a developmental process that culminated in a series of compromises between an individual's interests, capacities, opportunities and values. In contrast, the **structure-opportunity model** stressed the individual's structural content in influencing occupational choices. The structural content of an individual includes such factors as their parental socio-economic status, gender, and ethnicity which purportedly has a profound effect on socialization to particular occupations, access to opportunity, and subsequent decisions about career choices.
10. The term professions to denote certain occupations is used in a very specific way by sociologists. It is reserved for those occupations which have exclusive jurisdiction over certain kinds of services, are able to negotiate freedom from external intervention and have control over the content of their work activities in the delivery of services. For an occupation to be deemed a profession, it must meet certain characteristics. Many occupations meet several of the identifiable characteristics of a profession but they do not meet all. Sociologists

have developed an occupational continuum to identify how well occupations meet the identified characteristics of a profession. The continuum includes: old established professions, new professions, semi-professions, would-be professions, and marginal professions. Recently, some sociologists have argued that the professions are experiencing an erosion of their autonomy and monopolistic privileges. These arguments range from a **deprofessionalization** of the professions to a **proletarianization** of the professions.

11. **Work satisfaction** typically refers to a summary attitude of favourable or unfavourable feelings that people experience about their work. Overall, work satisfaction tends to be positively correlated with age and occupational status. Recent research on work satisfaction shows that higher satisfaction levels also tend to be associated with such factors as intrinsic interest in the work, level of control, level of pay and economic security, and opportunities for social interaction (Scott, 1989). Work satisfaction surveys, however, tend to be criticized because response rates are low and it is usually closely linked to life satisfaction.

References

Abeshouse, R. P.
1987 *Lifelong Learning Part One: Education for a Competitive Economy*. Washington, D.C.: Roosevelt Centre for American Policy Studies.

Anderson, Grace M. and Liviana M. Calzavara
1986 "Networks, Education and Occupational Success," in Lundy, K. L. P. Lundy and Warme B. eds. *Work in the Canadian Context: Continuity Despite Change*, Second edition. Toronto: Butterworths.

Armstrong, Pat and Hugh Armstrong
1984 *The Double Ghetto: Canadian Women and Their Segregated Work.* Toronto: McClelland and Stewart Limited.

Baran, Barbara and S. Teegarden
1984 "Women's Labor in the Office of the Future," in Kraft, Phillip, *A Review of Empirical Studies of the Consequences of Technological Change on the Work and Workers in the United States.* New York: Monthly Review, pp. 125–153.

Bell, Daniel
1976 *The Coming of Post-Industrial Society.* New York: Basic Books.

Blauner, Robert
1964 *Alienation and Freedom*. Chicago: University of Chicago Press.

Braverman, Harry
1974 *Labor and Monopoly Capital: The Degradation of Work in the Twentieth Century.* New York: Monthly Review Press.

Bryant, Clifton D.
1972 *The Social Dimensions of Work.* Englewood Cliffs: Prentice Hall.

Burman, Patrick
1988 *Killing Time, Losing Ground: Experiences of Unemployment*. Toronto: Wall and Thompson, Inc.

Calhoun, C. and M. Copp
1988 "Computerization in Legal Work: How Much Does New Technology Change Professional Practice?" in Simpson, R. and Simpson, I. eds. *Research in the Sociology of Work,* 4: pp. 233–259.

Cameron, Duncan
1988 *The Free Trade Deal*. Toronto: James Lorimer and Company.

Chen, Mervin Y. T. and Thomas G. Regan
1985 *Work in the Changing Canadian Society.* Toronto: Butterworths.

Christensen, Kathleen
1987 "A Hard Days Work in the Electronic Cottage." *Across the Board,* 23 (April), pp. 17–21.

Collins, Randall
1979 *The Credential Society.* New York: Academic Press.

Craib, Prudence W.
1986 "Canadian-based Research and Development: Why So Little?" in Lundy, Katherina and Warme, Barbara. *Work in the Canadian Context: Continuity Despite Change,* Second edition. Toronto: Butterworths, pp. 6–22.

Derber, Charles
1982 *Professionals as Workers: Mental Labor in Advanced Capitalism.* Boston: G. K. Hall and Company.

Faunce, William A.
1981 *Problems of an Industrial Society.* New York: McGraw-Hill.

Federal Government of Canada
1981 *The Task Force Report on Labour Market Development in the 1980s.* Ottawa: Minister of Supply and Services.

Form, William
1987 "On the Degradation of Skill." *Annual Review of Sociology,* 13, pp. 29–47.

Ginzberg, Eli, S.W. Ginzberg, S. Axelrad, and J.L. Herma
1951 *Occupational Choice: Toward a General Theory.* New York: Columbia University Press.

Glenn, Evelyn N. and Roslyn L. Feldberg
1977 "Degraded and Deskilled: The Proletarianization of Clerical work." *Social Problems,* 25: pp. 52–64.

Groff, W.
1983 "Impacts of High Technologies on Vocational and Education." *Annals of the American Academy of Political and Social Sciences,* 470, pp. 81–94.

Haug, Maria
1973 "Deprofessionalization: An Alternative Hypothesis for the Future," in Halmos, Paul ed. *Professionalization and Social Change.* Staffordshire: The University of Keele, pp. 195–211.

Hedley, R. Alan
1988 "Industrialization and Work," in Robert Hagedorn ed. *Sociology,* Fourth edition. Toronto: Holt, Rinehart and Winston of Canada, Limited.

Hodson, Randy
1988 "Work in High-Tech Settings: A Review of the Empirical Literature," in Simpson, R. and Simpson, I. eds. *Research in the Sociology of Work,* v. 4, pp. 1–29.

Hodson, Randy and R. Parker
1988 "Good Jobs and Bad Management: How New Problems Evoke Old Solutions in High-Tech Settings. In England P. and Farcas eds. *Industries, Farms and Jobs: Sociological and Economic Approaches.* New York: Plenum Limited, pp. 247–279.

Hodson, Randy and Teresa A. Sullivan
1990 *The Social Organization of Work.* Belmont, Calif: Wadsworth Publishing Company.

Jenkins, Clive and B. Sherman
1979 *The Collapse of Work.* London: Eyre Metheun.

Kraft, Philip
1979 "The Industrialization of Computer Programming: From Programming to Software," in Zimbalist, A. ed. *Case Studies in the Labor Process.* New York: Monthly Review Press, pp. 1–17.

Krahn, Harvey J. and Graham S. Lowe
1988 *Work Industry and Canadian Society.* Scarborough: Nelson Canada.

Kuttner, B.
1983 "The Declining Middle." *Atlantic*, July, pp. 60–72.

Lee, Richard B.
1981 "politics, Sexual And Nonsexual, In An equalitarian society," in Berreman, General D. ed. *Social Inequality: Comparative and Developmental Approaches.* New York: Academic Press, pp. 83–102.

Lenski, Gerhard
1966 *Power and Privilege: A Theory of Social Stratification.* New York: McGraw-Hill.

Marx, Karl
1967 *Capital, Volume One [1887].* New York: International Publishers.

Menzies, Heather
1981 *Women and the Chip: Case Studies of the effects of Information on Employment in Canada.* Montreal: The Institute for Research for Public Policy.

Northcott, Herbert C. and Graham, S. Lowe
1987 "Job and Gender Influences in the Subjective Experience of Work." *Canadian Review of Sociology and Anthropology,* 24, pp. 117–131.

Oppenheimer, Martin
1973 "The Proletarianization of the Professional," in Halmos, Paul ed. *Professionalization and Social Change.* Staffordshire: The University of Keele, pp. 212–224.

Pavalko, Ronald M.
1971 *Sociology of Occupations and Professions.* Itasco, Ill.: F. E. Peacock.

Piore, M.
1969 "On the Job Training in the Dual Labor Market," in A.R. Weber, F. Cassell, and W. L. Ginsberg eds. *Public-Private Manpower Policies.* Wisconsin: University of Wisconsin, pp. 101–132.
1970 "Jobs and Training." In S. H. Beer and R. H. Barringer eds. *The State and the Poor.* Wisconsin: University of Wisconsin, p. 53–83.
1975 "Notes for a Theory of Labor Market Stratification," in R. Edwards, M. Reich, and D. Gordon eds. *Labor Market Segmentation.* Lexington, Mass.: D.C. Health, pp. 125–150.

Rinehart, James
1988 "Forward," in Burman, Patrick. *Killing Time, Losing Ground: Experiences of Unemployment.* Toronto: Wall and Thompson, Inc.
1987 *The Tyranny of Work: Alienation and the Labour Process,* Second edition. Toronto: Harcourt Brace Jovanovich.

Ritzer, George and David Walczak
1986 *Working: Conflict and Change.* Englewood Cliffs, New Jersey: Prentice-Hall.

Rosenthal, Neal
1985 "The Shrinking Middle Class: Myth or Reality?" *Monthly Labor Review, 108* (March): pp. 3–10.

Rosenthal, Robert A.
1987 *Working: Sociological Perspectives.* Englewood Cliffs, New Jersey: Prentice-Hall, Inc.

Royal Commission on the Economic Union and Development Prospects for Canada
1985 *Report One.* Ottawa: Minister of Supply and Services.

Scott, W. Richard
1989 *Organizations: Rational, Natural, and Open Systems,* Second edition. Englewood Cliffs: Prentice-Hall.

Smith, Adam
1937 *The Wealth of Nations [1776].* New York: Random House.

Smucker, Joseph
1980 *Industrialization in Canada.* Scarborough: Prentice-Hall of Canada.

Speakman, Mary Anne
1980 "Occupational Choice and Placement," in Esland, G. and Salaman, G. eds. *The Politics of Work and Occupations.* Toronto: The University of Toronto Press.

Toffier, Alvin
1980 *The Third Wave.* New York: Bantam.

Toren, Nina
1975 "Deprofessionalization and Its Sources: A Preliminary Analysis." *Sociology of Work and Occupations,* 2, pp. 323–337.

Wallace, Michael
1989 "Brave New Workplace: Technology and Work in the New Economy." *Work and Occupations,* 16 (4), pp. 363–392.

Wilensky, Harold
1964 "The professionalization of everyone?," *American Sociological Review*, 70, pp. 137–158.

World Bank
1988 *World Development Report.* London: Oxford University Press.

13

The Sociology of Religion: An Introduction

Don Swenson

Orientation

This is the final chapter of the text that introduces us into a forth institution, religion. Again, the central concepts in sociology are revealed here as well. religion should be seen as an aspect of culture for its focus is upon world views and the living out of these world views. Its link to social action is through the first kind of social action as outlined in the first chapter, affective social action. It is affective in that, as we shall see, the genesis of religion is in the experience of the sacred which is an affective kind of a relationship. The structural dimensions of religion emerge when one looks at the construction of religious organizations.

I shall begin with outlining a definition of religion that will also frame the chapter. Emerging from the definition of religion, we will look at it from the inside. Topics to be covered here include: experience of the sacred, world views known as myths or, more commonly, belief systems, ritual, ethos (morality), and organizations. Another way to look at religion is to link it to other social institutions like politics, economy, family, and culture. Although this is important, at this introductory level this would make this chapter too complex.

I begin by presenting a definition... "religion is the individual and communal experience of the sacred expressed in myths, rituals, ethos and integrated into a social collective or institution." This definition is a synthesis of a number of definitions from a wide variety of sources from sociological and anthropological studies. As each of these elements constitute the contents of this chapter, I shall refrain from explaining their meaning now.

This definition constitutes what has been defined by sociologists as having substantive or functional interpretations. A substantive definition of religion focuses on the essence or nature of religion. Berger (1974) notes that it is seen in terms of the meaning of the contents of the phenomenon. The substantive approach comes from historians of religion like Rudolf Otto and Mircea Eliade. We shall meet these figures later in the chapter.

Functional definitions emphasize the effects of religion on people and on the social order. They may define religion in positive functional terms with religion providing meaning, social legitimation, social cohesion, integration and a source of morality. Functional definitions see religion as being a product of human activity, which in turn acts back on members of a society in ways that contribute to the maintenance of the social order. It is religion that is regarded as an important agent of socialization and a guardian of societal values. This approach has been codified by Emile Durkheim, Bronislaw Maninowski, and Karl Marx. However, for Marx, religion is seen to have a negative effect on people causing alienation and control.

These two ways of defining religion will also be how myths, rituals, and ethos will be defined. We begin with looking at individual and the social experience of the sacred.

Individual and Social Experience of the Sacred

From an historian of religion (Otto, 1958), I commence the investigation of the meaning of religion by outlining what the sacred or the holy (in Latin, *numen*) is. Durkheim (1965) aids us in a preliminary definition: "things separate and set apart." He interprets this to mean that the sacred is distinctly different from the profane or the ordinary. The contrast is between mundane or everyday life or other worldly or eternal life.

Otto (1958) expands on this. As depicted by Table 13:1, there are two dimensions: *mysterium tremendum* and *fasciandus*. As a believer approaches the sacred, two kinds of experiences are elicited. The first one is awe and distance. The religious person is in touch with a power, a force that is illustrated by terms like: august, a shuddering, dread, fear, being overpowered, a sense of being a creature and of relating to the sacred as being wholly other.

Table 13:1
Numen or The Idea of the Holy

Mysterium Tremendum	Fasciandus
Awe	Wonderfulness
Distance	Rapture
August	Becoming One with the *Numen*
A Shuddering	Desire
Dread	Blissful Excitement
Fear	Exaltation
Overpowering	Over Abundance and Plenty
Creature Fleeing	Love
Plentitude of Being	Mercy
Energy	Compassion
Wholly Other	Kindness
	Understanding

In contrast, the believer is fascinated by the sacred and is mysteriously drawn towards it. Feelings such as wonderfulness, rapture, desire, excitement, exultation, plentitude, love, mercy, compassion, kindness and understanding emerge.

Thus, a dilemma confronts the religionist: a drawing close to but, in the opposite, a pushing away. This forms the most fundamental dilemma of religion that is reflected in much of the research on religion.

Religious experience, then, is to be understood by a unique kind of human experience—the experience of the sacred. I shall briefly outline some of the philosophical and social scientific studies on religious experience to link this kind of experience to the lives of people.

In the late 17th century, Friedreich Schleiermacher (1799) attempted to justify Christianity against Enlightenment rationality that threatened its credibility by arguing that religion is best grounded in sentiments, not in ideas. People have experiences that cannot be comprehended within the bounds of the everyday world. As they reflect on such experiences, they come to conceptualize God in certain ways. According to Schleiermacher, science and philosophy may attack religious conceptualizations or ideas but they cannot undercut the experiences themselves (Proudfoot, 1985).

Those who follow Schleiermacher accept religious experience at face value. For them, religion cannot be destroyed by rational critique for it is grounded in the experience of believers. It was Schleiermacher who influenced some early social scientists who wrote about religious experiences, including social psychologist William James (1842-1910).

James considered experience to be the genesis of religion, arguing that the founders of every religion had some sort of direct, personal communication with the divine. The "divine," according to James, is "primal reality" that the "individual feels impelled to respond to solemnly and gravely" (James, 1902:38). It is the foundation of religious experience, which according to James are

> the feelings, acts, and experiences of individual men in their solitude, so far as they apprehend themselves to stand in relation to whatever they may consider divine. (James, 1902:31)

James envisioned religious experience as something that exists *sui generis*—as something that is really real. Conventional religion was but a pale reflection of the energizing experience that propelled the saints and prophets. As James describes it

> It would profit us little to study this second-hand religious life. We must make search rather for the original experiences which were the pattern-setters to all this mass of suggested feeling and imitated conduct. These experiences we can only find in individuals for whom religion exists not as a dull habit, but as an acute fever rather. (1902:24–25)

One approach to the study of religion has been to follow William James in taking experience as the core of religion. Although this tradition has been criticized for being too individualistic and subjectivistic, it has provided an important foundation from which to explore the origins and renewed fervor of religious groups.

As referred to in the definition of religion, it is presented as the "individual and social experience of the social." I refer to Weber's work to help us to understand the individual experience and Durkheim for the social experience.

Although Weber focuses on the individual person, he links religious experience of the individual to the social. His focus is on relationship between charisma, the affective action of religious leaders, and social organization. Weber's *charisma* appears to be similar to what Durkheim and Otto call the sacred. As Weber states:

> [Not] every person has the capacity to achieve the ecstatic states which are viewed...as the preconditions for producing certain effects in meteorology, healing, divination, and telepathy. It is primarily...these extraordinary powers that have been designated by such special terms as 'mana,' 'orenda,' and the Iranian 'maga' (the term from which our word 'magic' is derived). We shall henceforth employ the term 'charisma' for such extraordinary powers. (1947:400)

Weber terms the individual bearer of charisma a "prophet," citing such religious figures as Zoroaster, Jesus, Muhammad, and the Buddha (Weber 1947:339–40). According to him, charisma cannot remain in its pure form, but becomes routinized or institutionalized.

This is another important dilemma in religious experience: from beginning with charisma and to end in a routinized form of it. This insight helps us a lot to understand why religion can be a source of social change and vivacity or an inhibition to change and become "dead weight."

In somewhat of a contrast to Weber and to what the psychologists of religion say, Durkheim (1915:417) argues that religious experience is more of a collective one and less an individual one. For example, in his work on aboriginal peoples of Australia and North America, it is when believers in hunting and gathering societies gather together in a ritual, a religious ceremony that they are carried beyond themselves into another world. It is in this group ritual that they experience ecstasy, enthusiasm, effervescence, joy, interior peace, serenity and a sense of being 'transported into another world.'

In summary, Durkheim is saying that because of the group experience (not possible as an individual) in the celebration of ritual, the believers adhere to a conviction that the deity, filled with energy and power, is real and present to him or her.

Myths

The second element of religion is the belief system or, the term that I am using, myth. It is important to emphasize that when using the term "myth," it is not to imply that such beliefs are false or fictitious. Nor is myth intended as a synonym for fairy tales or folk narratives (Roberts, 1990:77). Myths are accounts or stories that undergird different religious world views. Their truth or falsity is not the concern of social science. All are essentially treated as being "true" in a sense because they are defined as being so by believers. Even false definitions of a situation have psychological as well as social implications. The social scientist's task is to determine the effects of myth on believers and their society. I shall discuss substantive and functional definitions of myth and conclude this section with research on changes in myths with the growth of modernity both in select Muslim countries and in Canada.

Substantive Definition of Myth

Religious myths once provided *the* paramount definition of reality for people in pre-modern societies. Although different cultures may have had very divergent ideas about the non-empirical world of their mythic figures, all shared the conviction that the spirits had an impact on life.

As with religion, the study of religious myths, as seen through the eyes of the scholar of mythology, Joseph Campbell (1964), may be approached using two perspectives: substantive and functional. The *substantive approach* attempts to define the essence of a myth. It seeks to clarify and illuminate, much as we have been doing in our present discussion of myth in this chapter. The *functional approach*, on the other hand, seeks to determine what effects myths have in the lives of people and the larger society. In other words, an important task of the functional perspective is to determine the purpose myth serves in maintaining the social order. While these two approaches may appear to be distinct, in actuality there is overlap. What may begin as a substantive approach may end in a discussion of the functions of myth; what is intended to be a discussion of the functions of myth may produce a tentative definition. Despite the fact that these two approaches are not mutually exclusive, discussing them separately does enable us to provide a comprehensive discussion of the nature and purpose of myth.

Mircea Eliade, an anthropologist who wrote extensively about religion of hunting-gathering and agricultural-pastoral societies, has provided us with a concise description of the substantive nature of myth:

> In short, myths describe breakthroughs of the sacred (or the supernatural) into the world. It is this sudden breakthrough of the sacred that really *establishes* (italics in the original) the world and makes it what it is today. Furthermore, it is a result of the intervention of supernatural beings that man himself is what he is today, a mortal, sexed, and cultural being. (Eliade 1973:70)

Eliade contends that myth presents a sacred history, a story of what took place in primordial time. It informs the believer of how, through the deeds of supernatural beings, the cosmos came into being. It represents a breakthrough, or more accurately, a "break into" the mundane world of the common place by non-terrestrial beings. In constructing his theory of myths, Eliade built on the work of Otto (1958), referred to above.

Functional Definition of Myth

Campbell (1964) explains the functional definition of myth. He divides these functions into three: cosmological, sociological, and psychological. The first one, cosmological, presents people with an account of the origins of the universe or of "making sense" of the cosmos. The prophet or seer has received some illumination, but the understanding of the seer must be translated into cultural images, symbols, rites and texts for it to become viable. Unless this is done, the vision will die with the visionary. There is a tension, however, between making the mystery available to the culture while at the same time retaining the awe of the mystery. This tension may be briefly demonstrated by what happened over time to the accounts of creation presented in Genesis. Most religions, including the Judeo-Christian tradition, have cosmological accounts of creation that attempt to capture its mystery. The stories are intended to help "make sense" of the origins of the world. At the same time they must capture the sense of mystery and awe reflected by the rhythm of life's polarities and paradox that includes birth and death, light and darkness, sowing and reaping, peace and war. When a creation story is twisted into the mold of history and science (as the book of Genesis has been countless times), a sense of mystery and awe is often lost. Paradoxically when the myth becomes rigid doctrine, its power to serve as an effective source of cosmology is weakened.

A second purpose of myth identified by Campbell is sociological that includes social control, social support, and socialization. Myth functions as an agent of social control in that it reinforces the existing social order. The ten commandments given to Moses on Mount Sinai warn people against such socially divisive practices as lying, stealing, and murder. Although generally functional for society in their power to bind people together, myths may also become dysfunctional (i.e., work against the good of the social system). Myth has been used to uphold anti-social practices, including slavery, the burning of women thought to be witches, spouse and child abuse, and unfair labor practices. Myth may function to support legitimate order in society, and it may be used to bolster illegitimate power. Emile Durkheim, a founding father of sociology, tended to emphasize the positive functions of myth for upholding the social order. Durkheim (Bellah, 1973) believed that religion had provided an essential moral base for all societies.

The sociological function of myth is built into a classic definition of religion advanced by Emile Durkheim. Durkheim (1965, p. 62) defined *religion* as "a unified system of beliefs and practices relative to sacred things, that is to say, things set apart and forbidden—beliefs and practices that unite into a single moral community called a Church, all those who adhere to them." In this definition we see that religion includes both myth and the rituals that reflect mythical beliefs. These beliefs and corresponding rituals are of a particular kind that pertain to the sacred (not the mundane or the secular). They function to unite believers into a single moral community; in other words, into a socially cohesive group. This community is both a source of support and an agent of control.

Myth not only functions on the social level; it also functions on the individual level. Campbell (1964) terms this the "psychological function" of myth. Myth may initiate the individual into the reality of his or her own psyche, guiding a person toward spiritual enrichment. Campbell asserts that in primitive and traditional forms of myth, the principle of personal development was often downplayed or even suppressed. In the modern world with its emphasis on individuality, myths are more likely to accent the development of full personal potential (Campbell 1968).

The psychological function of myth, however, is not restricted to Christianity nor to modernity. Eastern mythology traditionally has accented the growth of the individual person into the divine. The ultimate goal of Hinduism, for example, is for the soul (*Atman*) to become one with the universal soul (*Brahman*). A similar goal is held out in Buddhism where the follower is to become like the Buddha and to rest in *nirvana,* a state of quiescence. Perhaps what differs for the modern world is the increased primacy given to psychological functions (individual benefits) over sociological (collective needs) ones.

Changes in Myth

In a sociological study of Islam in Pakistan, Malaya, Turkey, Iran (before the revolution), Tunisia and Morocco, Kanwar (1974) found that modernization and secularization had taken their toll on the mythology and practice of Islam. These changes reflect new values, a changing concept of the state, ways of living, family life and education. It should be added, however, that since Kanwar wrote this text, there have been many changes in the countries he researched, particularly Pakistan and Iran, where there is a strong movement back to traditional Islam where the state and religion were much more linked.

Research in Canada by the sociologist of religion, Reginald Bibby (1987) also reveals a shift in myth. In previous times, according to Bibby and Durkheim, believers tended to accept the whole mythology of a particular religion. With the rise of modernity, however, they tend to become somewhat sophisticated and are more likely to select what is more suited to their own circumstances. Bibby uses the term "fragmented gods" to describe this phenomenon. He garnishes evidence from a number of Canadian national surveys.

Ritual

Consistent with the approach began in the discussion on the substantive and functional definitions of religion and myth, I continue to look at ritual in a similar way.

The elaboration of a substantive definition of ritual emerges from the works of anthropologists, religious studies scholars and sociologists. From several sources, a comprehensive description of a substantive understanding of ritual will be presented.

From the work of Geertz (1966), Davis (1948–1949), Hargrove (1989), Durkheim (1989) and Smith (1956), I present a substantive definition or ritual as:

> Repeated consecrated (sacred) behaviour that is a symbolic expression of the moods and motivations of religious participants and unseen powers. Ritual forms a bond of friendship, community and unity with the believer and her/his god. Finally, ritual transports the participant into another world (the world above) wherein there is peace and harmony.

To illustrate this definition, I will use Watts' (1954) study of myth and ritual within pre-Vatican II Catholicism.[1] In this religion, the historical myth-event of Christ takes on an eternal dimension that is not restricted to two thousand years ago but is something perennial, both in all time and beyond all time. This church follows an annual cycle called "the Church Calender" which begins with Advent, a period of preparation for Christmas, symbolizing one's personal death and the permanent coming of Christ's kingdom, and continues with Lent which prepares the participants for the death/resurrection myth of the Christ. The third period is the post-Easter period wherein the church members are reminded of the "mysteries" which they just experienced ritually. The final period is a post Pentecost time wherein the participant reflects upon the long period of history when the church exists in this "world" under the "power of the Holy Spirit." The cycle begins again to repeat the previous periods.

Just as there is a functional definition of religion and myth so also is there a functional definition of ritual. It accents what ritual does—its function both for the individual and for the social group or society. Eight functions of ritual can be identified from the literature (again, from a wide variety of anthropologists, religious studies scholars and sociologists): (1) remembering, (2) social bonding, (3) regulating the moral behaviour of members, (4) socialization and changes in social statuses, (5) psychological development, (6) bonding to nature (the ecological function), (7) being empowered, and, (8) evoking the nefarious.

Remembering

The remembering function recalls to the believer that which he/she tends easily to forget: the mythologies of the past. One example from the anthropological literature will illustrate this function. Geertz (1966) outlines an example of a collective ritual from Bali (an Indonesian island east of Java which has been Hindu since the 7th century A.D.). Two key actors who represent Rangda (a satanic figure) and Barong (a comic figure). The contest continues over a long time with one figure gaining the upper hand at one time and the other at another time. Most of the tribal members participate actively and are "drawn near" to the two main figures. As they participate, they move into a mass trance and enter "into the world of Rangda and Barong." The ritual functions to have the participants "remember" the original conflict between these two figures and to be present with them in that conflict. Rangda reflects the cultural trait of fear whereas Barong represents playfulness, exhibitionism, and extravagance: both realities close to the life experience of the people.

Social Bonding

Social bonding occurs because as one is bonded to her/his god so also is she/he bonded to other members of the social group or the society. Two examples from native American religions will aid us in understanding this function. Research on the Mohegan Indians of New England by Kertzer (1988:20-21) is a case in point. These people had been struggling to find an identity ever since their tribe was outlawed by the state legislature in 1880. By 1930 they had lost much of their identity and bonding through intermarriage, language loss, and cultural demise. The Monhegans solved this crisis by stressing rites and symbols that identify themselves as Indians and Monhegans. The central rite is the annual powwow wherein native dances are performed, local crafts are displayed, and native clothes are worn. These repeated rites, then, functioned to create unity and bonding among members.

Another example from American Indians peoples is the rite of the Sacred Pipe. Paper (1989) gathered together evidence that the most central and most universal rite of the North American Indians is the smoking of the Sacred Pipe. The rite has many elements that do not vary substantially from tribe to tribe and from region to region. At an appropriate time (for example in council), the Sacred Pipe is ceremoniously filled with tobacco and the shaman lights it from a fire. Then, he raises the pipe up to the zenith and down to the nadir as well as pointing it to the east, west, north and south. Thereafter, he passes it to all who are present and each smokes. The significance of the various gestures is in raising up to the zenith which symbolizes an offering to the deities and a resultant communion with them. The pointing to the earth signifies a unity with the earth whereas the circle pointing is a sign of unity with the whole of the universe. The sharing of the pipe is the sharing of lives: therein is the source of bonding and unity among the participants. Paper (1989:36) writes: "Basic to the ceremonial use of the Sacred Pipe is that it is passed among the participants: it creates social communion; it joins all into a sacred circle."

Regulation of Behavior

Another function is one of regulation of behaviour. For social life to be possible, it has been long understood by both anthropologists and sociologists that there needs to be some sort of common base, some sort of common value or moral foundation that integrates individual persons together. Wuthnow (1987), a sociologist of religion, sees that the central function of ritual is moral. In a simple word, ritual is that which maintains moral order or (1987:107) "Ritual regulates and defines social relations" and (1987:109) ritual is "a symbolic expressive aspect of behaviour that communicates something about social relations, often in a dramatic or formal manner." In the tradition of Durkheim, then, the moral function of ritual is to put order into human relationships, to provide a code whereby men and women can live by and interact together.

Socialization

Another sociological function of ritual is present when individuals are in the process of being socialized into being active members of a society. The literature on ritual terms these "rites of passage" and include such rituals that surround birth, puberty, marriage and death. An example of this is provided from a case study by Kligman (1988) who studied the marriage rites of a people called the "Ieud Maramures" of northern Romania. She analyses the ritual according to the three phases of separation, transition, and incorporation. The separation stage consists of the marriage preparation, the "dance of the groom's flag" and of the "dance of the bride's crown," a symbolic ritual of bride bargaining, the dressing of the bride and the mutual asking forgiveness of the parents both of the bride and the groom. The dance of the groom's flag consists of the friend's of the groom gathering to sew together a flag the evening before the wedding. This flag is symbol of colourful vitality and power between men and women. It is patriarchal in nature and is the dominant marriage symbol. It is carried by a flag bearer who leads the groom and together they go to the home of the bride on the day of the ceremony and lead the bridal entourage into the church.

It is in the home of the bride that the "dance of the crown" ritual is celebrated. Here the bride's maid, with another woman, hold the crown (made of flowers) and lead a dance of both men and women. The crown is a symbol of the bride's virginity and is shown to friends and the future husband.

The transitional stage consists of the actual church ceremony, post-ceremonial meals, gift exchanges between wife-givers and wife-takers, and rituals of asking for the bride and the "song of the hen." After the church ceremony, the bride returns to her parents home. It is late in the night that the groom comes to the house and asks the father for his bride. Through many tries, the father "gives" over the bride to the her new husband. After this, a meal is shared. Here the families are gathered and a roast chicken is prepared for food. All but the bride eat for the passing and the eating of the chicken symbolizes the virginity of the bride.

Now that the transfer from the family of the bride to the family of the groom has taken place, she is now brought to the groom's house where she is symbolically undressed. This is the new status and the woman now moves from a status of freedom and carefreeness to that of being a child-bearer and one having full adult responsibilities. The husband, now, is also no longer free and is also a full adult.

Psychological Development

Ritual also serves the individual to develop psychologically. In one way, it may help to elicit as well as to control emotions and, in another way, contribute to individual well-being. O'Dea and O'Dea (1983) provide us with an interpretation of religion being a response to people's experiences of "limit situations" or feelings of contingency, powerlessness and scarcity. Ritual practices can, as noted by Smith (1956), Kluckhohn (1968) and Hargrove (1989), reduce the anxiety produced by these feelings. Kluckhohn argues that rites remind believers of how the ancients did it. These ancients (he uses the example of the Navaho people) meet similar "limit situations" and conquered them. If the rites are performed properly, the participants can also reduce anxiety and be at peace.

Ecological

The ecological function of ritual is not common. What is understood by this is that for some religious participants, rituals put them in touch with nature, with the natural ecology. They function to form some kind of communion with the earth, the fields, waters etc. This function will be illustrated with an investigation of native American religion. As is well known from native studies, the aboriginal peoples of America and Canada have a profound respect for the natural environment. Paper (1989) describes the ecological and cosmological meaning of the Sacred Pipe. The bowl of the pipe (made of stone) is a miniature cosmos that is female. The tobacco is put into the bowl in minute pieces that symbolizes bringing the entire cosmos into the bowl itself. The stem (made of wood) of the pipe is male in nature and is symbolic of the trees, and the sky.

When the Sacred Pipe is smoked in a formal ceremony, there is signified a connection of the self (the participant) with the world of social relations (fellow participants, family, clan, and nation), to that of animals who are extensions of social relations (nature is depicted in personal, familial terms), to the earth, to the sky and to the whole of the cosmos. This ritual, in effect, then, is understood to integrate people with nature for all things are "relatives."

Empowerment

The seventh function is empowerment. The argument here is that when participants gather together they experience something they do not when they are alone: empowerment and a sense of having received a supernatural power. Two studies on the charismatic movement will illustrate this function. In her work on Catholic Pentecostals, McGuire (1982:7) identifies four characteristics of power among participants within a prayer group ritual: that the power of God is given directly to ordinary human beings (you need not be a professional cleric); that individuals have power to see the relevance of religion in their ordinary lives; that this power has a strong experiential component; and that all these beliefs (and rituals) compel members to seek out a community of fellow believers.

Swenson (1990) argued that through the central rituals of a small, evangelical/charismatic church, individuals gave witness to being empowered. The four key rituals were:

(1) holy communion, (2) the Sunday worship service, (3) adult baptism, and (4) membership ceremonies. The Sunday worship service is the rallying point, the core ritual that focuses within a few hours the drama of the people's Christian myth, the charismatic heritage, and empowerment for service. There are two pulpits in this ritual service: the "Word Podium" and the "Music Podium." "The Word Podium" symbolizes the importance of the literal word as found in the Christian scriptures. It is in this setting that the senior pastor spends about one-half an hour in teaching, exhortation, and preaching. This "Podium" is a focus of faith, of life, of empowerment and of action. The sermon is understood as having practical effects like touching people's hurts, and being a balm to soothe the brokenness experienced by members throughout the previous week.

Not as important, but still central, is the "Music Podium." Nearly equal time is given to worship songs. These have an effect of "clothing" participants with praise, wherein something happens in the spiritual realm and the worshipper communicates with the divine.

Evidence is that these rituals are vehicles of empowerment: assisting the participants in feeling stronger, less alienated, and more ready to serve others. It should be accented that in both cases, empowerment, although is personal, it is directed to the social group wherein the whole group (or church) becomes empowered as well.

Nefarious

The last function is negative and is the invocation of the nefarious. As religion can be dysfunctional both for individuals and societies, so also can ritual. This function will be illustrated from some studies of witch hunting rituals of early America. In Salem New England about 1650, a ritual of hunting for witches occurred. Weisman (1984), an historian, noticed a common characteristic of most of the women accused of witchcraft: they were older, single or widowed, and poor. The ritual process began with an accusation of one person against a particular women who had a rupture of normal relationships with the community. The accusation was countered by the accused which, sometimes, took on the form of curses, threats, and being outspoken in public. These actions of the accused brought upon herself more accusations from the larger community. She began to be labelled a "witch" not only by the one accuser but also by the community. Weisman interprets this level of accusation in terms of a symbol of conflicts within the community itself: of those who had means of living and those who had not. The woman began to be a "scapegoat" to fears and conflicts of the village.

The next stage evoked the judicial system of the colony. Courts were set up and witnesses for and against the accused were heard. If the evidence gathered confirms the accusation, she would either be imprisoned or executed—depending on the severity of the "witchcraft."

Rituals like this provide evidence that religion, in some circumstances, is harmful to persons. In this case, it is marginalised women who become victims.

Ethos

As myths and rituals are extensions of religious experiences so is ethos. The term comes from the anthropologist of religion, Geertz (1973). One may see this as a cluster of behavioural codes including values, norms, morals, and laws. Anthropologists and cultural sociologists have referred to values as providing a general orientation to life while norms as outlining more specific kinds of behaviour. Another way we may look at norms is to consider them as "the rules or standards that govern interaction" (Moot, 1965:24). A particular species of a norm is what a founder of American sociology, Sumner (1906), terms the *more* that has the authority of facts (1906:80). Mores, or moral codes carry more weight and channel human behaviour according to effects: rewards for conformity and punishments for disobedience. Laws are specific norms and mores are codified by some state or societal authority.

The cultural analyst Robert Wuthnow (1987) adds another important element to an understanding of morality: the provision for social order in a society. This recalls Durkheim who also saw morality as a basis of social solidarity.

In religious circles, these mores have even more of an impact because they carry with them some sort of divine approbation and legitimacy. A popular term to describe them as an *ethic* and a collection of ethics would be called an *ethical system*. For example, as in the case of the ten commandments of Judaism, conformity means long life and prosperity and disobedience connotes suffering, a shortened life and poverty (see Deuteronomy 28 in the Jewish or Christian Bible).

There appears to be a general consensus among anthropologists and sociologists of religion that the moral or ethical dimension is central to the understanding of religion. However, some dissenting voices include the 19th century anthropologist, Edward Tyler (1929) and the functionalist anthropologist, Bronislaw Malinowski (1932).

Inspired by Yinger's (1959) outline of the connection between religion and morality, the Rice University anthropologist Edward Norbeck (1961), saw some basis for Tyler's and Malinowski's position. For example, he found that, among the Inuit, morality is relatively removed from religious myths and to break a moral code is not to entail after-life punishment. However, in contrast to Tyler and Malinowski, Norbeck discovers that for the Manus peoples of Melanesia, morality is intricately tied to religion. Strict moral codes govern sexuality. To illustrate, one is guilty of sexual transgression even if s/he sees the private parts of the opposite sex by accident. Laziness, theft, and disobedience of elders incur illness as a punishment from the ancestral spirit. He writes (1961:184): "Any moral transgression is thus the concern of everyone and the compulsion to follow the code is strong. Public accusations of guilt, confession, and expiation also bring shame and loss of social prestige and serve to strengthen the supernatural sanctions."

Figure 13:1
The Sacred: Myth, Ritual and Ethos

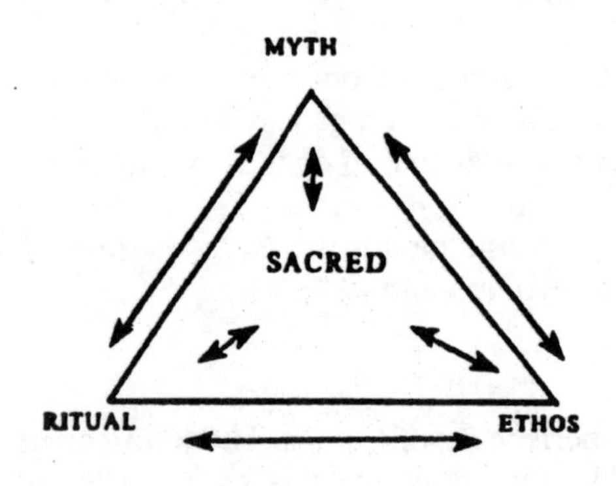

The bulk of the evidence does reveal that there is a substantial inter-connection between myth, ritual and morality in religion. Inspired by Geertz (1973), Figure 13:1 illustrates this connection.

We begin with the heart of religion, the sacred that is interactively linked to myth, ritual and ethos. Geertz (1973:126ff) explains the connection of myth, ritual and ethos in the following way. religion consists of a myth, ritual and a code. Myths provide believers with what "is," the factual, a view of reality and the ethos is the "ought" that flows from the myth. He writes:

> A people's ethos is the tone, character, and quality of their life, its moral and aesthetic style and mood; it is the underlying attitude toward themselves and their world that life reflects. Their world view (in our terms, myth) is their picture of the way things in sheer actuality are, their concept of nature, of self, of society. It contains their most comprehensive ideas of order....the ethos is made intellectually reasonable by being shown to represent a way of life implied by the actual state of affairs which the world view describes, and the world view is made emotionally acceptable by being presented as an image of an actual state of affairs of which a way of life is an authentic expression. (1973:127)

These world views, however, are not merely in the ideal realm. They are represented in symbols such as a Buffalo totem of the Sioux peoples of the American Great Plains, the cross of Western Christianity, the icon of Eastern Christianity, the serene Buddha statue in Burma or the crescent of Islam of Saudi Arabia. As we saw in the last section, rituals dramatize and make present the myth. This is to enable the practitioners to have a religious experience. Thus, the connection between myth, ritual and the ethos is profound. In other words, myth makes meaning of the cosmos, ritual enacts the myth, and ethos provides the quotidian channel to live out the myth. Again, we come full circle. Ideally, if believers know the myth in an experiential way, enact it through ceremonies and live it out in daily life, they increasingly come in contact with the sacred.

Linkage between Myth, Ritual and Ethos

What I propose to do in this section is to provide empirical evidence for these connections. The thesis is that myth and ethos mutually reinforce one another and ritual reinforces ethos. I shall provide evidence on the link between myth, ritual and ethos from an anthropological study of Buddhism in Burma and recent surveys in North America.

Buddhism has an ancient history and preceded the emergence of both Christianity and Islam. Founded by the charismatic leader, Gautama Buddha (563?–483? B.C.), Buddhism shares with the other Eastern religions a monism that does not posit a separate creator deity. Throughout its long history, Buddhism, like Christianity, has gone through many transformations and creations of different versions (sects of systems). Two major schools are identified: *Theravada* (or, sometimes called, *Hinayana*, the Lesser Vehicle or the way of the elders) and *Mahayana* (the Great Vehicle). The Theravada school predominates in Sri Lanka, Thailand, Burma and Indo-China. The Mahayana alternative is the Buddhism of North Asia in China, Korea, Japan and the Himalayas (Noss and Noss, 1984 and Florida, 1994).

The anthropologist Spiro (1982) illustrates the linkage between myth and morality through his field work among the Theravada Buddhist of Burma. In this work, Spiro identifies four types of Buddhism: Nibbanic, Kammatic, Apotropaic, and Esoteric. Each provides evidence of the vital linkage between myth and ethos or morality.

Morality is at the very heart of Buddhism for it is one of the three stages of salvation: *sila* (morality), *samadhi* (meditation) and *prajna* (wisdom). However, salvation from the world of suffering (in the hope to reach the "land of no suffering or nirvana") is centered on meditation in the original teaching of Gautama. Through meditation, one becomes detached from all things: both internal desires and external troubles. In the state of detachment, then, one practices the great precepts of Buddha, especially compassion towards all creatures.

Buddhism received the myth of *Karma* or the process of rebirth from Hinduism. Salvation consists in being freed from the karma that would reduce your social status in the next life. For example, through meditation and following the precepts, one can achieve a better state in another life cycle. Eventually, one is freed completely from Karma to enter Nirvana or eternal peace, calm and the total cessation of suffering. Spiro argues that for the various kinds of Theravada Buddhism in Burma, this process and goal is quite different.

Nibbanic (after *nibbana*, nirvana) Buddhism is reflected in monastic Buddhism where monks meditate several hours a day and obey the precepts. Kammatic Buddhism (after *Kamma*, one's Karma) is a routinized form of Buddhism which focuses not on achieving Nirvana but, rather, an improvement of one's karma. It is in this form of Buddhism that the linkage between myth and morality takes the form of a "salvation by works." By doing good works and in not transgressing the precepts that a better karma is assured in the next life.

Apotropaic Buddhism (from the Greek, a ritual designed to avert evil) is concerned with what happens in this world, in the everyday, the mundane. Both morality and ritual are designed to ward off evil and to protect the faithful against calamity and illness. It acknowledges the presence of evil spirits that one needs to be protected from.

Here, then, we see the unity and the inter-connectedness of myth, ritual and morality. The myth states that the world is suffused with evil spirits and that there is power in the Buddha statues, the monastery, the Buddhist teachings, and the precepts. By adhering to various rituals like reciting prayers and making offerings to the Buddha images, making offerings to the relics of the Buddha, and reciting the beads (repeating, for example, texts from the sacred canon) as well as obeying the five precepts, one is protected from evil in this life.

The forth Buddhist form in Burma, Spiro calls *esoteric* or *chiliastic*[2] Buddhism (1982:162). It is a syncretism of traditional Buddhist beliefs, local animistic practices, and quasi secretive sects. There is also a belief in a mythical magician or *Weikza* who has enormous supernatural powers. For esoteric Buddhism, morality is secondary while the practice of magical rites to invoke the Weikza is primary. In this case, morality is not connected to the myth but ritual is.

Survey research documents a reasonably long tradition of linking myth, ritual and morality. Gerhard Lenski (1963), in the late 1950s in Detroit, conducted research of 656 Roman Catholics, Protestants and Jews. He found that devotionalism (as measured by personal communication to God through prayer and meditation) was associated with an ethic of helping or humanitarianism. Allport (1966), in his study of religion and prejudice, found that even though religious affiliates were more prejudiced than non-affiliates, members who were most active in their churches were least prejudiced.

Later research is consistent with these studies of the 1960s. In a 1973 survey of San Francisco Bay area residents, Piazza and Glock (1979) found linkages between myth, measured by images of the divine, ritual, church attendance and daily prayer, and morality, willingness to perform compassionate acts. Those who had what the researchers called a "personal view of God" or a belief that God was active in their lives were more likely to attend church and pray and more likely to loan money to a co-worker without interest and give money to a stranger for bus fare. Morgan (1983) adds further credibility to the linkage between ritual and morality from data of a national representative sample (N=1,467). His findings reveal that those who pray frequently or those who have integrated prayer into their day-to-day lives are more likely to "stop and comfort a crying child," be a "good listener," "get along with loud and obnoxious people," and "turn the other cheek," than those who do not.

Lastly, another national study conducted by the Gallup organization (Poloma and Gallup, 1991), reveals similar results. Poloma and Gallup extend the measure of prayer beyond mere frequency to types of prayer: ritual prayer, reading from a prayer book or reciting memorized prayers, and conversational prayer, talking to God in one's own words. Two other types include petitionary prayer, asking God for favours, and meditative prayer, illustrated by those who spend time thinking about God, feel a divine presence, worship God, and try to listen to God speaking. A bivariate analysis[3] reveals that those who pray meditatively are more likely to forgive others who have hurt them and are less likely to nurture resentments than are those who use the other forms of prayer.

Substantive and Functional Ethos

In the first and second parts of the text, we have given both substantive and functional definitions of religion, myth and ritual. In a typology of morality, we also discover both substantive and functional elements. A substantive understanding of morality is a precept or moral code that is proximate to the sacred. The example given is from Goode (1951) who uses Durkheim's distinction between the sacred and the profane which is at the core of our text. Almost universally among primitive peoples, Durkheim (1965) and Goode (1951) observe that the profane must not intrude into the sacred. One might construct a moral code that would reflect the reality: "*You shall not let the profane intrude into the sacred.*"[4]

Functional morality is what morality is to do. Within functional morality, seven different forms appear: empowerment, bonding, ecology, social integration, worldly success, social control and alienation. An explanation will be given with empirical examples to illustrate each type.

The Function of Empowerment

The focus on morality in Durkheim's work is on social control. Not only do moral codes come from the gods to induce conformity, they also empower the conformists. To be an effective member of a society, Durkheim (1965) argues that one must not only conform externally but also internally. In the process of internal conformity or socialization, one becomes elevated and magnified. In addition, these moral codes become "moral powers" within us and we develop a moral conscience. By conforming to the codes, one senses a protection from the deities and one has confidence to meet the challenges of the everyday life.[5]

The Function of Social Bonding

The example of this function comes from Goode's (1951) analysis of the Murngin of Australia. These people consist of a large clan of about 40 to 50 thousand members who live in a geographical region comprising 360 square miles. The religious and social centre of the clan is a large water hole which is believed to house the unborn children. It is necessary that parents obey the codes of their clan in order to free the spirits of the children to become incarnated. After birth, a child must follow the age graded codes of his or her gender. In doing so, the child becomes bonded to his or her group. As an adult, a man grows into spiritual manhood and in so doing, increasing bonds with his fellows. Thus, by following the moral codes, he builds a bond with the spiritual world and with the world of his clan.

The Ecological and Cosmological Function of Morality

This function of morality connects believers to nature and to the cosmos. Obedience to moral precepts bonds people to brothers and sisters, to the earth, the water, the sky, the animals and to the stars. For example, Eliade (1959) argues that by following the codes of sexual intimacy, one becomes bonded to the heavens, for the heavens are to the earth as the male is to the female. Or, when one lives out a married life, one represent the divine wedding to the whole universe.

The clearest example of this function is from the Amerindian peoples. Before European contact, there were an estimated 4 to12 million people in North America who spoke 550 different languages. Even though there was a wide ethnic variation, they all shared some fundamental myths, rituals and ethical codes. The social historian of American religion, Albanese (1981, 1990) describes it in this way. "Nature Religion," the central concept, is a descriptor of a mythology of connectedness: the world and the cosmos is redolent with power, vivacity, unity, and purpose. The view is fundamentally a relational one that connects individuals, societies, nature and the universe into a sacred tapestry. Unlike Apotropaic Buddhism of Burma, the material world is a sacred world, a safe world, a world "peopled" with mysterious persons.

The fundamental value and explicit moral code for all these people, termed by Albanese (1990:26), is "the harmony ethic." In pragmatic terms, one is to respect and honour all around you: animals, plants, the earth, water and fellow humans. The well being of all persons depends fundamentally upon how well one lives out this basic precept. Not to honour nature (kill more than one can eat, cut down more trees than necessary, fish beyond the dietary needs of your group) is to cause disharmony with your fellow brothers and sisters. A specific code that is common among the Amerindians is to apologize to a animal if you have to kill it in order to live.

The complimentary ethic to this is what she calls the "ethos of reciprocity" (1990:27). If you follow the harmony ethic, you will, in turn, be treated well by your fellow humans, by nature, indeed, the whole cosmos will smile upon you.

The Function of Social Integration

Another function that removes morality further from delimitation is that of social integration. It is argued that as members of a social group, a tribe, a religious organization honour the moral codes that are common for all the members, then they will integrate more and more into the whole of the community. For the Inuit of the north, it is very important to avoid breaking the religious taboos. If one does, the spirits will be angered and will take their anger out on the members of the group (Norbeck, 1961:177).

Another example of morality influencing social solidarity is among the Kammatic Buddhist of Burma whom we met before. In what is called a Buddhist lent, people go on a pilgrimage throughout local villages to collect articles and money to give to the monasteries. The manifest function of the practice is to gain merit for one's better-future karma but the latent function (to use Merton's famous term) is the creation of village solidarity. In fact, Spiro (1982) notes that being a Buddhist adds to the solidarity of the whole Burmese society for to be Burmese is to be Buddhist.

The Function of Worldly Success

A further elaboration of morality is reflected in religion's tendency to affect change in peoples' mundane world. religion is pragmatic and it is effective in providing believers with a better place in life. Weber's (1958) study of Protestantism is a classic expression of this function. He argues that the Protestant ethic (as represented by the Calvinistic ethic of hard work and diligence that would bring eternal rewards) has a latent function: to empower people to succeed in wealth and status. It is too simplistic to think that if one adheres to this ethic one will prosper financially. However, the ethic becomes a moral force, a power to work hard, to be honest, to save, not to steal. An offshoot of this is success in the world. Weber goes to great lengths to present credible evidence to substantiate the thesis and his work has been replicated in many research projects since his time.

The Function of Social Control

We turn to Durkheim's research to illustrate morality as social control. In fact, as we have seen, it is at the very heart of his theory of religion. Again, society is a moral force coercing members to conform. It is in this conformity that society is made possible.

Norbeck (1961) portrays this function well in his analysis of the Manus people of Melanesia. The Manus, as we saw before in section 2, are very strict in regard to sexual mores. Again, each family has a guardian spirit who keeps a close eye on the actions of the family members. If members are obedient to the precepts (Norbeck identifies sixteen), they will have wealth and a long life. If they transgress, they will become ill, live a short life and be poor. Nordeck writes of the power of social control among the Manus:

> Any moral transgression is thus the concern of everyone else and the compulsion to follow the code is strong. Public accusation of guilt, confession, and expiation also bring shame and loss of social prestige and serve to strengthen the supernatural sanctions. (1961:184)

Most of the research using morality to control people is found in the literature linking religion and politics. The basic thesis is that political regimes use religion as an instrument of power and enforce it through the medium of religious morality (especially those that protect the power of the regime). Yinger (1959) refers to the Russian Orthodox Church of 1915 being used by the aristocracy to control the people. MacIver and Page (1957:318) expand this interpretation: "The religious codes often emerge as powerful engines of control to maintain the interests of the established order against the processes of change, as when the Russian Orthodox Church became a bulwark of the tyranny of the Russian Tzars."

The Moral Function of Alienation

The last function that we identified is really a dysfunction: alienation. Berger (1969) explains that religion (and religious ethics) is a product of social construction that occurs in conversations between persons, groups and institutions. In the process of this construction, some projections can become so reified as to appear objective and not dependent at all on social creation. The actor does not act but is acted upon and is but a passive receptor in the process. If this involves codes of behaviour, these codes become "alien" to the person and are dysfunctional to him or her.

A good historical example is the publication of *Malus Malifactorium* towards the end of the first Millennium of Christianity. In this document, there is an outline of how to identify and prosecute women who are suspected of witchcraft and sorcery (Mahoney, 1987). These particular codes illustrate how far removed morality can be from the sacred and are used to not only control people but to imprison them. This is the ultimate extent of the elaboration of ethos.

The Emergence of Formal Religious Organizations

This part of the chapter outlines how sociologists of religion have categorized and specified religious formal organizations. One might argue that religion becomes formalized according to different ways of meeting the need to have an elaboration of roles and institutionalized procedures on one hand and of maintaining the charismatic element on the other hand. The literature provides us with five basic ways in which formal, religious organizations emerge: sect, the church, cult, movement of renewal, and the denomination. These different alternatives will be outlined.

Sect

Using a wide variety of sources (Weber,1946; Troeltsch, 1931; Demerath III, 1965; Coleman, 1968; Wach, 1944; Stark and Bainbridge, 1979), a summary of a definition of the sect seems to encompass three domains: leadership, membership and the relationship to the environment. A sect is:

> A religious organization that includes members who are considered to be converted, who follow stringent rules of behaviour, who form a small, primary and intimate group, who opt for spontaneity rather than for formalized ritual and form an egalitarian moral community. The leaders of the organization protest against the "over accommodative" nature of the church type and tend to be lay, charismatic, non-professional and adhering to clear doctrinal statements. As a whole, the organization stands in a high-tension relationship to the environment and is organizationally precarious in that it endeavours to maintain the

pristine message while providing a sense of social order. As an organization, it tends not to accommodate to the external environment and may take a stance of indifference, intolerance or hostility towards that environment.

Table 13:2 illustrates the characteristics of a sect.

An example of sect is one located in a mid-sized city in Alberta. The sect's emergence is in a very different time in Alberta than were the ones illustrated above. It's formation is from several charismatic prayer groups within the United Church of Canada. For about 10 years, members of these prayer groups served in some United Church congregations in a hope to "renew" the churches. Increasingly, their gentle protest became nullified for the resistence to change overpowered mechanisms of protest. Also, the United Church of Canada was going through modernization processes such as questioning the literal meaning of the Bible, speaking of God in inclusive language, and allowing practising homosexual persons to be ordained ministers. Several members of these groups left the denomination and eventually invited a minister of a Pentecostal church (of the *Fellowship of Christian Assemblies*). From a small number of 40 members in the early 1980s, the sect has grown to over 300 members as of 1991. Swenson (1990) argues that there is significant evidence that most of these members came from the mainline churches (especially Roman Catholic, United, and Anglican) because they experienced deligitimation from their previous commitments.

A final question one may ask of the sect is to inquire where they get their members from? Bibby and Brinkerhoff (1973) asked this of evangelical sects in Calgary in the early 1970s. A common assumption was that they grew by reaching disillusioned Christians from mainline churches (like Roman Catholics, Anglicans, Lutherans or United Church members) and the unchurched community. What they found was that members of one sect grew primarily by reproduction and socialization of children and from what they call "the circulation of the saints." Members were not new members but were, rather, members of other evangelical sects. Their growth, then, was more of an actual fiction than a reality.

Table 13:2
Elements of a Sect

Leadership	Membership	Relationship to the Environment
lay	converted	high tension
charismatic	members follow the leader	non accomodative
non-professional	stringent rules	organizationally precarious
	they form into primary groups	indifference to the outside environment
	spontaneous	

The Church

From the same authors who informed us on what a sect was (with the addition of Clark, 1948) and using the same dimensions as the sect, I define the church as:

> The leaders of the church usually are priests or ministers who are professionally trained and hold not a personal charisma but a charisma of office. Authority is from "top-down" in a series of hierarchical rankings. There tends to be a liaison between the religious and the secular leaders. The religious leaders seem to be wanting the welfare of the larger society. These leaders tend to be conservative in doctrine especially in traditional societies but move towards liberalism in relatively open societies.
>
> Members are mostly members from birth and have an ascriptive status. The people appear to be socially controlled by the leaders, large in numbers and there is a relatively high level of organizational stability. Ritual is more important than spontaneity and the fellowships lean towards impersonality and a kind of collectivity. Church members tend to be ascetic in religious practices in traditional societies but are much more relativistic in the modern setting.
>
> The church accommodates itself to the external environment and thus may become overly secularized. It is a level of low-tension with this environment and because of its bureaucratic "weight" tends to break down.

Table 13:3 illustrates this definition.

To present an example of a church, Miner, a sociologist from the University of Chicago, (1939) offers an ethnographic analysis of this type of religious organization.

St. Denis was (is) a rural parish community about 80 miles downstream from Quebec city on the *Riviere Quebec*. Although the history of the community goes back to 1695, it was formally established as a parish in 1833. The economic base was entirely agricultural with the unit of the social life of the community being the parish itself. Because the civic boundaries of the community are co-extensive with the parish, we can rightly call St. Denis a church. The parish is the "first point of reference" of the people into which is

Table 13:3
Elements of a Church

Leadership	Membership	Relationship to the Environment
priest or minister	not converted	low tension
not charismatic	from birth	accomodative
professional	loose rules	tends to be secularized
hierachical order	control is from the leaders	heavy bureaucracy
liason with the secular order	ritual is vital	
conservative in traditional times	impersonal social group	
liberal in modern times	ascetic in traditional times	
	relativistic in modern times	

enmeshed the family. The family type is patriarchic-primogeniture (inheritance given to the first son). All of the other children (ranging in number from 5 to 7) were to leave the farm. One was to become a priest, another a nun, and the rest professionals or emigrants to the North Eastern part of the United States.

The role of religion was very powerful. Sacred beliefs supported the time-tested, successful right behaviour. The Sunday ritual, the Mass, was the key ritual attended by virtually every person in the parish. It this setting, the priest (called the cure) presented directives for a righteous life. This ritual functioned to create solidarity and cohesiveness within the group of believers. This ritual was augmented by sacred feasts which brought further integration. One such example is a celebration in the autumn called All Souls Day. In this ritual families were integrated with their ancestors in a series of prayers for the deceased.

This kind of religious organization permeates the daily life of its members. It is present as a powerful means of social control, and creates social solidarity and cohesiveness among a people. However, it is out of step with modernity which accents individual choice and personal freedom[6] and could be a type more of a historical past than a present reality, at least in North America and Europe.

Cult

Becker (1932), Mann (1955), Westley (1983), Stark and Bainbridge (1979 & 1985) and Johnstone (1992) are the authors that I shall call upon to present us with a understanding of what a cult is. From their research, we can identify several elements which converge around three domains of the cult: deviant beliefs, accent on the individual and the relationship with the environment. Table 13:4 and the following definition illustrate these domains:

Table 13:4
Elements of a Cult

Deviant Beliefs	Membership	Relationship to the Environment
deviant from the religious doctrine of the host society	converted	high tension
syncretic	achieved status	accomodative tendency varies with type of group
selection of beliefs from several sources	individual is considered to be divine or sacred	
hierarchical order	loose and informal social group	
	group tends to be informal	

> A cult is a belief system which is deviant from the traditional religious doctrines of the host society. Members tend to blend non-traditional with traditional tenets that make it a syncretic. There is a special accent on the individual who becomes almost sacred. This emphasis on the individual leaves the association thus formed in a loose, informal, organizational structure. Finally, the cult stands in a high tension relationship with the external environment.

With this background in mind, I will illustrate this ideal type with an empirical case study of new religions in Montreal, Canada. Westley (1983) researched six groups which are categorized as being part of new religions movements[7]: Scientology, Psychosynthesis, Arica, Est, Shakti, and Silva Mind Control. It is beyond the scope of this presentation to detail the unique elements of these religions. I will present the common characteristics such as beliefs and organizational features.

Using several authors (Stone, 1976; Ellwood, 1973; Gaustad, 1974 and Bach, 1973), Westley (1983) presents the following common characteristics of these groups: being drawn from the encounter group/therapy tradition; having the idea of pre- and post-existence in a spiritual state; the idea of a plurality of worlds, each with its own spirits and angels; believing in the Renaissance notion that divine and human consciousness are co-extensive; adhering to the intimate connection between the body and the mind; believing that bodily conditions are a direct reflection of mental states; and being part of the human potential movement which accents individual changes from an intense group encounter. These groups, what Westley calls "the cult of man," are

> a mixture of the late stages of the human potential movement, the positive-thought movement, and the occult traditions. The point of agreement of all six of these is that it is the human individual who is seen as sacred, as all powerful. This sacred power is seen as located deep within the individual personality. Actions in the outer world become significant, not in themselves, but only in terms of their impact on this inner self. (Westley, 1983:38)

There are several distinguishing organizational features that these six groups share together. To participate in the group activities, fees for services are asked. Rather than have teachings on certain themes common in churches and sects, the fee for service is offered in exchange for a course on a certain topic. Membership transience is another feature of these groups. In fact, as long as the individual grows or develops, the continued presence of the group is not necessary. Partial commitment or involvement is also common. One can come and go at will and one will not be asked "why did you miss the gathering last week?" (Westley, 1983: 39–58).

The belief system (the mythology) corresponds to this informal, loose kind of organization. Faith (as trust in a supernatural power or person) is substituted for learning scientific technology (one is reminded of the turn of the century cult, Christian Science). Rather than accenting healing that would integrate one into a community (as in the case of members of the Catholic Charismatic Movement), it is purification from polluting ideas, especially negative ones, that is important for members of these groups. One may argue that faith (as trust in a person or adherence to basic doctrines) is exchanged for knowledge.

Table 13:5
Elements of the MOR

Leadership	Membership	Relationship to the Environment
lay	conversion	high tension
charismataic	achieved status	low accomodative
not professional	small primary groups	non-schismataic to the Church environment
in liason with the larger Church	in liason with the larger Church	

Movement of Renewal

The fourth type of religious organization that is reflected in the literature is the movement of renewal. Its central feature is a protest from within an existing church that does not involve and secession or a schism but, rather, a desire and mobilization to change the tone, the emptiness, the routinized charisma of the church through a renewal of a tradition. The renewal movement members strive hard to maintain connections with the authorities of the church. Table 13:5 reflects the characteristics of a Movement of Renewal or MOR.

A current example of a MOR is the Catholic Charismatic Movement. Swenson and Thompson (1986) did a content analysis on key texts and magazines of this movement from 1967 to 1976. Using Wach (1944), Hill (1973) and O'Dea and O'Dea (1983) as a theoretical base, they review Catholic Charismatic spokespersons such as Ranaghan and Ranaghan (1969), Ford (1970), O'Connor (1971), Clark (1971), and Byrne (1971) to illustrate that the Catholic Charismatic Movement is a movement of renewal.

All of these spokespersons write of the need for members of the movement to remain loyal to the Roman Catholic Church in its leadership and its core beliefs. In their writings, Swenson and Thompson (1986) also observed that to legitimate the charismatic dimension of this movement in the eyes both of the followers and the church hierarchy, they take great pain in locating the charismatic dimension in the traditions of the Catholic church. Such "sacred pasts" consist of the New Testament, the early church, the monastic movement and the mystical saints of the medieval period. A recent past was the Vatican II council in the early 1960s. Relying on the documents (Abbot, 1966), these spokespersons make a case that the highest authority in the Catholic Church, the gathering of all the bishops and the Pope, approved of the vitality of the charismatic gifts.

Denomination

The term denomination was introduced into the sociology of religion by Niebuhr (1957). It is seen as one type of rountinization of charisma that represents an accommodation to the class divisions within a society. He argues that a sect exists only for the period of time of the reformer. Soon after the death of the reformer, the sect begins to accommodate itself to the host society and the denomination emerges. The denomination, then, is a routinized sect that reflects the class, ethnic, and racial divisions in a society.

Martin (1962), a sociologist from England, expands. He notes that sects do not necessarily become a denomination but may continue for many generations as, for example, established sects. What is unique about the denomination is that it has some features that are common to the church and sect type as well as having characteristics unique to itself.

Rather than presenting my usually summary definition of the different types of religious organizations, I choose to select Martin's own definition of the denomination.[8]

> It does no claim that its institutional borders constitute the one ark of salvation, its concept of unity is a unity of experience and it historical sense is likewise a unity of experience rather than an institutional succession. Its attitude to organization and to cultic forms tends to be pragmatic and instrumental, while its sacramental conceptions are subjective. This subjectivity is related to a fundamental individualism. In the field of eschatology its conceptions are traditional and in the field of moral theory its conception of the relation of faith and works is dynamic but balanced. (1962:11)

With this definition as a background, we will illustrate this type with a church from Canada: The United Church of Canada. On June 10, 1925, this church became a formal organization of three churches (Presbyterian, Methodist, and Congregational) and one small amalgam, the General Council of Local Union Churches. Grant (1967) argues that the union was not so much a result of ecumenism (it had not yet been born) but, rather, one of exigency and practicality. Canada was still a frontier expanding country at this time. Vast lands with small populations left rural areas with many churches in competition with one another and each with few members. Union, then, made a lot of pragmatic sense.

The *Basis of Union* presents a presbyterian polity wherein each congregation and pastoral charge (there were 4,200 congregations in 1990 and 2,400 pastoral charges or one or more congregations under a minister) has a representation and a voice in a particular presbytery (98). Each presbytery, in turn, has its own elected representatives in the conference (a union of local presbyteries and numbering 13). Finally, each conference has its elected persons to the national church, the General Council, wherein major decisions are made (Morrow, 1923 and Grant, Chambers, Forrest, Greene, Lee and White, 1990). One of the ways the early founders found consensus is that each church would not accent its own "brand" of Christianity. In other words, there were to be no "Wesleyans," or "Calvinists." A consequence of this meant a lessened emphasis on "ours" and "theirs" (Grant, 1967:101).

Morrow (1923) outlines a history of the discussions within each of the churches that eventually led to the union. The *Basis of Union* (Morrow, 1923:322–327) establishes both the doctrinal and political basis of the new church. All representatives agreed that the union was to be based upon the faith given by the apostles and prophets of the New Testament with Jesus Christ as the "corner stone." The Bible is understood to be the primary source and ultimate standard of the faith. In addition, the representatives hold allegiance to the early creeds and the teaching of the reformers. The document goes on to detail the common beliefs regarding God, revelation, the divine purpose, creation, the sin of man, the grace of God, the divine-human nature of Jesus, the Holy Spirit, the need for regeneration, faith, repentance, sanctification and prayer. The doctrines of the law of God, the meaning of the Church, the sacraments, the ministry, fellowship and the teachings of eschatology all follow basic reformation theology.

A significant contrast is found in the (unofficial) currently accepted "doctrines of faith." Grant et al present a creed in the following words:

> We are not alone, we live in God's world. We believe in God who has created and is creating, who has come in Jesus, the Word made flesh, to reconcile and make new, who works in us and others by the Spirit. We trust in God. We are called to be church: to celebrate God's presence, to love and serve others, to seek justice and resist evil, to proclaim Jesus, crucified and risen, our judge and our hope. In life, in death, in life beyond death, God is with us. We are not alone. Thanks be to God. (1990:160)

From this latter creedal document, one is able to see how very concerned the leaders of the United Church take a middle ground approach that is quite indicative of the denominational type. This church sees itself as only one way among many to salvation, being pragmatic, seeing the divine presence in others, accenting personal choice, and combining both faith and works.

Also, the rountinization of sect to denomination is also evident in the church. From a sect type of doctrinal stance common in the beginning of the church to a much wider basis of faith in the 1990s, one can see how much the church has adapted itself to the external culture.

Summary

What this section of the chapter has attempted to do is to present to students the variety and forms of religious organizations. One of the problems that the study of religious organizations faces today is that as there is an increase of the different kinds of organizations outside of the Judeo-Christian tradition, there is more of a need to take this diversity into account. This we might call the need of a next generation of sociologists of religion who would expand our horizons.

Conclusions

It is the hope of the writer that the student of introductory sociology has come to a better appreciation of the contents of the social scientific study of religion. Here, I have outlined an investigation of religion by using a definition and expanded on it from as wide a perspective as possible. There are many things that have not been reviewed, especially the link of religion to the other social institutions. Another chapter awaits this expansion.

Notes

1. Vatican II Council happened between 1963–1965 in Rome where all the bishops of the Roman Catholic Church met to update the teachings, rituals and organization of Catholicism.

2. The term refers to millenialism or religious beliefs that focus on the coming of the divine kingdom, the future order, the future heaven on earth.

3. The type of analysis that investigates to see if there is a significant relationship between two variables.

4. Another example of the substantive meaning of morality is from the Decalogue of Judaism. Of the ten commandments, the first three are ordinances specifically related to honouring Yahweh or the central sacred element of the religion.

5. This is reflected in the sacred text of Christians, the New Testament. It is told that after Jesus rose from the dead, he sent his Holy Spirit to his disciples. If they would obey his precepts, they would be empowered from "on high" to continue his mission upon earth.

6. Ten years later, Miner returned to the parish. Already by this time modern values and technology were invading the tight community.

7. although there is a wide variation of new religious movements, Wilson provides us with a general definition:

> that salvation is gained by becoming acquainted with a special, perhaps secret, knowledge from a mystic source; that ultimate salvation and knowledge comes from the liberation of powers within the self; that real salvation is attained by belonging to a saved community, whose life-style and concerns are utterly divergent from those of worldly people. (1979:63)

8. Some later work has been done on developing this type (Berger, 1961; Morika and Newell, 1968 and McGuire, 1992). However, these more recent references do not add anything substantially different than Niebuhr and Martin.

References

Albanese, Caherine
1981 *American Religion and Religions*. Belmount, CA: Wadswroth.

Albanese, Caherine
1990 *Nature Religion in America: From the Algonkian Indians to the New Age*. Chicago: The University of Chicago Press.

Allport, Gordon
1966 "The Religious Context of Prejudice." *Journal for the Scientific Study of Religion* 5:447–457.

Becker, Howard
1932 *Systematic Sociology on the Basis of the Beziehungslehre and Gebildelehre of Leopopld Van Wiese*. New York: Wiley.

Berger, Peter
1961 *The Noise of Solemn Assemblies: Christian Commitment and the Religious Establishment.* Garden City, NY: Doubleday.

Berger, Peter
1969 *The Sacred Canopy*. New York: Doubleday and Company.

Berger, P.
1974 "Some Second Thoughts on Substantive versus Functional Definitions of Religion." *Journal for the Scientific Study of Religion* 13:125–133.

Bibby, Reginald and Merlin B. Brinkerhoff
1973 "The Circulation of the Saints: A Study of People Who Join Conservative Churches." *Journal for the Scientific Study of Religion*.

Bibby, Reginald
1987 *Fragmented Gods: The Poverty and Potential of Religion in Canada.* Toronto: Irwin Publishing.

Byrne, James
1971 "Charismatic Leadership," Pp. 187–210. In Devin and Dorothy Ranaghan eds. *As the Spirit Leads Us*. Paramus, New Jersey: Paulist Press.

Campbell, Joseph
1968 *The Masks of God: Occidental Mythology*. New York: The Viking Press.

Campbell, Joseph
1968 *The Hero with a Thousand Faces*. Princeton, NJ: Princeton University Press.

Clark, S.D.
1948 *Church and Sect in Canada.* Toronto: The University of Toronto Press.

Clark, Stephen
1971 "Charismatic Renewal in the Church," in Kevin and Dorothy Ranaghan eds. *As The Spirit Leads Us*. Paramus, New Jersey: Paulist Press. Pp. 17–37.

Coleman, John S. J.
1968 "Church-Sect Typology and Organizational Precariousness." *Sociological Analysis* 29:55–66.

Davis, Kingsley
1948–49 *Human Society*. New York: MacMillan.

Demarath, N.J. III
1965 *Social Class in American Protestantism*. Chicago: Rand McNally.

Durkheim, Emile
1965 *The Elementary Forms of The Religious Life*. Translated by Joseph Ward Swain. New York: Free Press. Originally published in London: George Allen and Unwin, 1915.

Eliade, Mircea
1959 *The Sacred and the Profane: The Nature of Religion.* New York: Haracourt, Brace & World, Inc.

Eliade, Mircea
1973 "Myth," pp. 70–78, in *Readings on the Sociology of Religion* by Thomas O'Dea and Janet O'Dea eds. Englewood Cliffs, NJ: Prentice Hall.

Florida, Robert
1994 "Buddhist Ethics." *Religious Humanism* 28:107–114.

Ford, J. Massingberd
1971 "Tongues-Leadership-Women." *Spiritual Life* 17:19–23.

Geertz, Clifford
1966 "Religion as a Cultural System." Pp. 1–46 in Michael Banton ed. *Anthropological Approaches to the Study of Religion*. London: Tavistock Publications.

Geertz, Clifford
1973 *The Interpretation of Cultures*. New York: Basic books.

Goode, William
1951 *Religion among the Primitives*. New York: Free Press.

Grant, John W.
1967 *The Canadian Experience of Church Union*. Richmond, Virginia: John Knox Press.

Grant, John W., Steven Chambers, Dianne Forrest, Bonnie Greene, Sang Chul Lee, and Peter G. White
1990 *Voices and Visions: 65 Years of the United Church of Canada*. Toronto: The United Church of Canada Publishing House.

Hargrove, Barbara
1989 *The Sociology of Religion*. Arlington Heights, Ill.: Harland Davidson, Inc.

Hill, Martin
1973 *The Religious Order*. London: Heinemann Educational Books.

James, William
1902 *The Varieties of Religious Experience.* New York: Longmans, Green and Company [1920].

Johnstone, Ronald L.
1992 *Religion in Society: A Sociology of Religion*, Fourth edition. Englewood Cliffs, New Jersey: Prentice Hall.

Kanwar, Mahfooz
1974 *The Sociology of Religion*. Calgary, Alberta: Mount Royal College Press.

Kertzer, David
1988 *Ritual, Politics and Power.* New Haven: Yale University Press.

Kligman, Gail
1988 *The Wedding of the Dead: Ritual, Poetics, and Popular Culture in Transylvania*. Berkeley, CA: University of California Press.

Kluckhohn, Clyde
1968 "Myths and Rituals: A General Theory," pp. 137–183, in R.A. George ed. *Studies in Mythology*. Homewood, Ill.: The Dorsey Press.

Lenski, Gerhard
1963 *The Religious Factor*. Garden City, New York: Doubleday and Company, Inc.

MacIver, R.M. and Charles H. Page
1957 In J. Milton Yinger, Ed., Pp. 318–329, *Religion, Society and the Individual*. New York: MacMillan Company.

Mahoney, John
1987 *The Making of Moral Theology: A Study of the Roman Catholic Tradition*. Oxford: Claredon Press.

Malinowski, Bronislaw
1954 *Magic, Science, and Religion and Other Essays*. Garden City, New York: Doubleday Anchor Books.

Martin, D.A.
1962 "The Denomination." *The British Journal of Sociology* 13:1–14.

McGuire, Meredith
1982 *Catholic Pentecostals: Power, Charisma, and Order in a Religious Movement*. Philadelphia: Temple University Press.

McGuire, Meredith
1992 *Religion: The Social Context*. Belmont, CA: Wadswroth Publishing Company.

Miner, Horace
1939 *St. Denis: A French-Canadian Parish*. Chicago: The University of Chicago Press.

Morgan, S. Philip
1983 "A Research Note on Religion and Morality: Are Religious People Nice People?" *Social Forces* 61:683{693.

Morioka, Kiyomi and William H. Hewell
1968 *The Sociology of Japanese Religion*. International Studies in Sociology and Social Anthropology 6. Leiden, Netherlands: Brill.

Morrow, E. Lloyd
1923 *Church Union in Canada*. Toronto: Th omas Allen.

Mott, Paul
1965 *The Organization of Society*. Englewood Cliffs, NJ: Prentice-Hall.

Niebuhr, H. Richard
1957 [1929] *The Social Sources of Denominationalism*. New York: World Publishing.

Norbeck, Edward
1961 *Religion in Primitive Society*. New York: Harper and Row.

Noss, John and David Noss
1984 *Man's Religions*, 7th ed. New York: MacMillan Publishing Company.

O'Connor, Edward
1971 *The Pentecostal Movement in the Catholic Church*. Notre Dame: Ave Maria Press.

O'Dea, Thomas and Janet O'Dea
1983 *The Sociology of Religion*, 2nd ed. Englewood Cliffs, NJ: Prentice Hall.

Otto, Rudolph
1958 *The Idea of the Holy*. New York: Oxford University Press. [1923].

Paper, Jordon
1989 *Offering Smoke: The Sacred Pipe and Native American Religion.* Edmonton, Alberta: University of alberta Press.

Piazza, Thomas and Charles Glock
1979 "Images of God and Their Social Meanings," Pp. 69–91 in Robert Wuthwow ed. *The Religious Dimension: New Directions in Quantitative Research.* New York: Academic Press

Poloma, Margaret and George Gallup, Jr.
1991 *Varieties of Prayer: A Survey Report.* Philadelphia: Trinity Press, International.

Proudfoot, Wayne
1985M "Attribution Theory and the Psychology of Religion." *Journal for the Scientific Study of Religion* 14, 4:317–330.

Ranaghan, Kevin and Dorothy
1969 *Catholic Pentecostals*. Paramus, New Jersey: Paulist Press.

Roberts, Keith
1990 *Religion in Sociological Perspective.* Belmont, CA: Wadsworth Publishing.

Schleiermacher, Friedrich
1799 *On Religion: Speeches to Its Cultured Despisers.* Trans. Richard Crouter. Cambridge University Press: New York [1988].

Smith, W. Robertson
1956 [1989] *The Religion of the Semites*. New York: the Meridian Library.

Spiro, Melford
1982 *Buddhism and Society: A Great Tradition and Its Burmese Vicissitudes.* Berkeley: The University of California Press.

Stark, Rodney, and William Bainbridge
1979 "Of Chruches, Sects, and Cults: Preliminary Concepts for a Theory of Religious Movements." *Journal for the Scientific Study of Religion* 18:117–131.

Stark, Rodney and William Bainbridge
1985 *The Future of Religion.* Berkeley: University of California Press.

Sumner, W.G.
1906 *Folkways*. New York: Mentor Books.

Swenson, Donald
1990 "A Charismatic Church: A Cultural Analysis." Annual Meeting of the Canadian Sociology and anthropology Association, May, in Victoria, B.C.

Swenson, Don and John Thompson
1986 "Locus Theologicus and Constructing a Sacred Past: Charismatic Renewal among Catholics as a Movement of Renewal." Paper presented at the Annual Meeting of the Canadian Association of Sociology and Anthropology, Winnipet, Manitoba.

Troeltsch, Ernest
1931 *The Social Teachings of the Christian Churches. Vols I and II.* Translated by O. Wyon. New York: Harper and Row.

Tyler, Edward
1929 *Primitive Culture*. New York: Brentano.

Wach, Joachim
1967 *Sociology of Religion.* Chicago: University Press; Phoenix edition. Originally published in 1944.

Watts, Allan W.
1954 *Myth and Ritual in Christianity.* New York: Thomas and Hudson.

Weber, Max
1946 *From Max Weber: Essays in Sociology.* Edited by H.H. Gerth and C. Wright Mills. New York: Oxford University Press.

Weber, Max
1947 *The Theory of Social and Economic Organization* by Hans Gerth and Don Martindale. New York: Free Press.

Weber, Max
1958 *The Protestant Ethic and the Spirit of Capitalism.* New York: Charles Scribners and Sons.

Weisman, Richard
1984 *Witchcraft, Magiac, and Religion in 17th-century Massachusetts.* Amherst: The University of Massachusetts Press.

Westley, Frances
1981 *The Complex Forms of The Religious Life:* A Durkheimian View of New Religious Movements. Chico, California: Scholars Press.

Wuthnow, Robert
1987 *Meaning and Moral Order: Explorations in Cultural Analysis.* Berkeley: The University of California Press.

Yinger, J. Milton
1959 *Religion, Society and the Individual.* New York: MacMillan Company.

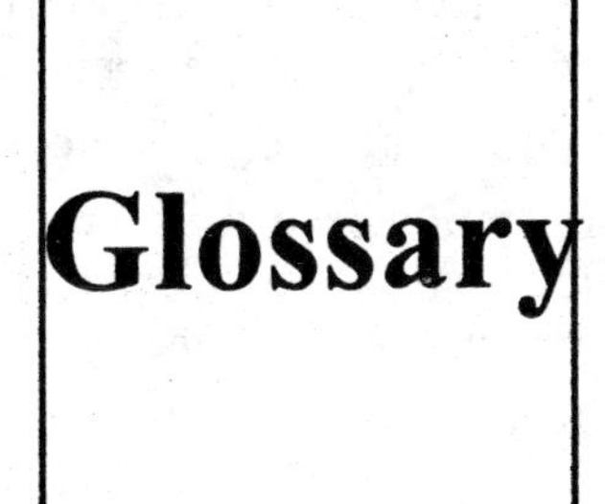

Glossary

Aboriginal: native, first in the land mass, original as in aboriginal Canadians consisting of Inuit, Indian and Métis peoples.

Achievement: class mobility based upon personal attributes like hard work and education.

Anomie: Durkheim's term for a condition of society in which people become detached, cut loose from the norms that usually guide their behavior.

Apotropaic Buddhism: from the Greek, a ritual designed to avert evil; is concerned with what happens in this world, in the everyday, the mundane; both morality and ritual are designed to ward off evil and to protect the faithful against calamity and illness.

Ascription: a status in society based upon what you are born with: sex, ethnicity, race and religion.

Back stage: Goffman's term to describe our behaviors that are performed outside of the view of others; where people rest from their performances, discuss their presentations, and plan future front stage performances (see **front stage**).

Blocked socialization: socialization that is substantially thwarted; typical among institutionalized and feral children.

Bourgeoisie: Marx's term to describe the capitalist class who are dependent upon the proletariat but also exploit them.

Charisma: Weber uses this term in the sociology of religion to describe a person who is extraordinarily gifted; one who has a divine or sacred gift; one who attracts followers because of this charisma.

Church: a moral community of believers; an routinized form of religious organization; with formal religious services; adapted to the social environment.

Class: strata in a society based upon income, prestige, education and occupation.

Cognitive development: socialization seen from how well the human person matures mentally; the rational development of individuals; a theory by Piaget that focuses on the ability of the child to develop logical thinking.

Cognitive culture: mental culture; ideas, mythologies, world views and ideologies.

Common law unions: couples who live together and who have an intimate, sexual relationship without being married.

Communication in marriage: Kurian's term to describe how married couples talk to one another, are open to each other and who are willing to lay bare their deepest concerns.

Conflict theory: a theoretical framework in which society is viewed as composed of groups competing for scare resources.

Consanguineal: bonds between persons normally found in families that reflect generational blood relations.

Construct: used in methodology to describe an abstract idea that can be used to develop theory; refers to the potential of being able to be measured in the empirical world.

Control variables: a variable that is held constant in an attempt to further clarify the relationship between two other variables (independent and dependent).

Correlation: the simultaneous occurrence of two or more variables; two variables which influence each other without knowing which one causes the other.

Counterculture: a group whose values place its members in opposition to the values of the wider culture.

Crime: deviance from the law.

Cult: a belief system which is deviant from the traditional religious doctrines of the host society; members tend to blend non-traditional with traditional tenets that make it a syncretic; there is a special accent on the individual who becomes almost sacred; this emphasis on the individual leaves the association thus formed in a loose, informal, organizational structure; finally, the cult stands in a high tension relationship with the external environment.

Cultural relativism: understanding a people from the framework of its own culture.

Cultural transmission: the transformation of one's culture to another.

Culture: a society's system of ideas, myths, world views, ideologies, values, attitudes, norms, and human made artifacts.

Culturally competent: describing the need of all adult members of a society to learn the culture of the same society in order to function well; in modern societies, this is the goal of educational institutions.

Demography: the social scientific study of a society's people: it includes topics like birth and mortality rates, migration rates, marriage rates, divorce rates.

Denomination: a type of religious organization that is adapted best to a democracy; it accents pragmatism, democracy, freedom of choicc.

Deprofessionlization: the erosion of autonomy and monopolistic privileges of the professions.

Deskilling: the process of breaking down a skill into its component parts with the intent of paying a worker less for labour related to that component.

Deviance: variation from a social norm.

Division of labour: the process in modern societies whereby more and more different kinds of work are required to meet the needs of a complex society.

Divorce: an official declaration by a state that a marriage has dissolved.

Empirical: information garnished from observations of the visible world about us.

English Great Rebellion: the Puritan revolt against the monarchy of England that happened between 1640 and 1650; it introduced more of a parliamentary system with a wider range of representation by the people.

Enlightenment: the dominant philosophy during the 17th and 18th centuries that focused on science, rationalism, secularism, and an optimism of progress.

Esoteric Buddhism: a cult in Buddhism that it is a syncretism of traditional beliefs, local animistic practices, and quasi secretive sects.

Ethnicity: a shared cultural heritage.

Ethos: an element of culture; a system of values, attitudes, mores, laws and codes.

Ethnocentrism: the practice of judging another culture by the standards of one's own culture.

Eugenics movement: a movement built on a science concerned with improving a breed or species, esp. the human species, by such means as influencing or encouraging reproduction by persons presumed to have desirable genetic traits.

Experiment: a research method for investigating cause and effect under highly controlled conditions.

Exploitation: from the sociology of Marx wherein it is argued that the bourgeoisie take from the proletariat a value of their labour that the proletariat should have for themselves.

Expressive abilities: in family and the study of intimate relations that accents nurture, care, emotion, and love.

Family: a group of intimate persons who are bound together by procreative, consanguineal, sexual, emotional and economic ties that, typically, include children who are socialized into being socially competent and who all live in a common residence.

Family violence: a range of negative behaviors including emotional, physical and sexual abuse inflicted on family members.

Fasciandus: from the work of the philosopher of religion who uses it to describe that part of the sacred which reflects the attraction of the believer to the holy.

Feminism: the study of women that includes the advocacy of gender equality between men and women ranging from the most intimate (as in families) to the most public (as in economy and politics).

Fieldwork: the kind of social scientific research which involves the researcher living among a people and observing them in their most natural of settings.

First Nations Movement: a movement among the First Nations peoples towards sovereignty over many of their institutions and ways of life.

Folkways: behavioral codes among a people that are flexible and malleable according to a wide variety of tastes. An example would be dress codes.

French Revolution: the revolution in France that began in 1789 that culminated in the demise of the monarchy, the secularization of the Roman Catholic Church, and the beginnings of democracy in that state.

Front stage: Erving Goffman's term to describe the kind of behavior that we present to others that is governed by the roles we fulfill; where the performances are given in front of others who are considered an audience.

Functional definition of ethos: what religious ethos does or what its social effects are.

Functional definition of ritual: the effects and consequences of ritual to people and to societies.

Functional definition of myth: what myth does in peoples's lives and how it affects institutions and whole societies.

Functional definition of religion: what the effects of religion are.

Gender: the cultural and social construction of sex.

Generalized other: George Herbert Meads term to indicate the norms, values, attitudes, and expectations of others "in general"; it is an important stage in the development of child as she or he relates to society as a whole.

Hawthorne effect: from the social research tradition wherein the presence of the researcher significantly influences the people he is observing and thus contaminates the results.

Hidden curriculum: the unseen and unwritten codes of schools that socializes children beyond what is explicitly taught.

Historical methods: methods in research used by investigators who study historical records like newspapers, church records, letters, diaries, and autobiographies in order to reconstruct the social life of people of previous generations.

Hypothesis: a proposition that is specific enough to be tested with empirical data.

Ideology: in culture a system of ideas; a more specific meaning is the system of ideas that a group of people use to control others.

Industrial Revolution: a process of economic change that began in England about 1775 that included large factories, steam engine power, wage labour and mass production of commodities.

Industrialization: the results of the industrial revolution.

Instrumental abilities: in intimate and familial relationships that accent a bond based on a goal or a purpose.

Intermarriage: marriage between persons of different religions, races or ethnic groups.

Kammatic Buddhism: a type of Buddhism in Burma wherein believers follow the customs and norms of the religion in order to achieve a better karma. This means that in the next reincarnation, if they follow the rules diligently, they will be reincarnated into a better life.

Labour force: those persons in a modern society who are currently or potentially working for a salary or a wage.

Labour markets: the economic arenas in which employers seek to purchase labour from potentially qualified employees who themselves are seeking employment, suitable to their present education, experiences, and preferences.

Laws: norms which have been legislated by a state.

Liberal feminism: generally considered to be the more moderate feminism based on the preposition that all peoples are created equal and should not be denied equality of opportunity because of gender.

Life chances: chances that individuals experience in their hopes and dreams for a successful life especially in their career and work aspirations.

Looking-glass self: Charles Cooley's term to describe social action wherein others become mirrors of us so that we learn from them who we are.

Marital power: the emotional, physical, financial ability of a married person to influence his or her spouse.

Marital roles: a set of specific right and obligations that a married person has in relationship to his or her spouse.

Marital satisfaction: a measure of the global well being of married persons that includes sexual, emotional, financial and intimate satisfaction.

Marriage: in most societies as at least one woman and one man who have established an approved relationship and who maintain a common residence.

Medicalization of problems with living: defining social or physical problems as medical problems and thereby including the health care system in order to meet these problems. An example is that in the United States in the 19th century, child birth was defined as a medical issue rather than a normal part of familial life. In effect, this eliminated the need for midwives.

Merchant class: the social class that emerged in Western Europe about the time of the age of discovery and the European exploitation of Africa, the Americas, and Asia; this class functioned as middle men who purchased the products from these lands and, in turn, sold them to Europeans; in doing so they incurred many profits.

Methodology: the whole scientific process of gathering data, analyzing them, and making the results known to the public.

Moral entrepreneur: those who act like economic entrepreneurs and try to "sell" or influence others regarding moral standards; an example would be the Catholic Pope who frequently speaks out on moral issues like abortion, euthanasia or the death penalty; another example would be feminists who appose pornography.

Mores: standards which members of a society consider to be an obligation.

Movement of Renewal: a type of religious organization that is a protest from within an existing church that does not involve and secession or a schism but, rather, a desire and mobilization to change the tone, the emptiness, the routinized charisma of the church through a renewal of a tradition; in it, members strive hard to maintain connections with the authorities of the church; an example would be the monastic movement within Catholicism.

Multiculturalism: as social policy planned to create ethnic or cultural heterogeneity.

Mysterium Tremendum: from the work of the philosopher of religion, Otto, who uses it to describe that part of the sacred which reflects awe and distance of the believer to the holy.

Mythology: a system of beliefs; a system of myths that describe breakthroughs of the sacred or the holy into the world; it is this sudden breakthrough of the sacred that really establishes the world and makes it what it is today; it is a result of the intervention of the holy that humans make themselves what they are.

New eugenics movement: made possible through screening techniques and fetal diagnostic technologies to determine various kinds of disorders like Downs Syndrome.

Nibbanic Buddhism: from *nibbana*, or nirvana; this kind of Buddhism is the closest version approximating the path of the Gautama.; it is the Buddhism of the monks who obey the five or eight precepts as a means to achieve nirvana; this kind of Buddhism as a morality that is primarily a form of spiritual discipline; it is a means to the attainment of a certain psychological state which is the first condition for the achievement of nirvana.

Norm violation: deviance from a norm.

Normative culture: that dimension of culture which includes codes of behaviour like values, attitudes, norms and mores.

Norms: social expectations of others that impact our behaviour.

Occupational segregation: from gender studies that refers to the practice of segregating women into predominantly female places of work (like nursing or elementary teaching) and men into predominately male places of work (like construction and mining).

Operationalization: from social methodology; it is the process of specifying how a construct can be measured.

Patriarchy: from the Latin and Greek words that mean, literally, "the rule by the Father"; in current diction it means an institution, organization or a society in which power is held by and transferred through males.

Pattern variables: from the work of Talcott Parsons and Seymour Lipset which illustrate cultural value patterns in modern societies.

Physical availability: from family studies; the term illustrates the physical availability of person in intimate relationships.

Political economy: a concept emerging from the work of Karl Marx and conflict theorists; it refers to the union of politics and economies from the capitalistic perspective; it indicates the integral union of the two insinuations in modern societies.

Post-industrial: a modern economy based upon information, service, and knowledge; most advanced capitalist nation states are post-industrial.

Post-positivism: science that focuses upon social models that are not rooted in empirical data sources; an era wherein sociologists use methods other than surveys and censuses to gather their data; close to qualitative research.

Prejudice: bias, preconception, slant, prejudgment, predisposition, one-sidedness, narrow-mindedness, bigotry; intolerance, unfairness, partiality, predilection, favoritism.

Primary sector: in modern economies, the sector that focuses on primary production of commodities like oil, grain, forestry, fish.

Principal of deterrence: a practice to encourage conformity to laws by inflicting punishment on the offender.

Profession: being reserved to those occupations which have exclusive jurisdiction over certain kinds of services, are able to negotiate freedom from external intervention and have control over the content of their work.

Proletariat: in Marxist class analysis those people who are wage earners and depend upon the bourgeoisie for employment.

Proletarianization: professions are losing control over the conditions of work and are experiencing a serious reduction in compensation.

Proposition: in sociological theory, a generic statement positing a relationship between two or more constructs.

Protestant Reformation: an important initial process that initiated the early modern period; the reform of Christianity that resulted in a succession from the Roman Catholic Church; the religious change that resulted, according to Weber, changes in the economic system of Europe from a traditional economy to a capitalist economy.

Psychoanalytic: a systematic structure of theories concerning the relation of conscious and unconscious psychological processes; the origins are in Freud's theories of personality.

Psychological availability: in familial and intimate relationships; the range of availability of a person to another psychologically or emotionally.

Punishment: a penalty inflicted for an offense, fault or a crime committed.

Qualitative research: investigation by which a researcher gathers impressionistic, not numerical data.

Quantitative research: investigation whereby a researcher collects numerical data.

Quiet Revolution: a period during the 1960s in Quebec which was one of rapid change from a traditional, rural, conservative and Catholic society to favor a ethic of Rattrapage, catching up, with social, political, and economic development in the rest of Canada and the Western world.

Race: a classification of modern humans, sometimes, especially formerly, based on an arbitrary selection of physical characteristics, as skin color, facial form, or eye shape, and now frequently based on such genetic markers as blood groups.

Racism: a belief or doctrine that inherent differences among the various human races determine cultural or individual achievement, usually involving the idea that one's own race is superior.

Radical feminism: that gender inequality is rooted in all of the social institutions of modern society and that it is patriarchy and not capitalism which is the root of the problem.

Random sample: in sociological research wherein a sample in which everyone in the target population has the same chance of being included in the study.

Regionalism: a concept that describes a people's tendency to identify with their region of residence and with those who live there with them; this identification may in turn lead them to 'think differently' about certain things than residents of other regions; in time, this regionally distinctive set of attitudes and values may lead them to behave differently as well.

Religion: the individual and communal experience of the sacred expressed in myths, rituals, ethos and integrated into a social collective or institution.

Religious organization: a cluster or a complex of ranked roles that are, in turn a cluster or a complex of norms that are routinized elements of charismatic or affective social action that is focussed on creating relationships of an individual to the divine, the cosmos, nature, others and oneself.

Religious experience: the feelings, acts, and experiences of people both privately and socially in so far as they apprehend themselves to stand in relation to whatever they may consider to be sacred.

Research process: a process in sociological methodology which involves the exploration of, description of, and explanation of social data.

Resocialization: radically altering an inmate's personality through deliberate manipulation of the environment.

Ritual: ritual is repeated consecrated (sacred) behaviour that is a symbolic expression of the moods and motivations of religious participants and unseen powers. Ritual forms a bond of friendship, community and unity with the believer and her/his god. Finally, ritual transports the participant into another world (the world above) wherein there is peace and harmony.

Role-taking: the process of becoming socialized into a social group, a culture, or a society that involves the taking of the role of others.

Routinization of charisma: Weber's term to describe a process that frequently happens within religious organizations; it includes the charisma of the original founder or founders becoming routine, ordinary, even profane.

Sacred: also called the holy; the term from Durkheim and Otto that specifies the religious object as separate from and removed from the profane; see **mysterium tremendum** and **fascinadus**.

Secondary sector: work in construction and manufacturing.

Sect: a type of religious organization that stands apart from the larger society.

Sex: the biological characteristic of being male or female.

Sexism: the belief that one's sex in innately superior to the other.

Significant other: an individual who significantly influences someone else's life.

Social action: human action that assumes that persons are free agents who, in their relationships with others, attach a subjective meaning to their behaviour and take into account the behaviour of others.

Social competency: the ability that a person has to relate well to others.

Social desirability: the tendency in social scientific research for the subject not to be honest with a researcher and to give what she or he would want to hear.

Social structure: every way of acting, fixed or not, capable of exercising on the individual an external constraint; or again, every way of acting which is general throughout a given society, while at the same time existing it its own right independent of its individual manifestations.

Socialist feminism: the understanding that gender inequality is rooted in the patriarchal, capitalistic relationships of power that is firmly held by men.

Socialization: the process by which people learn the characteristics of their group—the attitudes, values, and actions thought appropriate for them.

Sociobiology: a framework of thought that views human social behavior as the result of natural selection and considers biological characteristics to be a cause of this behavior.

Sociological theory: theory designed to offer explanations for social action, group behavior and societies.

Sociological imagination: C. W. Wright's term to describe human social action in terms of individual biography, social structure, culture and history.

Sociology: the science of the social group that ranges from a dyad of two persons to whole societies and accents understanding social action and social structure.

Sociology of medicine and health care: the study of both individual and institutional definitions of, and responses to, illness and injury.

Sociology of health and illness: the study of both individual and institutional definitions of, and responses to, illness and injury.

Statistics: a mathematical method used to analyze social data that is numeric in nature.

Stereotype: a cognitive structure that helps individuals to process information about the environment without reasoning about that information.

Structural functionalism: a framework for creating theory that envisions society as a complex system whose parts work together to promote solidarity and stability.

Subculture: the values and related social action of a social group that distinguishes its members from the larger culture.

Substantive definition of ritual: what ritual is; the reliving of the experience of the holy or the sacred.

Substantive definition of ethos: what ethos is; the living out in everyday life the experience of the holy or the sacred.

Substantive definition of religion: what religion is in itself; the core of religion is the experience of the sacred, both personally and socially.

Substantive definition of myth: what myth is; the stories of the sacred being manifested in human conditions and various situations.

Survey: the collection of data by having subjects answer a series of questions related to their social lives.

Symbolic interactionism: a theoretical orientation in which society is seen as composed of symbols that individuals use to create meaning, establish their world views, and inter-relate with one another.

Taboos: a norm so strong that it brings with it a revulsion if so disobeyed.

Technology: the tools and skills used in the process of work.

Tertiary sector: work in transportation, communications, commerce, finance, health, and education.

Unemployment rate: the number of individuals out of work and who are actively seeking work divided by the total number of labour force participants (including the unemployed).

Variable: a construct that is measured numerically; a construct whose value changes from case to case.

White collar crime: crimes like computer illegal access, stock market frauds, real estate fraud, lawyers embezzlement, and medical malpractice.

Work: continuous employment in the production of goods and services for remuneration.

Work satisfaction: the enjoyment or pleasure one receives from labour.

World view: a life orientation; a personal reflection on what a person believes about him or herself, others, society, the world, the cosmos and the sacred.

Index